TRIBES

*How Our Need to Belong Can
Make or Break the Good Society*

DAVID LAMMY

CONSTABLE

CONSTABLE

First published in Great Britain in 2020 by Constable

1 3 5 7 9 10 8 6 4 2

Copyright © David Lammy, 2020

The moral right of the author has been asserted.

A CIP catalogue record for this book
is available from the British Library.

ISBN: 978-1-4721-2873-7 (hardback)
ISBN: 978-1-4721-2874-4 (trade paperback)

Typeset in Adobe Garamond by Hewer Text UK Ltd, Edinburgh
Printed and bound in Great Britain by Clays Ltd, Elcograf S.p.A.

Papers used by Constable are from well-managed forests and other responsible sources.

Constable
An imprint of
Little, Brown Book Group
Carmelite House
50 Victoria Embankment
London EC4Y 0DZ

An Hachette UK Company
www.hachette.co.uk

www.littlebrown.co.uk

This book is dedicated to my wife Nicola and her late mother Julie, both of whom have been paragons of how to transcend difference to connect with people from all backgrounds.

Contents

1. A New Tribalism
   How we entered a new era of polarisation   1

MY TRIBES

2. Jerusalem
   The erosion of a once proud English community   33

3. Babylon
   The fluidity of British Caribbeans   63

4. Out of Africa
   Looking for belonging in my DNA   95

HOW BELONGING CAN BREAK SOCIETY

5. Alone
   How we created an epidemic of loneliness   119

6. Identity Crisis
   The politics of group identity   155

HOW BELONGING CAN MAKE SOCIETY

7. Encounter Culture
   Empowering our neighbourhoods   187

8. Rebuilding England
   How we can create pride in a civic nation state   227

9. Beyond Tribes
   Why and how we must move beyond tribes and replace
   them with communities   271

POSTSCRIPT   303

ACKNOWLEDGEMENTS   307

NOTES   311

INDEX   337

1

A New Tribalism

How we entered a new era of polarisation

'O mankind, indeed We have created you from male and female
and made you peoples and tribes that you may know one another.'

The Quran, 49:13

A cylindrical white package landed on my doormat. Each morning
for weeks I had been excited and nervous as I checked the post, in
anticipation of its arrival. The papers inside were supposed to tell me
where my ancestors came from. For my entire life I had described my
heritage beginning and ending in Guyana, the country of my parents'
birth. It was obvious that my ancestors had been involuntary participants in the transatlantic slave trade, but I had no idea where they
had been taken from. Our family history was not something I ever
discussed with my parents. As far as I am aware, they knew little
about their family tree more than a couple of branches back. I hoped
the DNA analysis inside the package would resolve my unanswered
questions.

The year was 2007 and I had been asked by the then prime minister,
Tony Blair, to lead on the UK's commemoration of the bicentenary of
the 1807 Abolition of the Slave Trade Act. I was given this honour

because I was the Labour government's culture minister and, as the *Daily Telegraph* had bluntly put it, 'a descendant of slaves'. Indeed, the previous year, in a speech highlighting the preparations that were being made to mark the bicentenary, I had talked about how little people knew of Britain's role in the buying, selling and exploitation of human beings from the sixteenth to the nineteenth centuries. The average Brit might have watched *Roots*, the 1970s TV series based on the eponymous Alex Haley novel. Or they might have heard of the role played by William Wilberforce in the abolition of slavery. But beyond these and a few other exceptions, a sort of collective amnesia has followed the slave trade in Britain.

At the time, the nation's obsession with genealogical studies and family history documentaries such as *Who Do You Think You Are?* was relatively new and exciting. So, when I received an invitation from the Science Museum in London to undergo a DNA test, I did not hesitate before agreeing. The Cambridge-based company offering the service, Roots for Real, specialised in uncovering genetic ancestry. They would give me a detailed analysis of my mtDNA, the genetic code of my maternal ancestry, and my Y-DNA, the genetic code for my paternal line.

When the Roots for Real 'home saliva' kits arrived six weeks earlier, I became gripped by the possibility of what the analysis would reveal. All that stood between me and an insight into my genetic roots were a bunch of swabs, some glass vials and a pre-paid return envelope. I immediately swabbed myself and, on the advice of the company's scientists, got saliva samples from my mother and maternal uncle. Then I sent the vials off to the lab and waited. A month and a half later, the results, which would match me to my long-lost cousins across the world, arrived.

I brought the package, along with the rest of that day's post, into my kitchen, brewed a cup of coffee and sat down. Opening the tube, I peeked inside and eagerly removed the printout. The analysis of my nucleic acids revealed that I was a 25 per cent match to the Tuareg tribe in Fafa, Niger; a 25 per cent match to the Temne tribe in Sierra Leone; and a 25 per cent match to the Bantu tribe in South Africa. One of the most surprising details was the reference to traces of Scottish DNA, which apparently come from my mother's side.

Of all the findings, the Tuareg element amazed me the most. I had been to South Africa and Sierra Leone, so I had at least a degree of familiarity with the Bantu and the Temne people. Niger had never been on my radar. When I tapped 'Tuareg' into Google and browsed several books I had ordered from Amazon, I felt a sense of pride as I read about their complex history and unique culture. It quickly became clear that the Tuareg are not easily characterised. They are an 'ethnic confederation' of Berber tribes, originally from North Africa. According to legend, they moved into the Sahara around AD 400.

The Tuareg do not perfectly fit the old-fashioned anthropological definition of 'tribe' because they are not a self-contained 'whole society'. Instead, they are a group of various tribes, which includes around 2 million people, mostly spread across Niger and Mali, as well as Algeria, Burkina Faso and Libya. Though they were once all nomadic, many have now moved into towns and villages. Today many live as minorities among larger, ethnically separate majorities, often marginalised by restrictive laws. Perhaps most interestingly, and fundamental to understanding the Tuareg, is that they do not all look as if they come from one ethnic group. A caste system separates the 'Bella', dark-skinned members who were once slaves, from the lighter-skinned members who tended to be slave owners.

Nevertheless, the Tuareg do have a distinctive culture. They share one language, or at the least one group of very closely related languages, called Tamasheq, which is written in its own ancient script.[1] They are sometimes known as the 'blue people' due to the distinctive indigo often used in their clothes. They practise Islam, but their own distinctive form, as part of the Maliki sect.[2] Many still retain beliefs in spirits and exorcism.[3,4] Interestingly, as I would find out, it is Tuareg men rather than women who wear the veil. What brings the Tuareg together is a shared set of numbers on their ticket in the lottery of life: their parents, their DNA and where they were born. I shared the most necessary condition needed to be classed a Tuareg, in my genetic code, but I had been raised in a wholly different environment which made that insufficient.

The DNA results gave me something I had longed for. Something more than a biography, a backstory or a culture. The results gave me the potential to discover more about my biological heritage. Suddenly, a genetic sense of self, an appreciation that I came from a specific group of people from a definable location, allowed me to identify as more than just a 'descendant of slaves'. Previously there had been a hole in my understanding of where I came from. This new information filled the gap. I began to empathise with the type of belonging about which I had sometimes been cynical. In the past, I might have rolled my eyes if someone told me they were descended from Viking, Norman or Celtic stock, but now I understood what they were getting at.

After rereading my results for the fourth time, I went upstairs to scan them onto my computer so I could email copies to my family. I then excitedly phoned every sibling, cousin, aunt and uncle I could reach. This was not just my story; it was my whole family's history. We all feel the need to belong. This is part of what makes human beings uniquely social animals. My whole family's reactions when we looked at the DNA results are evidence of this.

What did it mean that I felt this visceral connection to the Tuareg tribe? Clearly, I do not speak the same language, live in the same culture or share the same worldview as the Tuareg. Yet I could not deny my desire to somehow belong to their group.

DEFINING 'TRIBES'

When I was growing up in the 1970s and '80s, the popular scientist of the day was Dr Desmond Morris. An unusual character, Morris flitted between impressive careers as a zoologist, TV presenter and surrealist painter. His bestselling *The Naked Ape* was written in just four weeks in 1967. It made Morris stupendously rich, leading him to buy luxury cars, a yacht and move to a twenty-seven-room house in Malta. Morris's many books are based on the underlying premise that, despite 10,000 years of 'civilisation', our species' characteristics are predominantly defined by the hundreds of thousands of years that humans were hunter-gatherers, and the millions of years before in which our species' ancestors evolved. The implicit consequence of this is that the genetic features we have inherited are not designed for the modern world.

Morris's central premise – that our modern human experience is shaped by millions of years of evolutionary tinkering – has stood the test of time. And so has the man himself: Morris, now in his nineties, reportedly works from 10 p.m. until 4 a.m. every single night.

In *Manwatching: A Field Guide to Human Behaviour*, Morris explains that humans began as 'tribal animals, living in comparatively small groups, probably less than a hundred, and we existed like that for millions of years'. In our tribes, we knew everyone else. If we had any contact with outsiders from other tribes, we would aim to immediately drive them away from our space. To the tribe, anyone outside of its physical and conceptual boundaries is an outsider, even an enemy. And, in the tribal order of things, threats must be eliminated. A tribe does not only promote its own interests and vision for the world, it defines itself in opposition to the 'other'.

It would be wrong to frame the ancient tribes of our ancestors only in terms of their exclusivity. Cooperating in groups of this size is more inclusive than existing as individuals, or in smaller groups based around family, for example. Human psychology is different to other social primates, in that it makes larger, more cooperative societies possible. For anthropologists, the scale of human cooperation that has developed is an 'evolutionary puzzle'.[5] The most plausible theory to explain these changes is that they are the result of natural selection.[6] The development of tribes allowed individuals to learn from each other, increase genetic variation, and find strength in numbers against nature's threats. Our instinct to work in larger groups, which can be characterised as tribes, helped humans to survive and were the first steps towards the large and open societies we live in today.

As human societies advanced, the size of the human world expanded. The tribes of old were replaced by the 'great capital city'. Paint and piercings were replaced by 'flags, emblems, uniforms, anthems, marching songs and bugle calls'. Boundary lines evolved into national territories, trade agreements, customs arrangements, checkpoints, passport stops and border walls. But this has left 'the ancient tribal hunter', which Morris claims forms the basis of each of us, 'unsatisfied by membership of such a vast conglomeration of individuals, most of whom are totally unknown to him personally'. As Morris wrote in the seventies, in the twentieth century the only option was to join 'the local club, the teenage gang, the union, the specialist society, the sports association, the political party, the college fraternity, the social clique, the protest group'.

In the decades that followed, opportunities for engagement in civil and social organisations have rapidly declined. In the twenty-first century, it is harder to find belonging in local clubs, unions and other small groups. Instead, many of us attempt to satisfy our primal communal urges by joining different forms of 'tribes'. Some have tried to gratify their need to belong by finding pride in ethnic identities. Others have joined and begun to identify with subcultures online. The internet allows new groups to feel emotionally connected, while being physically far apart.

Tribal behaviour is on the rise in our politics and across society, as various scholars and commentators have observed.[7] Yet the term has become unfashionable among anthropologists. This is understandable: 'tribal' was originally used by Europeans as a catch-all term to describe their interactions with the non-white world. 'Tribalism' was everything Europe was not: uneducated, primitive, non-white. All the same, some anthropological definitions are worth looking at to help us understand what it means to say that modern society is becoming more tribal. The cultural anthropologist Aidan Southall usefully described a tribal society as 'a whole society, with a high degree of self-sufficiency at a near subsistence level, based on a relatively simple technology without writing or literature, politically autonomous and with its own distinctive language, culture and sense of identity, tribal religion being also coterminous with tribal society'.[8]

The term 'tribe', however, was never very effective at capturing the vast cultural and social diversity, richness and difference found in groups of people living on the continent of Africa and elsewhere in the so-called 'developing world'. For these reasons, by the latter part of the twentieth century, most anthropologists and historians had mostly stopped using the term 'tribe'. Today anthropologists use many other terms, such as ethnic group, nation, people, community, kin group and village.

Given its colonial baggage, you might ask why I have chosen to focus this book around the concept of tribes at all. I am not interested in rehabilitating outdated and racist uses of 'tribe'. I do not use it as a specific anthropological identifier to mark out certain groups of humans. Instead, I am using it as a metaphor to describe the creeping resurgence of our polarisation into groups at the beginning of the twenty-first century. In this era, 'tribal' identities are not exclusively the result of your ethnic make-up or the place you live. Instead, they are often the product of the tensions and splits in the modern world.

This is based on the theory of 'neo-tribalism', a term coined by French sociologist Michel Maffesoli in 1988, when he published "Le Temps des Tribus". After the book was translated into 'The Time of the Tribes' in 1996, it became a popular text among post-modernist students across the English-speaking world.[9] I remember staying quiet as a group of friends discussed the book, while I was studying for my postgraduate degree in the USA, in part because I did not buy its central premise. In 1996, at least to me, the world did not feel tribal, but open, hopeful and on track for progress. Neo-tribalism is an idea which I only began to take seriously more recently.

Maffesoli's neo-tribes are best thought of as 'communities of feeling'.[10] They are groups defined by the individuals within them sharing a particular emotional perspective of the world's meaning. The central feature of neo-tribes are social ties between humans. Instead of making decisions as individuals, its members make them while playing a specific role within a certain social group. Within these groups, an individual is likely to see their own identity purely in terms of the group identity. This is in part due to a kind of identity crisis that is spreading across society. In the era of rationalism, which followed the Enlightenment, we understood our identities in terms of our social position, class, or stable work function. As these rigid structures broke down – because of a combination of deindustrialisation, technological advance and even social justice movements – this stability was lost.

Individuals began to seek community and emotional connection with others in a neo-tribe, in part as a defensive rebellion against feeling like they had no clear identity.[11] Neo-tribalism, then, which I will refer to as the 'new tribalism', or later simply 'tribalism', is a backlash against the increasingly atomised and individualistic societies we created. The new tribes crave the benefits of community in a society of individuals because individualism went too far.

In the three decades since Maffesoli first conceived his theory, the trends leading to society's identity crises have deepened. Traditional lifelong job paths, and the class structures they were linked to, which were once the source of individual's identities, have declined further. Meanwhile, the technological and communications revolution has massively weakened the barrier to forming new tribes. Rather than relying on physical interactions and meeting places, new social ties and tribal groups can be formed around the world effortlessly, using the internet. What is consistent between old and new versions of tribalism is that both are appealing because they satisfy the very human desire to belong to something bigger than oneself. The dynamics of solidarity, faith and, at worst, blind loyalty in those who are like you appear to be much the same.

My desire to feel part of the Tuareg was reflective of the broader desire of many in modern, Western society to feel as though we belong to an exclusive group. It follows, and is in many ways a reaction against, the long period of individualism in which we were more focused on what separates us than what we have in common. As people have been pushed further into individualism by the logic of the market, their urge to belong has not been able to be satisfied by the community structures – like organised religion, clubs and unions – that once held us together. Instead they have looked to new identity groups in which to find belonging.

The reforms begun under Ronald Reagan and Margaret Thatcher are key drivers of the new tribalism. The era of 'neoliberalism' did not only change our society's economic systems: it changed our politics, our culture and how we view ourselves. Markets became stronger, but our communities became weaker. Individuals were encouraged to pursue personal success, but often at the expense of helping those around them. For some, the pursuit of individual success resulted in wealth, comfort and even fame. Many more were left behind, without the communal safety net which once might have caught them.

The backlash against an era of individualism and the resulting desire to belong to a particular tribal group can most obviously be seen in the growing antagonisms between those with opposing political identities like Leave and Remain, Republican and Democrat, Labour and Conservative. It may, however, also help explain why many of the most alienated in our society are attracted to the extremes of religious terror groups, resurgent white nationalist movements and inner-city gangs.

In this new era of tribalism, the rational is increasingly being replaced by the emotional. The logic of the global liberal order, which for so long enjoyed political hegemony, is being attacked in almost every modern democracy. The universal values that were its basis (all humans are of equal value, cooperation is better than domination, freedom is an intrinsic good) are now being questioned. This tension was obvious in the BBC's 2019 UK general election leaders' debate, where an impassioned member of the public bluntly asked the two Prime Ministerial candidates that, in light of the recent London Bridge terror attack, "Will you put public safety ahead of human rights?" Human rights are designed to protect individuals, but as this question highlighted, some are growing suspicious that a rights-based order poses a threat to their group.

IN-GROUPS AND OUT-GROUPS

Tribalism is natural. Humans intuitively sort themselves into 'in-groups' and 'out-groups'.[12] Our need to belong is hardwired into our brains.[13] Yet what these groups are based on – our nation, our skin colour, or even our football team – is somewhat arbitrary. We need to belong to groups, but there is nothing inevitable about the specific groups to which we belong.

Countless psychological studies back this up. In one such experiment, toddlers aged between four and six were divided in two. One group was given red T-shirts and the other blue T-shirts. Both groups were then shown images of other children, whom they had never met but were wearing either red or blue T-shirts. At no point did the teachers mention shirt colour, but by the end of the three weeks it was clear that children favoured other children wearing the same colour shirt as themselves.[14]

This type of behaviour has not only been demonstrated in children.

One study, by academics at Northeastern University in Boston, asked volunteers to answer questions before dividing them randomly into one group of 'over-estimators' and another group of 'under-estimators'.[15] They were then introduced to another person who they believed was also taking part in the experiment, but in reality their behaviour was guided by instructions from the researchers. Half of the volunteers were told that this additional participant was a member of their in-group, while the other half were led to believe he was a member of their out-group.

The volunteers from both groups then watched as this new member cheated on a simple task that they had earlier completed. At the end of the experiment, the volunteers rated the 'fairness' with which this additional member had acted. The results showed that volunteers were significantly more likely to excuse the unfair behaviour of the other member if they perceived them as belonging to their in-group.[16] We perceive objectively unfair actions as more acceptable, excused or forgiven when it comes from one of our own.

The desire for group membership is innate, but this does not dictate whether it is morally good or bad. On the positive side, it can help us foster solidarity with other people, as well as facilitate positive action. Being part of a group can discourage selfishness by instilling a sense that we are responsible for one another. It can encourage fidelity and loyalty, and create a whole that is bigger than the sum of its parts. Community can be an antidote to selfishness and individualism, creating secure networks and rich cultures. In fact, our urge to belong underlies much of what it means to be human.

Once we accept our innate need to belong, we can start thinking about which types of group identity to organise that urge around, and which to avoid. One positive way to satisfy our need to belong is to organise it around shared values and institutions. This can be inclusive to all those who wish to be a part of a group, rather than exclusive to those who happen to possess the required attributes. There are countless examples throughout history of positive, inclusive group identities. Consider, for example, what it means to be an American. The founding documents of the USA laid the groundwork for a group identity that was not based on specific, exclusive criteria, but instead offered a group identity for all those who wished to pursue "Life, Liberty and the pursuit of Happiness".

Inclusive group identities contrast with new tribal identities, in which individuals retreat into groups defined by a core similarity of experience found in shared religion, ethnicity or culture, in part caused by unease, confusion, pain or fear at the speed of change in the modern world. Our longing for belonging only becomes destructive when it is used to argue that one group is superior to another. It becomes toxic when it blinkers us: by being exclusive rather than inclusive. In these cases, community is distorted into a toxic form of tribalism. At its worst, tribalism can be blind, unquestioning, divisive, exclusive and hateful. Individuals who do not conform are likely to be ostracised. Those in the same tribe lower their moral standards for each other, easily forgiving – and even denying – their bad actions. Those perceived to be in an opposing tribe are often seen as wrong by default, regardless of the content of their argument. This form of tribalism does not seek to include others of different faiths, ethnicities or cultures around the values and institutions they share. Instead it denigrates and divides those who are different. Instead of seeing an action as right or wrong in itself, its value is assessed purely with regard to its instrumental effect on the tribe. 'Right and Wrong' are replaced by 'Us and Them'.

HOW WE GOT HERE

In 1962, President John F. Kennedy delivered one of those rare speeches that leave a lasting mark on history. Speaking from a podium at Rice University in Texas, in front of a crowd of 40,000, but a worldwide audience of many millions more, he put forward his case for 'why we go to the moon'. What stuck with me when I first watched that speech was not only the argument for space travel but Kennedy's articulation of the speed and scale of human progress:

> No man can fully grasp how far and how fast we have come, but condense, if you will, the 50,000 years of man's recorded history in a time span of but a half-century. Stated in these terms, we know very little about the first forty years, except at the end of them advanced man had learned to use the skins of animals to cover them. Then

about ten years ago, under this standard, man emerged from his caves to construct other kinds of shelter. Only five years ago man learned to write and use a cart with wheels. Christianity began less than two years ago. The printing press came this year, and then less than two months ago, during this whole fifty-year span of human history, the steam engine provided a new source of power. Newton explored the meaning of gravity. Last month electric lights and telephones and automobiles and airplanes became available. Only last week did we develop penicillin and television and nuclear power, and now if America's new spacecraft succeeds in reaching Venus, we will have literally reached the stars before midnight tonight.[17]

If we do the similar rough calculations today, less than two weeks ago the first commercial internet servers arrived.[18] A day and a half later we concluded the Uruguay Round of General Agreement on Tariffs and Trade which created the World Trade Organisation (WTO) – an agreement that liberalised trade and reduced tariffs for 123 countries – which China joined last week. We created the first iPhone about four days ago. Yesterday Uber deployed the first fleet of twenty self-driving taxis, and earlier today an artificially intelligent computer defeated the world's best human player at the ancient and nuanced strategy game, Go. The twin revolutions of technological advancement and economic globalisation have irrevocably changed how we live. Half a century on from when he condensed human history into fifty years, JFK himself would be in awe at how far we have come.

Though most people use it only to stay in touch with those acquaintances they may lack the time to see in person, today, through Facebook, you have the power to contact more than 2 billion strangers from the supercomputer that sits in your pocket. If you want to, you could start a business from Dublin that exports French wine to Mount Fuji in Japan with zero tariffs.[19] Online you can find a community of thousands, if not millions, who subscribe to your own niche interest, whether it is paranormal activity or gluten-free baking. In most capital cities across the world you can eat your exact favourite chain burger while watching your favourite TV show on Netflix. Low-cost air travel means you can fly from London to Morocco for less than a typically priced train ticket from London to Manchester. Continental Europeans can move across the mainland uninhibited – without any need for passports, let alone visas. If you are abroad, you do not have to be concerned that you might forget your family's faces, as you can video-call them with your high-definition camera for free. To gain a following, you no longer need to become a famous musician, actor, artist, politician or comedian, or work for a national newspaper. All you need to reach millions is an internet connection, a smartphone and an ability to engage other people.

As technology has progressed and globalisation has advanced, there have been many measurable benefits. Every single day between the year 1990 and 2015, 138,000 people were saved from the indignities of extreme poverty.[20] In 1945, half of the world's population was under-nourished, while today that figure is around one in ten.[21] Around 2.6 billion more humans have gained access to safe water since 1990. If you were born in Britain in 1840, you could have expected to live to around forty.[22] Today your life will on average be twice as long.[23] Literacy rates have spiked too, from 21 per cent in 1900 to 86 per cent today.[24]

But no change comes without disruption, so it should not surprise us that the remarkable shifts we are experiencing have also brought serious adverse effects. For a start, the benefits of technological revolution and economic liberalisation have been spread unequally. As Thomas Piketty's ground-breaking analysis in *Capital in the Twenty-First Century* showed, the rate of return on capital now outstrips the rate of growth, and inherited wealth therefore grows faster than earned wealth.[25] This means that if you are born into a rich family, you are likely to get richer, but if you are poor it is hard to move up, regardless of how hard you work. Poverty remains a grave issue for billions, including a significant minority in even so-called developed nations. In my own country, the United Kingdom, homelessness has more than doubled since 2010.[26] The effects of the financial crisis in 2008 are still being painfully felt, through austerity policies imposed across much of the Western world. Deprivation has contributed to an opioid crisis in the United States of America that is killing more than 130 people every day,[27] a surge in violent crime in the United Kingdom by 19 per cent in the past year, and left Greece and Spain with a youth unemployment rate of greater than 30%.[28]

As we have grown more connected in an increasingly globalised and digitised world, we have also grown more divided. Traditional pillars of community and sources of identity, which in Kennedy's day were strong, have begun to erode. As globalisation has spread and deepened, the nation state has lost importance. Governments and politicians gave up parts of their sovereignty and regulatory power to the market or supranational institutions in search of economic benefit. As trade and movement have become freer, the convention of national boundaries has broken down.

In 2016, the then British prime minister Theresa May said: 'If you believe you are a citizen of the world, you are a citizen of nowhere. You don't understand what citizenship means.'[29] This caused uproar precisely because it ignores the plurality of human identities. Theresa May was aiming to attack an 'international elite' class of cosmopolitans, but instead singled out a much broader group of the world's population. A poll for the BBC World Service in 2016 found that for the first time in its fifteen-year history of tracking the question, more humans identified as global citizens than as citizens of their own country.[30] By stating that you cannot be a citizen of the world and a citizen of a nation, Theresa May created a false dichotomy. Many of us identify with our localities and our nations, at the same time as being proud global citizens. We should not force those who do not have cosmopolitan urges to consider themselves as citizens of the world, but neither should politicians tell those who feel strong solidarity with the rest of humanity that this disqualifies them from belonging to a nation.

There is no denying that it is easier to become a citizen of the world if you have the cash to pay for it. If you are born into a wealthy family in north London's Muswell Hill today, it would not be unusual for you to go on to study in Paris, work in New York and retire to northern Italy. If you are born just a few miles away on the Broadwater Farm Estate, near where I grew up in Tottenham, it is possible that in your life you will rarely go beyond Oyster travel card Zone 3.

As the world has become increasingly globalised, the centrality of the nation state has eroded, yet alongside this erosion there has been no change to our human need to belong. The newly digitally connected, global world has only provided a coherent new identity for those who have the education and the means to exploit its advantages. University graduates who go on to become management consultants, lawyers, investment bankers, non-governmental-organisation (NGO) workers, media professionals and politicians are among the lucky few who belong to this group. Meanwhile, for many, economic stagnation following the global financial crisis combined with the decline in the importance of the nation state, have left few healthy contexts in which to find pride or identity.[31]

Work and travel opportunities are defined by your parents' wealth and social status and the strength of your education, but in other ways things have changed for everyone, no matter their social class. Solitude – when defined 'as a subjective state in which you're isolated from input from other minds'[32] – has become vanishingly rare compared with previous centuries. A typical family scene as we enter the third decade of the twenty-first century is a family eating dinner with the television on, while the parents scroll through Twitter, the teenagers Snapchat their friends and the youngest play mobile-phone games. Like most people, when I travel by bus, plane or train, I either work from my phone or laptop, pick up a free newspaper, or plug in my headphones to listen to music or a podcast. While this may seem like a remarkable improvement – an opportunity for us all to consume information and learn new perspectives at a newly rapid rate – it has also had negative effects. We have lost both connection, and the time for the reflection and mindfulness we need in order to process the stream of life's events.

Our media cycle has become dominated by a perpetual outrage culture. The launch of CNN in 1980, and with it the dawn of twenty-four-hour news coverage, changed how we digest information and perceive politics for ever. For decades prior to this, families got their news once in the morning from their daily paper or radio show, and maybe one more time with the evening news. News producers had to condense the day's news into one half-hour show. Now they had to fill twenty-four hour-long slots each day. Inevitably, this meant stories that previously were not deemed newsworthy became worth talking about. As different twenty-four-hour news stations began to compete with each other, sensationalism was incentivised. In the USA in particular, where impartiality rules are non-existent, TV news networks quickly became dominated by shows filled with partisan talking heads rather than fact-based news reports.

The internet and social media took the concept of twenty-four-hour news to a new level. You no longer need to tune in to cable TV to get your current-affairs fix; you can now get it at any point during the day on your mobile phone. Almost half of us check our smartphones before we get out of bed in the morning.[33] This has had the positive effect of democratising debate. You do not have to be a journalist or a public figure to find a platform to speak. Anyone with access to the internet can make a Twitter account. Initially, this revolution seemed like it could be the start of a new forum for open and constructive dialogue. Instead, social media has become a realm for anger, disagreement and shame. Few of us are innocent. I send an average of around six tweets per day, giving my reaction to the day's news stories, campaigning on my political priorities and calling out opponents when I think they are wrong. At the start of my career, I had to pitch to newspapers or give interviews to influence the public debate. Today my personal Twitter account has more followers than the individual daily circulation figures of *The Times*, the *Daily Mirror* and the *Daily Telegraph*.[34]

What's more, most of the time our 24/7 information windows do not take us down new roads of discovery. We are rarely offered new perspectives or differing views. The social-media algorithms that determine what content appears on our newsfeeds most often offer up opinions we already agree with. The result is that we get trapped in echo chambers of like-minded individuals, where we routinely congratulate ourselves and condemn those we disagree with. With self-reinforcing information flooding our minds at a rate and intensity unimaginable in the past, we have begun to adapt in strange and concerning ways. The more time a moderate individual spends online, and on social-media websites specifically, the more extreme their views and opinions are likely to become.[35]

As technology and globalisation have advanced, citizens of nation states have fractured into individualism. This has proven shallow. In the UK, the rate of depression among teenagers has shot up by 70 per cent since the early 1990s.[36] One in eight children in England have a mental-health disorder,[37] and 2.4 million adult Brits suffer from chronic loneliness.[38]

Alienation and isolation among those who do not have the social or financial capital to be part of the new global world has left a vacuum for new identity groups to exploit. Using exclusive identities, defined by ethnicity, culture or ideology, rather than broader inclusive identities, like an idea of the nation state built on institutions and values, extreme groups on all sides of the political spectrum have gained new support. In recent years, the liberal-democratic order, for decades accepted by many as a righteous force for progress, has been questioned. Populist resurgences across Europe, the United States of America, South America and beyond have begun to dominate the political agenda. The reaction to the injustices of the modern world has been a surge in ethnocentric identity politics. What started as a tool for oppressed minorities to win rights and opportunities has been warped by the new right to legitimise superiority and chauvinism. The civil rights movement Black Lives Matter is opposed by White Lives Matter, a group which describes itself as 'dedicated to promotion of the white race.' Meanwhile, feminism is attacked by 'male supremacists', including some of those who gather for the annual 'International Conference on Men's Issues'.[39]

From the retreat of moderate individuals into their own identity groups, religions and political movements to the rise of increasingly extreme white-supremacist neo-Nazi organisations, radical Islamic groups and gangs, the modern world is becoming increasingly tribal. This is not healthy for our democracy. There is a need for a renewal of the politics of the common good, an urgency for our communities and nations to find new ways to bring us together, rather than split us further apart.

Many of the solutions to the great challenges we face in the first half of the twentieth century will rely on economic reform, sound investment in the future and a radical redistribution of wealth from the 1 per cent to the rest. But economics is not everything. Culture also matters. For too long social democrats in Europe and Democrats in the United States of America have provided good economic policies, while leaving conservatives an open goal to put forward their ideas for what it means to belong to an identity. Donald Trump became President in 2016 with the slogan 'Make America Great Again,' which signalled that he would return something intangible he recognised was lost in the nation's culture. Similarly, the Leave side won the 2016 referendum with the slogan 'take back control', which connected with voters' emotions more effectively than the sober economic arguments cued by the Remain campaign's strapline 'Britain stronger in Europe'. A failure to provide a renewed and progressive path to identity and the common good, when combined with the consequences of vast advances in technology and globalisation, has allowed tribal politics to fill the cultural gap.

THE END OF BIPARTISANSHIP

'I've got a Lammy whammy in the paper against me when we're thirteen months from a general election. I'm disappointed . . . because you're supposed to be my mate. Because you're not a commentator, you're a Labour MP. Because you're trying to be a serious person in this party. Because we've got a general election to win. Because we've got the Tory press against us. That's why I'm disappointed . . . I'm very angry about it,' Ed Miliband said.

It was March 2014, four years into Ed's five-year stint as leader of the Labour Party, and the first and only time I was invited to his office in Parliament. It was immediately obvious that he had not asked me over for a coffee and a catch-up, or to discuss policy ideas. With the door left ajar and his team of advisers conspicuously listening in, it was clear that I had been summoned to be made an example of.

Ed was referring to an interview I had given the day before in which I'd responded to a journalist's question about his leadership by saying: 'I think we have been a very effective opposition, but in the next fourteen months we have to cross that Rubicon to being a government in waiting. I think that has yet to happen.'[40]

I told Ed that, as a backbench MP, I was simply giving an honest assessment of where we stood as a party in the minds of the electorate. I had not made a personal attack on him. I had not said that the public would not see him as a future prime minister. Looking like a prime minister in waiting has always been the challenge for any opposition leader. Many people did not even think Barack Obama looked presidential when he won the Democratic nomination in summer 2008.

I was upset by the seriousness with which he was taking what I had said. I was not involved in a plot to undermine Ed's leadership. Quite the opposite. Though I was not his closest political ally, I supported his agenda, and I was as fed up with the coalition government as anyone. I longed for Labour to get back into government.

'Labour MPs should not be saying "Labour should", "Labour must", because you are Labour,' Ed continued. 'You're a representative of the Labour Party. We're trying to win an election in an incredibly hostile environment. Everybody should be thinking: "What have I done today to help there be a Labour government?" That is what we need. Anything that detracts from that is unacceptable.'

During the Blair years, party discipline was just as strict. When I was first elected in a 2000 by-election aged twenty-seven, it was the first time I had ever even been to Westminster. I had much to learn, but it did not take me long to realise that toeing the party line, particularly in the media, was necessary for getting ahead in New Labour. Indeed, in Blair's first meeting with MPs, he stressed 'the importance of strength, unity and discipline'.[41] Implicit in this is a threat. If you show anything other than blind dedication to the party, you risk exclusion.

Typically, exclusion in British party politics has simply meant long spells on the backbenches, without being given a ministerial or shadow ministerial job. I've enjoyed long periods both as a minister and on the backbenches, but in recent years I have for the first time been threatened with actual exclusion, in the form of deselection.

Growing up in north London, I had many Jewish friends. I went to bar and bat mitzvahs. Reading Martin Luther King as a teenager, I became fascinated by the solidarity shown between black and Jewish oppressed people. One passage particularly stuck with me: 'My people were brought to America in chains. Your people were driven here to escape the chains fashioned for them in Europe. Our unity is born of our common struggle for centuries, not only to rid ourselves of bondage, but to make oppression of any people by others an impossibility.'[42]

So, when there was evidence of anti-Semitism within significant fringes of the Labour Party, I knew I had to call it out. When I went to a rally against anti-Semitism in Parliament Square in spring 2018, I was showing my solidarity with a minority I have supported all my political life. I marched with friends from my youth, from Stamford Hill, and the kind lawyers who sponsored my entrance as the first black Briton to go to Harvard Law School. By attending the rally, I was voicing my commitment to standing up for Jewish people and nothing else.

Despite this, my actions were interpreted as an attack on Jeremy Corbyn's leadership. One or two members of my local party decided that it was a treasonous offence, with one posting on the Tottenham Labour Facebook group:

> I want a candidate in the next election who wants Labour to win, not one who joins the extreme right wing attacks on the Labour movement. He can be triggered in December if we haven't had an election by then.[43]

Loyalty and discipline have always been important in party politics, but it is only in recent years that I have noticed it become so intensely tribal. At the point where MPs in a proudly and historically anti-racist party are threatened with deselection for attending a march against anti-Semitism, it is clear that tribalism has become a problem.

The problem goes far beyond the Labour Party. The 2016 EU referendum was a political earthquake that cleaved a new rift across the whole of the once-United Kingdom. In the lead-up to the vote, and the painful years since, my country has been divided into two camps, which the liberal *Economist* magazine presciently described in 2014 as best understood by contrasting Clacton and Cambridge.[44] The former, 'poor, nostalgic and occupied by white, working-class and mostly elderly folk', is mainly made up of people with communitarian values who distrust change and feel insecure about the future. The latter, with high investment, good transport links, international connections and openness to change, is disproportionately filled with cosmopolitans, who welcome the modern world and benefit from improvements to technology and the spread of globalisation. Indeed, in June 2016, 70 per cent of Clacton's residents voted to leave the European Union, while in Cambridge nearly 74 per cent voted to remain.

Tensions between the two tribes reached a tragic crescendo a few days before the 2016 vote, when my colleague Jo Cox, the Labour MP, was shot and stabbed to death by a far-right terrorist who shouted: 'Britain first.' While there have been no similar attacks on members of parliament since, the threat lingers. Barely a week goes by in which I do not receive a death threat or some piece of racist abuse. This ramped up during the recent years in which I have been a prominent member of the unsuccessful campaign to keep Britain inside the European Union via another referendum. Since 2016, Brexit has been at the centre of what commentators frequently refer to as a new culture war. How you voted has become an identity-defining issue that goes far deeper than the question of whether we remain part of a supranational structure.

The entrenchment of divisions in British politics is mirrored in the USA, where friends in Washington regularly tell me about the increasingly partisan nature of their politics. Throughout much of the 1980s and in to the '90s, several left-leaning Republican members of Congress and the Senate regularly voted for more liberal policies than certain right-leaning Democrat members, and vice versa.[45] They were what was known as the 'ideological middle'. The consequence was that coalitions could be formed across party lines to get specific bills passed. There was a reason for members to work together in the best interests of the country, as well as their own parties. Bipartisan work in Congress not only facilitated the smooth running of government, it also allowed for collaboration. Senator Sam Nunn, a Democrat, and Senator Richard Lugar, a Republican, for example, have been commended for their joint work to secure and dismantle the threat of nuclear weapons in the former Soviet countries.[46]

During Bill Clinton's presidency, and as we reached the new millennium, members of each party began to move further apart ideologically, until this middle ground eventually disappeared. According to the *Washington Post*, membership of the ideological middle plummeted from 344 (79 per cent of the House) in 1982 to just four (less than 1 per cent of the House) in 2013.[47]

Newt Gingrich, the former Republican Speaker of the House, is often cited as the man who broke American politics.[48] On election to Congress, Gingrich's plan was to blow up the ideological middle and use the resulting inefficiency to ferment populist dissatisfaction. To do this, he made use of the new twenty-four-hour news coverage. Gingrich told other Republicans to 'raise hell', to not be so 'nice' and to recognise that politics was ultimately a 'war for power'.[49] Forming a group of twelve disciple congressmen that he named the 'Conservative Opportunity Society', Gingrich achieved his goal of eradicating bipartisan spirit in Washington, and in so doing threw a spanner into the engines of US administrations for decades to come. After two decades in Congress, he told Conservative activists: 'The number-one fact about the news media is they love fights . . . When you give them confrontations, you get attention; when you get attention, you can educate.'[50] By the time Barack Obama became president in 2008, the idea of finding bipartisan support for a policy was farcical. He found it increasingly difficult, and often impossible, to push important reforms through Congress. Gingrich's political philosophy was a precursor to that of his friend and the current president, Donald Trump.

Worryingly, our increasingly tribal politics – on all sides of the political spectrum – are becoming more reminiscent of the political arena envisioned by Carl Schmitt,[51] a Nazi philosopher and political theorist who wrote about identity. In 1938, Schmitt asserted that because economics is defined by a distinction between profitability and unprofitability, aesthetics is defined by a distinction between beauty and ugliness, and morality is defined by a distinction between good and evil, there must also be a distinction that defines 'the political'.[52] Schmitt settled on the distinction between 'friends' and 'enemies', arguing that an individual's political identity comes in large part from their most ardent opponents. 'Tell me who your enemy is, and I will tell you who you are,' Schmitt said.

Schmitt saw the advance of liberalism as an 'onslaught against the political', which aimed to replace friends and enemies with economic rationalism and 'perpetual discussion'. He saw this as a negative trend that would replace all political problems with those which are technocratic and economic. Schmitt argued that suppressing the distinction between friends and enemies from the political would lead to even more destructive wars. Clearly it was his own conception of the political, and not liberalism, that can be more closely linked to the mass destruction of the Second World War. As 'Crown Jurist' of the Nazi government, Schmitt was responsible for defending Hitler's extra-judicial murders of his political enemies, as well as removing 'Jewish influence' from German law.[53] A resurgence of a politics based on the distinction between friends versus enemies, instead of rational debate and discussion, does not necessitate a return to the worst horrors of twentieth-century Europe, but it is concerning.

Unquestioning loyalty to a group matched by unthinking oppos-ition to enemies can undermine our ability for intellectual honesty. When issues are split into Labour versus Tory, Democrat versus Republican or Leave versus Remain, they are always oversimplified. We are not always able to make an honest assessment of the other side's policy idea. We judge an idea's merit according to its messenger rather than its content. This has the secondary effect of blinding us to bad behaviour within our own group. Members of a tribe are predisposed to closing their eyes when confronted with a fellow member's wrongdoing.

When anti-Semitism was exposed in the Labour Party, too many who had spent years righteously campaigning against racism simply dismissed, ignored or denied the problem. The leadership was far too slow to adopt the full International Holocaust Remembrance Alliance's definition of anti-Semitism. Some party members who displayed grotesquely anti-Semitic attitudes were handled too leniently, with dozens of cases left outstanding for far too long. When whistle-blowers who had worked within the party's HQ criticised the handling of anti-Semitism cases, a Labour spokesman attacked them for being 'disaf-fected former officials' with 'both personal and political axes to grind'.[54] This gross misjudgement by the party's leadership showed their tribal instincts to defend themselves had overtaken their commitment to taking allegations of anti-Semitism seriously.

Meanwhile, the same Conservative politicians who relish the oppor-tunity to point out these failures on the left make no effort to call out senior members of their own party. In recent years, the transformation of Boris Johnson from liberal London mayor to the talisman of the populist nationalist right as prime minister has occurred without any real complaint from the majority of his own colleagues.[55] I was able to work with Johnson amicably following the 2011 riots. We disagreed on many things, but I would never have accused him of racism or Islamophobia. Johnson's targeting of Muslim women in summer 2018 for electoral gain marked a concerning shift. Following Johnson's comparisons of Muslim women to 'bankrobbers' and 'letter-boxes', the silence of leading Conservatives was deafening. Once within a tribe, a member's desires, thoughts, intentions and wishes are filtered through the emotions of the group as a whole, and in opposition to those outside of it. In some cases it means that defending your group matters far more than external standards of right and wrong.

THE DEATH OF TRUTH

One of the ugliest consequences of the new tribalism is what the Pulitzer Prize-winning literary critic Michiko Kakutani has labelled 'The Death of Truth'.[56] The basis of liberal democracy is that its citizens work with some set of shared facts. When a politician or another public figure makes a claim, the press can scrutinise the truth of it and let the citizens know whether they were correct or mistaken. In the past, on the whole, countries with a free press would operate largely on this basis. This is not to pretend that we ever enjoyed perfectly objective news reporting – a right-wing newspaper or television station would inevitably put a different spin on a story to a left-wing newspaper or television station – but, ultimately, they would work off much the same accepted truths.

This is no longer the case. With the decline of traditional media and shared news sources, there is no such thing as the common adjudicator. Rather than most of the country tuning in to the *News at Ten*, individuals are now glued to unique feeds on their mobile phones that are based on personal preference. Disappearing into different silos, people's beliefs about facts are now often founded on their tastes or political opinions to a greater degree than on what can be established as true. A 2017 survey by the *Washington Post* found that 47 per cent of Republicans falsely believe that Trump won the popular vote in the 2016 presidential election.[57] Similarly, a King's College London study found that 64 per cent of Conservative Leave voters and 65 per cent of

Labour Leave voters still believed the debunked claim that the UK sends £350 million per week to the EU, two years after the 2016 Brexit referendum.[58] There is also a deluded group of individuals who think Arsenal are the best football team in north London.

The political leaders who have flourished in this era have mostly been those who are prepared to compromise over the truth. A much-cited statistic calculated by the *Washington Post* is that Donald Trump made 2,140 false or misleading claims during his first year as president.[59] That works out to 5.9 known public lies a day. Similarly, the two most prominent proponents of the Brexit campaign, Boris Johnson and Nigel Farage, were, at the most generous, ambivalent towards the truth – confident that even when others called them out on their lies, they would not lose support. Michael Gove, another major figure in the Leave campaign, displayed his disdain for the truth when he said in an interview that 'people in this country have had enough of experts'.

As Prime Minister, Johnson has continued to lie his way to electoral success. In order to avoid the Irish backstop created by Theresa May's Brexit withdrawal agreement, Boris Johnson accepted an amendment to introduce a border between Northern Ireland and the rest of the UK. Despite it being written in black and white in the new withdrawal agreement, Johnson repeatedly denied the creation of a border, in direct contradiction of his own Brexit Secretary, who admitted that businesses would now need to carry out 'exit summary declarations' when sending goods from Northern Ireland to the rest of the UK.[60] Perhaps Johnson felt he had no choice other than to lie. Only months earlier, in the Tory leadership contest, he had pledged, 'Under no circumstances, whatever happens, will I allow the EU or anyone else to create any kind of division down the Irish Sea.' Similarly, Johnson's 2019 general election slogan 'Get Brexit Done' was fundamentally dishonest. Voting Conservative in that election meant voting for years more negotiations in Brussels, and division in Parliament and the country, over the UK's future relationship with the EU. A more accurate slogan would have been 'Get the Withdrawal Agreement Done So We Can Begin Years More of Arguments About The Future of Brexit'. Unfortunately, as Johnson's landslide 2019 victory demonstrated, many voters either did not notice Johnson's lies, or simply did not care.

It is not only easily caricatured figures like Boris Johnson and Donald Trump who have flourished by treating the truth with disdain. Theresa May has a claim to being the UK's first post-truth prime minister. Throughout her premiership, May regularly denied what she knew to be true and happily reversed her previous statements without acknowledgement, explanation or embarrassment. A study by a team from the University of York found that in interviews Theresa May answered just 27 per cent of questions, either ignoring awkward ones or modifying them to suit her pre-prepared answers.[62] Politicians from all parties use similar tactics on occasion, but on this analysis Theresa May was the 'most evasive' Conservative prime minister in fifty years.[63] In 2015, Jeremy Corbyn defied expectations to win the Labour Party leadership with the slogan 'straight talking, honest politics'. However, many in the party and the wider public became disappointed by his failure to live up to this pledge. During the 2016 referendum, the lifelong Eurosceptic failed to convince the public that he had become an advocate of the UK remaining in the European Union overnight. In the years that followed, Corbyn's triangulation on Brexit was neither 'straight talking' nor 'honest'.

The changes to party politics in recent years provide a clear illustration of the corrosive effect the new tribalism can have on public discourse, but this is not only about politics. Affiliation with a certain political group only represents one sphere in which individuals who are reacting to the radical changes in the global and digital era are retreating. It also explains why we tend mostly to follow like-minded people on social media, why there is a widening divide between those who live in cities and those who live in rural areas, and why it seems harder than ever for us all just to get along.

The new tribalism is the enemy of the good society because it judges people not by the content of their character, or the calibre of their arguments, ethics or actions, but *only* by their affiliations with a specific group. It breaks down what is common between citizens of one nation, reducing the opportunity for reasoned and respectful dialogue, persuasion and understanding. It focuses on what sets us apart from each other, rather than on what we share.

FROM APATHY TO TRIBALISM

I am from Guyana, or at least both of my parents were. As the test I took revealed back in 2007, my DNA is a close match to members of the Tuareg tribe in Niger, West Africa, but I do not speak their language. I grew up in the British Caribbean community in a single-parent household in Tottenham, but I spent term time as a choirboy at a boarding school in Peterborough. I am British, English and a Londoner, but my answer to where I am from changes depending on how far I am from my first home on Dongola Road in Tottenham. I am a member of parliament for the Labour Party, but I did not spend my time at university wearing a red rosette and knocking on doors. I am a lifelong Spurs fan, but occasionally I lend my support to Peterborough United F.C. I have faith in Christianity and its traditions, but my views are progressive. I grew up working-class with no elite connections, but these days I am one of the Queen's Privy Councillors, and I am friends with the man who became the forty-fourth president of the United States of America. I am black, but I am happily married to a white woman, with three mixed-race kids.

These are several of my identities. Each classifies me according to a characteristic that qualifies me for membership in a specific group. My identities are fluid and cross-cutting, and a couple of them even contradict. There is no doubt that they have contributed to who I am today: the views I hold, the dreams I have and the prejudices I cannot shed. I am all my identities at once, but at the same time none of them on their own define me. They are socially constructed, in so far as they would be meaningless if it weren't for how they relate to other people.

Sometimes I use my group identities to make a political point. I make no apologies for this. Blackness is as rare in the House of Commons as it is in an Alpine ski resort. I am not the only black member of parliament, but we could probably all fit into one cable car. When I perceive an injustice towards the black community, I speak out against it not as an objective observer, but as a member of that group. Of course, there are times for cool, dispassionate and objective politics, but there are other occasions when it is important for politics to be about who you are, where you come from and where you belong.

When seventy-two people were burned alive by a preventable fire in a social-housing block made up disproportionately of black, Asian and minority-ethnic people, I spoke with a special passion reserved for those whose lives are just as precarious as mine was growing up. When it became apparent that thousands of British citizens were being subjected to the full force of Theresa May's 'Hostile Environment' because of their skin colour, I thought of my parents when I called it a national day of shame.

When I entered public life after the 2000 Tottenham by-election, triggered by the sad death of my formidable predecessor Bernie Grant, our main challenge during the campaign was to make sure that people turned out in what was traditionally a safe Labour seat. This was particularly difficult after our party's momentous landslide victory in the 1997 general election. In the end I won a comfortable majority, but only around one quarter of the electorate used their ballot papers. I remember being told this was the third-lowest turnout in a by-election since the Second World War. It was more evidence of an apathy in politics, particularly among young people, that was beginning to become a concern to broad sections of the media.[64]

Apathy was the subject of my maiden speech in Parliament.[65] I spoke about the lack of engagement between voters and politicians, and called for political parties to make more effort to get the public interested. There was a sense that most people no longer cared about politics because the two major parties agreed on too much. Some academics, politicians and journalists bought into Francis Fukuyama's thesis that the liberal democracy we had achieved marked the end of history.[66] There was excessive consensus. Not enough to argue about.

Indifference is poison to democratic politics. Meaningful options are vital if we are to offer people choice. Debate is necessary for us to further understanding, to synthesise opposing viewpoints and to come to wise conclusions. Yet complaints about apathy in our politics feel strange and foreign now.

Twenty years ago, when I first became an MP, I could never have predicted how far the mood would shift. Concerns about apathy have been replaced by deeper worries about toxic new forms of tribalism. Factions within political parties have become more bitter enemies of each other than of their supposed opponents. We have a resurgent, populist nationalist right that is anti-migrant, denies climate change and wants to roll back human rights. On the far left there is a dangerous minority who have confused anti-capitalism with anti-Semitism and have turned inwards, not wanting to reach out to the world. In between the extremes of far left and right, too many of us are guilty of jumping to conclusions based on who a person is rather than what they say.

Analysing the phenomenon of tribalism as though I am an objective observer would fail to recognise that belonging is deeply personal. A balanced account of why we have become more polarised, and what we should do about it must not only address the dangers of tribal membership and suggest what should replace it. It must also contain a personal exploration of the groups where I have found belonging. This should include all the virtues of group membership as well as its defects. I therefore begin this book with a section called 'My Tribes', where I retrace my sense of belonging in three groups to which I am personally connected. I do this to find out what we can learn from the differences between each of these tribes: what holds them together, how open they are to new people, how they are changing and what it feels like to be part of each of them. In the second part, 'How Belonging Can Break Society', I focus in on the loneliness crisis we are experiencing and address criticisms of identity politics. In part three, 'How Belonging Can Make Society', I put forward some ideas for how we can, together, move beyond tribalism for the benefit of all.

MY TRIBES

2

Jerusalem

The erosion of a once proud English community

'To be born English is to win first prize in the lottery of life.'

Cecil Rhodes

The first time I appeared on TV, I was wearing a dress. My parents, siblings and extended family had gathered round my Aunt Annette's TV set in Edmonton. She was my only relative who had a VHS video recorder. Aunt Annette had taped the 1983 Christmas edition of BBC's *Songs of Praise*, filmed in Peterborough Cathedral. No one in my street, let alone my family, had been inside that box before. I could not believe I was on BBC1.

I can't remember a day between the ages of eleven and thirteen when I wasn't singing. If I wasn't performing at Matins, Mass, Eucharist or Evensong, I was practising. Every day for three years. At home, there was always music playing. Changing vinyl records for my parents, I became a connoisseur of Marvin Gaye, Diana Ross and the Supremes. After Bob Marley died in 1981, 'No Woman No Cry' was played endlessly, as though it was stuck on repeat.

Most of all, I wanted to be Michael Jackson. I had a curly perm, a sequined glove and a badass moonwalk on the dance floor. But Aled

Jones, who was a chorister at Bangor Cathedral, had just got to number one in the charts with 'Walking in the Air'. With my baby face and angelic voice, my primary-school music teacher Mrs Shepherd, the local priest and my mother conspired to send me for voice trials. Miraculously, I was successful and was awarded a scholarship to cover my boarding fees at The King's Cathedral School, a state boarding school in Peterborough.

Singing inside Peterborough Cathedral, a magnificent twelfth-century building, is something I look back on with deep fondness and nostalgia. There were, of course, a few catches. On hot summer afternoons I would have preferred to play football with my friends outside rather than perform endless chants and vocal warm-up exercises. The race to see whose voice would break first induced real anxiety at a time when growing up should have been something we were excited about. And with my beaming grin resting on a white ruffled collar and cassock, I ended up looking more like Henry VIII than Michael Jackson. Fitting, then, that Peterborough Cathedral is where Henry VIII's first wife and queen, Catherine of Aragon, is buried. Just a few metres away from her tomb, somewhere along the pews, I had carved my name into the ancient oak. Decades later a BBC researcher, much to my surprise, located it for another episode of *Songs of Praise*. I had made my mark on Peterborough, as it would on me.

DISCOVERING ENGLAND

Taking the fifty-minute train from King's Cross to Peterborough these days brings back memories of when I had made the journey for my first school term in September 1983. I was eleven years old – excited, but anxious – about to start a life far removed from my parochial upbringing in a small corner of Tottenham. My parents, neither of whom owned a car at the time, accompanied me on the journey. Dad wore a pinstripe suit and a trilby. Mum wore a bright yellow, floral dress. These were the clothes they wore to church. They wanted to make a good impression, as for them my scholarship to King's was a huge achievement. None of my other siblings went to a school like this. For my mum it must have felt like vindication for the extra tests she set us after school while she was working her third job. My dad was more worldly

and experienced than my mother, but even he could not hide the obvious pride in his gleaming smile.

We arrived at the station and took a taxi to my new boarding house.
I pressed my forehead against the window, taking in the wide avenues
lined with trees and the spaces between each house. I had only seen this
kind of place in picture books and on television. I didn't realise that I
could have been awestruck much sooner if I had just gone about three
miles north of Tottenham to leafy Enfield. Through my eleven-year-old
eyes it seemed that the green suburban calm with its picket fences and
winding avenues was a world away from the bustling, chaotic, suffocat-
ing neighbourhood where I had grown up. Through childhood eyes, it
felt as though there was more room for sunlight to spread. There were
so many new sounds to hear. Lawnmowers, dogs barking, the crack of
a cricket bat meeting ball on a hot September day.

Soon enough, we arrived at the boarding house. I glanced at the
other boys waiting around with their parents. There was a strange antiseptic smell in the rooms that made me feel sick. As the time came for
them to leave, my mum began to cry, and then so did I. I wouldn't see
my parents for six weeks. I had never spent so long away from home.

As the only black boy, this was the first time I felt overwhelmingly
conscious of my skin colour. All of those with easily observable differences, whether camp, physically disabled or in my case black, were
quickly picked on. My difference was met with comments that ranged
from light-hearted teasing and banter to downright cruelty. It was the
era of British TV – from the comedy of Alf Garnett to *Love Thy
Neighbour* – in which black characters had begun to appear on shows,
but often only to be mocked. I remember the BBC children's show
Grange Hill featured one black character, Benny, but he was always on
the fringes, never in the centre of the action. That's how I felt at the
start of my school days in Peterborough.

Though I came to love my life in Peterborough and even became
head boy at the school, the first few weeks and months were difficult.
Mostly I stayed very quiet. In part because I was nervous and I didn't
know what to say, but also because I wanted to digest and absorb what
was going on. I was not the only child staying nearly mute in those first
few days. There was another boy who stood on his own without saying

much. On the second afternoon I mustered the courage to ask him his name. It was Jamieson. He spoke with a terrible stammer, as he told me where he came from. He was from a working-class background, not alien to my own. Soon I realised that he was funny despite his impediment, skilled at cracking jokes to deflect from his own insecurities.

In the first term, Jamieson and I stuck together at the boarding house. We attracted a few other boys and kept ourselves apart from the others. In break-time we would mind our own business and talk about the teachers, or football, but it didn't take long for us to attract the attention of older boys. One break-time a group from the year above came over and told us it was their job to make sure we weren't 'arrogant' and 'knew our place'. Our fear encouraged them, and they chased us down the school corridor and outside across the well-kept lawns and flower beds. The smallest of our number, Nigel, was quickly caught and thrown onto the ground. I kept running . . .

Finding an unoccupied common room, I barricaded myself inside with wooden chairs. I leant against them for what felt like hours but was probably no more than a few minutes. Suddenly there was loud knocking at the door.

'Open up!' a boy shouted as he burst in. His name was Tom. A tall thirteen-year-old with ginger hair, patchy stubble and wild eyes, he had cleared the first hurdle of puberty. Tom had legendary status in the school after scoring fourteen tries in his first rugby season the previous year. He grabbed me, threw me onto the floor and sat on me, pinning my arms down with his knees, and began slapping me on the face. I was writhing around trying to break free, but he was too heavy and strong. In those moments, I felt trapped, humiliated and afraid about what might happen next.

Suddenly we both heard a voice calling from downstairs. 'T . . . To . . . Tom,' the voice squeaked, 'Tom!' I recognised the stammer at once, but Tom was unnerved. He got up and sprinted away. It was, of course, Jamieson. This small act of heroism had saved me from a worse beating. I felt the intense solidarity that only comes through adversity. For Jamieson, it didn't matter where our parents came from, or what music we had grown up listening to. We were, on an important level, the same.

Even in the earliest weeks it was clear that this was not a place where you were supposed to be sensitive. There was not a moment to pause or reflect. I quickly learned that my insecurities, which related to my accent and my skin colour, were supposed to be hidden. Inside I worried that I would never fit in. There was a clear distinction between the day school, where we had lessons, and the boarding house – of which only around one fifth of the pupils were resident. While the day school was a gender-mixed and relatively open environment (for the 1980s), the boarding house felt more like an old-fashioned independent school. King's was state-funded and thankfully avoided the most archaic traditions of the English public school, but there was still a clear hierarchy in the boarding house. You rose in the pecking order according to some combination of your age, talent on the rugby pitch and ability to get girls.

It was still normal when I arrived to suffer corporal punishment for misbehaviour. The senior housemaster at the time favoured using the slipper, which was in fact an old-style rubber plimsoll, on our bare buttocks. Younger boys got his firm hand on their arse instead, as an apparently softer form of discipline. I never got the hand, but remember crying in anguish after being slippered. In 1982 the European Court of Human Rights had ruled that such beatings in schools could only be administered with parental consent, and by 1986, when I was fourteen, it was outlawed in all state schools in England and Wales.

Secondary school is when you're meant to start finding out who you are, but it was difficult to do this when 'who I was' represented the very kind of otherness I was trying to escape from. I was constantly told off for holding my fork in the wrong way. 'It's not a pen,' prefects and teachers would repeat. I didn't know what a butter knife was, or that dinner was called supper. I was surprised to learn that there are more varieties of cheese than Cheddar.

My family back home was a source of deep insecurity and awkwardness. I hated being asked whether I had brothers and sisters. Most of my friends had traditional families: two married parents and one or two siblings. It was complicated to explain that I had three half-brothers, two from my dad's first marriage and another from my mother's previous relationship. I also had a full younger sister, whom I was very fond of, but also a sister with whom I shared no DNA. Technically she was my brother's sister. From the age of twelve, I did not have a dad any more. And before he left, he and Mum had a tempestuous relationship. Dad was a drunk. When he came home from the pub, they inevitably fought and yelled. As a teenager already ashamed of my obvious differences, it filled me with dread.

I remember bringing friends back from Peterborough to my house in Tottenham for the weekend to celebrate my sixteenth birthday. We had a great time, but seeing my two worlds collide was deeply embarrassing nonetheless. My house had none of the mahogany furnishings, well-stuffed sofas or Agas that many of them were used to. We had lino on the floor and cupboard doors that came off when you opened them. Some of my friends were perplexed as to how we did our washing-up without a dishwasher. My insecurities about my home life were clearly visible to the older boys at school who picked on me in those early years.

Though I felt like an imposter, I slowly began to enjoy my new life: the structure, the ebb and the flow, of the English boarding school. The discipline, the hierarchy and the assumption of ambition showed me, even if I did not know it yet, that new opportunities were opening. As I came of age in the school, it was not only my accent that changed or my grades that improved. Singing every day in the cathedral choir ensured that I understood the importance of repetition in the service of excellence that would benefit me in later life. As culture minister decades after, I joked with my wife that I only had the discipline to go through my Red Box each day because of the strict routine I followed as a chorister. In fact, I doubt I would have become the MP for Tottenham if I had not spent my formative years in Peterborough. Spending time meeting the families of my day-student friends, I gained a new perception of what life could be and what middle England could offer. Stability, structure, calm, comfort, duty, service and tradition were instilled in me. I wanted to hold onto those values.

Jamieson became my best friend. He helped me find comfort in this strange place that soon began to feel like my new home. After a couple of terms, the people who had seemed intimidatingly bright and worldly to me in my first weeks now seemed normal. When the school holidays came, I did not want to leave. I often stayed with Jamieson at his parents' house in the Peterborough suburbs. His mother and father, Kathy and Clive, welcomed me into their lives with open arms. Many of my fondest memories as a teenager were of my time spent with them, eating roast dinners, playing in their garden, watching the football and, as I got older, getting ready to go down to the town's pubs and clubs.

ENGLAND IN DECLINE

A part of me will always be in the Fens. I've been going back to Peterborough regularly ever since I left. In this time, the train from King's Cross has speeded up, but the infinitely flat landscape and the sickly-sweet smell of sugar beet on arrival has not changed.

When I last visited Jamieson's parents after a long interlude, it felt like a family reunion. Five foot nine, in good shape but with greying hair, Clive stood proudly in his Peterborough United football shirt and jeans. I met him at the John Lewis car park after making the short walk from Peterborough station. He greeted me with a sloppy kiss on the cheek. We drove in his Fiat to the bungalow he shared with Kathy. Though different to the house I had stayed in as a child, it felt familiar. Their bungalow was immaculately clean, with photos of their children and grandchildren lining the walls, a large TV in the corner of the front room, a glass coffee table and a faux leather suite of one sofa and two chairs. We sat down and at once I fell into a state of contentment and belonging. I felt as relaxed as a teenager visiting his grandparents for Sunday lunch. It was a home away from home. They told me I hadn't changed a bit, and we reminisced about the past.

I had adored living in Peterborough – in my mind it was a suburban paradise – but the previous week I had read that *iLiveHere* had made the city the winner of its annual 'crap towns' survey. This 'award' was based on the responses of nearly 50,000 people, one of whom described Peterborough as 'the biggest dump in England with aggressive and inbred residents'. Another said: 'You feel totally isolated from the rest of the world and life in general, as though everything else is going on and you're not part of it as you're stuck in this dump. Take a trip into the town centre and it's like walking onto the set of the *Walking Dead* – every manner of inbred mutant adorns the streets.' The criticisms had been reprinted in the tabloid press, caricaturing the city as 'Britain's migrant squatter shambles'[1] and 'a city crumbling under pressure from immigrants'.[2]

'Peterborough was far safer in the fifties and sixties,' Kathy said, laying down a fine spread of freshly made sandwiches, quiche Lorraine and a pot of hot tea in the sitting room of their modest bungalow. 'I would go out till eleven o'clock at night, after I left school at fifteen, and come home on my own. Fine. I'd go into town to the skating and the dances. I'd get the bus home . . . I'd have ten minutes to walk home from the bus stop . . . no worries. But now . . . I wouldn't go out to the end of this road. Not because there's been anything here, but . . .'

'Peterborough was a nice town,' Clive said.

'Oh, it was lovely,' said Kathy. 'We first met in the dancehall in the centre of town. The Palais! We would meet up with a couple of friends, go to the pub, go and have fish and chips and then we'd go bowling. I remember when the first Chinese opened in Peterborough, down on Market Place, which would have been around 1965 or 1966. Later, when we had kids they used to play out in the street. You'd go shopping with them in a pram and leave them out the front of the shop and get your shopping . . .'

'You wouldn't do that today,' Clive said.

'It's scary now,' Kathy agreed.

Clive and Kathy pointed out that their children Jamieson and Sara took the short walk to school when they were just five or six years old. Even in Tottenham, in the 1970s, I can barely remember ever being taken to school by my parents. Today the school run has become like a scene from *Wacky Races* in which vehicles travel bumper to bumper, clogging up the streets with more speeding cars and pollution.

It is not only Clive and Kathy who are feeling insecure. In the UK, nearly two thirds of adult women and one third of men now feel unsafe walking alone after dark.[3] These fears are being passed on to the young, with three quarters of British children spending less time outside than prison inmates.[4] Knocking on doors across Britain at election time, I hear the same sentiments of fear and insecurity. At family weddings, gatherings and birthday parties in Chichester, Ludlow, Solihull, Birmingham, Southampton, Bristol, Bodiam and Edinburgh, I hear similar articulations of this feeling of apprehension. There is a general sense that while the technology we use, the food we eat and the TV we watch have improved, what lies outside the front door is in rapid and serious decline.

When I ask Clive and Kathy what the source of their anxiety was, they were quick to pinpoint immigration. Clive said 'Sometimes it's like being in a different country, really.'

The Tottenham I grew up in was a melting pot of ethnic groups: white English, African Caribbeans, Irish and Cypriots, to name just a few. By contrast, Peterborough was dominated by the white English. There were some exceptions. Peterborough has had a vibrant Italian population since the 1950s, when the London Brick Company advertised for workers in Puglia and Campania.[5] When I was there, I do remember a small West Indian community, which I sought out whenever I needed a haircut, as well as a growing Pakistani community. It was the 2004 enlargement of the EU, however, that made Peterborough a prime destination for Eastern European migrants. The original pulls were cheap housing, fast access to London and relatively high employment. The restaurant owner and chef Damian Wawrzyniak is a pillar of the local Polish community. He told me on a previous visit as we cruised down the multi-ethnic thoroughfare of Lincoln Road that Peterborough's total population of nearly 200,000 was made up of roughly 30,000 Eastern Europeans.

Though its centre is ancient, dating back to the mid-seventh century, Peterborough was paradoxically designated one of many 'new towns' in 1968. New houses, streets and neighbourhoods were built to accommodate overspill from London and Birmingham, where inner-city living was crowded and there was little space for new families. Plans were drawn up to create thousands of new homes and jobs.[6]

Like other new towns, including Stevenage, Harlow and Crawley, Peterborough grew rapidly as a result of a deliberate strategy to encourage people from the cities to move in. But in recent years the rate of change has been unprecedented. Many of the areas of the UK that reported the most dissatisfaction with immigration in recent years have experienced the least of it. Peterborough is an exception: 21 per cent of its population are non-British nationals. This is more than twice the figure for the UK overall.[7] Over the ten years from 2002, Peterborough was the fastest-growing city in the country, rocketing by 27,600 to 186,400.

The right-wing press has been quick to jump on the city as an example of the dangers of immigration and multiculturalism. Under the headline 'Peterborough: Brexit, migrants and last English pub left' in July 2016, the *Daily Mail* quoted Bram Brammer, barman at the Hand and Heart – said to be the last pub left in the city's Millfield area – as saying: 'English people are leaving and it's becoming ghettoised. The society's infrastructure has just been destroyed.'

These sentiments closely echo the words of hard Brexiteer and former Conservative Peterborough MP Stewart Jackson, who in 2006 described suburbs that were previously 'settled and peaceful' becoming 'ghetto-ised'. He then declared that 'resentment, anger and hostility is rising in the host communities' and claimed that the police spend time keeping 'disparate communities from conducting turf wars, which prevents them from tackling routine crime'.[8]

Clive sympathised. 'When I go into Peterborough every Monday, I go on the bus,' he said. 'The bus stops in Millfield, which is now all Eastern European.'

Clive said the same of Longthorpe, another formerly affluent suburb of Peterborough that had been 'taken over' by absentee landlords who, by renting to mainly Eastern European tenants in multiple-occupancy houses, had changed the face of the area in less than a generation. Thanks to the lack of affordable housing, this was a pattern that was being repeated throughout the area and had affected Clive and Kathy personally.

'We moved fourteen years ago because an Asian gentleman bought the house next door and put a dozen Eastern Europeans in it,' Clive said, 'They used to work shifts, so some used to be coming home from doing a shift and others would be going to work. So, we lost all the privacy. We went from having just one couple next door to having a bunch of blokes. It wasn't a very pleasant thing. They constructed a building at the bottom of the garden and had people in that. They didn't have planning permission for it. Foreigners get away with it. If I did something like that, I wouldn't get away with it.'

Clive said he felt abandoned by the British state. Not only did he believe that playing by the rules had put him at a disadvantage, he also felt that successive governments favoured migrants by allowing them to break the rules with impunity. Clive and Kathy had seized the opportunity of the 2016 referendum to give the British state a 'bloody nose' for what they perceived as mismanagement of the country's social and cultural evolution. They saw successive waves of economic migrants as being unable to speak English, not integrating sufficiently, taking up space and resources, gaming the state system and breaking the rules.

My 'Guardianista' north London friends would most likely have choked on their quiche Lorraine and spat out their tea at this point in Clive and Kathy's analysis. It is wholly understandable that the transformation of Clive and Kathy's street from a friendly family environment to one full of young, mostly male workers living chaotic lives, regardless of their background, causes concern and even alarm. My problem is with the false connection drawn between England's own decline in power and influence, of which the English are very aware, and immigration. Migrants are perceived as dynamic, energetic and on their way up, in contrast to the stagnating English, but it is not fair to blame English inertia on migrant success.

Clive and Kathy are not the only ones to blame what they perceive as injustices related to immigration on successive governments. In fact, political scientists have found 'strong evidence' to suggest a general growth in discontent with politics in the fifty years preceding Brexit.[9] A National Centre for Social Research report provides evidence that this trend has been accompanied by a distrust of politicians in general terms. The proportion of those surveyed who trust the government 'to place the needs of the nation above the interests of their own party' fell by more than half, from 38 to 18 per cent, between 1986 and 2013. The political scientist Matthew Goodwin has argued that 'one major driver' of Britain's 'growing crisis of distrust' in the 2000s, as measured by the data above, is 'the pace of immigration'. While Goodwin admits that the global financial crisis, the Iraq war, austerity and the MPs' expenses scandal – among other factors – also played a role, 'it is immigration that seemed to encapsulate the failure of a remote political class to respond to their concerns'.[10]

Immigration was certainly the biggest factor for Clive and Kathy when they joined 60.9 per cent of Peterborough in voting for Brexit. They felt that their local area and way of life was not just changing, but declining, as a result of large-scale immigration facilitated by free movement and reduced national sovereignty. Populist nationalist parties across Europe and beyond have capitalised on this kind of discontent, by challenging the legitimacy of the establishment and calling out politicians, civil servants, experts, intellectuals, judges and the media for working against what they perceive as the popular will. The Brexit vote was just another manifestation of an environment in Europe that has allowed populist parties to triple their vote in the past twenty years.[11]

It is easy to brush aside feelings of insecurity about immigration by dismissing them as merely the result of inequality and economic discomfort. And, in many cases, economics does play a large role in driving what on the surface look like specifically cultural grievances. One of the main reasons people voted against our EU membership in 2016 was related to fears about the effect of immigration on areas like public services and housing. And while it is true that the effects of austerity have created widespread feelings of discontent for which immigrants are easily, though incorrectly, scapegoated, the NHS is not strained by immigration, as Nigel Farage has suggested. In fact, our health service is reliant on migrants. Around 139,000 of the 1.2 million people employed by the NHS are foreign nationals.[12] Similarly, it is deeply unfair to blame migrants for our housing crisis, when 28 per cent of construction workers in London are non-UK EU nationals.[13] Austerity, a decision made and enforced by national governments, is a much more convincing explanation for our straining public services. Government spending on the NHS has fallen in real terms by 13.5 per cent from £439 per head in 2010 to £379 in 2017.[14]

While many cultural grievances do have economic roots, it is simplistic to suggest that this is all that is going on. Culture does matter. As retired homeowners with good pensions and no mortgage left to repay, Clive and Kathy's complaint is not correlated to their bank balance, but to the behaviour of those they share a street with, the appearance of their high street and whether they feel safe walking home at night. While the left have held their noses and turned away from such complaints, the populist nationalist right have been able to exploit their recognition of these kinds of cultural concerns. As the writer Anthony Barnett noted in his book *The Lure of Greatness*: 'One reason the right won such dramatic successes in 2016 in England is that their opponents on the left fled the field of meaning and identity.'[15] Conversations with Clive and Kathy make it clear that we need to do more than offer economic, rationalistic arguments to explain away feelings of discontent. The most rational way to vote might be to read each party's manifesto – or at least their key pledges – and vote according to what is most beneficial either to you personally, or to society as a whole. But in the privacy of the polling booth, people are not making calculations, or producing impact assessments. Voters often follow their emotions. As well as stating our position on how to fix inequality and end poverty, as a society we also need to formulate policies, build institutions and provide healthy ways to satisfy our human desire for identity and belonging. If we do not, the populist nationalist right fills the gap. Tribalism and toxic polarisation become inevitable.

UNDEREMPLOYED

For many of the people I met in Peterborough, an inability to find reliable work was the main source of their anger and discontent, particularly when they see so-called foreigners busily employed.

'I haven't been able to find any kind of work for the past year, not even cleaning toilets,' one young man living in Peterborough told me. 'The only work about is temporary. And when I do get a bit of work from an agency, I'm normally pushed out after a few weeks for someone who will do it cheaper. If you want me to be completely honest, mate, there's too many people round here. We've got to boot out some of the foreigners, if I'm honest. It's not about their race or country or anything like that, but there just ain't enough jobs.'

There is no denying that in terms of job opportunities, as young adults, Clive and Kathy had more options. Companies such as Hotpoint, Baker-Perkins, Perkins-Diesel and London Brick provided thousands of jobs for the people of Peterborough in the post-war period. By the 1980s, the likes of Thomas Cook and EMAP publishing signalled a second wave of investment and opportunity.

'You were inundated with jobs,' Clive, who has been retired for the past eight years, told me. 'You couldn't not find a job. You could leave school, find a job, find another job . . . I weren't a clever dick, I must say. My first job was working at a motor factory supplying garages with car parts and HGV parts. I did that for four years, then at nineteen I went into the glass trade, and that's where I finished up. I've worked in glass and glazing near enough all my life. When I first went in the glass trade, the firm I worked for – Thomas Bennett's – were Leeds-based, but they opened a branch in Peterborough. I was with them for twenty years.'

Clive's mum died when he was nineteen, shortly after he'd met Kathy, who also left school at sixteen and went straight to work. 'Three pound, nine-eleven was my first pay packet,' Kathy said, 'but when I left EMAP in the wages department in 1969 to have Sara [their first child], I was earning £12 a week. These days the young ones don't have it so easy. You can't just walk into a steady job like we all did.'

The industrial economy that once bred feelings of community, solidarity and patriotism is now small. In the UK, manufacturing output accounts for only around 9 per cent of the UK economy.[16] Where once people might have felt represented by their trade unions, now membership is at an all-time low.[17] The feeling of agency that Clive and Kathy felt early in their careers has become rare, if not impossible to find. It has been replaced by a kind of impotence.

Outside of big cities like London, Manchester and Birmingham, decent jobs are becoming increasingly rare. The transition from a Fordist economy based on manufacturing to a knowledge economy based on the transfer of information, creativity and technology has led to more centralised clusters of wealth.[18] The most ambitious people in today's economy do not simply want to live in places like London or New York. They are obliged to live and work there to tap into centres of economic opportunity and innovation. Clusters of jobs, talent and opportunity inside dynamic cities consistently secure investment that disproportionately outweighs those parts of suburbia that used to be home to specialised areas of manufacturing. It needs to be said that the decline of traditional working-class jobs in places like Peterborough has more to do with technological advances than it does with Eastern Europeans moving in next door. A full quarter of checkout assistant jobs in the UK were lost due to automation between 2011 and 2017.[19]

Regardless of its causes, many of those who would have found steady work in previous decades are left behind in former industrial areas. At less than four percent, unemployment in the UK is at its lowest for decades.[20] What this hides is a chronic problem of underemployment: where part-time workers want full-time jobs, gig economy workers want to enter the career economy, and zero-hours contracts are replacing 40 hours contracts. There are still 300,000 more part-time workers in the UK who would like a full-time job than before the 2008 financial crisis.[21] And an increasing proportion of the best jobs are found in a few city centres.

As an MP, I have tried to address the inequalities of class and geography as well as ethnicity. When I ran a campaign to promote fair access to Oxford and Cambridge, the UK's two top universities, the data I found on class and geographical background was just as shocking as that on race. My Freedom of Information requests in 2017 found that Oxford made more offers to applicants from just five of the Home Counties (Hertfordshire, Kent, Surrey, Hampshire and Oxfordshire) than to every region of the north of England combined. Cambridge made nearly 5,000 offers to applicants from eight areas in southern England, while students from eight local authority areas across the North, the Midlands and Wales received just eight offers. Oxford is just as bad. Applicants from Salford, Middlesbrough, Hartlepool, Blackpool and Stoke combined received eight times fewer offers than Richmond, in London, alone.

'The North–South divide makes the UK more regionally divided than any comparable advanced economy.[22] When I publicised the university entrance data, I expected the media to pick up the geographical inequality angle at least as much as on my findings that black and other ethnic minority students face disproportionately high barriers to entry to Oxbridge. The truth was that broadcast and print publications were not interested in geography. They cared far more about race. Though the media was lukewarm to the North–South divide that this data clearly highlighted, I expected a northern Labour Party colleague to use the data and front a public debate. It never happened. It is no surprise that some of the so-called white working class are abandoning the Labour Party when we miss basic opportunities to make a young person from that background think that our politicians speak for them.[23]

After its designation as a new town, many people from Birmingham, as well as East Enders and working-class north Londoners, migrated to Peterborough. The city's population of around 80,000 in 1967 soon doubled.[24] What struck me was how Clive and Kathy spoke of what we would now call a 'white flight' to Peterborough, which back then was a typical English market town inhabited solely by East Anglians. Clive and Kathy did not see those escaping Birmingham and London's poverty, poor housing and low standard of living as a threat. To them, these arrivals, while not East Anglian, were still English.

'A lot of them used to move over to Westwood 'cause Peterborough Development Corporation in those days built a load of properties where the Londoners used to go,' Clive explained, adding that development of the area had started in the mid-1960s on what had been home to RAF Peterborough. Since 2005, Westwood has been home to Her Majesty's Prison, Peterborough, the UK's first purpose-built unisex prison.

'In them days, we [East Anglians] had everything in common,' Clive says. 'The only sport was football. We used to live and breathe football. So, all my work colleagues and people I grew up with in school . . . well, what did we use to do on a Sunday and a Saturday? Play football. We had the harmony of playing football together and enjoying the social side outside of football, going to the pub. We had a lovely time. When Kathy and I were courting, big groups of us would go out to see live music, dancehalls . . .'

After slight nudging, Clive admitted to having been a rocker rather than a mod. He had been the proud owner of two motorcycles: 'There used to be about twenty of us on motorbikes. We used to meet on a weeknight at a pub up the road called the Swiss Cottage then go and hang out at the café. There was always trouble with the mods in those days . . .'

Clive chuckled and became sheepish when I probed him about how 'involved' he got in such trouble.

'They were good days, happy days. I mean, look at London now. It's terrible, what with these stabbings. It's rife, isn't it? So, so sad. No need for me to tell you how bad it is. What I put it down to is past and present governments have let us get to this position. They've let us down. Law and order.'

The early 1970s were an exciting time for Peterborough. Having rebranded itself, the city saw increasing development of new housing and facilities. The jewel in the crown was Queensgate Shopping Centre. Completed in 1982 and boasting more than 100 stores, it advertised itself on local radio station Heart Cambridgeshire as 'the capital city of shopping'. Now owned by the American venture capital firm Invesco, I visited Queensgate in the run-up to Christmas. It was doing a roaring trade among its diverse consumer base sauntering from John Lewis to Primark to M&S in search of festive high-street bargains. While the items for sale, the clothing styles and the food on offer had changed, the experience was hardly different to how it was in the 1980s, when as a teenager I used to hang around there with groups of school friends.

While the Queensgate Shopping Centre has continued to flourish, it does not reflect broader trends in Britain's retail sector. The financial crash in 2008, leading to stagnating wages and limited credit, has shrunk consumer confidence across the country, with high-street shops hit the hardest. Ordnance Survey data for 2019, covering eighty-eight cities and towns, shows that the average town centre now has forty fewer shops than it did in 2013.[25] This amounts to one in five shops closing in five years.[26]

Boarded-up shops are occasional rather than usual in Peterborough, but the city centre has lost the vibrancy and variety it once had. The number of individual retailers selling clothes, food and jewellery has shrunk. Poundland, Paddy Power and a pawnbroker's now sit facing each other on one street corner: a typical scene of discount stores, gambling and access to fast cash that is repeated in town centres across the country.

THE POSH

Even in late retirement, having played football to a semi-professional standard, Clive still manages to jog six to seven miles twice a week. Most of my own sporting activity these days, outside of running across the House of Commons to make votes, tends to be as a spectator, so I declined his offer to go running. Instead, I readily took up his invitation to see Peterborough United, aka 'the Posh', versus Oxford United in a League One match.

Navigating our way through the dense Saturday afternoon traffic from Clive and Kathy's bungalow via Deansgate to the Posh's London Road Stadium, it was clear that Peterborough had grown far busier and more metropolitan over the almost four decades since had I first arrived. Regardless, whether on foot or in Clive's car, getting around never felt like an issue – certainly when compared with the footfall of my own constituency. Peterborough has a population density of 579 people per square kilometre. Of the 326 districts in England, it has a middling ranking of 166. Haringey, the borough in which my constituency sits, comes in at number twelve, with 9,163 people per square kilometre. Overcrowding is relative.

On our road trip to the Posh, and then our walk up to the ground, through the turnstiles, over to the bar and then to our seats up in the stands, the multicultural environment of Deansgate soon gave way to a practically all-white crowd. In fact, I spotted more people of colour on the pitch than I did among the 7,027 supporters on the terraces. I did not feel uncomfortable. For the most part, I felt invisible to those around me. According to the last UK census in 2011, 86 per cent of the population identified as 'white', markedly down from the previous census in 1991 in which 94 per cent of respondents identified with a white ethnic group. The 2011 census shows that Peterborough was 82.5 per cent white, which is just below the overall UK figure. The next census in 2021 will make for interesting reading.

As we settled into our seats for the 3 p.m. kick-off, Clive had no explanation for why Peterborough's growing ethnic minority population was largely absent from the crowd, even though football is by far and away the most popular sport among ethnic minorities in Britain, on both a participant and armchair-supporting level.

'I can't really say why more ethnic minorities don't come to the football,' Clive said. 'I know the club tries to get more in, especially from the local Asian community, but you can only do so much, eh?'

Ten minutes into the game, Posh took the lead and set up an exciting contest in which Oxford equalised just before half-time. After seventy-five minutes, Posh went 2–1 up from a spectacular thirty-yard shot from twenty-two-year-old striker Siriki Dembélé. Born in the Ivory Coast, schooled in Scotland, Siriki was now plying his trade in East Anglia. As Clive quipped, he was a 'positive example of immigration'. But it's true – as 33 per cent of professional footballers in the UK come from an ethnic minority background, there has been an incalculable boost to race relations. It is much harder to hate people of colour when your ten-year-old son is running around in an England shirt with 'Dele Alli' emblazoned on the back. But football clubs, as commercial entities, can only do so much. The reality is that much of their work on detoxifying racism in football is about brand management, not social cohesion.

The Posh looked set to seal the three points before an eighty-eighth-minute penalty earned the visitors a deserved draw. During the match, the banter flowed thick and fast between the surrounding home fans – a mixture of wisecracks, in-jokes and typically ironic observations about mistimed tackles, errant shots and footballers' hairstyles. The chanting between the Posh and Oxford's small but vocal away supporters was lively but good-natured. If you closed your eyes, it could have been one of many mid-league football stadiums in action around the country that Saturday. This made me think: is there anything about Peterboroughians that sets them apart from other Englishmen?

'We call a spade a spade,' Clive said. 'We're straight-talking. What you see is what you get. People say, for instance, that Northerners are friendly or East Enders are a bit "tricky". But I think we're losing that now. I remember a few years ago Ray Winstone saying during an interview that wherever he lived [in the UK] he didn't like what he was seeing and wanted to move away. He said, as an East Ender through and through, that his culture is going. We're finding that in Peterborough.'

LONDON BRICK

After failing to get good enough grades for sixth form, Clive's son and my best friend from school, Jamieson, got his first job at London Brick. The company, situated in Fletton just outside of Peterborough, has been in operation for more than 140 years. It dominated British brick production for much of the twentieth century.[27] Around its peak in 1973, the London Brick Company sold 2.88 billion bricks, which represented close to half of the total UK brick market.[28] It claims to have produced the bricks to build more than 5 million homes. But today London Brick has reduced its operations. One of Peterborough's oldest and formerly largest employers now exclusively produces bricks for the renovation, maintenance and extension of houses that have already been built.

The rapid decline in London Brick's output in recent decades is symptomatic of declining manufacturing across the UK and much of the Western world, as cheap labour, in Asia in particular, and technological innovation have steadily replaced the manual jobs that once supported so many families in this region. Between 1960 and 2015, the UK experienced a steeper decline in manufacturing employment than any so-called 'advanced economy', except for Switzerland.[29] In the past decade alone, we have lost more than 600,000 of these jobs, meaning that fewer than 3 million Brits are now employed in the manufacturing sector.[30]

Even so, seeing some of Britain's remaining manufacturing workers in full swing at the site of London Brick is still an incredible sight. Visiting on a mild winter's day, I took a deep breath and paused as I took in the huge clay quarry, surrounded by low buildings with high chimneys caked in orange dust, which tower over the surrounding Fenland. Workers wearing fluorescent orange jumpsuits and white helmets were operating heavy machinery, walking around with clipboards overseeing the complex operation or rooted to their spot, meditatively sorting bricks.

'I don't follow politics. I don't understand politics,' said Rob, a London Brick supervisor who has been with the company for fifteen years. 'I've never voted in my life. So, I will never moan about politicians or what they do.'

Rob was born and raised and still lived in Whittlesey, a six-mile, twenty-minute drive east of Peterborough. My contemporary, in age at least, he spoke quickly and confidently about his outlook on life as he handed myself and my researcher a hardhat, work boots and overalls in preparation for a tour.

'The way that I see it, it doesn't matter who's in office. I still have to pay my taxes. The hospitals or whatever affects me, I've got to pay it anyway. People higher than me, with more money, millionaires and all that, perhaps they have a choice and understand it a bit better. They've got the money to do what they want. Me, I come to work. I go home. I eat, sleep. Weekends or whatever, I enjoy myself. That's how I see my life.'

Despite what seemed like an 'ignorance is bliss' approach to life, Rob was astute when it came to understanding the effects of key economic variables such as interest rates. For the past twenty years, interest rates have been relatively low, and apart from fluctuations in supermarket prices and petrol, it is the one piece of economic information that cuts through to the general population.

'In the building trade, we're the first to see the effects [of economic changes]. When we don't sell bricks, we know there's something happening out there, and we start stockpiling. We've got a little bit less than we started out with at the beginning of the year, so it's been a good year. When I first started here fifteen years ago, we had a hundred and twenty million bricks stood down between this yard and the Saxon brickyard [in his native Whittlesey] when it was open. Now we've got something like forty million on the ground.'

Rob also avoids reading newspapers: 'I used to read the *Daily Star*, the *Sun* and the *Mirror*, but only because people bring 'em into work. I look on Google at what's happening during the day . . . I used to watch the news, but I don't watch telly no more. There's nothing on there. If there's anything I want to watch, I just stream it or download it from the internet.

'I used to be up on current affairs when Maggie Thatcher was in office. I could've told you all of her cabinet, even though I didn't like politics – because they was always on the news. What's real, what ain't?'

Now that people can choose from multiple platforms how and when they want news, information and entertainment, those focal points no longer exist. Instead each of us follows a unique combination of outlets and personalities that often reinforce and strengthen our previous convictions. A few scheduled televised events – usually of a significant sporting or political nature – still have a big draw. World Cups, elections, royal weddings are still watched on TV more than online platforms because we want to engage in such activities as they happen and as a shared activity. But these opportunities are fewer and farther between. Watching a stream off your laptop does not have the same social appeal as gathering around the TV set. It is unlikely that we'll ever see another televisual event of such an historic, epic scale as the 1969 Apollo 11 moon landing, an event that reverberated around the world for years after and, for a brief time, reminded us all of the best of human endeavour.

Closer to earth, Rob took me out onto the vast site that forms the nucleus of London Brick, which started life in 1900 after the developer-architect John Cathles Hill bought the T. W. Hardy & Sons brickyard in nearby Fletton. It's now owned by Forterra plc following a series of mergers and acquisitions.

'If people want to come over here and better themselves, then that's fine. They wanna work, put into it. That's fine. My former partner, he come over here [from the Philippines], we got married, he worked. My partner now [from Brazil], he's working. They're not from the country, but they're here and they're putting into the system.'

Rob was married with a wife when he first started at the firm but came out five years earlier. 'Coming out in this environment was all good,' he said. 'There was always that bit of banter, but I just put it out on Facebook. I didn't want to be telling one person after another. So I just wrote a status saying, "I'm here, I'm queer, I'm going nowhere! You got a problem, come and see me." That's exactly what I put. But these guys down 'ere, for all the trouble that they give, they didn't hassle me about that.'

Rob reminded me of what my friend Jamieson used to tell me about working at London Brick. The banter, as in many working-class industries in Britain, could be fierce, and to the uninitiated it could even seem overly aggressive or cruel. But there is an adversarial nature to life in Britain that is a curious feature of our national identity. Whether you call it 'banter', 'wit' or 'pulling your leg', not being able to take a joke is seen as a distinct weakness in British life. It stands to reason, then, that migrants without a great understanding of the English language or our singular brand of humour are at a distinct disadvantage. But perhaps more important is a sense that ordinary Brits, because of what is cited as 'political correctness', feel unable to express themselves using the language they have been raised with. In the culture wars that rage among British politicians, social commentators, stand-up comedians and the like, freedom of speech has become a key battleground. The irony, of course, is that people can and do say what the hell they want these days. The only caveat is that polite society now expects them to govern their tongues in certain obvious and generally public places. As Rob said: 'If I didn't know them blokes out there, I could get them into a lot trouble for the things they come out with.'

In a frank end-of-year statement, Stephen Harrison, the CEO of Forterra, said that the building trade as a whole was still recovering from the long cold winter of 2017–18: 'As construction sites strive to make up lost time, haulage capacity and availability of labour have come under significant pressure. The combined effect has meant that our sales were behind forecast for the first half of the year.'

Six years earlier, the company had stopped paying their stackers at a per-brick rate and introduced a set rate of sorting 18,000 bricks per day into twenty-one units at £25 per hour for a twelve-hour shift. Four days on, four days off. Do the arithmetic and that equates to around £72,000 per year. As back-breaking as it is, you don't have to be Arnold Schwarzenegger to stack bricks – it's all about core strength and technique. It is also one of the few labour-intensive, unskilled jobs that is currently impossible to automate at the stacking level. A robot just cannot separate the wheat from the chaff with the accuracy of a human.

Out in the grey, dusty, sprawling yard, Rob introduced me to Steve, who'd been with London Brick for fourteen years. Now fifty-six and originally from Cheshire, he had lived in Peterborough since moving down from Merseyside in 2000 via Greece. Steve was more upfront than Rob about why, though he did not vote, he had supported Brexit: 'I don't like having rules made for me by people who weren't voted in. Simple as that. Whether they live in a different country or not. If the European Commission was voted in by the people that they're making rules for, fine. I'd still prefer our country to make our own rules, but to have an unelected bureaucracy telling you what to do is undemocratic.'

Steve's first reason for supporting Brexit was driven not by disdain for free movement, but by the idea that we had experienced vast and deep changes to our society and that the people making those decisions were not even elected. Changes are one thing, but when it feels like they are imposed, rather than chosen, it is harder to accept. My own belief is that the democratic deficit in the EU is exaggerated by those who ignore the fact that decisions are made largely by democratically elected national leaders at the European Council level and are scrutinised and ratified by democratically elected members of the European Parliament. I do not deny that this deficit exists. Giving the public more of a say, and a sense that they are closer to what is going on in Brussels, is a vital part of necessary reform.

'To be honest, I found Farage to be the most persuasive,' Steve added. 'I don't particularly like the bloke, but a lot of what he says I totally agree with.

'It's the [political] hierarchy that's been more divisive. I think the ones at the top who are delaying it and trying to force us to remain, still, are purely in it for what they can get out of Europe. They all want their nice, cushy jobs in Brussels. I don't see any reason why it has to be made so complicated. Yes, there'll be hard times, but Britain doesn't stay down for long. It never has. We'll come good again.'

Among those who have lost faith in the establishment, it is not true to say that they have lost hope. In fact, they hold enduring optimism in Britain and England as a whole. Possibly a hangover from the British Empire, there is a nostalgic belief in a time when we were one whole, coherent and 'successful' community. They have certainly lost hope and trust in Westminster.

'They're all in it for themselves,' Steve continued. 'The vast majority may have started out with good intentions, but I think the majority of politicians, at least in higher ranks, are just in it for themselves.

'Traditional Labour values have almost gone. I've got kids, stepkids, grandkids. What do I think about life for them? Pretty shit, really. Too much technology. Life is not what it should be. They spend far too much time sat behind a screen. My kids are all grown-up. They came along before it got so bad. They wanted mobile phones at fourteen. Now, kids want mobile phones at five, and it is hell to pay if they don't get 'em. Most parents give in to them.'

The dissatisfaction many people feel about the future is tied up with how they perceive the prospects for younger generations. When they spend time with their children or grandchildren, they are perplexed by the hours they spend online, staring at a tablet, laptop or phone. I feel the same with my own children. In 2018, children spent an average of two hours eleven minutes per day online, in addition to an estimated one hour fifty-two minutes watching TV.[31] This fundamental shift towards screen time, and away from more natural forms of human engagement, is a unique phenomenon in the long history of the human species. Nevertheless, technology is just one of the major changes to our way of life that is producing anxiety.

Just like Clive and Kathy, Steve was concerned about immigration: 'I don't think diversity has, as a lot of people see it, been a particularly good thing. Diversity has to go both ways. At the moment, what we see a lot is certain parts of the community seeming to take over, and they seem to want everything their way but don't want to give in the other way.

'It's the usual thing. Don't raise a Union Jack, don't raise the Cross of St George, because it might offend somebody, but they can put the rising moon or whatever it is . . . they can do what they want. They can burn poppies, they can burn flags, they can do what they want. But if you do it to them, you get locked up. It's not a race thing. I've got lots of friends that are Asian.'

While Steve's account of the behaviour of people he does not perceive to be part of his own culture felt exaggerated, it is undeniable that Britain and England in the twenty-first century have been deprived of much of the symbolism that has traditionally been an important element in defining nationhood. The Cross of St George has been discarded by mainstream politicians, elites and society more generally. Following this it has been picked up, appropriated and exploited by cynical right-wingers. Newspapers like the *Daily Mail* have run headlines like 'Who will speak for England?' And playing on the fears and anxieties of those who identify as being English, more sinister groups like the English Defence League, the British National Party and the UK Independence Party have sought to perpetuate toxic ideas of nationhood defined by ethnicity, rather than by shared faith in values and institutions. Pride in England itself has become a loaded concept.

With Christmas just around the corner, the secularisation of the festive season came up: 'I'm not religious in any way whatsoever, but this is a Christian country. It's always been a Christian country. Why the hell can't you celebrate the nativity? I'm not religious, but it doesn't offend me.'

A picture was emerging of many different social and cultural developments occurring at the same time that were forcing a level of change that ordinary people found overwhelming. It's not all about migration, religion, the internet or cultural changes. Rather it's the quantity of factors happening simultaneously, and the speed at which people are expected to adjust. Diversity, immigration and technological progress can be hugely positive, but when they break down shared ways of life and social cohesion, it is understandable that people get defensive and threatened. How much change is too much? And when do the negatives outweigh the positives?

Aside from at tea breaks and lunchtime, there was little interaction among the stackers piling up the vast numbers of red bricks. It seemed like a solitary, almost monastic job, what with the repetition of the work, the penitence of having to work in all weathers come rain or shine and the almost Benedictine lack of conversation. Perhaps this is why the workers were so up for talking to me.

'I'm thirty-five, but still in me prime, mind,' Johnny joked as I interrupted his stacking by introducing myself. Another born-and-raised-East Anglian, Johnny explained that he was now on his second stint at London Brick, having previously worked at the Saxon brickworks. 'When I finished school, I did an apprenticeship in welding and then got a job down here when I was twenty. I was here for eight years. I was in this yard for four, then went over to Saxon when the robots came in for four years, then they shut Saxon, and I went and done various other things and came back here three years ago.

'I love it down here. It's great. Come down, hard work, can be, but they pay you for it. When I got made redundant and went out there doing various other jobs, the money you'd get paid compared to down here . . . It's hard work, and it does take its toll on ya, but it's great. Love it.'

Married with two young kids, Johnny complained about costs going up but was resigned to the notion that 'they always go up anyway'. Most of his mates worked at the brickyard and the ones who didn't, while they weren't doing 'the crap work I do', didn't earn the money he earned either.

'I'm a firm believer in PMA, matey – positive mental attitude. It could always be worse, you know what I'm saying?

'Look, it don't matter where you come from, there's always gonna be lazy buggers. I know of people from Peterborough who just want the quick money . . . They're not prepared to put the graft in. You gotta earn it. You go out and buy something cheap, expect it to break. You want the money? Go out there, do the work and get the money. If somebody else wants to do the work . . .'

Johnny points out a slightly younger, strapping lad working another mound of bricks in the near distance: 'It's like Tom. He's from Lithuania. He wants to do the work. Top lad. It's a laugh. We have a giggle. Everybody's here for the same reason: money.'

Johnny explained that there is no tension on the site with Eastern European workers. In the past, many Italian migrants had worked at London Brick, and at its Bedford site there was a significant Asian workforce. It is dangerous to characterise everyone in one place as though they all have the same attitudes to complex issues like immigration and Britain's place in the world. In a city where 60 per cent of voters supported leaving the European Union, 40 per cent supported remaining. Some are anxious about the changes society is undergoing and end up retreating into smaller groups. Others are bursting with hope and generosity, focusing their energies on their family, earning money and living their lives.

EROSION

In recent years I have met with people from all walks of life during my visits to Peterborough, from the dean of the cathedral to students at the local education centre, my old teachers, UKIP party members in a Brexit debate, workers at London Brick and the parents of my best friend from school. I did not find a middle England that was angry, on the verge of violent protest, bitterly racist or bigoted. There was real kindness and generosity among everyone I met. People were more open to speaking and sharing their points of view than I ever could have expected.

While I was overwhelmed by the kindness that strangers and old friends showed to me, the frustration that is emerging in Peterborough makes me concerned about the future of England. I cannot pretend that I did not find fear, loss, decline and tribal instincts, particularly on the issue of migration, among some of those who showed me kindness personally. While Peterborough's unemployment rate is only slightly above the national average,[32] there was a feeling that many of the jobs available offered poor conditions and bad pay, unlike the few lucky enough to earn high salaries at London Brick. Coming of age in Peterborough in the second decade of the twenty-first century feels as though it offers fewer opportunities than it did when I was here in the eighties, or in the sixties or seventies before that. And where once a sense of community flourished, now it is a rarity. Pubs are closing and the streets are increasingly segregated into different ethnic areas, while the Posh function as a sort of last frontier for white Peterborough. There is little that is new to entice and engage the whole community. Parallel lives are being lived by groups increasingly afraid of one another.

There is no denying that immigration to Peterborough has been rapid and that it has significantly impacted on the city's social and demographic fabric. It makes sense that some are convinced by polit-icians who call for an end to freedom of movement and for reduced immigration, when successive governments have failed to give the help and assistance required to sustain public services. Politicians and certain sections of the right-wing press have cynically and opportunistically jumped at the opportunity to portray the area as 'overrun, collapsing and overwhelmed by the presence of migrants'.[33] The Peterborough I found was not collapsing, but instead facing the predictable problems that accompany any major transition.

Nevertheless, changes in cultural and religious norms, migration and the economy have simply become too much to deal with for many people. Frequent EDL marches, hate crimes and even physical violence against Eastern European migrants and minority ethnic groups show the most extreme consequences of a divided, increasingly tribal England.[34] For most law-abiding citizens, however, it has simply increased fear, distrust and unease.

For all the vast technological progress, increased global connection and economic progress that has occurred in Britain – and the rest of the world – in the past half-century, many people feel that it has not been worth the cost. So much, including community, respect, shared values, common bonds and mutual understanding, has been overlooked at the expense of 'rational' economic policy that has disproportionately bene-fited those at the top. The sense I got from the people I spoke to in Peterborough was not only that England's best days are behind it, but that they are on track to get a whole lot worse.

It is ironic that the Eastern European migrants that many are disturbed by are themselves doing their best to live the small 'c' conser-vative middle England dream. Moving from formerly Eastern bloc countries to the modest Fenland city, most take entry-level jobs, performing manual labour or other so-called low-skilled work. Like my mother, they work several jobs, including late-night shifts, and live in cramped conditions as they establish themselves here. A decade or so later, as they scrimp and save, rise to management positions or start their own businesses, they may be able to afford their own house. The aspirations that drive them – wealth, security, comfort for their families and home ownership – are strongly redolent of the Thatcherite ideals.

What is missing in this England is any arena that allows those with competing visions for our future to communicate and share: a space for Clive and Kathy to mix with the dozen or so hard-working Eastern European migrants crammed into the small family home next door; a place for the young from the cities to interact with older generations who live in market towns; institutions and shared experiences across all social classes that would provide us with the opportunity to arbitrate our differences and remind us of what we share in common.

Returning from tea at Clive and Kathy's house to arrive at King's Cross, where I began Christmas shopping for my wife and children, it was undeniable that these are different realms within the same country. The energy, the confidence and the dynamism of London are not replicated in the same way elsewhere. The economic problems my constituents face in Tottenham are the same as those that afflict the people who are in a precarious position in Peterborough, but who they blame is different. While my constituents look towards the government of the day as the cause of their problems, more in Peterborough singled out immigration. The England that once knew itself from one generation to the next is threatened with implosion caused by a cultural, as much as an economic, imbalance. We have drifted so far apart that we no longer recognise each other's fears and dreams.

3

Babylon

The fluidity of British Caribbeans

'Why you wan' the whole world when ya have a likkle piece a hope
here?
Stay. Stay and fight, man.
Fight till you look 'pon what you wan' see.'

Andrea Levy[1]

There was no pomp or circumstance. No traffic-stopping crowds. No
parade of weeping, crying, shouting, dancing or laughing mourners.
Instead there was a mood of solemn resignation among the small gathering of close family and friends shuffling out of the rain and into the
sterility of Hendon Crematorium in North London.

To the uninitiated, a traditional African-Caribbean funeral can be
bizarre, given its emphasis on celebrating life rather than lamenting
death. This is not to say that mourners are not bereft. Grief is grief in
any culture. But the vast majority of African-Caribbean funerals I
attended growing up were accompanied by gospel, old Caribbean spir-
ituals and jazz bands that would not have been out of place at dusk in
New Orleans. Tots of rum are thrown into the grave as the coffin,
covered by the flag of a Caribbean island, is lowered. The colours mix

in harmony: black represents strength, gold means warmth, red is energy and green is fertility. Mass graveside turnouts run into the hundreds, as the wider community comes together in a show of solidarity.

My own mother's funeral cortege was led by a white horse-drawn hearse through the streets of Tottenham after a two-hour Catholic mass accompanied by a full classical choir as well as the London Gospel Choir. Her coffin bearers wore black tails and top hats.

Dorothy Monica Nelson's funeral, however, was different. It was a glimpse into a growing trend of the 'Afro-Saxonisation' of British Caribbean births, deaths and marriages. 'Mum would turn in her grave if she thought I'd even so much as flirted with the notion of a lavish funeral,' her son and my good friend Geoff told me, comforting himself. 'She wasn't that type of woman. She was of that frugal, make and mend, squirrel it away generation.'

More and more African-Caribbean Brits now opt for functional and secular funeral rites, a trend that has been replicated across British communities over the past few decades. This final signifier of cultural identity has been abandoned in part because of spiralling costs and economic insecurity. When African-Caribbean constituents come to my advice surgeries with concerns about a death in the family, time and time again the same issues arise. A loved one has died intestate and there is little in the way of a legacy to pay for 'a decent send-off'.

It was not only her muted funeral that marked Dorothy Nelson out as British, however. After arriving in 1962 with her first-born child, Dorothy spent most of her life in north and east London. She got married in the city and had two more children, Victoria and Geoff. By the late 1960s she and her husband had bought a Victorian end-of-terrace house in Leyton, east London. This predominantly white working-class area was undergoing a demographic shift at the time thanks to the arrival of West Indians, followed by Southeast Asians from inner-city London. She worked on the factory floor of a medical-equipment company, then as mail-room messenger in the Foreign and Commonwealth Office, and later in care work.

'I didn't choose the music,' Geoff told me, visibly self-conscious, as we entered the chapel to the strains of Pachelbel's *Canon in D*. 'If it was up to me, it would've been Stevie Wonder or Bob Marley playing.'

Geoff and I had grown close over the past twenty-five years because we had so much in common. Both from north-east London, both the first in our family to go to university, both black British and both second-generation Guyanese. Just as Geoff's parents had come to the UK in the early spring of 1962, my father had come to London from Guyana in 1956 and his second wife, my mother, later in 1971. Our parents were unsung members of a quiet minority of British Caribbean people now referred to as 'the Windrush generation'. The vast majority of this generation worked hard, paid their taxes and hardly ever complained, even while withstanding grotesque prejudice and racism.

As Geoff steadied himself to deliver his mother's eulogy, he averted his gaze from the coffin, as though he couldn't face the finality of it. Straightening himself, he spoke of a life that, while obviously unique, had much in common with working-class people across Britain. It was heart-breaking to hear his gratitude for his mother's sacrifices and his regret that the particular sorrows his mother faced might have affected her quality of life. He ached that there were not more moments of shared happiness.

When I look back on the first eleven years of my life, it was without doubt narrowly parochial. In fact, even this description is probably generous. My life was more or less entirely confined to the N17 postcode in Tottenham. My mother, who had only been in the UK for sixteen months before I was born, imported many of her Guyanese habits to our small terraced house. She took pride in her newly purchased red-brick home, as well as the furnishings she had bought in the Jones Brothers department store on Holloway Road. All available surfaces were covered with china ornaments, snow globes, crucifixes and other religious artefacts.

I vividly remember sitting in the front room with my feet sticking to the plastic covers purchased to protect the new deep-pile carpet and my head resting against the lace doily coverings on the PVC sofa. Our mahogany record player took centre stage in the room. I remember the large speakers that provided me with a knowledge of reggae, calypso, soca, and deep Motown soul. My mother was an expert cook, and she lovingly prepared Caribbean dishes for us. She bought those ingredients and groceries in Tottenham's West Green Road, Dalston's Ridley

Road Market and Brixton's Coldharbour Lane. In the early years, all her friends were black. Arriving in Britain with few contacts, she used her culinary skills to quickly acquire new friends among her colleagues on the London Underground, where she first worked. Jamaicans, Bajans, St Lucians, Antiguans and Trinidadians joined us Guyanese for 'cook-ups' and 'soirees' in our small home. All of them became 'Uncle' or 'Auntie' to me and my siblings.

The Caribbean ex-patriates gathered in my mum's kitchen romanticised their home countries to each other and 'talked up' a big nationalistic rhetoric for their various islands. Outside of this space, their national identities were subsumed into a broader pan-Caribbean identity that was based on a shared history of slavery, colonialism and emancipation. You only have to look at the large carnival parades such as the Labour Day Parade of 1940s New York, the Notting Hill carnival in London or the Caribana in Toronto to see how infectious and adaptable Caribbean communities have become. At these kinds of events, they may arrive as St Lucians, Bajans, Jamaicans and Guyanese, but they leave as West Indians. Nothing is more emblematic of this than when West Indians come together for the cricket. When each island plays each other in the Caribbean Premier League, they go at each other as fiercely as the most loyal fans in any sport. When the Windies play, all are unflinchingly united behind one multi-national team.

My mum was the eldest in a family of seven children. Her own mother's early death meant she had a powerful sense of work and duty, which she retained throughout her life. She was house-proud and spent endless hours applying Dettol antiseptic to every surface before she wiped them, not realising that the hypersensitive cleaning habits she had learned in the tropics were not necessary in mild, damp England. As children, we were not free from the gruelling cleaning regime. If she met with any protest, she would remind us that having a clean home not only cultivated responsibility and self-respect but provided a kind of domestic order that protected us from the mess of the outside world.

We felt safe and loved, but nothing she could do made us feel truly Guyanese. We lived in the paradox of parallel identities. As second-generation immigrants, we primarily identified as young, black and

British. As soon as black-and-white television turned to colour, *Top of the Pops*, *Morecambe and Wise* and *Blue Peter* became at least as influential on us culturally as our parents. All of our schoolteachers were white, and our church had a largely white congregation, headed by a fantastic Welsh Anglo-Catholic vicar. Lots of our friends and neighbours on my street, as well as the local Broadwater Farm Estate where my cousins lived, had African or Caribbean parents, but many were Irish, cockney, Cypriot, Indian and Asian, too.

My alternate worlds were sometimes very confusing. I remember in 1982, aged ten, when the Falklands War broke out, proudly announcing to a group of friends and relatives in our front room my sympathies for Argentina. I confidently explained that it was because as Guyanese we were also South American. My mother jumped out of her chair and slapped me firmly around the head, commanding me not to repeat it in school for fear that the teachers would report her to social services and she would be thrown in jail for treason. It was a deeply confusing time for me. I felt prohibited from feeling really British, but at the same time I had to be patriotic to the country in which I lived. Those times when I did feel Caribbean-South American, I was told to hide this feeling away. It was only a year later when I had landed with a bump at boarding school and slowly made new friends, some of whom had fathers in the RAF and armed forces who served on the frontline defending the Falklands, that the reality of my folly sunk in.

The truth was, for all my mother's outward strength and her work ethic learned as a young motherless girl, she was shy and reticent. She grew nervous around white authority figures – teachers, civil servants, doctors, policemen. Often, she was right to treat them with caution. I watched them misunderstand, mimic and mock her accent. I remember her recalling how she was cruelly ribbed for her pronunciation and spelling of her new daughter's name when she went to register the birth of my little sister.

With his extra fifteen years in Britain, my father was more educated, urbane and confident then my mother. He won everybody over with an intellect he wore lightly, as well as his humour and charm. With women, Dad was flirtatious and cheeky. He acquired white British friends easily. Frequently without warning, he brought them home to my fidgeting mother and her divine cooking.

On her own, or in the company of her children, Mum viewed life like a picture postcard from the 1950s. She was a hopeless romantic and liked nothing more than to disappear into the old black-and-white films that would play on television on a weekend afternoon. She swooned at the male leads and heroes like Rock Hudson, Bing Crosby and, her favourite, Sidney Poitier. She played numerous ballads and classics on her vinyl record player and devoured Mills & Boon romantic novels. She often told the story of travelling to the UK in the same plane as Shakira Baksh, who had been crowned Miss Guyana two years earlier and had subsequently been pursued and then married by the British actor Michael Caine. Mum told an exaggerated version of this story, with a hint of jealousy, so that the listener almost assumed that Michael Caine had chosen between my mother and Shakira. 'Darling, in another world, you could have been Michael Caine's son,' she would say within earshot of my father.

Beyond her cleaning obsessions, she loved shopping. Her favourite was W. H. Smiths, from where she was obsessed with buying us extra maths books, comprehension exercises and set exams so that we could get ahead at school. She would set revision exercises for us whilst she was out on shift-work in the evenings or at the weekends and mark them on her return home. She also loved to buy dresses and garments in the rag trade area of Fonthill Road in Finsbury Park, or the shops alongside Walthamstow Market in the East End. She loved a bargain and would march us through nearly every shop as she tried on all the items that she fancied one at a time. When more than one store had the same item, she would always return to the one where it was being sold for the cheapest price.

Looking back, so much of this was about her own desire for upward mobility. Education was fundamental. She had left school at sixteen, so she was determined that her own children would not. She would also say that 'whilst we might be poor', we must never 'look or smell poor'.

It was only after she died that I came to appreciate how much of her life she had given up when she left Guyana. Many West Indians who emigrated from the Caribbean for a better life in the UK, Canada or the

USA faced tremendous resentment from those relatives whom they had left behind. My mother's case was even more poignant, as she left behind my brother Desmond, her first son, aged ten at the time, born out of wedlock in circumstances she rarely chose to discuss. She ached for Desmond. Some days she grew gloomy and depressed and her eyes welled up as he came to her mind or she spoke about him. She told a desperate story of wanting him to come to England after she left to marry my father, but it was not straightforward. UK immigration law required that my father adopt him, but the process was complicated and expensive. And her paternal grandparents and stepmother were formidable in their demand that they raise Desmond back in Guyana, at least initially. Months of course turned into years, and the sacrifices of immigration and hard work in a new country left their mark. I didn't meet my elder brother properly until I was eighteen. To this day, it is still remarkable to me that he speaks of my mother with so much love and fondness, love that was established in those early years with her in Guyana and then maintained over time by letters, gifts and a Post Office saving bond.

My mother's job on the London Underground offered a dependable, steady income, but one not always sufficient to support us in the way she would have liked, particularly after my father abandoned her. Dad had fallen on hard times. His work as a taxidermist dried up in the 1980s animal-rights era, his drinking habit got considerably worse, and he was getting into heated rows and fights with my mother. He said he wanted to move us all to the USA. If we had done so, we would have followed a lot of West Indians who, during the early 1980s, moved to the USA and Canada in order to escape the recession facing the British economy at that time. He went ahead of us but slowly dropped out of contact. Months turned into years, and years turned into decades. My mother made a formidable single parent, and when we got news that Dad had died penniless eighteen years after he'd left, I still did not know whether he had ever really intended to come back.

Slowly, as the seventies turned into the eighties and then the nineties, my mother's West Indian attributes blended more and more with British influences. She began to take pride in her Sunday chicken and lamb roasts. She threw out the old furniture, ornaments and plastic coverings, replacing them with flat-pack Ikea. The Dettol was swapped for French polish. In later life, she suffered from ovarian cancer. One of her best friends from work, Maureen, a white East Ender, insisted on caring for her when my siblings and I were busy at work. She wheeled her to the local park to smell the fresh spring daffodils and brought her shepherd's pie and toad in the hole.

Cosmopolitans – those who feel comfortable anywhere, seeing themselves as citizens of the world more than of one specific place – are most often characterised as being a highly educated and wealthy elite. I can confidently say that this class exists, as these days I am very much a part of it, but this description fits both my and Geoff's parents, too. British Caribbeans have proved themselves as worldly as any management consultant, media personality or investment banker. The Windrush generation were not rich, and their children have faced disproportionate economic hardship. Despite this, we have been able to flex and adapt to Britain, making it our home. Undeniably that adaptability has much to do with the history of slavery, indentured labour and colonisation, which enforced integration on African, Indian, Chinese, European and Native American peoples, to name but a few. This is, of course, not a history I'd ever advocate repeating, but the spirit of openness of British Caribbeans remains an example to us all.

NATIONAL SCANDAL

On a crisp spring morning in 2018, I was sitting in the House of Commons chamber with a knot in my stomach. I was waiting to ask the home secretary an urgent question about the government's Hostile Environment policy that had led to the abuse of thousands of British Caribbeans in what became known as the Windrush scandal. Since then, the Home Office has admitted that it wrongly deported or detained at least 164 British citizens. Many more victims were made homeless, jobless, left destitute and denied access to public services by their own government. At least eleven died before they received any justice. We do not know the true number of those affected by the scandal, as the Home Office records are somehow incomplete. But we do know that there are more than 5,000 cases of individuals alleging that they were in some way seriously harmed by the contempt their own government showed them.[2]

Shortly before I stood up to speak that day, I feared I would be overcome with emotion and have to restrain myself from crying. I could not stop thinking of my mother and my aunts who had come to Britain from the Caribbean in the 1950s and '60s as part of the Windrush generation – women who had toiled tirelessly as nurses in the NHS, who had bent their backs working painfully long shifts and whose hands bore calluses resulting from their seemingly unending workloads. I thought of their struggle to be accepted in Britain. How as black women they were unable to be promoted from State Enrolled Nurses to State Registered Nurses. I thought of how hard they had worked to be recognised as part of this country and how painful it would have been for them to learn that seventy years on from their arrival they were still not British in the eyes of their government. I thought about how it would feel for British citizens like them to sit in detention for days on end, only to be manhandled onto a flight bound for a country they hadn't seen for decades. And so it was with considerable emotion that I stood up to speak. I told Amber Rudd, the home secretary: 'This is a day of national shame, and it has come about because of a "hostile environment" and a policy that was begun under [your] prime minister. Let us call it as it is. If you lie down with dogs, you get fleas.'

As soon as I had made the speech, my office in parliament was inundated with calls from journalists asking for interviews. Increasingly it became clear that this was a major news event, and there were signs that pressure was building on the home secretary, who would later be forced to resign. On top of media enquiries, my office started receiving calls from around a hundred people a day who had themselves been victims of the government's immigration policy. People called and wrote in from all over Britain, telling us how they had been living in fear and forced into hiding by the Hostile Environment. We heard from mothers whose sons were about to be deported the next day and from black Britons paralysed by fear of detention.

The response was unprecedented. For months, my parliamentary researcher Jack had been in contact with Amelia Gentleman, a journalist from the *Guardian* reporting on the effects of the Hostile Environment policies. We had written letters to ministers and asked parliamentary questions, but to no avail. It seemed as though the government's Hostile Environment would always be a fringe issue, taken up only by migrants' rights organisations and given occasional exposés in the *Guardian*.

Before the scandal broke, we had a steady trickle of Windrush cases, but afterwards it became a flood. Within weeks we had twenty-three new cases. Many of the people affected had been working and paying their taxes in Britain for decades but had found themselves deprived of their rights, living underground and in some cases even driven to homelessness. My casework team were in constant communication with the Home Office's Windrush Taskforce, which routinely failed to act with the urgency required. Every case revealed a life shattered by the Home Office, plunged into uncertainty as a result of the government's Hostile Environment.

The Windrush scandal occurred because Britain has consistently ignored its own history of Empire and imperialism, and its role in enslaving 12 million Africans and subjecting them to colonial rule. It forgot that the people invited to Britain from Commonwealth countries in 1948 had had their British identity thrust upon them centuries ago when they were stolen from their homes and sold as slaves. The Windrush story did not begin in 1948, but in the seventeenth century, when British slave traders stole millions of Africans from their homes, shipped them to the Caribbean and sold them into slavery to work on plantations. The wealth of the United Kingdom was built out of the forced labour of the ancestors of the Windrush generation. The Windrush generation and their children, like myself, live in the United Kingdom today because British people exploited the land of our ancestors, not the other way around. There is no British history without the history of the Empire. As the late Stuart Hall put it: 'I am the sugar at the bottom of the English cup of tea.'

If the Home Office was to be believed, the detention and deportation of British citizens who came from the Commonwealth from 1948 to 1971 was an administrative error. But the Windrush scandal was not a bureaucratic mistake, nor was it the folly of a few Home Office officials who misunderstood the guidelines. It was the result of a body of legislation designed to create a Britain hostile to migrants by denying them access to public services. In recent years, it had got dramatically worse because of a calculated plan by the then Conservative Home Secretary Theresa May to pander to anti-immigrant sentiment and to legislate against ethnic minorities by asking them to prove their 'Britishness'.

As the son of two Guyanese migrants, I was able to understand the sacrifice the Windrush generation made for this country because each day of my youth I saw it in action in my mother. I saw it when she returned home briefly in between shifts as a home help for the disabled and as a care assistant at an old people's home. I saw it in her spare time, when she left us at home while she sold Tupperware door to door. And I saw at first hand the pain and strain that living in a new land put on so many in my father, who regularly came home drunk, angry or afraid.

Growing up in the 1980s, I lived in fear of the National Front. Enoch Powell's 'Rivers of Blood' speech was made just four years before I was born. It had its desired effect of 'fizzing like a rocket': fermenting and legitimating an ugly racism that made us feel unwelcome. I've lost count of the times I've been told to go home, or had my Britishness questioned. When you hear enough of this stuff, a small part of you, in your darkest hours of insecurity, can even start to believe it. For some Windrush citizens, the question may have lingered: did I gain an identity when I moved to this island as a British and Commonwealth citizen, or am I merely an intruder? The Windrush scandal confirmed our worst fears. The British state did not recognise people like us as British citizens after all.

The government's insult to the Windrush generation was not only financial, though it forced many people into destitution by preventing them from getting jobs in the legitimate economy and denied them the welfare payments that the unemployed need to survive. And it was not only to do with their freedom, though many were detained in Britain's brutal immigration detention estate and others were deported to countries they had not set foot in since they were children. It also cast doubt on their very identities. It said to those hard-working British Caribbeans, who had answered the call of a desperate United Kingdom, that they did not belong here. It questioned whether my parents, and by extension whether I, could be black and British at the same time. Being told

so often to 'go home' made many descendants of the Windrush generation wonder whether they had a home at all.

HOPETOWN

Hopetown is a quiet village on a small strip of land in the north-eastern
corner of Guyana, sitting on the Atlantic coast. It lies in the shadow of
Georgetown, the capital, which is just fifty miles away. Underneath
Hopetown's modesty lies great beauty. People's backyards give life to a
forest of fresh fruit and vegetables. My favourite is the sapodilla, a small
brown fruit, bursting with sugary sweetness and organic purity. A place
of humility and humidity, Hopetown is built on rich, red soil. The air
is pungent with the distinct smell of country life: lots of families keep
cows, goats and chickens. But while Hopetown is rustic, it is not calm.
Loud and lively carnival music mixes with the cries of the yellow-
headed caracara, the loud taps of the blood-coloured woodpecker and
the sound of children spilling out onto the streets as they walk to
Hopetown Primary School.

The village means a lot to me because it is where my father, also
named David, was born, as well as where my mother grew up and is
buried. I have visited Hopetown regularly since I was eighteen years
old. Most recently I have gone to tend to her grave, but also to speak to
my cousins, uncles and aunt. Everyone in the village seems to be related
to me in some way. People there knew my grandmother, Susannah, a
powerful matriarch in the 1930s and '40s, as well as my mother's stepmother, Clarabelle Thompson, who was a local magistrate.

Hopetown is a place I go to when I want to connect with the majority of my extended family. The Thompsons, the Johnsons, the Semples
and the Grants are all important figures in the stories I hear whenever
I visit. People in Hopetown look at me and tell me they see my ancestors looking back. Even though I have never lived there, people in the
village treat me as if my parents never left the country behind half a
century ago.

Occasionally my visits have coincided with the lively annual festival
that celebrates the village's emancipation. In 1831, the British government seized three colonies occupied by Dutch settlers to form British
Guiana: Essequibo, Demerara and Berbice.[3] On the west coast of

Berbice lay four cotton plantations: numbers sixteen, seventeen, eighteen and nineteen.[4] They were owned by a British MP named James Blair, who entered Parliament in 1818 to protect the interests of slave owners.[5] Pseudo-emancipation came in 1834 with the passing of the Abolition Act.[6] I say 'pseudo' because slaves were bound by a further four-year apprenticeship period.[7] 'Slavery', in formal terms, ended, but subjugation continued. The apprenticeship period essentially 'tutored' slaves in freedom, as if forced labour was something from which people had to be weaned. Instead of forcing slaves to work for nothing, they coerced them to work for scraps. Workers eventually managed to transcend the cruel exploitation by saving their paltry wages until full emancipation came in August 1838. Pushing a wheelbarrow filled with $2,000 worth of coins to Mr Blair, forty-nine freed slaves purchased the former plantations to trigger their physical and economic liberation.[8]

I am very proud of the fact that my ancestors were among those forty-nine freed slaves who seized the means of their own futures. By 1841, the Johnsons (on my father's maternal lineage) and the Thompsons had helped set up an entire village. Driven by the prospect of a better life, they had risen to build a home. They called it Hopetown.

Hopetown is just one of forty-one villages in Guyana founded by African slaves.[9] In the years that followed, thousands of 'Liberated Africans' were brought over to replace or supplement the workforce that had dwindled since emancipation.[10] Between 1841 and 1865, 13,563 indentured African workers, including my paternal grandfather's family the Lammys, came to Guyana from southern Africa, as well as from Rio de Janeiro, West Africa and the Bahamas.[11] You can see further evidence of Guyana's fluid heritage by looking at its birth registers, which were enacted after the 1868 Registration of Births and Deaths Ordinance. Relationships formed between Sierra Leoneans, Angolans, Congolese, Krus, Akus, Portuguese, Cape Verdeans, Indians, West Indians, Creole natives of Anguilla, Barbadians, Kittitians and British Guyanans.[12]

This hybrid condition is replicated across the twenty-eight nations and over 7,000 islands of the Caribbean. Belize, which is 50 per cent mestizo, 25 per cent Creole, 11 per cent Maya, 6 per cent Garifuna and

10 per cent Syrian–Lebanese, Chinese, East Indian and Mennonite, is a great example.[13] Suriname censuses report its people as 40 per cent Hindustani, 31 per cent Creole, Africans and persons of mixed European descent, 15 per cent Javanese, 10 per cent Maroon, 2 per cent Amerindians, 2 per cent Chinese, 2 per cent Lebanese and 1 per cent white. The country also has a significant number of immigrants from Madeira and the Netherlands. By the end of the nineteenth century Caribbean island societies – whether Anglophone, Francophone or Hispanic – were characterised by gentle waves of migration. From the 1880s onwards, Caribbean people migrated to avoid the repercussions of failing sugar prices by moving to Cuba and Brazil, where sugar was doing well, or to the mainland, in order to escape a series of natural disasters that destroyed the livelihoods of small farmers. And when economic or political opportunities arose, Caribbean people followed. Two hundred and forty thousand labourers from Jamaica and Barbados helped with the construction of the Panama Canal between 1881 and 1915. Thousands more moved to Costa Rica, Guatemala and Honduras to work for the United Fruit Company plantations. Many thousands of Puerto Ricans relocated 'home' to North America, where they were given US citizenship in 1917 for their contribution to the First World War.

Like so many of the countries of the Caribbean, Guyana was also home to incoming migrations of East Asian and Indian workers. On 5 May 1838, the first Indian indentured labourers stepped onto British Guyanese soil.[14] In the seventy-five years that followed emancipation, more than 238,000 Indian workers were also imported as cheap labour to replace and supplement the dwindling workforce.[15] They were predominantly poor and labelled 'untouchable' by the Indian caste system. As the backbone of an immigrant workforce, Indian migrants toiled under harsh contract laws. In return, they received low and unstable wages determined by sugar prices. Known by the Guyanese as a period of struggle, sacrifice and resistance, these indentured workers engaged in numerous strikes and protests to ensure not only the survival of the sugar industry but their role within it. From a position of exploitation, Indian workers soon gained a foothold in the Guyanese economy. By the end of the nineteenth century, their descendants expanded their economic role beyond plantations. They became bankers, tailors, goldsmiths, taxi drivers and boat manufacturers. My great-grandmother was half Indian, so my mother took great pride in reminding me of this heritage.

This history explains why modern-day relations between the Afro-Guyanese and Indo-Guyanese populations are fraught. To the newly freed slaves in Guyana, Indian workers were perceived as rivals. As both groups later became free from direct exploitation, suspicion turned into resentment. As a community that emancipated themselves from literal chains and started from scratch to design and inhabit their own villages, the Afro-Guyanese population were sceptical of a self-organised community who were able to work, save and buy land with what they perceived as relative ease. With increasing intensity, anti-immigrant rhetoric pushed the Indo-Guyanese into isolation.[16]

Ethnic tensions between Indians and Africans in Guyana were socially and politically cemented during the struggle for Guyanese independence. Initially united under the Progressive People's Party, Cheddi Jagan, an Indian dentist, and Forbes Burnham, an African barrister, stood together on a platform of national emancipation from the British.[17] In 1953, the PPP secured 'home rule' status, a first step towards their goal of independence, which at this point was a chance not only for sovereignty but for unity. Nevertheless, home rule left behind a fractured, divisive and tribal landscape. By 1955, the PPP had split, with Burnham breaking off to create the People's National Congress. Jagan was left to front the PPP as leader, and Guyanese racial tensions were now codified into their party-political system. What had the potential to be a project of unification eroded into a bitter battle for control. Commencing in 1961 after Guyana was granted autonomy, the second step towards independence, Jagan's prime ministership was marred by violence and strikes. Covert CIA operations allegedly helped to incite racially charged protests and riots, likely due to Jagan's close links to Cuba's Fidel Castro.[18] Burnham snatched power away from Jagan in 1964. Presiding over Guyana's full independence in 1966, this was a post he held right up until his death in 1985.[19]

Unsurprisingly, Burnham's alleged collaboration with foreign forces, which resulted in deadly ethno-political violence, did not bode well for

Indian–African relations in Guyana.[20] Electoral contests were heavily framed as a struggle between Africans and Indians.[21] In 1973, the army shot dead two Indo-Guyanese poll workers, known as the 'Ballot Box Martyrs'.[22] Many Indians felt increasingly unsafe and unwelcome in an independent nation dominated by twenty years of Afro-Caribbean leadership, so much so that many chose to return to India.[23] The end of Burnham's reign did not mark the end of racially divided politics in Guyana. When the PPP gained power after the first reasonably free elections in twenty-eight years, racial tensions were far from neutralised. The 'us versus them' narrative did not dissolve, but simply reversed: the PPP would go on to hold power for twenty-three years, finding its electoral support from Indo-Guyanese voters.[24]

Even today, when there is a multi-ethnic governing coalition, the old tensions are re-emerging. The Afro-Guyanese leader has been widely accused of excluding the PPP from cross-party talks and has drastically increased Indo-Guyanese unemployment after slashing subsidies for the sugar industry.[25] Guyana remains divided. Afro-Guyanese people typically live in the cities, where they monopolise government and security jobs, while Indo-Guyanese people inhabit remote, rural areas.[26] Political and racial divisions have become rooted in the Guyanese consciousness. The diversity endemic to Caribbean history, culture and life was not harnessed, but exploited. Without effective, inclusive leadership, tribalism can and will happen, even in a community that is mixed.

Watching my teenage boys put down their smartphones and game consoles to fish and swim in the Essequibo river when we visited at Christmas in 2018, Guyana felt a world away from the political tribalism of Westminster. Christmas and New Year had brought colour and music to street and village life. There was a carnival atmosphere. My eldest enjoyed staying up late, dancing amongst stoned Rasta men and eyeing up girls for, it seemed, the first time.

As I looked out of my hotel window one day at the panorama of Georgetown towards the seawall and the Demerara river in the distance, I thought about my mum and dad running down those streets dreaming of another life somewhere faraway. Somewhere like England.

LEGACY

Nearly half a million people left the Caribbean to settle in the UK between 1948 and 1970. There have been books, exhibitions and documentaries about the experiences of the Windrush generation, a square in Brixton named after them and even a Windrush Day on 22 June.

I am well aware of the limits of using the Windrush label to refer to an entire generation of Caribbean immigrants, when only a fraction came over on the *Empire Windrush*. And I also recognise that they were not, by a long stretch, the first black immigrants to arrive in Britain. I have publicly encouraged commemoration and celebration of this post-war period, using the evocative term 'Windrush', because in my short lifetime I have come to know just a few of these men and women whose contribution to British society should not be forgotten. I have benefited immensely from their experiences before me and have seen how the thinkers, writers, entertainers and political leaders who emerged from this period have shaped British public life.

I was fortunate, for example, to follow in the footsteps of the late Labour politician Bernie Grant, who was elected as the member of parliament for Tottenham in 1987. Bernie came to Britain in 1963 from Guyana as part of the Windrush generation and is my distant cousin. He found work in British Rail and the Black Trade Unionists Solidarity Movement before entering local politics, where he went on to become a nationally famous politician. He was a tireless anti-racism and anti-apartheid campaigner, feminist ally, supporter of revolutionary governments and a loud advocate for multi-racial school curriculums. He gave a voice to so many people throughout this country and provided an inspirational vision of what it means to live in Britain today.

One of the Windrush generation's foremost intellectual contributors to twentieth-century British thought was Professor Stuart Hall. His remarkable contribution earned him a permanent place in the academic canons of anthropology, cultural studies and social history. Stuart's thinking continues to influence a generation of teachers, social workers, students and activists. If you need any proof of his unpredictable, exceptional and open mind, he is the man who gave us the idea of multiculturalism and coined the term 'Thatcherism', and he offered a nuanced critique of both British socialism and the ideology of New Labour.

Stuart left Jamaica in the fifties to study at Oxford and became internationally renowned in the field of cultural studies through his prolific writings and lectures. One of the last times I saw him was when he came to see me in the House of Commons in 2016. He was alarmed that following the 11 September 2001 attacks on the USA, amidst a trend of rising Islamaphobia and anti-refugee sentiment, British multiculturalism was under threat. The sustained attack from both left and right against multiculturalism was, in retrospect, a little bit like the demonising of the EU during the Brexit campaign. Multiculturalism was portrayed as some sort of doctrine of politically correct madness imposed from above.

David Cameron, pandering to the populist nationalist right, had had begun to criticise a 'creed of multiculturalism for contributing to a deliberate weakening of our collective identity' prior to the referendum.[27] When Stuart came to see me, Trevor Phillips, the former chair of the Equalities and Human Rights Commission, whose parents came to London in the fifties from Guyana, had recently intensified his critique on multiculturalism, partly endorsing Cameron's comments that state multiculturalism had failed.[28] He would later go on to call multiculturalism a 'public fiction'.[29] According to Trevor, multiculturalism overlooked the possibility that minority groups such as Muslim communities simply 'see the world differently from the rest of us'.[30] Stuart wanted to make it clear to me that he strongly disagreed, and that it was my job as a minister to defend multiculturalism from these kinds of critique.

Undoubtedly, many people found Trevor's opinions refreshing. He was brave, bold and provocative. Still, his criticisms were qualified with a recognition that the government needed to take discrimination, racism and economic marginalisation seriously. But in Stuart's view, Trevor was refusing to recognise the very existence of multiculturalism. For Stuart, multiculturalism was a bit like democracy: an organic, malleable, hotly contested process that contained within it vastly different interpretations and versions. Stuart felt that Trevor was overriding these kinds of nuances to deliberately maximise the inflammatory nature of his remarks. Rather than targeting 'problem communities', we needed to look to the reactionary, regulatory and discriminatory forces inherent in our society. Even now, I can hear Stuart arguing that multiculturalism is a fact – the processes of colonialism, slavery and globalisation mean that it is here to stay. Stuart and I did not always agree, but I learned so much from him. He was part of a long socialist tradition of great thinkers from the Caribbean that included people such as Hubert Harrison, Cyril Briggs, Claude McKay, Frantz Fanon and Richard B. Moore.

Since my parents' arrival, the British Caribbean community has undeniably integrated into the British way of life. The literature of C. L. R. James, Benjamin Zephaniah and Zadie Smith has shaped what it means to be British. In politics and in culture, Stuart Hall, Bernie Grant and Linton Kwesi Johnson shifted the framing of the debate not only about race, but about class and working life. The remarkable sporting achievements of Jessica Ennis, Frank Bruno, Linford Christie, Kelly Holmes and Raheem Sterling make people from all backgrounds proud to be British. A generation of prominent artists, writers, sports people and cultural thinkers have shaped post-war British culture in ways that are hard to measure.

But celebrities are never the true measure of integration. The contributions made by those who have climbed to the top of the social hierarchy do not really tell us much about those whose feet are on lower rungs of the ladder. To me, the presence of loud British Caribbean football fans in most Premier League stadiums across the country is far more illustrative of our integration than the athletes they are applauding. And it is the countless British Caribbean postmen and women, security guards, teachers, caterers, bar staff, barbers, labourers, lawyers, shop assistants, nurses, journalists and council workers – who are the true measure of how Caribbeans have become British. Working hard to pay their mortgages, socialising in pubs and getting married across ethnicities, these are everyday people living quintessentially British lives.

The government's own definition describes integration as happening when 'people – whatever their background – live, work, learn and socialize together, based on shared rights, responsibilities and opportunities'.[31] It is about shared access and having an equal stake in and engagement with society. And despite its somewhat abstract foundation, integration can be measured according to tangible indicators, at least according to the Home Office.[32]

The first indicator is language, which is the most basic tool that enables people to become socially connected with others. After white British people, black British people are the ethnic group most likely to speak English as their main language – the proportion is 98.5 per cent compared to just 92.3 per cent of citizens across England and Wales as a whole.[33] Of course, the fact that so many black people speak English as their first language is not a quirk of fate, but a direct result of Britain's colonial history.

The next indicator is employment. According to the 2011 census, 67 per cent of black people were in employment.[34] That is around 500,000 people, and it is among the highest rates of any ethnic-minority group.[35] Black people became a vital part of our economy from the moment they arrived on British soil, taking ownership over their own means of integration. One of the most prominent contributions they continue to make is to an institution that is quintessentially British: the NHS. Today, many more women are following in the footsteps of people like my aunts: 29 per cent of black women do much-valued human health and social work.[36] What a group gets out of public services is as much an indication of integration as what they are putting in. It is notable, then, that a slightly higher percentage of blacks reported a positive experience of GP services in 2018 than did the average across all groups.[37]

Over time, the British Caribbean community has become less visible, even as its contribution to our society has become greater. In part at least, this is because we have integrated and intermixed.

CREOLE

British Carribeans have, in the most literal sense, mixed with white Brits. Caribbean and African communities that first became embedded in Britain as dockworkers and manual labourers during the industrial revolution took the lead. Places like St Paul's in Bristol, Tiger Bay in

Cardiff and Toxteth in Liverpool are all thriving, identifiably mixed-race communities, and proof of what happens when different groups merge into one healthy community. Despite this, mixed-race categories did not even exist as options on the national census as recently as 1991.[38] Now nearly one in sixteen children under five are mixed race.[39] In London it is one in eight.[40] In fact, Britain now has the highest rate of interracial relationships in the world, ten times the European average.[41]

During the first decade of the new millennium, the number of people in England and Wales living with or married to someone from another ethnic group increased by 35 per cent to 2.3 million.[42] That means that one in ten people living as part of a couple are with someone from another ethnic group.[43] By the end of the twenty-first century, one in three Britons will be mixed race, with this number rising to 75 per cent by 2150. This figure is staggering, and while statistical projections are fallible, it is grounded in straightforward logic. The offspring of a mixed-race individual can only ever be mixed race, yet the offspring of an individual who is not mixed race has a rising chance of being mixed race, given that the non-white share of the UK population is on the rise.

Of course, interracial mixing does not in itself lead to reduced prejudice and discrimination. When I was twenty-one, I went backpacking in New York with a white girlfriend. Not having to visit Guyanese cousins in Brooklyn and Queens for once, I was excited to be in the city as a young adult with no family slowing me down. We stayed at a youth hostel in Manhattan. We could not wait to hang out on 125th Street. We had planned months earlier to visit the famous Apollo Theater and the Studio Museum in Harlem, and generally immerse ourselves in African American culture. As we walked and talked in Harlem's wide streets, we felt more and more uncomfortable. The fact that we were arm in arm meant we got stares and even heckles of 'jungle fever' thrown at us. Spike Lee's movie with this as its title had only been out for a couple of years, and though we might have been overly sensitive because we were young, we felt keenly aware that our mixed-race relationship was a point of contention.

Fast-forward ten years: after having different black, Asian and white partners, I met, fell in love with and married a white woman. Society's attitudes towards interracial couples had improved, but not much. Blog sites and even friends questioned my intention to leave a black woman and then marry someone who was white.[44] Nicola and I were both conscious that our children would grow up in an environment that required them to think about identity. I was familiar with both the academic and the practical side of structural, conscious and unconscious racism, having studied and experienced it. Nicola, despite her own diverse heritage of white South African, Russian and Jewish antecedents, decided to make a conscious effort to learn more about race. Inevitably there have been interesting discussions about race and identity at our dinner table. The point at which my children seriously started questioning why Mummy is described as 'white' and Daddy as 'black', even though these descriptors are hardly accurate, came at around the same age they began to doubt whether Father Christmas existed. It is hard to explain to children this age that the concept of race is a social construction.[45]

It is no wonder, then, that the writer Afua Hirsch characterises her formative years as a time of great confusion. She remembers telling her mother that 'we don't fit in anywhere – black people don't see us as black, white people don't see us as white'.[46] Far from belonging to both racial groups, mixed-race people can sometimes feel as though they belong to neither. It is not so much an identity crisis as an identity deprivation: mixed-race people often find themselves existentially homeless. At best, the racial identity available to mixed-race people is one that is divided into slices like a pie chart. But their experiences will not be felt in this segmented way. They are members of a minority ethnic group, a lived and loaded experience that cannot be reduced to a DNA percentage. At the same time as being cast as 'other' by a census-driven society, they are also refused access to any distinct cultural home. People of mixed race have found it difficult to articulate multiple belongings, and so their identity is reduced to a statistic. Afua Hirsch was herself struggling with the prospect of 'erasing' her white father by identifying as black.[47] The fact that she felt as if she even had to 'pick a side' is testament to the fact that society is governed by simplistic and crude ethnic categorisations.

Across the pond, people of mixed heritage encounter a different kind of disorientation. Dating back to a 1662 Virginia law on the treatment of mixed-race individuals, the 'one-drop rule' puts anybody with a mixed-race background into the non-white box.[48] In other words, any traceable African ancestry is enough for someone to be 'black'. This has considerable social force even today. Studies consistently show that people who have a fifty–fifty mix of two races are almost never identified as white. Obama, whose mother is white, is widely celebrated as the 'first black president'; Tiger Woods, who is also mixed race, is identified as one of the most successful black sportsmen.

Between 2001 and 2011, the percentage of the UK population that identified as mixed race doubled from 660,000 to 1.2 million.[49] But the growth in Britain's mixed-race population is just one plotline in a much larger story, which concerns the changing nature and complexity of the black population as a whole. From 1948 until the introduction of the Immigration Act in 1971, some 304,000 Caribbean-born people lived in Britain. At its height in 1976, the UK's Caribbean population was 603,600. Until the turn of the century, Caribbean people were in the majority in the black British community.[50] But that has now changed. The black British community is historically comprised not only of black people of Caribbean descent, but also of those from anglophone countries in Africa – predominantly from Ghana, Sierra Leone, Southern Africa and Nigeria, as well as newer migrants and refugees from Somalia and Zimbabwe.[51] And while the percentage of the UK's black Caribbean population stagnated between 2001 and 2011, the percentage of the UK's black African population doubled.[52] At the same time, African and Caribbean people have intermarried, leading to the sharing of political and cultural space. Third- and fourth-generation black Britons would not even bother to ask 'where are you from?' any more. A British regional accent tells you all you need to know.

ABSORPTION

It may not be that the British Caribbean identity is eroding, but rather that it was never really given much chance to grow in the first place. It is difficult for British Caribbeans to find solace in the cultures to which they have historical ties, not least because many cannot afford to visit the places their ancestors left. Moneyed holidaymakers and offshore tax dodgers can afford the luxury of heading west for sundowners at Sandy

Lane in Barbados or banking appointments in the British Virgin Islands, but relatively few black Britons can afford the prohibitive costs of taking a family 'back-a-yard'. Meanwhile, Caribbeans who have the desire to travel to Britain have to negotiate an obstacle course for a visa that most often ends in disappointment. While their ancestors scrimped and saved to afford the boat fares and plane tickets to get to Britain during the Windrush generation's 1948 to 1973 social evolution, second- and third-generation 'Afro-Saxons' now find themselves culturally drifting away from their country of origin, which is physically out of reach.

British Caribbeans, then, feel a sense of split loyalties between Britain and the old country – between the everyday realities of life in the UK and the romance of a forgotten culture. Stuck in a kind of limbo, the British Caribbean community has become a victim of its own integrationist success. While the growing British African community has generally been protective of its culture, the static Caribbean community continues to mix with others. As a result, both Britain's growing mixed-race and African communities have edged the Caribbean community in terms of visibility.[53]

I would not say that the British Caribbean community is fading away. That would be to deny the lasting impact of West Indians on British culture. Instead of disappearing, then, I would instead describe British Caribbean culture as being in transition. As the first- and second-generation Windrush citizens get older and even die, the West Indian community as we once knew it is changing. Migration from the Caribbean is barely a trickle now. What we do have is a new generation of young people who are building on the culture of their forebears, as demonstrated by the constant reinvention of British Caribbean food, theatre, music, art and carnival. Alongside this is a kind of absorption. For many people, especially younger generations, West Indian culture is being absorbed into a far more thrusting black, American experience. As was the case for many of the Windrush generation, the black dynamic of America has far greater natural appeal than Britain's confused, rootless and identarian cultural landscape.

As first- and second-generation British Caribbeans die off, or return to the Caribbean, the links their offspring have to their culture inevitably become more abstract. Gentrification has also played a role in this process, by pricing out British Caribbean communities from the areas they once heavily populated, such as in Notting Hill, Brixton and Handsworth. Instead they have moved to suburbia or more multicultural areas, which include a diversity of African communities, as well as many others. The amalgamation of Caribbean, Anglo-Caribbean, African and Afro-Saxon has created a sort of black super-identity. Its roots are not just demographic change and internal migration, but also African American cultural imperialism. The factors have resulted in the emergence of a black British identity, which is most highly visible in music, sport and the wider entertainment industry.

It is unsurprising that the British Caribbean community is characterised by flux, fluidity and rapid change, given its relatively short history. British Caribbeans should be applauded for their innovative response to social circumstances and economic challenges they have only recently gained a legal right to confront. African Americans are still coming to terms with the legacy of slavery, Jim Crow segregationist laws and a state law-enforcement and prison industrial complex that appears designed to disenfranchise black people. In a similar way, British Caribbean people are still trapped in the pernicious story of colonialism, as written by colonialists. Seventy years on from the arrival of *Empire Windrush*, British Caribbeans, and black people in Britain as a whole, continue to experience open hostility in the media, through political campaigns and unfair treatment in the criminal-justice and mental-health systems, as well as racial harassment at work and on the street. The Hostile Environment has created an othered group so separate and removed from its 'host' that hostility, rather than hospitality, has become the default response.

'Our community is hurting,' Geoff lamented at the end of his mother's funeral. 'We bear the scars of fractured, dysfunctional and damaged families because we're continually going through the grinder from slavery, to indenture labour, to colonialism, to post-colonial IMF and World Bank penury to coming here as cheap labour . . . After decades of being here, we're still treated as second-class citizens. For many people like me, and younger generations, we're neither fish nor fowl.'

Integrated, intermixed, absorbed, but not always accepted, the story of the British Caribbean tribe is a paradox. By some measures Britain has successfully managed to lead the way in inclusion and integration; in many areas black Britons remain locked out. It is still the case that for many older white people in particular, an English or British identity requires a heritage that relies on race rather than shared values.

When I first went to school in 1976, black children notoriously experienced systematic prejudice and considerable intellectual discrimination from our teachers. Such treatment led to low expectations and self-fulfilling prophecies. When I reached sixth form and began to consider my future career, advisers bizarrely suggested that I become a fireman. While I have nothing but respect for those prepared to put their lives on the line to serve in the fire service, I have enough self-awareness to realise that I would not be much help waddling up the stairs of a burning building. My dream was to become a barrister, a career path these advisers did not deem appropriate. I guess the image of a black man in a fancy white wig and black robes was just too much for them.

It is still the case that young people have an uphill battle to raise expectations and break down these barriers. One of the main problems that persists is the disproportionate rates of exclusion from our schools. Last year, black British pupils were permanently excluded at nearly three times the rate of white British pupils.[54] Separated from mainstream education, it is no wonder that these pupils continue to underperform.

Importantly, there is some hope. The education gap is narrowing. In 2004, 23 per cent of black pupils who defined themselves as having one or more black Caribbean parent in England achieved five or more A*–C GCSEs, compared with 42 per cent of white pupils.[55] By 2013 it was 53 per cent, compared with 61 per cent of their white peers.[56] And the percentage of black children going into further education or employment at age eighteen is just 1 percentage point below the national average.[57]

Outside of schools and onto the streets, the wider black community continues to face further prejudice. The last time I was stopped and searched was during the 2005 general election campaign. In a car with my brother, a magistrate, we were pulled over by an armed policeman.

'Stop, stop, stop! Put your hands up!' he shouted aggressively.

The officer apologised once he realised I was an MP, but this was no one-off. I have been stopped and searched around a dozen times by the police, for no good reason. The first time, aged twelve, I could not have looked less like the picture of a criminal. I was a somewhat lanky, nerdy-looking boy with big hair, an old T-shirt and NHS prescription glasses the day I was harassed by men in blue while walking towards West Green Road. The three officers who jumped me that day frisked me down over my balls and buttocks with such force and familiarity that I wet myself. Black people in Britain are now more than eight times more likely to be stopped and searched than white people.

It is no surprise then that black people have consistently expressed less confidence in the police than other groups.[58] The disproportionate use of stop and search is based on and perpetuates a climate of suspicion of black men. It breaks down trust in those whose job it is to protect. Feeling safe and secure is fundamental to integration. It is difficult to feel connected to those around you if you are constantly looking over your shoulder and are systematically discriminated against.

As my 2017 review into the criminal justice system found, trust is not only low among black defendants and offenders, but across the entire BAME population. It revealed that 51 per cent of ethnic minorities believe 'the criminal justice system discriminates against particular groups and individuals'.[59] And who can blame them when we have greater ethnic disproportionality in our justice system than even the USA?[60] While culturally, and in terms of identity, British black communities provide stories of integration's success, in terms of opportunity and justice, we have too often been shut out.

YARDIES

Amani Simpson, now twenty-eight, was just fifteen years old when he left London and travelled to live in a small suburban flat in Peterborough, miles from his British Jamaican parents' home in north London, to deal class-A drugs.

Amani had not suffered the same economic hardship as many young black boys growing up in London. He was raised in comfort by two loving parents in Winchmore Hill, a middle-class area in Enfield. His dad worked as an engineer for an electronics company, while his mother was an entrepreneur, owning a blinds and curtains company. For most of his childhood, life seemed to be going well. He worked hard at junior school, played sports and learned the violin. Aged eleven, he started at a good grammar school, the type that well-to-do parents fight to get their children into.

Nevertheless, Amani immediately felt out of place. He did not speak or dress the same as his black peers at school, several of whom came from nearby estates. Amani started to get bullied and quickly began to feel alienated. At home his parents showed that they loved him, but that was not enough.

What appeared to be a normal, if unhappy, life for a middle-class black boy in north London deteriorated fast. At the age of fifteen, after being involved in a street robbery, Amani was arrested outside his house holding an imitation firearm. As he was weeks away from his sixteenth birthday, he was spared jail and given 100 hours of community service. His parents, shocked by their son's actions and exhausted by endless fights, were distraught as the painful decision was made to move him into a residential home.

A man in his mid-twenties began to groom Amani, promising him a new pair of trainers in return for running petty criminal errands. Amani started to make money and enjoyed the 'freedom that came with the lifestyle'. Before long, aged sixteen, he was running a drugs operation that spanned the small city of Peterborough out of a flat he shared with two adult drug addicts. Amani had made the journey from London to the Fenland city twenty years after I had, in very different circumstances. For a while, he enjoyed his new-found status, money and freedom. Having never quite fitted into school in London, he felt he was being 'noticed for the first time' and young people in the area 'respected him'.

Amani's time as one of Peterborough's major drug dealers was relatively short. After three months, he was nearly arrested. Scared and cornered by the justice system, he was forced to reflect on his choices.

He decided to call his father and ask for a second chance. With the security of good parents and a new-found resolution to do right, Amani managed to rebuild his life. As a result of attending Connexions, a youth-advice service created by the New Labour government, he found a mentor, Alain, who gave him confidence and helped him mature.

A few years later, at the age of twenty-one, Amani was involved in an argument that would change the course of his life once again. He was stabbed around thirty times. The thickness of the puffa jacket his mother had bought him miraculously saved his life. Only seven of the potentially fatal blows made real impact. Miraculously, he survived the attack and was subsequently discharged from hospital.

'I had two or three opportunities to go home that night, but I stayed on in the wrong place at the wrong time with the wrong focus and ultimately paid the price for my choice,' he told me in my Westminster office.

Today, Amani tours schools across the UK, providing inspiration for pupils to stay away from crime, drug dealing and gangs. His story shows the dangers of what can happen when individuals feel isolated and cannot establish for themselves a healthy identity that would help them to foster a sense of belonging. Some young black men in London join criminal gangs, becoming what are colloquially known as 'Yardies', just as young Muslims in Trinidad may join ISIS and a disenfranchised white person in the southern states of the USA may turn to a white nationalist hate group like Stormfront. All these scenarios can in part be explained by the phenomenon of the new tribalism, in which some groups are defined by their common angst and struggle to fit in, according to a violent and divisive set of norms.

For many others, however, poverty and deprivation are the chief drivers of crime. In total, 35 per cent of black households have a weekly income of less than £400, which is the highest percentage out of all ethnic groups.[61] In my constituency, where there is a large black population, 42.57 per cent of children live in poverty. You are more than twice as likely to be unemployed in this country if you are black (9 per cent) than if you are white (4 per cent). As the poverty of the black British community has become further entrenched, the opportunities open to members of that community have diminished. Between 2012 and 2016, 600 youth centres shut down, 3,500 youth workers lost their jobs, and 140,000 youth centre places disappeared.

A surge in violent crime has accompanied the growing drugs trade in Britain. Last year there were more than 37,000 recorded knife offences in England and Wales alone. This was more than a one-fifth increase on the previous twelve months. The year 2018 saw the most fatal stabbings since records began in 1946.[62] Meanwhile, gun crime has gone up by 20 per cent.

Britain's criminal underbelly isn't created by young men moving across county lines to sell cocaine and weed for the sake of it. It runs far deeper, reflecting what happens when a whole generation of young black Britons are shut off from mainstream society. With very limited opportunities to get good jobs or feel a part of the communities in which they live, it is natural that many retreat into the tribal community of the gang. The young and the vulnerable respond to poor employment prospects and limited opportunities by following the examples of those around them.

Sociologists such as Joan Moore interpret gangs similarly, but with different language, as the logical conclusion of a 'global city'.[63] On this account, 'peripheralisation' pushes large swathes of society – generally immigrants, ethnic minorities and the working class – out of mainstream modern life. Social mobility becomes restricted; as inequality rises, new barriers to attainment are erected and educational mixing declines. As the empowered wealthy classes gain new skills and opportunities, those on the precarious fringes can either live in near destitution on benefits and poorly paid employment, or turn to crime as a means of filling the gap.

It is wrong, however, to simplify the driver of gang activity as purely economic. While the worst-off are the most vulnerable to the attraction of criminal gangs, others are pulled towards it because they failed to find belonging anywhere else.

Amani's story tells of a wider vulnerability of disconnected young people around the world. Consider how a line of cocaine makes its way from the forests of Colombia to a young drug dealer like Amani, and then eventually to the nostrils of a middle manager in Peterborough in a pub toilet on a Friday night. It starts in a country in which average life expectancy can be as low as sixty-eight in rural regions, and in which decades of guerrilla violence have stunted the everyday economy – despite major economic advances in recent years. For a young man in the Colombian forests, getting involved in the cocaine trade might be the only way to provide for his family, or even to keep himself safe, but it also might be the only means of identification he can find. His involvement in crime might start as a way of putting food on the table, but it is easy to see how it becomes who he is.

Eventually, the shipment of cocaine that some young Colombian has facilitated makes its way to a north London high street. Imagine that you are a young black boy in a care home, with no parents, no GCSEs and no path towards a fulfilling life. Statistically, you are likely to be racially profiled by the police, unlikely to be admitted to a Russell Group university and will probably face precarious employment opportunities. When you see your peers gaining money, power, friends and prestige through selling drugs, you might well be tempted to join in.

Every step of the way, the supply line of cocaine from Colombia to an English pub toilet is populated by young men who, for various reasons and in different ways, lack the opportunity to build worthwhile lives. The research database Havoscope estimates that the global black market for goods and services is now worth at least $1.63 trillion, or at least 11 per cent of global GDP. The proliferation of the billion-dollar drug economy in recent decades shows what can happen when we disenfranchise young people, by excluding them from the 'good jobs' offered by globalisation, as well as the benefits of strong community institutions. This is how the black market, or underground economy, is created.

The emergence of a precarious class of young people on a global scale is therefore inextricably linked to organised crime and the black-market economy. Increasingly there is a race to the bottom in which drugs, prostitution and modern slavery offer vulnerable young people not only a better-paid option than bad jobs on the margins of capitalist society, but a sense of belonging. This is as true in rural Colombia as it is in the East End of London.

LOSS

If the British Caribbean community is defined by its flexibility and ability to blend with new cultures, the people I met in Peterborough were, at times, the opposite. While generosity, kindness and optimism still remain in England, those who feel excluded can easily drift into misplaced nostalgia, looking backwards and bewailing the future. With trust in our institutions eroding, opportunities limited and culture changing, it is no surprise that there has been a renewal of the defensive but also destructive urge to belong to groups based on exclusive characteristics. In part this is because the roots of English identity are many centuries old, and laced with stories of victory and dominance.

The other side of the same coin is that the Caribbean story must always start with forced mixing, subjugation and oppression. But the openness and cosmopolitan freedom of British Caribbeans means that our identity is quickly eroded as each generation passes. This is a weakness as much as it is a strength. The faith and optimism the English tribe has to 'go it alone' can at times be divisive and self-defeating, but it also allows for confidence and defence of what is shared. The truth is that in this confusing modern world of globalisation and rapid technological change, both communities could learn from each other – both are suffering from a loss of identity and both would benefit from a new way to belong.

After exploring the British Caribbean and English tribes I had grown up in, I still felt like something was missing from my journey to understand my own identity. I felt a longing to understand where I came from. I remembered the DNA test I took years earlier, which had revealed that my roots were linked to a particular tribe, from a particular ethnic group, in a particular village, in a particular country in West Africa. I wanted to go to Fafa in Niger. I needed to meet the Tuareg.

4

Out of Africa

Looking for belonging in my DNA

'God has created lands with lakes and rivers for man to live. And the desert so that he can find his soul.'

Tuareg proverb

It was only mid-morning, but we were already a hundred miles east of Niger's capital, Niamey, on a desert road. The former French colony is the poorest country in the world.[1] It is a place where infant mortality is still high, leaving the fittest to tough it out in one of the most challenging environments on earth. Sat in the back seat of an ageing Toyota Land Cruiser, the air-con struggling to mitigate the forty-degree heat outside, I figured we were no more than forty miles away from what most regional experts would call 'hostile territory'. Accompanied on my mission by six men, all black and all Muslim, I felt safe and excited, but deliriously hot.

My original plan had been to go to Fafa, the small town which the DNA test I had taken years earlier had identified as the source of 25 per cent of my DNA. Unfortunately, the trip was deemed too unsafe because of Islamist insurgents and bandits operating in the area. One such outfit was Boko Haram, the Islamic terrorist group and ISIS affiliate responsible for more than 20,000 killings and hundreds of kidnappings. Having displaced in excess of two million people, in 2015 it achieved the status of the world's number-one terrorist organisation, not least because of its use of child suicide bombers, a strategy that accounted for one in five of its explosive attacks.

After long discussions with representatives of both the Nigerien and British governments about what to do, we decided it would be impossible to reach Fafa without risking serious jeopardy. Following the kidnapping of an American Christian missionary and the killing of two Nigerien security staff, reportedly by the jihadist group the Movement for Unity and Jihad in West Africa (MUJAO), dozens of soldiers were now deemed necessary if we were to go all the way to Fafa. This would have made the journey somewhat more expensive and far more conspicuous. Even a backbench MP like me was a valuable scalp to the likes of MUJAO, Boko Haram, marauding groups of Al-Qaeda offshoots or other miscellaneous bandits roaming the Sahel.

To get closer to Fafa, even if we could not reach it, we drove north in a convoy of two cars. Outside of Niamey, there were few houses or businesses. The structures we passed were mostly makeshift and rudimentary. At one point we pulled over in our Land Cruiser to make way for a boy of about twelve pushing a rickety cart filled with packets of chewing gum, matches, bootleg Viagra, condoms and assorted pocket-sized products. Mostly, though, the desert roads ran for miles, with few signs of life. Although by then many Tuareg people lived in towns, some were still nomadic. The arid desert was punctuated by occasional Tuareg shelters, in small encampments that guarded half a dozen goats. The strong winds that blew whipped up the sands and covered the small mud and brick settlements in red dust.

Ironically, my journey to find my roots in the old tribalism was blocked by one of the most dangerous examples of the new. I was stopped by a man-made barrier of internecine violence and rebel activity. Extreme Islamist terrorist groups in the region had exploited the vulnerabilities of some of the poorest people in the world, who were locked out from the benefits of technological advancement and globalisation, and provided them with an appealing narrative based around a return to a purer time. The offer of Islamist terrorist groups to the young, isolated and disaffected has many parallels with the proposal made by resurgent white nationalists to those who feel alienated and isolated in the Western world. Both seek to divide, scapegoat and indoctrinate people, thereby forging loyalty to an extreme and violent way of life.

MEETING MY TRIBE

After travelling so far, it was frustrating to find my tribe out of reach. But even though I did not reach Fafa on my journey, I did find my ethnic tribe in Niger's capital. I met them in the dark complexions of the Tuareg board members of the Timidria NGO. I saw them in the faces of the artisans in the craft market, the barber who cut my hair, the youths milling around government offices awaiting travel permits, the believers amassed on the street during prayers and the women sauntering along the roadside. I recognised myself in ways I only ever had before in my mother, my siblings and my wider family. Noses, ears, eyebrows, hair – identifying features which, in a Western context, get lumped together as being 'black', but in Niger are viewed in a more nuanced way. Woven in amongst Niger's 18 million people, made up of twenty-three ethnic groups speaking eleven languages, were my ethnic roots.

I returned to Timidria's HQ in the centre of town, on a dusty road that also served as a makeshift playground. The children's broad smiles and chubby cheeks belied their shabby clothes. Poverty is often disarming in this way: although it is a cliché, people can be happy despite their tough circumstances. At street level in Niamey, there are conspicuous signs of modernity, including electricity, mobile phones and traffic jams, but the country's United Nations Development Programme rankings paint a bleak picture overall. Life expectancy is just over sixty years. On average children spend less than five-and-a-half years at school. Gross national income per capita is only $908. My return ticket to the country cost more than the average Nigerien's annual salary.

Walking around Timidria's spartan office, I came across a map of Niger, which encompasses both the hostile Sahel to the north and a thin strip of green delta rising from the banks of the River Niger to the south. At first glance, the country's borders appeared as though drawn by a drunk. A series of jagged edges contrasted with ruler-straight, arbitrary lines that went on for hundreds of miles. The map clearly illustrated the 'Scramble for Africa': the invasion, occupation, division, colonisation and annexation of the continent by Europe's superpowers during the New Imperialism of 1881 to 1914.

In 1870, 10 per cent of Africa was under European control.[2] By 1914, it was 90 per cent. Only Abyssinia (now Ethiopia), present-day Somalia and Liberia were independent. The Berlin Conference of 1884 regulated Europe's colonisation of, and trade within, Africa.[3] The partition of Africa was designed to avoid significant conflict over the continent's vast natural resources, but instead it cemented several decades of imperial rule. Today, many of the borders appear arbitrary, because the people who imposed them did so with limited knowledge of the continent's geography, ethnic groups and cultural differences. It reminded me of an 1885 quote from Lord Salisbury, then British prime minister: '[W]e have been engaged in drawing lines upon maps where no white man's feet have ever trod; we have been giving away mountains and rivers and lakes to each other, only hindered by the small impediment that we never knew exactly where the mountains and rivers and lakes were.'[4] The result was increased conflict between partitioned ethnic groups.[5]

My fixation with the map was broken by a gentle tug of the arm. It was Alhousseini. He began to ply me with facts, figures and stories. These ranged from the perils of Niger's French colonial past to the increasing influence of neo-colonialism from Saudi Arabian Sunnis on the one hand and Iranian Shias on the other. Both branches of Islam want greater cultural, political and economic influence over the population, which until relatively recently had practised a largely tolerant form of Sufism. On one visit out of town with Timidria, I was struck by the number of small mosques, presumably paid for by these competing sects of Islam, that surrounded us on a desert road heading north. As in much of sub-Saharan Africa, Islam was competing for the control of public morality.

Alhousseini then began to tell me the history of the Timidria NGO itself, which was founded in 1991 by the human-rights activist Ilguilas Weila. He explained its name was Tamasheq for 'solidarity' and that the organisation was 'born out of the Azawagh Liberation Movement'.

Liberation, empowerment and enfranchisement have always been a focus of my politics: from the racial struggles my parents endured, to my awareness of the 1980s race riots in St Pauls in Bristol, Moss Side in Manchester, Chapel Town in Leeds and Brixton in London, the anti-apartheid movement, and the anti-racist movements I'm involved in to this day. But I am not an expert on the political struggles going on across the continent of Africa. Even though I am descended from slaves who had been wrenched from West Africa to the New World at some point during three centuries of human trafficking, I had no idea that Niger, the land of my forefathers, still practised slavery today.

Despite government claims to the contrary, and slavery being illegal in Niger since 2004, Timidria estimates that there are still around 40,000 people in Niger in some form of human bondage.[6] Slavery is enabled by the Tuareg caste system. Dark-skinned members were traditionally enslaved by lighter-skinned masters.[7] Dark-skinned people, in general, continue to hold the lowest positions in Tuareg society. Those darker-skinned people, my DNA results suggested, are my distant cousins.

Economic difficulties and a distinct cultural identity had pushed the Tuareg to rebel four times since 1962. During one such rebellion, lasting from 2007 to 2009, the Tuareg people living in the Saharan regions of northern Mali and Niger sought independence from their national governments.[8] While fighting was mostly confined to guerrilla attacks and army counterattacks, large portions of the desert north of both Mali and Niger were no-go zones for the military, and civilians fled to regional capitals like Kidal, in Mali, and Agadez, in Niger. Niger saw heavy fighting and disruption of uranium production in the mountainous north, before a Libyan-backed peace deal, aided by a factional split among the rebels, brought a negotiated ceasefire and amnesty in May 2009.[9] In a variant of Stockholm Syndrome, many enslaved Tuareg fought alongside their 'white' or lighter-skinned masters during the various rebellions. Today, many slaves remain loyal to their masters because of a combination of fear, hopelessness and dependency. But this odd allegiance ultimately helped to inspire Niger's anti-slavery movement.

Alio, a weathered forty-six-year-old and key member of Timidria, who had fought with the liberation movement in 1991, said: 'Timidria was born out of this liberation movement because you had black Tuaregs fighting alongside their white masters who then said: "Well, hang on a minute, we're fighting against marginalisation, yet we're being marginalised within our own group."'

WAHAYA

In Niger, many women and young girls are sold into sexual and domestic slavery. Nobody knows the exact number of slaves in Niger, but in 2008 Anti-Slavery International estimated the number at around 43,000.[10] Girls from the 'black' Tuareg group are sold by their Tuareg 'masters' to wealthy men, including religious leaders, usually from the Hausa ethnic group from northern Nigeria. Disturbingly, the slave masters view the purchase of young women as a sign of prestige. Typical prices range from between £200 and £500. During one investigation, Anti-Slavery International found that 43 per cent of those sold were between the age of nine and eleven years old and more than 80 per cent were sold before the age of fifteen.[11]

Once sold, the girls are known as *wahaya*, or fifth wives, because they are additional to the four wives legally allowed in Niger and Nigeria under Islamic practice. No actual marriage ever takes place, so their status and role is far lower than that of an official wife. They are treated as possessions of their masters and have none of the legal rights or securities that come with marriage. It is common for the 'master' to begin sexual relations with the girls as soon as they reach puberty. The girls are forced to work without pay and are never allowed to leave their family home except to do jobs for their masters. Many are also forced to wear a massive brass ankle ring to signify their slave status. *Wahaya* are regularly raped and abused by their masters, as well as being mistreated by the legitimate wives, who view *wahaya*, as well as their children, as competition.

In 2014, a sixty-three-year-old slave owner was jailed for four years for keeping a fifth wife – the first case of its kind in Niger, thanks to Timidria's efforts and the support of Anti-Slavery International. 'They worked me like a machine,' said fifty-year-old Koulouwiya, who Timidria had liberated from a community near Tchintabaraden. Talking to me in guttural Tamasheq, through an interpreter, she said: 'Whatever I owned, they owned. They gave us the leftovers to eat, the scraps from their table.'

In order for Nigeriens to be emancipated from this kind of mental and physical slavery, the victims had to find ways to protest and stand up for their rights. It was also necessary for elites to champion change, though this was much rarer.

Moustapha Kadi, a descendant of the elite that has ruled Niger for centuries, was an exception. In 2003, following the official abolition of slavery in his country, he publicly freed his family's slaves. I listened intently to Moustapha's clipped French as he recounted in detail what led to his Damascene conversion. While the stories of ex-slaves were moving and important, hearing a former slave master speak was unusual and therefore carried even more impact. There was something remarkable about this man. What had made him, in the face of centuries of tradition, go against the culture that had made him a master and those around him his servants? What had made him renege on his membership of the Tuareg elite?

'Going back to my childhood, I used to play with the children of slaves,' Moustapha said. 'My father was an MP who was also born into a traditional chiefdom. He had a huge house. We would play together on a full football-sized pitch! We pretty much had more than everyone else who had money.

'Our family's slaves and their children lived with us. I started noticing that we had clothes, but the slave children didn't. I never felt my mother's back, because a slave would always carry me around. My mother, whose name was Rosalind but whom everyone called Rose, was never in the kitchen. I would see that it was the slaves who were carrying the children and working in the kitchen. On one occasion, I asked my mother why she didn't carry me: "Why is it that even when these women's own children are crying, they have to carry me?" She never answered. I saw others would be punished, beaten, when they did something wrong.

'One day, while on my way to secondary school, which was out of town, I met one of our slave girls by the road. When I saw her, she burst into tears. I asked her: "What's going on? Where are you living at the moment?" I followed her to where she stayed. It was a brothel. I said: "This is where you live?" She said: "Yes," and I started crying. I asked her why she was here. She said she had fled slavery – she'd escaped. As a child, I was completely overwhelmed. Since then, I've always thought, is there anything worse than slavery, something so bad that it could send a young girl into prostitution? I felt obliged to fight it.'

Moustapha explained that before she died, his mother had given him the authorisation to free all the slaves. But it came at a devastating personal cost. He was cast out of the community and ostracised by his family. Rumours even circulated that maybe he had slave blood in him, which was why he had freed the slaves. Worse still was the impact it had on his elderly mother.

'I was alone, because I was against everyone. I believe the shock of me freeing our slaves contributed to my mother's death. One week after I freed ten slaves, my mother passed away. People accused me of declaring war on the traditional chiefdom I belong to. There are people still in slavery that support and celebrate the system, and accept their status as slaves.'

Having been very close to my own mother, who died in 2008, I couldn't imagine how Moustapha must have felt, believing that emancipating the family's slaves had contributed to her death. But it also seemed absurd. How could seeing this good deed prove fatal? At the very least, Moustapha's perception illustrated the huge difficulties of being stuck within a group where wrongdoing is occurring, as well as how brutal and unexpected the consequences of breaking out from it can be on those involved.

LASTING EFFECTS

People were enslaved across West and Central Africa before the trans-atlantic slave trade.[12] Yet, it is hard to say to what extent indigenous slavery contributed to transatlantic slavery. I do not believe it is fruitful to hierarchise different forms of exploitation. It goes without saying that all forced labour is inherently wrong. We should not be afraid to analyse how different forms of human ownership vary. The principal difference between indigenous slavery and the chattel slavery that followed it was that it was not until the latter that people became the full legal property of their owners.[13] Chattel slavery, or transatlantic slavery, coincided with the rise of plantation agriculture and became central to the Western economy.[14] It led to the commodification of humans, who were bought, sold and transported in huge numbers across land and sea.

Wherever there is slavery, there is commonly a narrative of supremacy underlying it. Yet it was not until the construction of a unified racial identity of blackness that slave owners could legitimise this exploitation. In previous eras of slavery, hierarchies were typically based on fiefdoms and chiefdoms, as opposed to the explicit construction of racial inferiority that was used to justify the transportation of black bodies across the Atlantic. The consequence of the latter was the complete destruction of communities and cultures.

Chattel slavery was also far more profitable than the slavery that preceded it, as it became the foundation of the plantation industry. Humans became units of global capital, subject to the whims of an increasingly competitive market. In the seventeenth century, a slave could be sold for $5 to $10. By the mid-nineteenth century, that figure rose to $1,500.[15] It's this kind of profitability that helped turn the USA, Britain, France and others into the economic powerhouses they are today.

It is important to recognise the unique history of transatlantic slavery to avoid the kind of historical denialism that is increasingly common. In the run-up to the 2019 election, I criticised the Brexit Party MEP Anne Widdecombe for comparing Britain leaving the EU to 'slaves' rising up 'against their owners'. I tried to articulate how offensive it was for Widdecombe to equate Brexit with the emancipation of my ancestors. In response, Daniel Hannan, a former Conservative MEP, replied: 'Slavery was, alas, near-universal. It was practised on every landmass. I am descended from slaves. So, reader, are you.' It is undoubtedly true that before transatlantic slavery, all kinds of slavery existed. White people were enslaved during the Roman Empire, the Ottoman Empire and the Viking Age. This is something I hear a lot, particularly when I draw on slavery in the past to discuss racial injustices in the present. For some, it is difficult to see the relevance of slavery to discussions of race when white people, as well as black, have been enslaved at various points in history. How can transatlantic slavery be unique when slavery has happened everywhere? But equating the experience of direct descendants of transatlantic slaves with those who guess that one of their ancestors going back thousands of years was probably enslaved somewhere is a pretty glib attempt to deny a real injustice.

The notion of 'race' was primarily invented to justify the enslavement of African people.[16] This is why it is still extremely hurtful to call a black person a 'nigger', the sole purpose of which was to denigrate and dehumanise in an effort to further justify the subjugation of one group of people by another. For this reason, the N-word will remain a signification of white supremacy, because that's what the word was invented to serve.

The long-lasting, unique effects of the transatlantic slave trade are not somehow undermined by the existence of other injustices, not least because different things are unjust for different reasons. The enormous chasm between those communities that profited and others that were made destitute did not simply disappear with time. Nor did the construction of racial superiority. Despite abolition, the racialised hierarchy created by the transatlantic slave trade continues to generate enormous racialised inequality to this day.

ANTI-TRIBALISM

The independence that followed colonisation in most African countries was not characterised by peace, stability and people coming together. The arbitrary borders and nation states drawn up by departing colonisers cut across ethnic identities, heightening tensions. In many African nations, conflict and division followed. The ethnic-based violence that broke out after Niger and Mali's independence in 1960, and in the Democratic Republic of Congo around the same time, was typical.

For ill-informed onlookers in the Western world, tribal conflict following independence in post-colonial African nations must have looked almost inevitable. It was not. In 1966, Botswana became one of the last African colonies to become independent from Britain. After witnessing what had happened elsewhere on the continent, the first leaders of the newly independent Botswana recognised that their own fledgling nation could face similar problems. Indeed, in Botswana at the time, there were more than twenty tribes, split by culture, language and tradition.

To avoid tribal conflict, Botswana's early leaders devised a strategic approach intended to create a national identity that bridged the gap between different ethnic groups. The government worked to assimilate all tribal groups into one broad 'Tswana' culture. This policy excluded tribal identities from official records, passports and driving licences, as well as the national census, unlike in most other African countries. The Tswana language, Setswana, and English were made the only official languages. No other language could be used in official settings or taught in schools.

Even though Botswana was carved up and glued together by the clumsy hand of its former rulers, like so many other African nations were, it was able to achieve decades of relative harmony. Evidence of ethnic tensions in Botswana did not begin to emerge until the late 1990s.[17] Even then, the levels of discord never reached the same intensity as in many other post-colonial countries. For decades, Botswana has been known as one of Africa's 'most stable' countries.[18] From its start as one of the world's poorest nations, it is now classed by the World Bank as 'upper middle-income'. Botswana is also the thirty-fourth least corrupt country out of 180, according to Transparency International, making its government one of the most trustworthy on the continent.

The widespread plundering of natural resources in Africa by multinational corporations is well-documented. For many nations, what should have been a source of national prosperity ended up becoming a catalyst for conflict. Again, Botswana was able to buck the trend, at least to an extent. In 1967, just a year after the small southern African state became independent, an enormous diamond mine was discovered in Orapa, around 250 miles from Gaborone, the capital. By the early 1980s, the combination of diamond, copper and manganese mines made up 50 per cent of Botswana's GDP. Seretse Khama, the first President of Botswana, from 1966 to 1980, was able to compel De Beers, the company that discovered the mine, to work with the government in a joint venture. With profits split fifty–fifty, the people of Botswana, not just boardroom executives, were able to benefit from an industry that produces around one quarter of the world's diamonds. It is in stark contrast to how private companies were allowed ransack resources in other African nations.

Of the various causes of conflict on the continent of Africa, the battle for resources is only matched by disagreements over land. In Botswana's neighbour, South Africa, land reform remains an explosive political issue, dating back to the racist 'Natives Land Act' of 1913, which prevented black people from buying, or even renting, land in so-called 'white South Africa'. This resulted in the forced removal of black people from their homes. Disputes over land also remain at boiling point in Zimbabwe, where white Europeans were historically treated as politically and economically superior. Botswana itself managed to reduce disputes over land by distributing it to all those who wanted it. Crucially, the government mandated that everything beneath the surface of the land owned by individuals belonged to the state. This was vital in the diamond-rich nation. By spreading land across the population and taking ownership of what lay underneath the ground, the government made sure that neither were the subject of tribal competition.

To foster belonging between members of different tribes, the Botswanan government also introduced what is known as the 'transfer policy'. This obliged all civil servants to relocate to regions that homed different ethnic groups from their own for a few years at a time. This served two purposes. First, it meant that all areas had a good supply of doctors, teachers and other civil servants. Second, and even more importantly, it forced people from different tribes to mix.

For society, this has obvious benefits, but for many of those forced to move, it is a great burden. Speaking to National Public Radio (NPR) in the USA about her experiences of the compulsory transfer programme, one Botswanan teacher, Carol, who was forced to move to a small village in a region she did not know, said: 'I was angry with the minister of education. I was angry with everyone . . . I didn't even want to be a teacher any more. At times, I would just go to class, I would look at these kids, I would just give them a book to read, and I would go back to my room.'[19]

When Carol received a letter saying she would be transferred with immediate effect, she was a teacher in Gaborone, the capital city. She loved her profession and had an active social life in the city, where all her friends were based. Being forced to move to a remote village, Lentsweletau, turned Carol's life upside down. It alienated her from friends and family and made her dislike the job she once loved.

Then one day everything changed for Carol: she fell in love with Thabo, a man from the village. With Thabo making introductions, she began to socialise with other villagers: going to parties, weddings, funerals and even being invited to be a judge in a local beauty contest. One woman gave Carol a piece of land on which she built a house. After interacting with them, her view of the village and its people completely changed. 'They are loving people. I love them. I love them,' she told NPR. This story is not as unique as it sounds. Of those who take part in the programme, around 20 per cent stay where they were transferred in order to get married, according to the country's foreign minister, Unity Dow.

In this way, Botswana's tribal tensions could be said to have been soothed in part by compulsory movement, cross-pollination and individuals falling in love. But what lessons can we learn from this to help us to bridge divisions, based on political, religious or other differences, in our own societies? The first is that creating relationships that go beyond the groups we come from, or naturally fall into, is not inevitable. We are programmed to feel comfortable with those who are similar to us. Moving between crowds does not always happen naturally. Sometimes it requires encouragement and even compulsion. Second, the experience of being among those who are different will initially be difficult, but that does not mean it will not become rewarding. Carol hated leaving behind her home at first, but later she grew to love the village where she was forced to move. Third, what is beneficial for society is not always preferable for the individual. To create a more united nation, sometimes it may be necessary for individual citizens to sacrifice their own comfort, as Carol and so many other public servants have done in Botswana, at least for a while.

SUPREMACY

In Niger, as in western Europe, the USA and across the world, the most pernicious form of tribalism is based on the notion that one group of humans is inherently superior to another. On race, this myth is relatively straightforward to disprove. The consensus in human genetics today supports the 'Out of Africa' theory, which emerged in the 1950s, proposing that all human beings ultimately descend from a single tribe from present-day East Africa.[20] It is from this very specific location that all human beings emigrated, populating the entire globe. When two strands of the human species separated, there remained a remarkable amount of genetic similarity between distinct populations, wherever they ended up. Every *Homo sapiens* ultimately descends from a single thread.

Human beings across the planet are remarkably mixed. Different ethnic groups have consistently swapped DNA at every opportunity. Scientific evidence clearly shows that different human tribes have sex nearly every time they meet. Whether brought together through trade, war or exploration, our ancestors had sex. A lot of it. For example, when fifteenth-century Portuguese explorers sailed their ships around Africa into the Indian Ocean, at every port they founded they mixed with the local population. This created distinct groups of people, such as in Brazil, Goa and the Cape Coloured grouping in South Africa. This process of travelling, mixing and travelling again was repeated throughout human history, from the Bantu-speaking migration from West Africa to southern Africa to the steppe-based Caucasians moving into Europe and the Spanish conquistadors entering southern America.

Charles Darwin's great assertion in *On the Origin of Species* was that a species develops according to the challenges it confronts in its environment over a long period of time.[21] Crucially, humans were shown to be no different from any other animal in this model of evolution by natural selection. The theory caused a sensation when it was first proposed by Darwin: it made possible a new explanation for the apparent differences between humans and their various socio-economic circumstances. White Europeans, who had practised rampant exploitation of black Africans for slave labour, now had a pseudo-scientific justification for seeing other 'races' as genetically inferior. How else could they have achieved such greater economic prosperity and military might?

This reinforced the racial pecking order that was constructed to justify slavery in the first place. The greater economic power enjoyed by white people who enslaved Africans was proof, it seemed, that they were the superior race. The fact that black people were enslavable was all the evidence slave-owners needed to substantiate the racial hierarchy used to justify this exploitation in the first place.

It is easy to forget that supremacist conclusions were scientific orthodoxy in the nineteenth century. One theory of human development from those days claimed that Europeans, Asians and Africans look different because early members of these different strands of the human species were derived from different bipedal primates. This is the opposite of what we know now.

It is disturbing to consider that something similar to this theory is still taught today in China. Chinese textbooks treat it as fact that the Han ethnic group arose from genetic mixing with *Homo erectus*.[22] The fact is that *H. erectus* was a distinct species that died out, and the visible characteristics of the Han ethnic group are easily explained by variation within the species rather than the confluence of an outer species. The currency of this flawed theory is worrying because it suggests that the persistent conflation of genetic heredity and race is set to persist.

The truth about the relationship between skin colour and genetic ancestry is that although different skin colour is not random across different genetic ancestries, genetics is far more complex and far messier than our simple conception of ethnic groups. The genetics that determine skin colour are a tiny part of our overall genetic heritage. In cosmopolitan cites, such as London, New York or São Paulo, skin colour tells us little more about the rest of someone's DNA than their height or hair colour. The origin of the genetics of red hair is confidently assigned to the western fringe of Europe, but we don't use red hair as a definition of an ethnic group with all the baggage this entails. Variation within an ethnic group far exceeds the uniform differences between two groups.

The idea – known as eugenics – that human 'stock' could somehow be 'improved' through the systematic suppression of reproduction in some ethnic groups while encouraging reproduction in others was sadly considered a reasonable scientific rationale in the 1920s. It reached its nadir in the Holocaust. The term 'eugenics' was invented by Charles Darwin's half-cousin, Francis Galton, who combined Darwin's theory of natural selection with the fixity of genetic inheritance to justify his own theories about how to manipulate and 'improve' human beings on a national scale.[23] Galton laid the foundations for some of the key elements in the field of statistics in this unsavoury quest, but the conception that human stock could be improved was neither scientifically justified nor ethical. Despite this, University College London established a professorship of eugenics in Galton's name after his death.

Charles Darwin himself had relatively progressive views for his era. He argued for the abolition of slavery and spoke fondly of his taxidermy tutor John Edmonstone, a freed black Guyanese slave who became a friend and influenced Darwin's switch in focus from medicine to natural history.[24] Unlike Darwin, Galton was clearly racist. He openly spoke of his own prejudice, describing Arabs as 'little more than an eater up of other men's produce', Hindus as lacking in 'strength and business habits' and 'Negroes' as inferior.[25, 26]

The racial basis of eugenics is now unilaterally discredited, but the idea of the genetic improvement of the human species still has considerable currency. People in positions of power are still motivated by the notion of genetic hierarchies. Take Dominic Cummings, Boris Johnson's most senior political adviser on entering Downing Street in 2019. During Cummings's tenure as Michael Gove's special adviser, he wrote a 237-page thesis, entitled 'Some Thoughts on Education and Political Priorities', which argued that 70 per cent of a child's academic performance is attributable to genetics. A child's genetic make-up, Cummings believes, is far more important than the teaching they receive. Cummings even cites Galton in an attempt to bolster his ramblings.[27] He then draws the wrong policy inference from this piece of science – that teaching is not important – when genetic studies do not support this point of view.[28]

The 'scientific evidence' to which Cummings refers is complex to navigate, in particular on educational attainment. First, as Cummings himself admits, genetic heritability studies are wildly inconsistent and give varied results. Second, Cummings is referring to a measure of 'heritability', which is a simple-sounding English word but one that is in fact used to describe a complex concept, in this context within the specific environment of the UK educational system. Geneticist Steve Jones says 'almost everything is genetic, but we usually deal with it by changing the environment'.[29] The use of heritability as a measure for children's intelligence is particularly misleading. Jones explains that children respond much more readily to their circumstances than adults. For example, the IQ of a poor child adopted into a wealthy household rises significantly. Cumming's obsession with IQ, therefore, is less about scientific understanding and more about pushing a dangerous, elitist narrative: that a natural hierarchy of inequality must be preserved.

On the second page of his writing on the subject, Cummings argues that 'the spread of knowledge and education is itself a danger and cannot eliminate gaps in wealth and power created partly by unequally distributed heritable characteristics'. This narrative is highly contentious, not least because some people still try to promote an underlying genetic basis to broad ethnic classification and traits. For many people, 'genetics' is synonymous with 'ethnicity', from which follows a neat and tidy explanation of why certain 'ethnicities' (crudely, people with a certain skin colour) are predominantly in positions of power, influence and money. This neo-Darwinian conception of ethnic 'destiny' is simply false and not at all Darwinian. In fact, the genetic make-up of Afro-Caribbeans and African Americans is intertwined with European genetic ancestry, and modern geneticists do not use ethnicity as an important way to characterise humans at a genetic level.

Importantly, intelligence is not a single trait. It is made up of thousands of different variants that do not correspond to one particular ethnicity or another. As Kevin Mitchell, associate professor of genetics and neuroscience at Trinity College Dublin, has argued, it is 'inherently and deeply implausible' that there are 'systemic genetic differences in intelligence between large, ancient populations'.[30] Therefore, differences between different racial groups is in fact strong evidence that racial discrimination – both overt and unconscious – continues to run rampant. This is the case not only in communities traditionally thought of as 'tribal', but across most corners of the globe.

BELONGING

As my time in Niger drew nearer to a close, I began to feel a sense of belonging to the Tuareg. I had gone to Niger in search of a hitherto unknown aspect of my identity and an understanding of tribal dynamics, in part for self-affirmation but also to learn lessons about the increasing tribalism that has surfaced at home. And in some ways going back to my roots did affect my sense of self. I now had an entirely new sense of identity, outside that which was shaped by the markers that I had up until then associated with: Tottenham, Britain, Guyana, my class, my 'race', my social network and my status within a political elite. I felt as though I had gained a new layer to my identity that was real and tangible, made of flesh, blood and genetic code.

People who are descendants of slaves are often very conscious that they do not know their historical roots. They are forced to hold on to recent cultural icons who share their own heritage, because they do not have any information about the ancestors who preceded them. Growing up, I had in this way found pride in the oratory of Martin Luther King, the inner strength of Rosa Parks, the musical defiance of Bob Marley, the grace of Muhammad Ali and the poetry of Maya Angelou, to name but a few.

The greatest lesson I took away from retracing my roots to Niger is that our urge to belong is a paradox. It can be deeply destructive, as in the case of the enslavement of perceived inferior castes of the Tuareg. But belonging is also a source of comfort, solidarity and shared experience, underpinned by great bodies of tradition and custom. Breaking bread with nomads and city dwellers across Niger was deeply moving, and allowed me to feel connected to the genetic heritage I had only recently become acquainted with. I heard moving stories of those who had fought and escaped modern slavery, as well as those who had engaged in it but had had Damascene conversions and stopped. It reminded me that no culture is static, and even those that harbour the most medieval of practices can and do change.

'Very, very beautiful!' cried Alhousseini as Barkoji and Ali wrapped the long white turban, or *arshash*, around my head in ever more intricate twists and turns. Away from the assembled farewell party in the courtyard outside Timidria's office, I had slipped into my long flowing white robe (known as a boubou), for which I'd been measured two days earlier. I had no idea that the boubou and now my head-wrapping were in fact part of a ceremony, a rite of passage that in an informal but nonetheless moving way was now initiating me into the Tuareg tribe. A few turns into wrapping the *arshash*, Barkoji took my right hand and placed it on my head to keep the cloth in place. I was all but mummified. Outside, I could hear the infectious beat of *tendi* drums, tambourines, hand clapping, singing and high-pitched ululating.

'Do I look the part?' I asked, of no one in particular. Alhousseini, Ali and Barkoji exchanged words in Tamasheq, laughed and gave what appeared to be signs of approval. I stood up, slowly, almost unsteady under the weight of a new mode of self-expression, like some sort of metamorphosis in reverse. Rather than shedding a skin, I was gaining one, in the form of my Tuareg self. As I walked through the power-cut-darkened corridors of Timidria's offices, I could hear the mesmerising sound of the women performing out in the courtyard. The noise rose and rose until I reached the exit and was hit by a wall of piercing sunlight, drums, shouts, clapping and stomping feet.

I took my seat in the front row and centre of a couple of dozen gleaming white plastic chairs. We faced a colourful array of women wearing flowing gowns of crimson, red and gold, elaborate headscarves and veils, bangles and intricate hairdos. Some were tattooed with henna. Two of the four elders were playing the drums while conducting a dozen women who sat in a semicircle a few feet away. They rocked from side to side as the music ebbed and flowed.

At various times, a lone woman, either encouraged by the others or on her own whim, would break from the group with an elaborate flour-ish and move into the centre of the floor to dance with total abandon. After a few minutes of ecstasy, she would slip back to rejoin the group, receiving a chorus of approval. These women clearly had not got the memo from the Shia or Sunni fundamentalists about Niger's emerging Sharia dress code or behaviour befitting a Muslim woman. Nor had they shown any of the usual austere stiffness that visiting parliamentar-ians are often welcomed with. They weren't so much performing for me as performing with me. No sooner had I lowered my generous frame into my chair than I was being ushered up on to the stage to clap, dance and display the moves I had honed on the dance floors of my youth. I pray that no one had a camera.

As a politician, I am used to being 'presented' and occasionally offered up as a sacrificial lamb to crowds of overfed foreign dignitar-ies, hostile strangers, concerned constituents, angry detractors, disgruntled locals or cynical factory-floor workers. Politics is often described as 'show business for ugly people', as if all the average MP wants to do is get his face on telly. If I'm honest, most of the time in these situations I feel eager to be elsewhere, not because I am uneasy around people, but because my time is so often pressed. The real business of politics is done behind the scenes, not in front of a camera, so there's always an urgency to be at the next meeting, brief-ing or negotiating table. But here, in the moment, I wanted time to stand still. I wanted to savour this rite of passage, this coming of age. Unlike most of my encounters with strangers, the like of this might never happen again. And yet I felt an inner conflict that I couldn't quite shake off, even as all eyes were on me and I was being initiated into the Tuareg.

I felt an immense sense of belonging that day in that dusty compound on a side street of Niamey. The laughter and celebration and poignancy of the moment were real, but I also felt melancholy about the identity my ancestors, who were forced to leave Niger, had lost. Ironically, my position as part of the 'global elite' gave me the political and economic privilege of being able to go almost anywhere I wanted to go on the planet. The people surrounding me, however, would be lucky to cross the border from one stretch of desert into another. What did such limitations mean to them? I couldn't understand their language or their rituals, other than through the filter of the translators among them. With both my parents long dead now, and my grandparents too, my antecedents were a distant memory. I could not help but feel mildly embarrassed that my new cousins were so impressed that I was happy to describe myself as the descendant of slaves – to cling on to my heritage, my history – when some of them might well be willing to sell everything they had and risk their lives in a rubber dinghy for one shot at reaching Britain, a United Kingdom in which my own West Indian tribe now felt it was losing its own identity, as a victim of its own integrationist success. A country which had become divided and polarised, along its own tribal lines.

After Alhousseini had delivered a glowing introduction, and Anti-Slavery International gave a summary of their work in Niger, I stepped up, in full Tuareg regalia, in front of the assembled crowd. I started by explaining, with the help of a translator, how my DNA tests had led me to Niger, how somewhere along my maternal line a Tuareg ancestor had been taken from Niger on a journey that would result in my birth, following a genetic path from West Africa across the Atlantic to the New World and back again to Britain – a round trip of some 9,000 miles.

'Thank you for the welcome you have given me. It is wonderful to be back home after all these years!' The joke reached the smattering of those who understood English seconds before those needing a translation, like a linguistic echo. I went on to explain how I couldn't really put into words how spiritually enriching my visit to Niger had been. 'But what an honour it is for me to go back to the United Kingdom, to stand up in our historic parliament and make the case for the Tuareg people and against slavery in the United Kingdom and Europe,' I said. I was on a roll. I spoke of my immense gratitude 'to my brothers and sisters at Timidria' and all that they'd helped me to understand, in such a short time. My initiation into the Tuareg was not an artificial ceremony for the 'big man' from London, cobbled together to massage my ego. It was a genuine, heartfelt rite of passage I shall always cherish.

Finally, taking a deep breath, looking around at the crowd of strangely familiar dark faces staring back at me in reflection, I said: 'This has been one of the most special moments of my life. When I stand up in Parliament in the months ahead, because I now know who I am, I stand much taller.'

HOW BELONGING
CAN BREAK SOCIETY

5

Alone

How we created an epidemic of loneliness

'I have seen that in any great undertaking it is not enough for a man to depend simply upon himself.'

Lone Man, Teton Sioux

It was a bitterly cold spring morning, around 5 a.m., when I left the comfort of my north London home. I dragged myself outside into a careworn Prius cab destined for Heathrow, to catch a flight to Washington, DC, for a work visit. I slumped into the back seat of the taxi an exhausted mess, desperately trying to avoid eye contact with the driver, just in case he recognised me and wanted to chat about the sort of issues I deal with in constituency surgery: housing problems, welfare complaints, an issue with the council. While I love that part of my job, on this particular morning I was tired and hoping to zone out. The driver was a slight man, Asian and in his fifties. About ten minutes into the journey, he summoned the courage to ask me if I was the MP for Tottenham. I replied that I was. He told me he was a constituent and introduced himself as Tariq. There goes any chance of sleep, I thought to myself, but as we wormed our way through the darkened streets of suburban London, he narrated one of the most heartbreaking stories I have heard in nearly twenty years of being an MP. As soon as I boarded the plane, I wrote down every single detail I could remember.

Tariq explained that he had moved to the UK with his brother from Bangladesh in the early nineties as a young man. Arriving with a determined work ethic, an entrepreneurial attitude and a bit of luck, they were both able to build lives and eventually grow families close to one another in north London. Other family members soon followed them to the UK. Some settled in various boroughs of London, while several others chose to live in Birmingham. Tariq's own children inherited his mindset, working hard at school and both graduating from university. His adult son was now a pharmacist and his daughter an accountant. Life was far from perfect, but they could not complain about the opportunities they had made for themselves in the UK. Growing up, Tariq's children had spent their lives between their family home and his brother's house. They were one large family, enjoying meals together, gathering for religious festivals and watching TV in each other's front rooms.

In his early childhood, Anwar, Tariq's nephew, was almost as much a part of Tariq's family as his own children. He was a quiet but kind boy who enjoyed many of the same interests as his three elder siblings and two cousins. He loved football, rap music and cartoons like *The Simpsons*. Looking back, Tariq said it was clear that Anwar's teenage years were more difficult than for others in the family. He did not make new friends easily, feeling awkward in large groups. Academically, too, he achieved less success than his siblings and cousins. Anwar became frustrated when teachers told him off and easily upset when peers made fun of him. At home and at school he often lost his temper. Three or four times he was involved in fights so serious that the school phoned his parents.

It was not all bad. Anwar was never in trouble with the police, did not get heavily involved in drink or drugs, and in flashes at home he continued to show the kindness he had possessed ever since he was a young boy. After leaving school with few qualifications, he worked for a couple of years in retail, earning a small but reasonably reliable wage. As he grew a beard, he started to act more maturely. He began to take his religion more seriously, spending a lot of time in the local mosque.

His mother and father grew proud of their son, who never missed a day of work and practised his religion diligently.

It was only after a couple of years of working life that Anwar started to worry his family again. Abruptly leaving his job at a local clothing store, he showed little interest in finding another. He began to spend more time in his room alone, staying up late, watching YouTube videos and chatting to people through messaging apps on his phone. His father and uncle Tariq worked every hour they could and paid little attention to the rapid changes Anwar's mother was recognising in her son. One night there was a confrontation when Anwar's mother burst into his room, demanding to know what he was doing. He refused to say. The next day he fitted a lock to his door.

A few months later, Anwar had teamed up with a second cousin in Birmingham and flown to Spain. From there they travelled to Turkey and on to Syria to join the self-styled ISIS. He became one of around 900 British citizens to leave the UK to join ISIS since 2012.[1] You do not become a radical Islamic terrorist overnight. Usually individuals are enticed through a long process of indoctrination and socialisation that can go on for months and years.[2] This probably happened to Anwar late at night, on his smartphone, Tariq speculated.

Gripped by the growing emotion in Tariq's voice as we paused because of an accident on the road, I learned how this humble man's whole world had fallen apart. He explained that the entire family was distraught, knowing that even the best-case scenario would be a disaster for Anwar. If he and his second cousin did manage to come home in one piece, they would be assured of a quick arrest, a humiliating trial and lengthy imprisonment.

Tariq felt responsible for failing to intervene and change the trajectory of these young men's lives. He felt selfish because he had failed to understand Anwar, to get to know him before it was too late. And he felt helpless because, for all his hard work and law-abiding citizenship, he was utterly powerless in the face of a force that overrode his own will.

By holding down multiple jobs, both Tariq and his brother had abdicated their responsibility as the family's patriarchs. I could empathise with why they had done this. As first-generation immigrants, the two of them were much like my mother, in that they knew that to get ahead they had to work twice as hard as those around them. They saw their primary duty as to provide for their family, and they were not afraid of working all hours to do so. They could not have known that providing a positive example of hard work might not be enough to keep young, impressionable minds on the straight and narrow. Neither Tariq nor his brother can be blamed for Anwar's terrible decision, but there is little doubt that the lack of significant, close and empathetic male role models in the young man's life contributed to his radicalisation.

With no understanding of how to be, or where to belong, Anwar was left at the mercy of ISIS's twenty-four-hour online propaganda machine. Images of dashing jihadist protagonists and an evil Western enemy were alluring. The choice he faced was whether to continue in a low-paid, uninspiring job, with little opportunity for career progression, no friends and little meaning, or to live life as a hero, taking part in what he had become convinced was a moral struggle and adventure in a foreign land that was also his land. With a distant father, a mother who had little cross-cultural confidence in understanding her son's world and no strong group of friends or community to belong to, Anwar and his cousin were easy prey.

When I asked Tariq whether Anwar's decision to join ISIS was connected to the boy's mosque and its activities, he claimed that, if anything, the mosque was probably the only reason he had not gone sooner. Tariq said it had been exceptional at challenging the hateful ideology of Islamic fundamentalism and provided at least some of the belonging Anwar craved.

As we approached the airport, I wanted to ask Tariq dozens more questions. Who, or what, had got to Anwar? How had a virus like ISIS managed to defeat the vaccine of a safe, stable, loving home? Where was the community leadership and the oversight? Did Anwar ever have a partner? Was that even possible in his world? Did Tariq see how emasculating it could be for a young man to have no emotional outlets and no opportunities to develop empathy on his own terms? Above all, I asked myself, how many more people born and bred in this country have fallen victim to violent extremism?

FEAR AND LOATHING IN WALSALL

A few months later, I was in Walsall Magistrates Court. I spotted the overweight, red-faced man as soon as I made my way through security. Despite having never met David Hall in the flesh, I knew him at once from the sagging cheeks and badly dyed auburn hair on his Twitter profile picture. He certainly knew who I was. Just before Christmas a year earlier, the seventy-two-year-old retired engineer from Wolverhampton had sent me what he claimed was a 'friendly warning' via email. In reality, it was a threat:

> As you attack the White population of Britain in your aims to gain Black Supremacy in this country, remember what happened to Jo Cox. I AM NOT ONE OF THEM but there are those out there who would like to see you suffer the same fate. Be careful!!

He signed off: 'D. W. Hall (a well wisher).'

Jo was a Labour MP and someone I admired hugely for her tireless anti-racism and pro-EU campaigning. I had known her husband, Brendan, for nearly two decades, as he had led the campaign bus full of Labour students that helped me get elected for the first time in the 2000 Tottenham by-election. A week before the 2016 EU referendum, a fifty-two-year-old neo-Nazi walked up to Jo in the street as she was about to hold her regular constituency surgery in Birstall, West Yorkshire. In broad daylight and at point-blank range, he shot her with a sawn-off rifle, before stabbing her multiple times. She died instantly.

Many people thought Jo's death would somehow be a game-changer. I for one believed that her sacrifice would remind the British public of the dangers of nationalism and where it can lead. I was wrong. As David Hall's email made clear, far-right extremists were emboldened by Jo's murder. It would signal a new era of threats and abusive behaviour towards MPs. In May 2019, Met Police Commissioner Cressida Dick warned that abuse against MPs had reached 'unprecedented' levels since the Brexit vote.[3] My parliamentary colleagues and I were the victims of 342 crimes in 2018, more than double the 151 in the year before.[4]

I was not the only politician Hall had threatened. He also sent an abusive email to the MPs Nicky Morgan, Dominic Grieve, Anna Soubry and Heidi Allen with the subject line: 'YOUR BACK STABBING TREACHERY', which read:

> You deserve to be HUNG for your attack on our democracy yesterday. WE VOTED OUT OUT OUT!!!!!!!!!!!!!!!!!!!!!!!!!! and your attack on the British VOTE to leave the PARASITIC FRAUDSTERS in the EU amounts to an act of TREASON.
>
> In WW2 you would have 'SWUNG' for this act of TREACHERY – You join a long list of British TRAITORS – MAY YOU BURN IN HELL FOR ETERNITY.

Months earlier, in July 2017, Hall had emailed my colleague Eleanor Smith MP – the first African-Caribbean to represent a constituency in the West Midlands – in response to her criticism of the Black Country's flag:

> How dare you !!!!! HOW SODDING WELL DARE ATTACK OUR FLAG!!! As a Labour/Communist and RACIST you come to MY COUNTRY AND ATTACK OUR CUSTOMS, and EVEN the IDENTITY OF OUR FLAG. I think that YOU MUST HAVE ENRAGED EVERY SINGLE WHITE PERSON IN 'MY' TOWN.
>
> YOU MUST HAVE YOUR ARSE KICKED OUT OF POWER AND BE PUT BACK ON THE FIRST BANANA BOAT TO THE JUNGLE CLEARING YOU CAME FROM!! Our Enoch Powell was dead right in his 'River of Blood Speech' 1968 when he said the streets of Britain will RUN RED WITH BLOOD AND YOU HAVE BROUGHT THAT REALITY ONE STEP NEARER WITH YOUR VILE RACIST RANTINGS !!!!!!!!!!!!!!!!!!!!

I made the decision to attend Hall's criminal trial with the intention of putting a face to the threats I receive every week. I wanted to understand what would drive someone to such extreme actions. What emerged was not a pantomime far-right villain, but a sad and lonely man, channelling his personal frustrations against public figures.

In court, David Hall's young Asian probation officer recounted his client's life story. Hall had lived alone in the same house in Castlecroft, Wolverhampton, for forty-eight years, and had no family except for a daughter who had long since emigrated. After retiring seven years earlier, Hall had almost no social contact. He had become a daily drinker. The vulnerability of his solitude had resulted in him being scammed by a woman over the internet. Physically he was not in great shape either, taking medication for blood pressure and experiencing chronic pain following a hip and knee replacement.

A long-time UKIP supporter, Hall had previous for threatening behaviour following a tussle with an Asian neighbour who took umbrage at his distribution of party literature on lamp posts in the surrounding area. On the surface, Hall was no different to legions of other UKIP supporters, frustrated with the changing face of modern Britain and seeing multiculturalism as an existential threat. But he had crossed the Rubicon. He was not acting like some harmless 1970s sitcom character. He was no Alf Garnett or Steptoe from *Steptoe and Son*. He had not confined his opinions to the privacy of his living room or to local pub banter. He had threatened and racially insulted sitting members of parliament with grossly offensive and menacing messages.

The police were duly notified, and on 30 January 2018, Hall was arrested by West Midlands Police and charged with seven counts of improper use of a public electronics communications network.

All the way up to his day in court on that morning in June 2018, Hall had pled not guilty, arguing a democratic right to free speech. It was not so much a defence but a justification for threatening and abusive behaviour. Reactionaries and racists have a tendency to foam at the mouth about 'political correctness gone mad', contradicting the common sense, decency, tolerance and respect they like to extol as traditional British values. They fail to recognise that the process of putting threatening thoughts down on paper, in text messages, emails, newspaper articles, reports, books and so forth, are material actions, not abstract ideas swirling in the privacy of their heads. To say that the written word has little or no effect on human behaviour is to deny the impact of everything from the development of Egyptian hieroglyphics and Sumerian literature right up to our online discourse on Twitter or Facebook Messenger. In other words, saying that words lack the power to heal or maim contradicts reality.

Hall's 'free-speech' defence might have felt righteous to him as he sat at home, but under the scrutiny of the court, and with a throng of media waiting outside, he performed a volte-face. With me and Nicky Morgan giving evidence, and the threat of a longer sentence if he failed to acknowledge any wrongdoing, he changed his plea to guilty.

As I watched Hall shuffle into the courtroom ahead of me in his faded leather jacket and worn-out sandals, I felt sorry for him. He cut a pathetic figure. I recognised that his vicious messages were an expression of the impotence he felt about a world changing at a rate he could not comprehend and in a way that flouted the worldview he had absorbed as he grew up. Like others in his generation, Hall was raised with a perception of Britain as white, dominant and proud. His assertion that 'our' Enoch Powell was right to forecast immigration leading to blood on our streets exposed a man long convinced of white supremacy and trapped in a view that skin colour determined an individual's ability to contribute and be a functioning member of our society.

As well as his probation officer, Hall's own solicitor, Mr Adil Khan of Mian & Co., was not white. Individuals from 'othered' groups had made their way to positions of authority, while he had not. The irony of the situation was almost beyond comprehension. How must Hall have felt? An avowed racist, past his best and angry, in the dock for the words he had used against a black British lawmaker, being defended by not one but two Asian professionals?

The probation officer said that Hall was now a changed man who no longer took an interest in politics. She said that Hall felt he had 'never had anyone to challenge or moderate his thinking', which is no surprise given that he had spent most of his time alone for the better part of half a century. Hall had told the probation officer that 'prison would destroy him', but despite his pattern of offending she concluded that he posed a low risk of offending and a 'medium risk of harm to political figures'.

For all his bluster about 'back stabbing treachery', 'treason' and 'traitors', Hall had waved the white flag without giving any explanation to the court for his actions, except for mitigation from Mr Khan. To the fifteen or so people in court, Mr Khan argued that Hall had realised that his actions were 'a big mistake' and accepted responsibility. Hall still maintained that he had exerted his 'freedom of speech', and shook his head when the prosecutor, Matthew Brook, outlined the facts against him.

Sentencing Hall, Mr Paul Wooding said: 'This was a series of highly offensive emails sent to public servants involving a racial element. For these reasons we deem it so serious that it has crossed the custody threshold.'

Hall was given a nine-week jail term suspended for twelve months, and ordered to complete twenty-five days of rehabilitation work and pay £735 in costs and a victim surcharge.

LONELINESS

Neither Anwar nor David Hall's stories would have been possible thirty years ago. Indeed, ten years ago they would both have been very unlikely. There has never been a time at which the radicalising content of social media – from the right, the left and indeed from extreme religious groups – has been so accessible, engaging and persuasive. At no other point in history has it been possible for individuals to splinter into so diverse a spread of tribal communities through their 4G connection and mobile phones. Finding belonging in your locality has never been so difficult, but finding it in a global, organised supremacy group has never been so easy.

In step with our exponentially increasing access to radicalising content, the practical challenges associated with committing to a life associated with a hateful ideology have diminished. If Anwar had been a young adult in the 1990s and wanted his jihad blessed by Al-Qaeda, he would have needed to make contact with a mufti in Afghanistan, travel to meet him, and probably spend months networking and building trust. In today's world, an aspiring Islamic extremist only needs to find the right internet forum to direct themselves to armies of recruiters on encrypted messaging apps. In Hall's case, having the ability to fire off toxic messages to members of parliament without even having to leave his front room must have given him a rare feeling of immediacy and power in an otherwise detached and powerless life.

While advances in technology have made it easier than ever to contact other human beings, meaningful human connections have never been so rare. The tribal politics we are experiencing is at least in part a result of the individualistic society we have created. Both Islamic extremists and white supremacists find their belonging in a hateful ideology that values one group, whether defined by ethnicity, religion or some other shared characteristic, above any others. But why do they need to do this? The new tribalism comes from 'the shift from a longing for independence from a society made up of communities to a longing for belonging in a society made up of individuals'.[5] To understand how David Hall and Anwar's longing for belonging attached itself to far-right and Islamic-extremist tribes respectively, we need to analyse what it is about society that has caused so many individuals to have their cravings to belong left unsatisfied in the first place.

There are many different definitions of loneliness, ranging from the personal to the political, but most are centred on the absence of depth, richness or meaning in an individual's social connections. It is more clearly understood as an emotional state in which people have less social contact than they desire. Basically, if you feel as though you are lonely, you are lonely. You cannot measure an individual's loneliness by the number of friends, close family members or acquaintances they have. On social media, an individual can appear to have hundreds of friends, seemingly spending all their time at restaurants, on holiday and at parties, but this does not show us how they feel. Inside, they may be isolated, lonely and lacking in meaningful connection. Similarly, someone else may maintain no social-media presence and see only a few close friends but feel completely contented with the relationships in their life.

While it is impossible to tell from the outside which individuals have less social contact than they desire, there is no doubt that collectively as a society we are in the middle of a loneliness pandemic. More than 9 million people in the UK report that they 'are always or often lonely'.[6] Older people are the worst affected, with 1.2 million experiencing it chronically.[7] A staggering 41 per cent of Brits say the television or their pet is their main source of company.[8] This is not a problem unique to the UK. A recent survey of 20,000 people in the USA found that nearly half of Americans experience loneliness.[9] A government survey found that 541,000 people in Japan live as modern-day hermits – *hikikomori* – withdrawing from all social contact and not leaving their homes for months or even years at a time.[10]

The effects of loneliness can be physically as well as mentally catastrophic. Brain-imaging studies have shown that loneliness can prompt negative responses linked to fear and rejection, as opposed to the positive responses experienced by in-group members associated with trust and identification.[11] This may help to explain why living alone and having poor social connections are as bad for your health as a fifteen-per-day cigarette habit. Loneliness can make you more susceptible to dementia, depression and heart disease. It is worse for you than obesity, and it can increase your risk of early death by 29 per cent.[12]

The married psychiatrists Richard S. Schwartz and Dr Jacqueline Olds have suggested that the extent of the loneliness epidemic is masked by large numbers who are instead diagnosed with conditions like depression, anxiety and post-traumatic stress disorder.[13] Between 2008 and 2018, prescriptions for antidepressants in England almost doubled – more than 4 million people in England are now regular users.[14, 15] In the USA, there is a similar pattern, with antidepressant use jumping 65 per cent in the fifteen years up to 2017.[16] The widespread use of anti-depressants, which often contain opiods, has contributed to the opioid crisis, which in the USA caused nearly 50,000 deaths in that year alone.[17] It may be that 'a great many people who think of themselves as depressed have in fact a sense of isolation at the core of their feelings'.[18] The antidote endorsed by society? More individualism! In the past year alone, a record 3 million self-help books were sold to stressed-out Britons, making it one of the fastest-growing genres in the publishing sector.[19]

'Self-help books completely respond to the time that they were written and they tend to prey on people's fears and anxieties about that time,' Jessica Lamb-Shapiro, author and reader of hundreds of self-help books, told *Time* magazine.[20] The titles of four of Amazon's bestselling self-help books in 2019 are revealing in terms of identifying which fears and anxieties are being targeted: *You Are a Badass: How to Stop Doubting Your Greatness and Start Living an Awesome Life*; *Unfu*k*

Yourself: Get Out of Your Head and into Your Life; *The Subtle Art of Not Giving a F*ck: A Counterintuitive Approach to Living a Good Life*; and *Can't Hurt Me: Master Your Mind and Defy the Odds*. Besides a high frequency of swear words, the most obvious common thread between these titles is that they are all about what 'you' can do on your own. The goal is exceptionalism, individual glory and personal success. This is markedly different from Dal Carnegie's 1936 classic *How to Win Friends and Influence People*, which focused not only on the self, but also how you interact with other people.

I am no stranger to loneliness. By my early twenties, the conflicting juxtapositions in my life – Tottenham and Peterborough, British Caribbean and English, working class and middle class – had left me confused and isolated. I pivoted between them often, which left me with a nauseating confusion about where I belonged. From being the only black boy at my school in Peterborough, I became the only black Briton at my law school. I rarely if ever felt like part of the crowd.

After graduating from law school, I moved to California. In my head I wanted to become Jonathan Rollins, the young black lawyer played by Blair Underwood in *LA Law*. This was the late nineties and the middle of the dotcom bubble. I was part of one of the first intakes that were more excited about joining a firm in Silicon Valley than one in New York City. What I found in Silicon Valley, however, was not the life I had dreamed of. There was immense pressure on junior lawyers, who were expected to perform Herculean tasks from day one. A tough hierarchy separated us from our more senior colleagues. Instructions from partners were to be followed without question or a murmur of complaint. Clients were God. Thirteen-hour days in the office were typical. More often than not, I worked on Saturdays and Sundays. Without any family, and with a tiny social network in the city, work became my life. Every conversation I had was shallow.

I began to self-medicate with alcohol and cigarettes in the few hours I had off before going to bed at night. All this did was make it harder for me to get up when the alarm went off in the morning. There was no breakdown or single catastrophic event that forced me to seek help: I simply was not happy. I felt isolated and was part of a toxic culture in which I needed to be medicated to survive. After a while, I went to the doctor, who prescribed me the antidepressant Prozac. It soon dawned on me that half of the lawyers at my firm were on the same medication. The doctors were handing it out like candy.

The Prozac dulled the pain of gruelling legal work and softened the unhappiness of missing my friends and family back home in the UK, but it did not cure me. I felt numb. Though I started to experience fewer dark moments, I also lost the ability to reach sustained happiness. The dry mouth, sleepless nights and non-existent sex drive were constant reminders of just how bad it made me feel. After a year and a half, I decided to stop taking Prozac and moved back to London. Here I reconnected with the relationships that made my life worth living.

We talk a lot about social mobility in the UK, but we do not address the way in which it can be dizzying as well as giddying. There can be real moments of peril as you leave behind the friends you grew up with and take advantage of opportunities in new environments that are foreign to you. At times I felt like I was losing my sense of who I was, who I was meant to be and which parts of myself I was meant to leave behind. Throughout my life, I was lucky enough to be blessed with a formidable mother, as well as wonderful teachers, professors and youth workers, who were determined to see me succeed. Without any one of them, my life would have taken a very different path.

It is impossible to get inside the heads of either Anwar or David Hall, but both appeared to lack meaningful social relations. Hall was retired and had no close family or friends. Anwar lived at home with his parents but did not have candid or open relationships with them. I can only speculate that loneliness drove them both to their respective extremes, but this possibility is backed up by research. Academics in social science and psychiatry have shown that loneliness is a significant contributing factor to the susceptibility of an individual to radicalisation, so it might well be the 'elephant in the room' of an increasingly polarised political climate.[21] Social isolation, it is clear, leads to people becoming less empathetic, with less chance of dialogue with those who may disagree. Dr Jacqueline Olds told *Salon* magazine: 'I think comparing notes in a civil way is the antidote to a polarised society in which we don't understand a point of view other than our own. If we are so lonely that we have no one to compare notes with, we tend to become more polarised.'[22] This chimes perfectly with Hall's probation officer when she said he 'never had anyone to challenge or moderate his thinking'. But this does not answer why so many of us have become so lonely in the first place.

STILL BOWLING ALONE

Religious faith in the world is rising, with more than 84 per cent of people in the world identifying with a religious group. In the West, however, it is in decline. In the USA, there has been a 20 per cent fall in church membership over the past two decades.[23] In the UK, only 1 per cent of eighteen to twenty-four-year-olds now identify as being members of the Church of England. In every western European country except Italy, even those who do identify as Christian are more likely to be non-practising than to attend church regularly.[24] People are not abandoning their faiths for atheism. Instead, young people are far less likely to become religious in the first place. When older generations of Christians die, members of the generation that replaces them are considerably less likely to believe in God. It is not only church coffers that have lost out as a result of the increasingly empty pews. In recent centuries, religion has played a central role in building communities and relationships; providing inspiration for art, music and architecture; as well as helping people to move beyond narcissism and selfishness. Without organised religion, or a secular alternative, it is much easier to become convinced that we are simply individuals, without responsibility for society as a whole.

The decline of church membership is just one example of a society that has become more individualistic. It is mirrored by declining trade-union numbers and a fall in membership of youth clubs and other similar organisations.[25] Robert Putnam was the first well-known proponent of the idea that the groups, clubs and organisations that once held our social fabric together have faced a sustained period of decline. In *Bowling Alone*, Putnam argued that being a member of a group encouraged trust and reciprocity, which in turn benefited both individuals and wider society. He used a bowling league as an example of a social club that one could join voluntarily. The decline in popularity of US bowling leagues in favour of bowling alone was the perfect metaphor for a broader trend that Putnam perceived as having arrived at the end of the twentieth century. In the two decades since, there is little evidence that we are moving towards more communal living again. In fact, the opposite is true. Since the 1970s, Americans have been losing trust in each other. Today barely more than three in ten say 'most people can be trusted'.[26]

Our working lives, too, have become more fractured and less reliable sources in our search for belonging. The most idolised figures in the workplace are now more often entrepreneurs and start-up founders than leaders who have risen to the top of large corporations after decades of dedicated service. According to government figures, the number of businesses in the UK grew from 3.5 million at the dawn of the new millennium to 5.7 million in 2018.[27] Start-ups are to be welcomed, but the cult of the entrepreneur has also had other effects. Disruptive tech unicorns like Uber and Deliveroo have made lives easier for customers, while undermining existing taxi and food-delivery services, which once provided more stable and secure employment to their employees. Outside of tech firms, many workplaces have become less stable places for developing social relations. At the bottom of the lunch-queue hierarchy, employees on precarious zero-hours contracts move from job to job, trying to scrape together enough income to pay the bills. Instead of having the opportunity to build strong relation-ships with co-workers, they are confronted by a constantly moving conveyor belt of bosses and colleagues.

Worse still, our individualistic work culture means that lacking work stability or being poorly paid is perceived as an individual's fault for not working hard enough. Requiring flexible employment hours because you care for a family member is seen as a weakness rather than an achievement in itself. Big companies, which once rewarded employee loyalty with jobs for life, gold-plated pensions and a Rolex on retire-ment, now view their role as generating peak economic productivity. Board members want to maximise profits, not be burdened by contracts that give workers security and stability.

The Tottenham riots in 2011, which were the focus of my first book, were one expression of the decline of mutuality in our culture.[28] Many of those who participated in the looting did not have jobs, a decent education, homes or the opportunity to acquire through hard work any of the goods they were stealing. It was not their fault that, in effect, they were isolated from progress in the modern world. They had no stake in society. But on top of being born into tough circumstances, these individuals made poor choices. They showed no care for their neighbours: the shopkeepers, the police officers, those whose homes they burned down. The riots represented the worst excesses of personal greed in a society that tells its citizens to look after yourself, take what you can and pay no heed to others.

Parallels can be drawn with the financial crisis that erupted in 2008. It too illustrated the worst consequences of our overly individualistic society, but in an entirely different context. The crash was in part exacerbated by light-touch financial regulations, but the real catalyst was personal and institutional greed. While those on the streets of Tottenham in 2011 might explain away their actions by pointing to their sense of desperation, the bankers on Wall Street and in the City of London who formented the crash have no such way out. This is an important difference. But what unites these bankers and rioters is that neither showed any concern for their fellow humans, any respect to those with whom they shared connections, nor any pretence of responsibility for the society of which they were a part.

What this tells us is that deeply harmful consequences can emerge if individualism trumps collective belonging. If we leave individuals to fend for themselves in this way, it should not be a surprise when some people quench their thirst for social belonging by feeding off opportune scraps. An individualistic society that erodes a sense of commonality leaves people like Anwar and David Hall hungry, desperately looking to satisfy their need to belong wherever possible. It just so happens that for Anwar and David these places of belonging were extremely dark.

NEOLIBERALISM

'I'll be honest with you. I have no fucking idea what neoliberalism is.'[29]

The comedian David Baddiel is not alone in his ignorance of the meaning and origins of neoliberalism. And at least he was honest. Many people who fling the term around on Twitter and in the wonkish pubs of Westminster show few signs of understanding its meaning. For some of them, neoliberalism has become a catch-all explanation for everything wrong in our society. This usually comes without any recognition that inequality existed before the neoliberal era and will, in all probability, outlast it too. The term is best understood as a broad label for the economic consensus of free-market capitalism that followed decades of high public investment (referred to as Keynesianism) after the Second World War.

As I remember researching for commercial law in the third year of my law degree, Keynesianism promoted proactive government policies to stimulate the economy following the Great Depression of the 1930s and the Second World War.[30] This was an era of state investment, employment policies, welfare systems and relatively high taxes, which coincided with a 'golden age' of unprecedented growth. Keynesianism eventually ran out of steam, and people consequently lost their faith in the power of governments. The neoliberal alternative was less 'red tape', lower taxes, more flexible financing and more free trade across as well as within borders. The dominant ideology became one of deregulation, financialisation and privatisation. Individuals, rather than groups of people, were able to make their own financial decisions. The era of full-throated neoliberalism ignited under Thatcher and Reagan eroded key state institutions, taught us to rate competition above the common good, and provided no clear path for how we are meant to define and find belonging outside of wealth and personal 'success'. As Thatcher infamously said:

> There is no such thing as society. There are individual men and women, and there are families. And no government can do anything except through people, and people must look to themselves first. It's our duty to look after ourselves and then also to look after our neighbour.[31]

Naturally a right-wing economic philosophy, neoliberal policies became so popular that centre-left parties from the USA to Germany and the UK embraced so-called 'Third Way' politics – a political philosophy that combined some of the chief tenets of neoliberal economics with socially progressive policies. Indeed, in Tony Blair's first general election campaign in 1997, he pledged to maintain Margaret Thatcher's trade-union legislation and not to return to the high tax rates that preceded her. Twelve years after she left office in 2002, Margaret Thatcher was asked about her greatest achievement. She replied: 'Tony Blair and New Labour. We forced our opponents to change their minds.'

It is too simplistic to suggest that because New Labour incorporated certain pro-market reforms into its own policy agenda, it was entirely neoliberal or Thatcherite. In fact, much of what Blair did in power was in no way 'neoliberal' and could be more accurately described as being socially democratic. After all, it was this government that introduced a national minimum wage, limiting the freedom of the market to determine how much an individual deserves to get paid. This flagship policy was in direct opposition to the philosophical underpinning of neoliberalism, which dictates that the market should be left to determine the price of everything: including goods, services and labour. New Labour also introduced tax credits to benefit the worst-off, vastly increased spending on welfare, poured investment into schools and hospitals, dramatically reduced the number of people who slept rough on the streets, and made substantial reductions to pensioner and child poverty. It may be in vogue for ardent left-wingers to write off New Labour as 'neoliberals' little different to Thatcher's Tories, but the record shows this is simply not true.

For a while, the neoliberal aspects of Thatcher, Major and Blair's governments appeared to offer tangible benefits. The liberalisation of trade increased wealth. Easy access to debt helped less well-off people borrow significant amounts of money to purchase their own homes. On many measures, we became safer, richer, more connected, freer and with more opportunities to live well than in any other era in human history. Economic growth, for a while, seemed unstoppable. Inequality in the UK and the USA rose, but it was justified as the result of people's freedom to make their own choices. Meanwhile, light-touch financial regulation allowed banks to get away with leveraging huge lending compared to the equity they owned. On top of this, impartial regulators encouraged financial institutions to sell dud loans and mortgages to trusting consumers with the promise of a better life. Hard-working people and families inevitably ran up high debts and took out subprime mortgages they could not afford.

The true cost of rising public and private debt did not become apparent until the financial crisis, which culminated in the 2008 crash. Bankers, on the whole, escaped with their astronomical bonuses intact. Normal working people paid the largest price, particularly under governments that followed the economic crisis by imposing a decade of brutal austerity. Between September of that year until the end of 2009, households in the USA lost an average of nearly $5,800 each.[32] In the UK, 1.3 million people were left without work as a result of the recession.[33] Almost 9 million US workers lost their jobs.[34] In total, slower economic growth cost the USA an estimated $648 billion.[35] In the Eurozone, recession and stagnation lingered for many years after the initial crisis. It took eight years for the Eurozone to return to the size it had reached before the crash.[36]

The economic consequences of the financial crisis and the recession have rightly been identified as a result of neoliberal policy choices. The effect the same economic model had on the hollowing out of cultures and communities has been just as destructive. Changed structures of employment made workers' rights contingent on their utility to the industry's productivity, as economic efficiency became the paramount goal. During the 1960s, Britain's coal industry provided more than 500,000 jobs at 483 facilities,[37] but as railways started to move towards diesel and electric power, the coal industry became less economically viable, so the communities that had built up around it were forced into collapse. By the end of Margaret Thatcher's tenure, just 133 mines remained. The result was a loss of more than 300,000 jobs. Once proud mining and manufacturing towns not only lost their incomes, they lost their centre of social activity, camaraderie and solidarity.

Cultural loss can be understood in terms of the value given by society to certain acts and behaviours. A culture disintegrates when society changes so drastically that previously significant actions are no longer seen as worthwhile.[38] The development of the modern economy has imposed a kind of 'cultural death' on mining villages across the world, as well as in manufacturing communities that formerly relied on large, stable workforces.[39] When these workforces become obsolete, communities suffer from a kind of cultural loss that leaves those who depended on it alienated.

They are alienated not merely because the industries on which they relied have been decimated, but because the traditional working-class identity to which these industries were tied has been left in a state of ambiguity. There has been an expectation that individuals should 'reinvent' themselves, but there is no obvious focal point around which to do so. Even though many people still have to sell their labour to get by, it sounds old-fashioned to speak of working-class communities nowadays.

This relationship between work and identity hits quite close to home for me. I didn't realise it until I read Marx in my last year of school, but my family when I was growing up could be said to be part of the proletariat. A class of wage-earners, the proletariat's only possession of significant value is their power to work – they have to sell their labour to survive. My mum's situation was almost impossibly tough, but at least her multiple jobs had a degree of certainty. If she continued to turn up at the same time every day and do the work, she would continue to be paid. She could in turn find pride in the permanence of her working identity. Many in 2018 lack that luxury. If my parents were members of the proletariat, today's struggling masses are the 'precariat'.[40]

In order to define the 'precariat', according to the economist Guy Standing who coined the term, we need to understand how traditional class structures have broken down. The 'working class', or the 'proletariat, are terms that have been fundamental to our understanding of class structures since the nineteenth century. Since the beginning of industrial decline, however, these labels have been losing political relevance.[41] These days there are many more class groups. At the top sit an elite class made up of the superrich. Below is a 'salariat', which includes well-paid public and private-sector employees like me, who enjoy good benefits, paid holidays and pensions. The 'proficians' sit at a similar level to the salariat. Rather than steady jobs and benefits, proficians utilise high skills to work as consultants, independent workers or on short-term contracts. They are footloose and not tied to a specific company or organisation but make good money and live comfortable lives. Below the salariat and proficians sit manual workers and labourers who make up what's left of the traditional working class. This group is shrinking in size and influence, as jobs have disappeared and labour unions have declined.

Below them is the growing precariat class. It is loosely defined as a social class without security or certainty in the workplace that suffers from the financial and psychological consequences of this. These workers are often part of the 'gig economy' – working unstable hours according to the demands of the market or the whims of their bosses. The phenomenon is particularly acute in the north-east of England. The number of workers on zero-hours contracts in the region shot up by 11,000 to 45,000 in 2016 alone.[42]

Since 2016, the sharp erosion of steady low-skilled jobs has shown no signs of slowing down. In 2019, there are a record 4.7 million workers in the UK's gig economy – twice the figure estimated three years earlier.[43] It is impossible to predict accurately the scale of the impact that artificial intelligence and automation will have on jobs in the long term. The worst-off are expected to be the most affected. Jobs with annual salaries of less than £30,000 are almost five times more likely to be replaced by automation than jobs paying more than £100,000.[44] As much as 74 per cent of jobs in transportation and storage and 59 per cent of jobs in the wholesale and retail could be replaced, making these sectors the most at risk.[45] In total, 30 per cent of UK jobs could be at 'high risk of automation' by the early 2030s, compared with 38 per cent in the USA, 35 per cent in Canada and 21 per cent in Japan.[46]

A new generation, the precariat, is made up of those who lack the necessary skills, and social and financial capital, to compete in an increasingly competitive world. They are the babies of neoliberalism. They have no stable working identities, no access to property ownership and often no place to call home. Inevitably, many seek to satisfy their need to belong by other means.

ANTISOCIAL MEDIA

An incredible 95 million photos and videos are shared on Instagram each day. Facebook users click 'like' 4 million times every minute.

Every second, 6,000 tweets are sent. Social media teaches us to flaunt what we look like, what we're doing and what opinions we have. Egocentricity is rewarded with likes, comments and shares from others. In an era where it is more difficult than ever to find belonging at work and in our communities, social media has filled the gap.

Social media is both a symptom and a compounder of individualism. This technology has emerged at the dawn of a new crisis of narcissism. A US-wide study based on the Narcissistic Personality Inventory test – which measures an individual's sense of authority, self-sufficiency, superiority, exhibitionism, willingness to exploit others, vanity and entitlement – showed twice as many American college students answered narcissistically in 2009 than in 1982.[47] Most people will score more than zero on the test, but the proportion of us getting high scores is rising. According to a study by the US National Institutes of Health, nearly one in ten people in their twenties show narcissistic traits, compared to just 3 per cent in their sixties.[48] A level of self-assurance is important, but a world where 10 per cent of young people walk around thinking they are extraordinary will inevitably leave many disappointed. People may be filled with a grandiose sense of importance in their twenties, but when they reach middle age and their achievements do not match up with their egos, many become depressed.[49]

Individuals of all ages market their lives as though they were commercial products.[50] There has been a rise of influencers on platforms like Instagram, Snapchat and Facebook. At the top end, global celebrities such as Kim Kardashian market and monetise what many perceive as an 'ideal' life. After Kardashian posted an image on Instagram of her wearing Fendi clothes, internet searches for the brand increased by 16 per cent the following month.[51] But it is not only ultra-celebrity influencers that have grown in number. More and more of us are now narrating idealised versions of our own lives on apps. Selfies – 90 million of which are taken every day on Android devices alone – have become the defining images of our times.[52]

Social media has paradoxically managed to tie us all to an international network whilst simultaneously pulling us apart. The result is not only alienating but also polarising. Algorithms and personalised newsfeeds most often affirm and amplify, rather than challenge, an individual's beliefs. As a result, we are now witnessing a 'globalisation' of tribal identities, brought to us by the age of hyper-speed broadband. The original pioneers of the internet saw their mission as to create a 'global conversation', a world of harmonious interconnectivity. The pedlars of tribalism have learned to exploit these new networks to create global discord. While at its best the internet is a great unifier of humanity, in many ways it is now making us more divided than we ever were before.

The most used social-media websites, including YouTube, Facebook and Twitter, have become breeding grounds for radicalisation. But it is not only those who become extremists who are affected. Almost all of us have our biases confirmed in the echo chambers we create for ourselves online. Often this leads to us becoming entrenched in our opinions, as we are literally unable to see or understand the other side's position.

It would be wrong of me to write about the phenomenon of increasingly polarised behaviour online as though I were a passive observer rather than an active participant. I knowingly engage in Twitter spats myself. Over the past few years I have swelled my following on Twitter through being unafraid to speak my mind and call out powerful figures on the other side of the argument. When I first started using Twitter, I would post relatively mundane updates about events I was attending or how I was voting, but now I understand it as a useful way for me to represent my constituents and supporters, as well as to bring minority opinions into the mainstream. To this day, my most popular tweet – receiving almost 58,000 retweets and 150,000 likes – reads as follows:

Trump sharing Britain First. Let that sink in. The President of the United States is promoting a fascist, racist, extremist hate group whose leaders have been arrested and convicted. He is no ally or friend of ours. @realDonaldTrump you are not welcome in my country and my city.

In tweeting this, I was not reaching out to Donald Trump for a rational discussion or asking for common understanding. Instead, I was calling out grossly offensive and dangerous behaviour that amplifies and emboldens the British far right. Twitter users seem to flock to this kind of direct conflict, with far more alacrity and interest than to constructive debate. For the record, my first-ever Tweet – 'finishing the last few bits of work before the festive break and exploring the potential of Twitter' – quite understandably received a grand total of zero likes.

Ben Nimmo, information defence fellow with the Atlantic Council's Digital Forensic Research Lab, explained to me the dynamics behind this in simple terms: 'The nature of social media is that the more extreme the post is, the more shares, likes or retweets it will get.' Nimmo, who is described in the press as a world-leading troll detective, added: 'Anger is a potent selling point.' The new currency of anger is what leads online detractors like @smith21477413 to tweet: 'Deport Lammy,' followed by: 'I'll fly over Somalia in my helicopter and push you out.' It is also why I receive vastly more engagement when I tweet an attack on a direct political opponent like Nigel Farage or Boris Johnson than if I post an informative thread on the causes of Britain's violent crime epidemic or provide data on the systematic failures of the UK's top academic institutions to provide access to students from all social, geographical and ethnic backgrounds.

After the 2016 Brexit vote, I ramped up the intensity of my own Twitter activity. I was mortified that Nigel Farage's xenophobic campaign had won a victory that could permanently alter the character of the country I love. Following the referendum, the Labour Party entered a period of introspection and factional infighting, as Owen Smith challenged Jeremy Corbyn for the leadership. At a time of national crisis, I could not bear the prospect of yet more internal navel-gazing within the party. I was becoming increasingly concerned by an emboldened Farage and a rising populist nationalist right in Britain. In particular, the effective takeover of the Conservative Party by the European Research Group worried me. In this period, Jacob Rees-Mogg emerged as the leader of the highly Eurosceptic and right-wing grouping. Rees-Mogg's Victorian dress sense matches his arcane views, which include opposing abortion, even in the case of rape, being against same-sex marriage and describing the rise of foodbanks as 'uplifting'.[53] I was even more concerned by the company he kept. In 2013, Rees-Mogg faced mass criticism for appearing as the guest of honour at a dinner of the Traditional Britain Group, which advocates for black Britons to be deported, despite being previously warned about the group's far-right links.[54] More recently, Rees-Mogg used his Twitter profile to promote the AfD, an overtly far-right and Islamophobic party in Germany.[55] At the beginning of the 2019 general election campaign, Rees-Mogg was strongly criticised for arguing that the victims of the Grenfell Tower fire lacked 'common sense' for not ignoring the fire service's advice to 'stay put'.[56]

In spring 2019, my campaigning against Brexit reached one of many crescendos in front of an enormous crowd of marchers in Parliament Square. Estimates of the number of people who came out to march to demand a People's Vote just one week before the originally planned Brexit date of 29 March 2019 vary from a few hundred thousand to a million. Regardless of the specific numbers, a potent cocktail of frustration, anger and hope for a future without Brexit had motivated more people to take to the streets than I had ever seen previously. The energy of the marchers was palpable. EU flags flew alongside Union Jacks. The marchers were covered with blue-and-yellow face-paint. 'Bollocks to Brexit' and 'Put It To The People' banners mixed with homemade signs painted on to cardboard. People from all ages, and from all parts of the UK, had come together to demand a referendum on the outcome of the Brexit process, with the option to Remain in the EU.

I was one of a few MPs lucky enough to be given a platform to speak. I began my speech by running through some of the most destructive lies told by the Brexiters in government. Afterwards, I delivered a pre-prepared line: 'We will not let the nativists, the nationalists and the isolationists take us to a hard Brexit.' Looking out into the crowd, I saw the statues of Winston Churchill and Nelson Mandela looking back. I could not help but draw comparisons with today. I said:

I'm just looking over there at Winston Churchill. On the 30th of September 1938, he stood up in Parliament and he said we would not appease Hitler. I'm looking across to Nelson Mandela who would not give in to apartheid. We say we will not give in to the ERG. We will not appease. We will not appease.

A few weeks later, early on a Sunday morning, I was sitting in a BBC studio to pre-record an interview with Andrew Marr for the *Marr Show*, one of Britain's highest-profile political TV programmes. Halfway through the interview, Marr surprised me by playing a clip of my speech at the rally. He followed it by saying: 'By implication, you're comparing the ERG to the Nazi party, or at least to the South African racists. Now whatever you think about the ERG, that was an unacceptable comparison – wasn't it?'

'Andrew, I would say that that wasn't strong enough,' I responded, refusing to back down.

When I said my comments were "not strong enough", I was saying that the sentence "we will not appease" was not strong enough. It is not enough simply for us not to appease the ERG – we need to actively work to defeat their nationalistic vision. Andrew gulped, having clearly expected some form of mealy-mouthed apology, or at least an evasive politician's answer. Instead, I continued: 'We must not appease. We're in a situation now, and let me just be clear, I'm an ethnic minority. We have in the ERG, in Jacob Rees-Mogg, someone who is happy to put onto his webpages the horrible racist AfD party, a party that's Islamophobic and on the far right of the German citizenry. They're happy to use the phrase "Grand Wizard". KKK is what it evokes to me when I think of that phrase and the Deep South. I'm sorry, but very, very seriously of course we should not appease that. Of course, we should not appease that.'

I went on to highlight Boris Johnson's close links to Steve Bannon. At the time, Johnson tried to deny his ties to Donald Trump's white supremacist former adviser. Later it emerged that Bannon had helped Johnson write his resignation speech from Theresa May's cabinet.[57]

After the Marr interview, there was considerable outrage from certain sections of the right-wing press and political establishment. By pointing out leading members of the Conservative Party's links to the extreme right, I was accused of sowing division myself. Boris Johnson complained my words were causing 'toxic polarisation'. This was particularly ironic from a man who had previously compared the EU to Hitler's project.[58] Others, including the New Statesman, the Guardian and the Independent published comment pieces praising my stance.[59] The former Conservative deputy prime minister, Michael Heseltine, was also supportive, pointing out 'chilling' similarities between today and the 1930s.[60]

There are of course huge differences between the bloody fascism of the twentieth century and the current day. All the same, there are worthwhile comparisons to be made with the conditions that led to the rise of fascism in the past. The most extreme Brexiters have created a false narrative of betrayal by immigrants and foreign elites. In the 2019 general election, Boris Johnson cynically attacked European migrants, when he said EU citizens who had made the UK their home have treated the country like 'their own' for too long. Others have demanded that opposition politicians abandon the Parliamentary process and instead obey a poorly defined 'will of the people'. They have based the project on a nostalgic notion of an ethnically hierarchical past, by calling for 'Empire 2.0'. Some have even threatened violence – in the wake of the Brexit vote Nigel Farage threatened to 'don khaki, pick up a rifle and head for the front lines' if he did not get his way on Brexit.

Hannah Arendt, the holocaust survivor and political theorist, described how Nazism was legitimised and spread by different tiers of organisations. She wrote that fascism relies on 'more respectable forms, until the whole atmosphere is poisoned with totalitarian elements which are hardly recognisable as such but appear to be normal political reactions or opinions'. In effect, by legitimising more extreme right-wingers, mainstream politicians like Johnson and Rees-Mogg provide cover for the thugs on the ground. It is no surprise that Boris Johnson's ascendance to become prime minister has found support from far-right groups including Britain First.[61]

I am no wallflower online, at rallies or in the media. I try my best to avoid blind loyalty to any particular tribe. I make a concerted effort to call out failures within my own tribal political identity in the Labour Party. In the wake of the Labour Party's disastrous 2019 election result, I condemned the 'leadership's failure to deal with the stain of anti-Semitism', 'hostility to institutions such as Nato', 'failure of competence' and Jeremy's 'mind-boggling decision to abdicate leadership' on Brexit.[62] I admit it is always more difficult to criticise those who you perceive as belonging to your tribe. Attacking an individual from within your own group carries the risk of ostracism, as your peers and friends may accuse you of betrayal.

While this is clearest in politics, we all carry conscious and unconscious loyalties to those we perceive to be on our side. One such manifestation of this is in-group and out-group behaviour online. It is only by recognising that we have these tribal urges to unfairly privilege those we perceive to be part of our in-group that we can transcend them.

Donald Trump has become known as the first Twitter President. Using a pattern of generalised outrage followed by escalation towards specific individuals and institutions, Trump uses Twitter to attack those he sees as being a threat.[63] One of the president's main targets on social media is what he describes as the 'fake news media'. After years of tweeting outrage at negative coverage and hostile journalists, Trump had prepared his followers for more specific calls for limits on the free press. In October 2017, he exploited this by tweeting a threat to shutdown NBC: 'With all of the Fake News coming out of NBC and the Networks, at what point is it appropriate to challenge their License? Bad for country!'

Cognitive linguist George Lakoff has identified the major types of tweet Trump uses to assist his political purposes.[64] The first is to frame an idea or story pre-emptively. Now followed by more than 62 million people, the president is able to set the agenda of a story in a way that is favourable to him. On the release of findings from the Muelller report into whether Trump had committed crimes before and during his presidency, he tweeted: 'No Collusion, No Obstruction, Complete and Total EXONERATION.' This was simply untrue. In fact, the Mueller report was unable to exonerate Trump of allegations of obstruction of justice.[65]

Trump also uses controversial tweets to divert attention from serious or negative stories. As Lakoff points out, one of the most blatant examples of this came during a period when Trump was under pressure to answer questions around Russian hacking and conflict of interest. Rather than addressing these concerns, Trump launched an extraordinary attack on the actress Meryl Streep following her speech at the Golden Globe Awards. The president described the three-time Oscar winner as 'the most over-rated actresses in Hollywood'. Journalists who should have been focusing on the serious allegations regarding Trump's conduct were inevitably drawn towards the 'shiny object' of the A-list fallout. By doing this, the press not only fails to report more deeply on the serious news, but it provides cover for the existing negative story. Rather than holding power to account, they protect it with fluff.

It is not only the fault of aggressive individuals for compounding tribalism online. The design and configuration of social-media websites both amplifies and artificially inflates our already naturally tribal instincts. The motivation is profit. There are at least three ways in which social-media companies exploit our natural human tendency to divide into in-groups and out-groups. The first is through algorithms that automatically promote extreme or divisive content, as well as tending towards only showing us content that we agree with. When I was a boy, my whole family listened to a wide range of music on our stereo. These days my teenage son listens to music via Spotify on his own through headphones, with the streaming service's algorithms barely straying from his favourite genre: grime music. The second is the way in which closed-group forums – whether on an encrypted chat app like WhatsApp, Signal or Line, or on a closed Facebook group – tend towards the viewpoint of the most extreme member of the group. The third is in allowing content producers that build vast audiences on these platforms to legitimise, promote and repackage bigoted ideas. I will address each in turn.

Social-media websites are run by profit-driven companies whose main motivation is to extract maximum attention from their users in order to maximise advertising revenues. Former Google engineer turned whistle-blower Guillaume Chaslot has explained how sites like YouTube, which he worked on, do this. The French programmer explained that he saw at first hand how the algorithms used by YouTube recommend more extreme videos to viewers to exploit our natural curiosity towards extremes. When the *Wall Street Journal* conducted an investigation aided by Chaslot, it found that YouTube 'fed far-right or far-left videos to users who watched relatively mainstream news sources'.[66] If you started watching a video about either Hillary Clinton or Donald Trump during the 2016 US presidential election, you were significantly more likely to be recommended a pro-Donald Trump video next.[67] Similarly, the investigation found that if you looked up videos on the flu vaccine, you were likely to be shown anti-vaccine conspiracy theories in the video that followed.

Even on subjects entirely unrelated to politics, YouTube serves up increasingly extreme content. When researching YouTube, I came across the Turkish academic and technology commentator Zeynep Tufekci, who found that if you search for videos about vegetarianism you will soon be directed to videos on veganism. 'It promotes, recommends and disseminates videos in a manner that appears to constantly up the stakes,' Tufekci mused.[68] As a result of her findings, she added: 'YouTube may be one of the most powerful radicalising instruments of the twenty-first century.'

It is not only video-hosting sites or public platforms that encourage polarisation and entrench divisions. Closed-messaging services and private groups also play a major role. There is not one political faction in British politics that does not have its own WhatsApp group. When seven MPs left the Labour party out of opposition to our party's Brexit position and failures over the anti-Semitism crisis to form the Independent Group, watching them being booted out of various Labour WhatsApp groups felt particularly final.

Within these groups of MPs, just like groups of friends, football fans or activists, tribal instincts are undoubtedly encouraged. The radicalising nature of closed groups has been studied long before social media achieved widespread use. Cass Sunstein, the American legal scholar whom I met in London before he was made Barack Obama's adviser, is most famous for popularising 'Nudge Theory', a concept that encourages governments and other authorities to frame decision-making in a way that encourages people to behave in a positive fashion without using overt coercion or significantly altering economic incentives. Nearly a decade before publishing his book *Nudge*, Sunstein detailed 'the law of group polarisation' in a seminal 1999 paper. In it, he argued that individuals within a closed group shift towards the most extreme position of the other members of that group. This phenomenon assists in explaining 'extremism, "radicalisation", cultural shifts, and the behaviour of political parties and religious organisations'.[69] And although it was five years before Facebook was founded by Mark

Zuckerberg and ten years before the creation of WhatsApp, Sunstein already perceived that his observation about the behaviour of closed groups was closely 'connected to current concerns about the consequences of the internet'.[70]

Earlier this year, an anonymous but friendly stranger emailed me to inform me about 'The Jacob Rees-Mogg Supporters Group', a Facebook group which he or she said was 'an absolute pit of neo-Nazi style racial hatred'. The emailer added: 'They loathe you on there, I'm sorry to say, and you're a frequent topic for racial and violent abuse.'

Intrigued to see the extent of the threats directed at me on the closed forum, I asked him to send over screenshots. What I found in the 'taster' of the unofficial fan Facebook group included comments calling me a 'Muslim plant', a 'nigger', an 'African dictator' and a 'sub saharan oaf'. Each of these posts received 'likes' and approval, and apparently no condemnation.

Further research showed that I was by no means the only target of abuse on the page. Other politicians, including Anna Soubry, Jess Phillips and the London mayor Sadiq Khan, received similar treatment. The murder of Jo Cox was described as a 'false flag' attack by some, and, like David Hall, others used it as a warning to other MPs.

According to press reports, one user, 'Lee', posted that he wished to 'do the dirty work' for migrants that 'won't go back to their desert piss stinking pits'.[71] He added: 'German SS Einsatzgruppen will seem like a fucking boy scout outing compared to us pissed off Brits.' Meanwhile, a user called 'Julie' told other users to learn how to shoot. 'Lena' put herself forward to make Molotov cocktails and 'David' suggested strapping 'a big kitchen knife' onto scaffolding poles.[72] Other posts incited violence, civil war, burning foreigners, hanging MPs and blowing up Parliament.[73]

Neither Jacob Rees-Mogg nor the Conservative Party itself has had any involvement with the fan Facebook group, and both have strongly condemned death threats on the site. Rees-Mogg did tell the news website *Tortoise* that 'the vast majority of posts and comments are perfectly fine and abide by the rules'.

What may have started out as a relatively benign forum for like-minded Conservatives to discuss the news and issues of the day has since descended into a deluge of death threats, Islamophobia and incitements to violence. This is extraordinary for the supporters of an MP in what has traditionally been a moderate, centre-right political party. Some of the users may not have been Conservative members, but many were. After the Facebook group received widespread criticism, the party was forced to suspend at least fourteen members for Islamophobia.[74]

Given Sunstein's 'law of group polarisation', it is very likely that the Jacob Rees-Mogg Supporters Group did not simply attract far-right members from across the country, but helped to create them. In a closed group, where the opinions of the group as a whole shift towards those of the most extreme member of that group, it might have taken only one or two members espousing racial abuse and inciting violence for other members to themselves become radicalised in an auction of extremism. Of course, this phenomenon is not tied to one political party, ideology or group. It is a pattern that might also explain why some on the far left of British politics have begun to confuse anti-capitalism with anti-Semitism.

Outside of closed groups on public-streaming platforms, we are increasingly pushed away from moderate content towards more extremist material. A report by *Data & Society* detailed how people searching for videos that discuss conservative and libertarian ideas are quickly led to extreme white-nationalist content.[75] In addition to algorithms that promote more extreme content, mainstream right-wing internet figures with enormous global audiences, who themselves do not explicitly espouse racist or alt-right views, have a habit of inviting those who do onto their shows. In the ensuing conversations, they often fail to properly challenge dangerous ideas.[76]

Dave Rubin, a comedian and political commentator who has found an audience of more than a million subscribers on YouTube with his talk show *The Rubin Report*, is just one example highlighted in the *Data & Society* paper. Rubin describes himself as a 'classical liberal' and does not appear himself to expound overtly racist views. He does, however, invite guests onto his show who do promote toxic, supremacist ideologies.

In 2017, Rubin invited Stefan Molyneux, a far-right Canadian YouTuber who promotes deranged conspiracy theories about 'White Genocide' and 'The Great Replacement', onto *The Rubin Report*. On the show, Rubin discussed Molyneux's belief in scientific racism – the belief that some races have higher IQ results than others because of genetic rather than environmental reasons. As discussed earlier, these conclusions are entirely bogus, given that there is almost no link between skin colour and genetic ancestry, except for the properties of skin colour itself. During the interview Molyneux said he was 'heart-broken' when he learned about the 'link' between race and IQ, saying: 'This is one of the most difficult facts I've had to absorb in my life.' One part of the conversation went as follows:

Rubin: But is there evidence that it's genetic?

Molyneux: Yes.

Rubin: Genetic in what regard? I mean if we took the brain of a twenty-five-year-old black man and the brain of a twenty-five-year-old white man, what is it that they're doing that . . .

Molyneux: They're different sizes.

Rubin: Yeah?

Molyneux: Yeah.

Rubin never properly challenged Molyneux on his barbaric and ludicrous claims about different races having different brain sizes.[77] By failing to challenge or denounce them, supposedly moderate right-wing online political commentators legitimise and promote dangerous far-right ideas.

UPDATING THE RULES OF THE INTERNET

It is not exactly clear what David Hall or Anwar were reading or watching online. Nevertheless, it is undeniable that many people are being pulled to further extremes by content and media published by companies that did not even exist twenty-five years ago. On the surface, Anwar and Hall could not appear to be more different, but their stories share some essential similarities. Both are individuals pushed to the brink by some combination of a political economy that favours efficiency over cooperation; the existence of increasingly accessible and alluring radicalising content online; and a lack of social connection that carries with it a very high risk of loneliness.

YouTube has 1.9 billion monthly active users, including 73 per cent of US adults. Facebook has 2.38 billion monthly active users. Twitter has 330 million.[78,79] Only a tiny percentage of this number have been radicalised by extreme content, but all of us have been affected. Technology has progressed at dizzying speed, while politicians and other regulators have sauntered behind, too often unable to grasp the scale of the problems we are facing. If lawmakers are serious about tackling loneliness, tribalism and polarisation, we need to think seriously about how best to regulate the communications technology that has transformed how we live our lives.

Regulating any kind of speech is inherently controversial, for good reason. Limiting what we can say in person or online has costs: it curbs freedom of expression, which is fundamental to any democracy, and it sets a precedent for government intervention that totalitarian regimes around the world can use to legitimate unjustified censorship. Nevertheless, it is a mistake to treat free speech as though it takes priority over all other values. In most societies, we have limits to the freedom of expression, where it contradicts other values or causes serious harm to others. Hate speech is a prime example. Threatening or abusive speech or writing against a group, particularly on the basis of sexuality, race, religion or gender, is prohibited in many democracies. We also have laws against defamation in order to prevent individuals and organisations from making false statements about others in a way that unjustly damages their reputation.

For years, Silicon Valley leaders lobbied against government regulation, perceiving it as a threat to innovation and the spread of ideas. Tech companies argued that their sites were more analogous to telephone lines than newspapers. They facilitate communication, they said, but do not curate it, and should not therefore be held responsible for individuals who use their platforms to commit crimes. The problem with the telephone-line analogy is that you cannot simply pick up your landline phone and listen to endless content produced by extreme terrorist groups, white supremacists, anti-Semites or anarchist revolutionaries. And you are not limited to contacting one person at a time, as on a phone line. You can speak to millions instantly, all around the world.

Facebook and YouTube employ tens of thousands of staff globally, who remove millions of pieces of violent content each month. A great deal of toxic content slips through the net or is left online for too long before it is removed. In recent years, a growing consensus has formed that social-media giants have not been doing enough to remove hateful speech from their platforms. Bob Iger, the CEO of Walt Disney, said: 'Hitler would have loved social media ... It's the most powerful marketing tool an extremist could ever hope for.' In 2019, Facebook CEO Mark Zuckerberg himself called on 'governments and regulators' to update the rules for the internet to address four major areas: 'harmful content, election integrity, privacy and data portability'. Some have criticised Zuckerberg's intervention as an attempt to shift responsibility away from super-wealthy tech companies like his own and into the hands of government. Regardless of Zuckerberg's motives, action is needed.

Australia has been one of the countries to move fastest on regulating social media. In 2019, its parliament passed legislation that introduced large fines for social-media companies and their executives for failing to take down 'abhorrent violent material' from their sites.[80] It is no coincidence that this legislation was passed less than one month after an Australian white nationalist terrorist used Facebook to livestream himself gunning down fifty people at two mosques in Christchurch, New Zealand. The law, which was fiercely opposed by tech-industry giants like Facebook and YouTube, goes further than in any other democracy in forcing platforms to take responsibility for the content they host. Similarly, at the start of 2018, Germany introduced laws that mandated every social-media company which has at least 2 million registered German users to review all complaints and remove any post that is clearly illegal within twenty-four hours.[81] Companies that fail to meet these targets can face fines of up to €50 million.

While new laws at the national level make a powerful statement, their effectiveness is limited. As Susan Benesch, Associate Professor at Harvard's Center for Internet and Society, told the *New York Times*: 'The platforms would likely move their offices out of countries that pass such laws to protect them from prosecution.'

The EU's General Data Protection Regulation (GDPR), which established world-leading rules on how companies and organisations store and use data, is a powerful example of how supranational legislation is most effective for regulating the internet. It transformed how companies store user data and set new requirements for notifying users of data breaches. And the effects went beyond the European Union. Given the size of the EU bloc, several companies, including Microsoft, felt obliged, or simply found it easier, to offer the same level of privacy protection to all its users across the world. Legislation to tackle hateful content and political disinformation would be most effective if it was introduced at the supranational level, too.

The internet has made our world much smaller, by allowing us to communicate instantly across continents. Government regulation at the national level, as in countries like Germany and Australia, is a positive step. And yet it is not sufficient. The crisis of the new tribalism is a global phenomenon in part because the internet platforms that inflame it are global. Now that we have seen the great harms social media can produce, as well as the gains, we need to work across national boundaries to produce new rules. Without enforceable laws, the internet will remain a chaotic and dangerous Wild West.

6

Identity Crisis

The politics of group identity

'The longer they talk about identity politics, I got 'em.'

Steve Bannon

I woke up at around 5.30 a.m. that morning – a few hours after the catastrophe had started. Compulsively, as I do every morning, I grabbed my mobile phone. It was vibrating more urgently than usual. Nicola's phone was buzzing even more regularly. I shook her awake. Immediately our eyes were transfixed by our five-inch screens as we thumbed through messages, notifications and newsfeeds, periodically breaking our gazes to look at one another's state of total shock. Tears were rolling down our faces.

The already viral images we were confronted with were horrific. Clouds of dark grey smoke rose towards the blue dawn sky. The outline of Grenfell Tower had turned black, pockmarked by fluorescent orange squares of furious light.

In my youth I had spent much of my time in one of London's many towers of Babel. As a child, I lived in the shadow of the Broadwater Farm Estate, whose residents included my cousins, aunts and many family friends. Other relatives and friends were scattered across

London's other housing estates: Lansdowne Green Estate in Stockwell, the Andover Estate in Islington and the Clapham Park Estate in Lambeth – as well as Kensington's Grenfell Tower Estate. When Grenfell went up in flames, people from communities like the one I grew up in immediately felt as though we knew someone involved. The people who were burned alive were people just like us. At the time, 159 social-housing blocks in the UK had the same 'ACM' combustible cladding as Grenfell.[1] All were vulnerable to going up in flames.

For Nicola and me, this wasn't just a feeling. The reason my wife's phone had been rattling incessantly was the stream of message notifications she was receiving from concerned friends of Khadija Saye, who lived on the twentieth floor of Grenfell Tower. Khadija, just twenty-four, had become a family friend after my wife spotted her obvious talent while a judge on an art prize. Nicola nurtured her, giving her a job as an assistant at her art studio and offering Khadija her first real break in the art world. I met her countless times. Khadija's infectious personality and creativity seemed to promise a shining future.

Khadija's early life had mirrored my own in so many ways. We both grew up poor and black in inner-city London. Both of our parents arrived as immigrants but separated under the pressure of living in the city. Just as my mother had been for me, Khadija's parents were ambitious, taking her to IntoUniversity, an amazing after-school club. This helped her, like me, to win a scholarship to a prestigious school outside of London. Khadija attended Rugby School Sixth Form, following in the footsteps of such famous alumni as Prime Minister Neville Chamberlain, the novelist Salmond Rushdie and the poet Rupert Brooke. With all its difficulties and opportunities, this experience showed Khadija what was possible. I identified with her quiet determination when I met her. Though she was ambitious, in many ways she remained vulnerable, with an acute and sometimes debilitating dose of imposter syndrome which she tentatively raised with me on more than one occasion.

In the days following the fire, I tried my best to voice the implications of the deaths of Khadija and the seventy-one other victims of gross negligent manslaughter, in one of the richest boroughs of one of the richest cities in the world. I wore myself out doing countless newspaper and TV interviews, in between supporting Nicola and mourning Khadija's death. Against my better judgement, I agreed to do a final interview with Jackie Long, from *Channel 4 News*, in Victoria Gardens, just outside Parliament. My voice cracked and I fought back tears as I said: 'This is a tale of two cities. This is what Dickens was writing about in the century before the last, and it's still here in 2017. It's the face of the poorest and the most vulnerable. My friend who lost her life was a talented artist, but she was a young, black woman making her way in this country and she absolutely had no power, or locus, or agency. She had not yet achieved that in her life.'

What I found most difficult to express when I talked about Khadija's lack of agency was that at this point in her life she was still in an extremely precarious position, and absolutely reliant on, as well as trusting of, the authorities above her. When she complained about the poor state of the tower, along with other residents, she was ignored. Kensington and Chelsea Tenant Management Organisation, which supposedly managed the building on behalf of the Kensington and Chelsea Borough Council, had received warnings about serious fire-safety failures months and months before the blaze. They chose not to act. A report showed that the residents' right to life and right to adequate housing were breached before the fire started – authorities ignored the evidence presented to them proving the cladding was unsafe.[2] When the establishment told her what to do, she listened. I remember like yesterday how in my own family we would all respond promptly to the commands of an establishment figure in a suit or an official in uniform. When the fire officers told her to remain in her room, she did exactly that. How I wished she had ignored that command when she first smelled smoke and ran with her mother out of the building to save her life.

A few weeks later, when it was announced that Sir Martin Moore-Bick would head up the inquiry into what happened at Grenfell Tower, I alongside much of the Grenfell community felt a deep ache of disappointment. Like so many, I feared this scandal was being kicked into the long grass like others had before it with yet another long inquiry or review. I had watched my good friends and colleagues Andy Burnham and Steve Rotherham struggle for years to get justice on behalf of the

Hillsborough victims. The same establishment class that had controlled every aspect of Khadija's life, and in her death had tragically failed her, would now assume the authority to rule on the numerous failings that led to that gruesome night. With trust at an all-time low among the survivors of the fire and the families of the victims, this felt deeply wrong. Expressing my frustrations to Sophie Ridge on *Sky News*, I said: 'He is a white, upper-middle-class man who I suspect has never, ever visited a tower-block housing estate and certainly hasn't slept the night on the twentieth floor of one. I hope he would do that in the days ahead.'[3]

Not everybody took kindly to the way in which I expressed my grievances. In his conspiratorial look at the 'liberal-left and the system of diversity', author Ben Cobley chastised my words as an example of identity politics' most flagrant excesses:

> Here we see Lammy interpreting Grenfell not just through the prism of skin colour but of gender and class too, treating the fixed (and quasi-fixed) identities of the people involved as primary to the disaster itself and the response required. He assigns the categories of 'white', 'male' and 'upper middle class' to an order that was responsible for the disaster. He also demands an identity-based response, narrowing down to gender and skin colour in prescribing that only a woman or someone of non-white skin should be allowed to decide what happened at Grenfell.
>   . . . There is a distinct tribal aspect to it: of shared assumptions, shared language and a shared value system, not based on *belonging* to a certain fixed identity group, but on politicising various fixed identity groups – assigning favour to one group (including women and non-white-skinned people) and disfavour to another (notably the white-skinned and male). Across the spectrum of left-wing and liberal politics – from far left and environmental activists to centre-left types, Liberal Democrats and even 'liberal' or 'progressive' Conservatives.[4]

By questioning the judgement of the appointment of a 'white upper-middle-class man' to head the Grenfell Inquiry, I was supposedly contributing to a kind of 'identity-based favouritism.'[5] At a time of mourning, I was criticised for making the event too political and, even worse, too racial. I was apparently putting race on the table at a time when what was needed was an objective, calm and colour-blind response.

I fundamentally disagree with Cobley's critique of my handling of Grenfell because I did not introduce the "prism of skin colour" to this tragedy. The faces of the victims and survivors beaming out of our television screens had already generated a debate about race and class. The tragedy disproportionately affected ethnic minorities: just seven of the seventy-two victims of the fire were white Britons.[6] Moreover, in a population where 13 per cent of people are not white, ethnic minorities make up just 7 per cent of court judges.[7] The inequalities in our judiciary deserve to be under scrutiny in a case where the same ethnic groups are the most likely to have been harmed, but the least likely to be in charge of deciding what went wrong. Every major public inquiry – Grenfell, Leveson, Chilcott, Al-Sweady, ICL, Fraser, Taylor and Hutton – has been headed by a white, middle-class man. Why are black legal professionals always overlooked for these leadership positions? And why are those who condemn me for asking this question almost always from the same racial group that is typically in charge?

Part of the answer is 'white fragility', a term coined by Robin DiAngelo, a university academic, who wrote a paper and then a book informed by her experience of running diversity workshops across corporate America.[8] DiAngelo, who is herself white, describes white fragility as being 'a state in which even a minimum amount of racial stress becomes intolerable, triggering a range of defensive moves', including 'the outward display of emotions such as anger, fear, and guilt, and behaviors such as argumentation, silence, and leaving the stress-inducing situation'.

Cobley was exhibiting white fragility when he complained that I was interpreting Grenfell 'through the prism of skin colour'. The truth is, I didn't make an intentional decision to analyse Grenfell along racial lines. I say this not to imply I made a mistake, but because, as somebody who is black, my experience of the world is unavoidably shaped by race. So, when something like Grenfell happens, it is unthinkable, if not impossible, simply to 'put race to one side'. It would be wrong to expect me to react to events like Grenfell through a colour-blind prism because it would deny the reality of difference.

COLOUR BLIND

The sentiment behind colour-blindness is often an admirable one. If we contend there is no such thing as race, how can there be racism? If we do not hold conscious prejudices against another race of people, how can we be racist? Indeed, the roots of this way of thinking may well date back to a line in Dr Martin Luther King's famous 'I Have A Dream' speech, in which King said he hoped his children would one day live in a world where his children 'will not be judged by the color of their skin, but by the content of their character'.[9]

At the time of King's speech, in Western societies like the USA, conscious racism was much more socially acceptable than it is today.[10] People were more open about expressing their beliefs that black people are inferior to white people. Before the Civil Rights Act was passed in 1964, a year after King's speech, outright discrimination against black people was not yet illegal. Once overt racism became unlawful, people were more frightened to be open about their belief in racial superiority. In the decades that followed, all around the developed world, overt and conscious racist behaviour decreased.[11] But reducing King's campaigning, writing and thought to this one line is a vast oversimplification. It hardly needs to be stated that King did not win huge victories for the civil-rights movement by pretending as though race did not exist. Colour-blindness was not for him a means of tackling racism, but a desirable end state after racial prejudice had been defeated.

More importantly, colour-blindness cannot solve unconscious prejudice. Pretending not to see race is not helpful when addressing the problem of why ten out of thirty-two colleges at Oxford University failed to give a place to any black British pupils in 2015.[12] In fact, colour-blindness here simply perpetuates this injustice. If we are not allowed to identify the systematic failure of our elite academic institutions towards a specific ethnic group, we cannot begin to address that problem. Simply saying that we do not see race, or gender, or sexuality, or a distinction between disabled and able-bodied people, does not change the truth that these socially constructed groups do matter. It is undeniable that the experience of being a man in most societies is different to the experience of being a woman. We know that being transgender holds challenges that do not exist for those who have a gender identity that matches the one they were assigned at birth. Similarly, being black is different to being white. Though class categories are often fluid, being middle class is different to being working class. And everyone's specific combination of identities will vary their experiences. Though I am black, I am also male, straight, able-bodied and I have huge social advantages thanks to my position as a member of parliament. Pretending that any or all these identities do not exist does not bring us closer to objective, calm reasoning. Instead, it distances us from the truth.

Throughout the twentieth century, we saw that progress in social justice is inextricably linked to recognising our identities. This is true in terms of rectifying racial injustice, but also in terms of women's suffrage, LGBT+ emancipation and the rights of the disabled. You cannot secure progress for a specific oppressed group if you fail to recognise the existence of that group. Women could only win the right to vote by campaigning for men to grant them this right, as men controlled all the means by which to do this. They could not win control over their own destiny by playing dumb to the reality of social differences. Likewise, if we refused to recognise homosexual people as a distinct identity group from heterosexual people, how would the campaign for gay marriage have been won?

For those from privileged positions, the continued importance of identity categories is understandably hard to recognise. The identity groups to which they belong are the default in our culture. They are not told, as my own mother taught me, to behave extra deferentially around authority figures in order to stay out of trouble. Instead they have the luxury of thinking of themselves merely as people or, more accurately, as individuals.

Ever since the enlightenment, our society has been shaped by the notion that the individual is supreme. We all make our own choices. We have vastly different personalities. Each person's identity is unique.

In many ways, this is an appealing destination, but it is simply not reality for many historically oppressed groups.

Not thinking about your own identities in this way is not *per se* an issue or a fault. It only becomes a problem when an individual privileged enough to ignore their own identity groups assume that all of us have the luxury of doing this. The truth is, ethnic minorities have been longing for this kind of 'uniqueness' for a long time. White populations in former colonial countries have comfortably felt like people first; but too often ethnic minorities have been made to feel like they are black or brown first and people second. This is what makes my political interventions on race issues so alien to some people. It is based on experiences they will never truly understand.

Nothing is more illustrative of this than when I criticised the British television presenter and filmmaker Stacey Dooley for perpetuating a 'white saviour' narrative. The phrase 'white saviour' refers to a white person who performs an action demonstrably to help non-white people but does so in a way that is in fact self-serving and can create more problems than it solves. This idea has its roots in 'The White Man's Burden', an 1899 poem by Rudyard Kipling written to encourage US colonisation of the Philippine Islands.[13] In February of 2019, I used the term to respond to an Instagram picture posted by Stacey Dooley while she was filming with the charity Comic Relief. Stacey was standing with her eyes looking straight at the camera, her teeth shining in a smile, while holding a black toddler on her hip, with its finger in its mouth, looking down to the ground, against the dusty backdrop of an African landscape. Her chosen caption was 'OB.SESSSSSSSSSSED ♡'. What was Stacey obsessed with, I wondered. The child looked confused, confounded and downbeat. It certainly was not a photo that I or anyone I know would post of their own child online. In the image, Stacey had all the agency. The child had none.

I tweeted: 'The world does not need any more white saviours. As I've said before, this just perpetuates tired and unhelpful stereotypes. Let's instead promote voices from across the continent of Africa and have serious debate.' I had hoped to ignite a discussion about the role that Comic Relief plays in shaping perceptions of the African continent. For years, Comic Relief had used its privileged prime-time slot on the

BBC to tattoo images of poverty on public perceptions of Africa. The continent was painted as one homogenous blob of pain, suffering and starvation, instead of fifty-four independent and diverse countries. Rather than giving Africans a voice to narrate their own stories, British celebrities with little knowledge or understanding of the countries they visited were flown out to speak on their behalf.

As I was referring to in the tweet, I had raised these issues with Comic Relief on numerous occasions in the past. In March 2017, on the morning of the charity's annual fundraiser, I had written a Guardian article on the subject.[14] Later, I made a short film about it for BBC Politics. When I watched the show in 2017, I was appalled by what I saw. Comic Relief's films that night showed three different images of dead African children.[15] Two of them died during filming. Neither the BBC nor Comic Relief would ever have considered showing a video of a dead British child. If they had done, there would have been mass public outrage. In fact, the films that aired that night to raise money for domestic, British charities – focusing on homelessness and drug addiction – gave the individuals who were suffering far more agency. No celebrity spoke for them.

What made the night even worse was Ed Sheeran's video, which showed the world-famous singer-songwriter meet and attempt to save children from the streets of Liberia by temporarily putting them up in a hotel. There is no doubt that Ed had good intentions, but Comic Relief had forced him into a situation where the film became about his own personal angst, rather than the plight of the children. Was he going to pay for their rooms in a hotel for ever? I was not surprised when an aid watchdog later branded the video 'poverty porn'.[16]

Following my criticisms of Comic Relief in 2017, I had twice hosted meetings with senior representatives from the charity in parliament. I spoke directly with the charity's then CEO, Liz Warner. I stressed that Comic Relief is the first real way in which British children are introduced to all fifty-four countries on the African continent.[17] And I outlined how important it was that the charity use its unique platform to teach people about the complexity of African life, which goes far beyond mosquitos, starvation and HIV. Comic Relief, and other charities like it, should not be afraid to talk about the triumphs of African nations, even if these successes aren't always the product of Western charity. For example, six of the world's top-ten fastest-growing economies in 2019 were African: Ghana, Ethiopia, Ivory Coast, Djibouti, Senegal and Tanzania. And between 2019 and 2035, the UN predicts that the world's ten fastest-growing cities will all be African.

In our meetings, Warner assured me they recognised the problems I and others had raised and would make a concerted effort to put African voices, rather than British celebrities, at the centre of their future films and fundraising efforts. You can imagine my disbelief, then, when I saw Dooley's Instagram post. It was more of the same. After my comments, Comic Relief tried to claim that I had 'not responded' to their invitation to make a film with them. This was simply untrue, given I had explained why I did not want to participate when we met in my office both times. Anyway, sending me, someone who has never lived in Africa, to make another film perpetuating the same stereotypes was not the solution.

I could list hundreds of racist tweets, emails, letters and phone calls I received in response to my criticism of Stacey Dooley and Comic Relief. 'You should be grateful for what Comic Relief has done for your people,' someone wrote. Demanding gratitude for help provided to a continent I have never lived on did not exactly undermine my point. The message continued, 'Give it a break Lammy; Dooley was doing some good. In any case, Africa and the Caribbean for that matter are a mess, these places need aid and assistance. They are poorly governed, their people ill-disciplined and poorly educated. They need all the help they can get! You would be better off trying to sort out the mess that many Blacks in the UK have got themselves into re crime and poor education. The pathologies of many Black families would be the place to start.' This message was meant to convince me that I was wrong to criticise Comic Relief for spreading negative stereotypes about black communities. Others said it was 'racist' to ever refer to skin colour: and that to overcome prejudice I should strive to be 'colour blind'.

Many people who see themselves as progressives or liberals also made this argument, and became extremely defensive. This gets to the very heart of the phrase 'white fragility'. Ever since the civil-rights movement, racism has been interpreted more and more narrowly as a moral transgression. To be implicated in any form of racism is to have your overall moral integrity challenged. Any suggestion of unconscious bias is too uncomfortable to consider, as it is interpreted as an allegation of direct, overt and malevolent racism. In this situation, it is much easier just to shut the conversation down completely than engage with the points raised. That is what made it so difficult for some people to engage in discussions about the white-saviour complex. They perceived it as a personal accusation of conscious racism, when in fact it was an example of something much more subtle and endemic.

Richard Curtis, multimillionaire screenwriter and co-founder of Comic Relief, was the prime example. I had known Richard casually for fifteen years because he was friends with my wife. He had always struck me as sincere and well-intentioned, while possessing the characteristic confidence and ease typical of a high achiever who has been educated at Harrow and Oxford. He is funny and charming, but not the best listener.

When I bumped into Richard in parliament some weeks after my comments had blown up in the media, he was furious. He was particularly angry that I had organised a letter to the BBC asking questions about the justification for handing such a huge and unique platform to the charity without any real scrutiny. Richard kept saying to me that I should have rung him up and had a private conversation before going public. He wanted to have the opportunity to talk me down. I responded that I had been making the point privately and publicly for years, even discussing the issues with top Comic Relief staff in my own office. Clearly Richard did not understand my role as a representative. He was prepared to ignore the fact that ethnic-minority communities had been switching off Comic Relief in droves because they did not want their children to be bombarded by unrelenting, unrepresentative images of poor black people.

On one level, I can understand Richard's sensitivity: he had helped set up an enormous charity to assist the most vulnerable people in the world. He had been made a Commander of the British Empire. He was well-connected to A-list celebrities and politicians across the globe. He may well have thought who was I, a mere backbench MP, to challenge him? Despite this, I was surprised that he was unwilling to talk about race, even though the people his organisation aimed to help are vulnerable partly because of the historical and structural racism inherent in colonialism. In our discussion, race only became relevant to him when he mentioned Lenny Henry. It was as if having a black friend who supported him somehow meant he did not have to engage in any discussion at all.

When Richard met my wife Nicola at Michelle Obama's UK book launch, he berated her, even telling her that in his entire life no one had angered him more than I had. This is white fragility at its most predictable.[18] For those who have enjoyed the privilege of not seeing race their whole life, the notion of a white saviour is incredibly discomforting, especially in a context where they feel like they are helping others. But for those black communities that have been racialised ever since they were colonised, the notion of a white saviour is about the structures that keep them poor. If assistance is offered, it needs to be on the terms of those being assisted. If we are prepared to help, we should also be ready to listen.

Those who criticised my response to both Grenfell and Comic Relief invoke much of the same rhetoric in order to challenge the notion of 'identity politics'. This term has become pejorative for some on the right of the political spectrum, and an increasing number on the left. 'Identity politics' is a broad term that signifies political movements in which oppressed groups mobilise and adopt political positions with the aim of correcting a perceived shared injustice. The premise that underpins identity politics is that there is some deep similarity, or essential continuity, between the experiences of different individuals within one oppressed group. It suggests there is something unique about the experience of being black, female, disabled, a refugee or LGBT. I am unashamed to admit that in recent years many of the issues I have campaigned on – from Grenfell to Windrush, fair access to universities and even in part my opposition to Brexit – have been linked to my identity as one of very few black UK politicians from a deprived social background.

Colour-blindness may be an appealing target for a society without prejudice, but in the present, where conscious and unconscious racism are part of our day-to-day reality, it only handicaps progress. Even so, I recognise that there are legitimate criticisms of basing our politics around specific characteristics, rather than working to unite all groups around something more inclusive. With this in mind, it is worth examining the roots of identity politics, as well as its limits.

THE ROOTS OF IDENTITY POLITICS

Until the mid-twentieth century, 'identity' was not discussed in relation to politics, sexuality, ethnicity, gender or tribe. The close link between identity and an individual's nationality, or physical characteristics, or cultural interests, is uniquely modern. Some people see the politics that has come about as a result of this change as a force for good: a way to achieve justice and equality in an unbalanced world. Others see it as a force for evil: the reason and legitimator for the increasing division and tribalism in our politics. I do not believe that there is any simple answer. Identity politics is not intrinsically right or wrong. Instead, like all other manifestations of power, it has the potential for good as well as for abuse.

The twentieth-century psychologist Erik Erikson is thought of as a forefather of modern identity politics. He is credited as the first to clearly articulate identity as being deeply related to our social relations. In a 1957 essay, Erikson suggested that people first 'observe or impute to a person certain characteristics' which can provide an answer to the question 'who are they?' Such characteristics could be a person's skin colour, accent or even clothing style. Once this has occurred, 'these observed or imputed characteristics are . . . interpreted in terms of a set of culturally prescribed categories'. In simple terms, our myriad identities are those features that can be interpreted by others as an answer to the question: who are you?

From this, Erikson derived the notion of an identity crisis:

While the patient of early psychoanalysis suffered most under inhibitions which prevented him from being what and who he thought he already knew he was, the patient of today suffers most under the problem of what he should believe in and who he should – or, indeed, might – become.[19]

According to Abraham Maslow's hierarchy of needs – a theory of what motivates humans – once a person has achieved some level of economic and social security, the question of how to live a meaningful and satisfying life becomes more urgent.[20] It is this realisation that has led different groups to begin mobilising to correct a shared injustice. Once the basic rights, freedoms and a baseline of security and shelter have been achieved, human beings begin to consider their personhood: what makes life meaningful and worthwhile, and how can I get there? If you are part of a disadvantaged group, other questions instantly follow. Why am I, and people who look like me, disproportionately ignored, cast out, paid less, less often put in positions of power or influence, and even treated more harshly by the police?

These questions lie at the root of much of modern-day identity politics.[21] With the #MeToo movement, women have been speaking out about systematic sexual harassment within many industries. The Black Lives Matter movement was about demanding that black people be treated with equal dignity and respect by the police, in the context of often lethal prejudice. While the Windrush campaign was primarily about demanding that all British citizens be given their rights in the face of systematic abuse by the Home Office, it was also about a deeper call for the recognition of Windrush citizens' contribution to Britain.

I'm not sure if my mother ever made it to a place of sufficient economic and social security necessary to have an identity crisis as described by Erikson. She was too busy working three jobs. My father, on the other hand, may well have been asking such questions of 1970s Britain, as he walked out on my family to live in the USA. For many Windrush citizens, similar questions must have been somewhere in their minds, either at the surface or buried deeper within.

Like myself, Erik Erikson grew up in the context of contradictory cultures, and throughout his life he experienced profound personal changes. His mother was a Jewish Dane named Karla Abrahamsen. Karla was married to a Jewish stockbroker, Waldemar Isidor Salomonsen, but at the time of Erik's birth the couple were estranged. Despite this, at birth Erik took the Salomonsen name. He never knew his biological father, a non-Jewish Dane, whose identity Karla kept secret throughout her son's life. Fearing the stigma that accompanied unconventional family relationships in the early twentieth century, Karla moved with her son to Karlsruhe in south-west Germany. Here she started a new career as a nurse. Within a few years, she married Erik's paediatrician, Theodor Homburger, who himself came from a highly respected Jewish family. Still an infant, Erik's name was quickly changed to 'Homburger', and the boy was raised believing that the German Jewish doctor was his biological father.

Erik's genes quickly caught up with him.[22] He 'was blond and blue-eyed, and grew flagrantly tall'. At the temple he was teased by the other children for his Scandinavian looks, while at school he remembers being ridiculed for being a 'Jew'. I experienced similar feelings of dislocation each time I swapped between my British Caribbean and white English tribes in Tottenham and Peterborough. When I first started at boarding school, I had what felt like out-of-body experiences, as I intensely scrutinised how I was speaking, acting and holding myself, in a desperate attempt to fit in. But after a couple of years, I began to feel more at home in Peterborough than I did in Tottenham. By age fourteen, when I returned home in the holidays my primary-school friends noticed I sounded considerably more middle-class than they did. It was so alienating to see my friends look at me in a different way, as if I was a different person. And they were not looking at me like I had grown physically or had a different haircut. They were looking at me like I had left parts of myself behind. It was a lonely time. In some ways I was part of two tribes, but I often felt like I belonged to none. Erikson's feelings of dislocation and insecurity were of course different to my own. He was the product of two distinct ethnic groups, like my own mixed-race children. This prompts the question: do you belong in both of the cultures your parents came from or in neither? I cannot speak for Erikson, of course, but I suspect the most frustrating part for him wasn't so much seeking an answer to this question, but the feeling that he had to answer it in the first place.

As a child Erik did not flourish in the classroom, instead excelling in art. In the freedom of young adulthood, he led a Bohemian life travelling around Europe, funded by selling his artworks along the way. His life changed in 1927 when he met Anna Freud, who invited him to try psychoanalysis. He was so taken by the discipline that he quickly enrolled in psychoanalytic training. Although he held no undergraduate degree, Erikson's first paper was published just three years later. He was elected to the Vienna Psychoanalytic Institute in 1933. In the same year, no doubt in part due to fear of the rising Nazi Party, he emigrated to the USA. Joining Harvard Medical School, he began a successful academic career that included stints at Yale and the University of California, alongside a successful clinical practice. When he first arrived in the USA, Erik changed his name again, becoming Erik Erikson. As his daughter later joked, this suggested that he had become his own father.

There is no doubt that Erik Erikson's personal history influenced his own complicated sense of self, but it also pushed him to consider the identity of social groups in a new light. Erikson's work on race theory is often overlooked, but he made a direct contribution to how we think about social justice today. In *Identity: Youth and Crisis* (1968), Erikson explained that identity was at the centre of what he then described as the 'Negro Revolution'. In the book, he discussed African American identity with extensive reference to the legacy of slavery and Jim Crow, a programme of state and local legislation in the American South that mandated racial segregation in all public facilities, ranging from schools to transport, toilets, restaurants and even drinking fountains.[23] He argued that this past had constrained the options for African American identity to either a negative identity, based on oppression and opposition to the structure of mainstream society, or a lack of identity altogether.[24] For African Americans to gain 'emancipation from the remnants of colonial patterns of thoughts',[25] he argued that they had to assert their own agency and value in society.

Erikson's view was in direct opposition to a liberal colour-blind view of society. It saw the purpose of emancipation as being a means to combat the continued existence of oppression coming from the white majority. And it recognised that slavery was not only an historic truth, but a legacy that still shaped social reality today.

Erikson had the insight that it is right to discuss identity groups within their own unique historical contexts. He argued that the modern-day identities of African Americans were rooted in the 'historical trauma' of colonialism and slavery. Unlike other communities that Erikson studied, like the native American Sioux and Yurok tribes, for

African Americans there was no sense of 'loss'. Instead, there was a sense of 'never was'. This made the need to assert African American culture even stronger. This distinction remains vital in helping us to understand the dissatisfactions of different tribes in today's political climate, and rings especially true within the British Caribbean community. For the traditional English working classes, there is undoubtedly a sense of loss in terms of how they identify themselves. For first- and second-generation immigrants in this country, there is a sense in which their identity 'never was', at least in terms of how it works in relationship with England or Britain.

While Erikson's work provides a clear foundation for identity politics, it was arguably not put into explicit practice until decades later. The civil- and LGBT-rights movements, as well as second-wave feminism, all sprang up from the recognition of shared injustices and common experience. In the early years of these movements, identity consciousness was less explicit. When Martin Luther King made the world pause to listen to his dream, he did not ask for recognition of his skin colour, context or history, but the opposite.

King ignited passion across the country in a way that transcended group divides and set out a vision for a colour-blind America. This put the ideals of universal equality and fairness front and centre of discourse in the USA. As I discussed earlier, I interpret King's words to mean that a colour-blind world is a desirable end-state, where all racial prejudices have been defeated. Colour-blindness is not a means to defeat the real prejudices that exist. Ignoring the inequalities in how different ethnic groups are treated will not fix them, but perpetuate their existence. King's own actions and activism would have failed if he had pretended that in the world he lived in, he could not see differences between how black and white people were treated in twentieth-century USA.

What colour-blind universal liberalism can do is win legal equality for all minority groups. It has transformed the lives of many and has led to the proliferation of universal human rights, beyond the USA and Europe and across the developing world. Even with these rights won, oppression persists. Without the recognition of different group identities, the universalist conception of rights puts too little focus on structural inequalities.

For this reason, when the likes of Thatcher and Reagan came into power, they too embraced a universalist colour-blind agenda but were able to use it as an excuse to block progress and refuse to intervene as racial inequalities persisted. Opponents of social justice began to accuse progressives of being obsessed with difference and entrenching divides in society.

To this day, I am criticised whenever I mention race, as though by simply using the descriptors 'black' or 'white' I am engaging in toxic prejudice. During the 2019 general election, I tweeted the shocking statistic that 51% of people in youth prisons are black or minority ethnic, far outweighing their presence in the general population. Very predictably, I was quickly criticised for 'pulling the race card' and 'stirring up division', for daring to point out gross disproportionality in our prisons.

Social conservatives can easily hide behind colour-blindness to legitimise inequality. In doing so, they are intentionally oblivious to context. If after centuries of oppression you start treating everyone the same, it is inevitable that advantages for the privileged groups will continue. The whole structure of society has been built in a way that is cumulatively advantageous for specific groups and cumulatively disadvantageous for others.

For decades, those on the left of politics understood this in terms of class. A boy born into a working-class family in a former industrial town, where no one has gone to Oxbridge in thirty years, does not have the same opportunities as a private-school boy from the Home Counties with professional parents. And this became entrenched within the identity of the institutions themselves. In a self-reinforcing cycle, the same structural disadvantage that gave kids less chance of going to university also began to reduce the willingness of state schools to encourage candidates to apply in the first place. It is true that we have eventually extended this analysis to other identity groups, such as those defined by race, gender and sexuality. Just as the working class is disadvantaged in a capitalist system, so a woman in a man's world or a black man in a majority white country will tend to enjoy fewer chances than an individual from the dominant group. The outcome is that we realised that if we wanted to right historical injustices, we had to come up with a new strategy. This is why, gradually, our focus has moved from class to identity.

COMBAHEE RIVER COLLECTIVE

The first political activists to consciously use the term 'identity politics' and to theorise its meaning were a group of black feminists called the Combahee River Collective.[26] The group, named after the site where Harriet Tubman led a campaign that freed more than 750 slaves in 1863, started meeting in Boston in the mid-1970s. They were frustrated that the broader feminist movement, which was predominantly white, had overlooked their experiences of oppression. Prominent members of the group included the scholar Barbara Smith, the poet Audre Lorde, and Chirlane McCray, who would one day become the First Lady of New York City.

The Combahee River Collective issued 'A Black Feminist Statement' in 1977, clarifying their political intentions and in so doing articulating the first incarnation of overt identity politics:

> The most general statement of our politics at the present time would be that we are actively committed to struggling against racial, sexual, heterosexual, and class oppression, and see as our particular task the development of integrated analysis and practice based upon the fact that the major systems of oppression are interlocking . . .
>
> We realize that the only people who care enough about us to work consistently for our liberation is us . . . This focusing on our own oppression is embodied in the concept of identity politics. We believe that the most profound and potentially the most radical politics come directly out of our own identity, as opposed to working to end somebody else's oppression.[27]

Ultimately, the motivation behind the Combahee's statement is equality for all people. It is just that their means of achieving this comes through the politics of the group. The concept of oppression itself relies on notions of equality and liberty. If you view the world in terms of natural hierarchies, where humans are naturally unequal, then it makes no sense to talk about oppression in a pejorative sense. If you do not believe that all humans have the right to some basic level of freedom, then you may not see anything wrong with one group being forced to work for another. In my experience, advocates of identity politics focus on liberating certain oppressed groups only because they believe in equality and liberty for every human being. The value of identity politics can therefore be assessed by the results it produces. Does it lead society more closely towards the ideals of equality and liberty, or away from them?

Identity politics has played a key role in the huge progress achieved by black people, by women, and by gay and transgender people over the past century. It is easy to forget that not long ago, if you were a woman, your quality of life was not determined by what you could contribute to society, but by who you married. Gay people had to live in secret and could be imprisoned simply for falling in love. The disabled were ridiculed, cast out and denied the chance to work. Meanwhile, ethnic minorities were subjugated, oppressed and at worst enslaved.

The great story of the twentieth century is one of self-actualisation characterised by the brave sacrifices of a few courageous leaders – Emily Wilding Davison, Mahatma Gandhi, Harvey Milk and Martin Luther King, to name but a few – and the silent revolution of the majority who heard their call: the millions who took to the streets, wrote letters and stood up to be counted. At the dawn of the millennium, in December 2000, the Netherlands became the first country to legalise same-sex marriage. In the two decades that followed, more than two dozen countries have followed in its trail. We should not underestimate the power of identity politics for allowing groups of human beings to liberate themselves.

IDENTITY UNDER ATTACK

Despite its many victories in recent years, and its transformative power in the latter half of the twentieth century, identity politics is under attack, not only from conservatives, but also from some on the left. Following the twin shocks of Brexit and Donald Trump's election to the US presidency, a spate of influential articles, journals and books were published arguing that the rise of the populist right was the fault of the left for its shift to identity politics. I first took these arguments seriously when Bernie Sanders made them to me. I met him on a visit to his office in the Dirksen Senate Building, after I spoke at the Congressional Black Caucus in autumn 2017. Bernie stressed his view that progressives 'need to move beyond identity politics'. He was echoing what he had previously said publicly: 'It is not good enough for somebody to say, "I'm a woman, vote for me." No, that's not good enough. What we need is a woman who has the guts to stand up to Wall Street, to the insurance companies, to the drug companies, to the fossil fuel industry. In other words, one of the struggles that you're going to be seeing in the Democratic Party is whether we go beyond identity politics.'[28]

I agree with Bernie that being black, or a woman, or LGBT, is not enough to be worthy of getting elected. The value of diversity is not innate: it comes from what individuals from different groups can contribute – through different life experiences and cultural knowledge. Nevertheless, going 'beyond identity politics' to only focus on class issues is often motivated by a false distinction. Class, gender and race oppressions, for example, often overlap. Ethnic minorities are disproportionately members of the working class. And this extends beyond just race. The Gay and Lesbians Support the Miners alliance formed precisely because they had a shared experience of alienation and exploitation. Class inequalities are not a reason to leave identity politics behind.

Mark Lilla, an American liberal academic, goes further than Bernie. He argues that the Combahee River Collective's declaration is at the root of where liberalism went wrong: interpreting it as a manifesto for a politics of selfishness and obsession with one's own group, at the cost of providing a broad agenda that unites different tribes. In the days following Donald Trump's election victory, Lilla penned an op-ed for the *New York Times* in which he wrote: 'In recent years American liberalism has slipped into a kind of moral panic about racial, gender and sexual identity that has distorted liberalism's message and prevented it from becoming a unifying force capable of governing.'[29] In his subsequent book, *The Once and Future Liberal: After Identity Politics*, Lilla pushes these ideas further.[30] He argues that recognising group identity has created a new politics of division and the end of young liberals believing 'they share a destiny with all their fellow citizens and have duties toward them'.

Lilla went on to assert that the election was lost because of Hillary Clinton's focus on diversity, 'calling out explicitly to African-American, Latino, L.G.B.T. and women voters at every stop'. This relentless focus on oppressed groups alienated the many Americans who did not identify with these groups, and those who were looking for a united vision of the USA, in contrast to Trump's own divisive tactics.

There is broad consensus that Clinton's failure to provide a message that united her country is a large reason why she suffered the unexpected defeat in 2016. It is lazy, however, to blame this failure on identity politics. Lilla's understanding of the Combahee River Collective is a misapprehension of its purpose.[31] When the statement declares 'We believe that the most profound and potentially the most radical politics come directly out of our own identity,' they are referring specifically and only to black women. They are not, as Lilla suggests, providing a manifesto for every specific group to campaign and do politics only on behalf of their identity group. The reason why the Collective believe their group is in particular need of this action is clarified later in the statement: 'If Black women were free, it would mean that everyone else would have to be free since our freedom would necessitate the destruction of all the systems of oppression.'

The purpose of identity politics, at least in its original incarnation, was for black women to work to end their own oppression, because if they, as one of the least privileged groups in society, could do this, it would mean the total breakdown of existing structural oppressions as we know it. Understood properly then, identity politics is a self- and group-focused means to a selfless end. The purpose of identity politics is to stand up for those groups who have traditionally been oppressed in order to compel the whole of society to be more equal. The assumptions behind the Combahee's actions are universalistic: every individual and group deserves equal rights and opportunity. It is only historical and contextual inequality that forces them to mobilise for the interests of one group – black women – in an attempt to bring them up to the same level as others.

It is telling that one identity group happens to criticise identity politics more than any other. Ironically, many of those who lambast identity politics engage in the very methods they ridicule. That is, they want to monopolise victimhood. What we have here is a belief that, in the wake of identity politics, they have been left behind. And in some cases, this belief is grounded in an unwillingness to understand what oppression really means. It is no coincidence that this is the group that, more than any other, has governed, controlled and dominated history, across vast swathes of the world. While white, straight, well-educated and wealthy men have been able to self-actualise for centuries, many of the rest of us have not. Much of what oppressed groups demand through identity politics is simply to be given the same agency and power to be oneself.

This is not to say that liberal critics of identity politics do not have a point. Like any system of change, identity politics has excesses. It can be abused and manipulated in ways that are at best ridiculous and at worst appeal to our basest instincts. Identity politics succeeds when it targets a specific injustice. It fails when it forgets our common human-ity. In recent years, sentiments such as 'all men are trash' or 'white people are trash' are symptomatic of the latter. These phrases have increasingly become an acceptable part of online discourse among certain sections of the left. Salma El-Wardany writes:

> If you listen carefully on any given day, you'll hear the words 'men are trash' like a gentle hum vibrating across the globe. An anthem if you will. A call to arms and a battle cry. A sign of solidarity even. Enter any room, social event, dinner party, creative gathering and you'll hear the phrase from at least one corner of the room, and you'll naturally gravitate towards that group of women because you imme-diately know you've found your tribe . . .
>
> So when women across the land cry out, 'men are trash', what it really means is, your ideas of manhood are no longer fit for purpose and your lack of evolution is hurting us all.[32]

It is my view that generalising about an entire gender or race to label them 'trash' serves no valuable purpose. It stokes divisions, shuts down dialogue and contributes to an already toxic discourse. The defence of those who use such phrases is that they are figures of speech, used ironically or to express a subtler meaning in just a few words. Though its negative effects may be less – given the structural realities of oppression – this is the same rationale used by members of the alt-right who make racist or sexist comments online to provoke. They too claim that their rancorous remarks are figures of speech or jokes. If you want to say 'Your ideas of manhood are no longer fit for purpose,' say it. It undermines your point to say 'all men are trash'.

In 2015, Goldsmiths University's elected diversity officer, Bahar Mustafa, caused outrage when she went further, tweeting the hashtag '#KillAllWhiteMen'. This was not an isolated incident, as she had previously called someone 'white trash' on Twitter and reportedly posted on Facebook: 'Omg . . . Kill them all. What's wrong with white people?'[33]

Attempting to explain her position to *Vice* magazine, Mustafa said: 'The #KillAllWhiteMen hashtag is something that a lot of people in the feminist community use to express frustration.'

This is no defence. The frustration Mustafa experiences is understandable, but the way she expressed it was shameful and has no place in our politics, on the right or the left. This form of extreme rhetoric borders on hate speech. Indeed, Mustafa was investigated by the Crown Prosecution Service, though charges were eventually dropped.

The prevalence of this type of extreme identity politics should not be overstated. It does not exist in a large section of society and is predominantly limited to the fringes of the media, and universities. But its influence can be damaging. Not only does it provide the right with a means to delegitimise genuinely righteous and progressive movements, it also provides nuggets of radicalising material for them to exploit. Individuals confronted with these unpleasant generalisations are more likely to find the extreme right appealing. As the Stanford psychologist Alana Conner explains:

Telling people they're racist, sexist and xenophobic is going to get you exactly nowhere. It's such a threatening message. One of the things we know from social psychology is when people feel threatened, they can't change, they can't listen.[34]

A study she cites illustrates that while some individuals have predispos-itions towards intolerance, these predispositions require some kind of stimulus to be triggered.[35] The most common action is a staunch, aggres-sive defensiveness of their own group.[36] This is part of the reason why Trump's campaign was so successful. He was able to accuse the other side of incivility and use it as proof of how 'threatening' they were.[37] As one Trump supporter put it: 'Every time Democrats attack him, it makes me angry, which causes me to want to defend him more.'[38]

In recent years, the UK has become a key breeding ground for far-right extremism. Three of the five far-right activists with the biggest online reach in the world are British.[39] Their views are scarily penetrat-ing, with 52 per cent of people living in England believing that Islam poses a threat to the West.[40] The hate spread by far-right activists is by no means confined to the online sphere. Twenty-eight far-right sympa-thisers were convicted or arrested for violent or terrorist offences in 2017.[41] When identity politics eliminates common ground between humans, leaving no place for empathy or dialogue, it becomes counter-productive and entrenches the very division and hate it aims to prevent.

Others argue that the problems identity politics creates are deeper than its excesses and the far-right activism it encourages. Francis Fukuyama, the man who declared 'the end of history' in his 1989 essay and 1992 book, is one such critic.[42, 43] He is known for arguing that liberal democracy was 'the final form of human government'. In the context of the fall of the Berlin Wall and the beginning of rapid global-isation and democratisation, liberal democracy seemed a plausibly final destination for how countries would be run. The optimistic title has left Fukuyama open to criticism after every global event that under-mined his thesis. The global financial crisis, war in the Balkans, Russia's annexation of Crimea, the rise of authoritarian China and the election of Donald Trump have all been used to prove his theory wrong. Fukuyama believes he's been hard done by:

Most of these criticisms were based on a simple misunderstanding. I was using the word history in the Hegelian-Marxist sense – that is, the long-term evolutionary story of human institutions that could alternatively be labelled development or modernization. The word end was meant not in the sense of termination, but 'target' or 'objective'. Karl Marx had suggested that the end of history would be a communist utopia, and I was simply suggesting that Hegel's version, where development resulted in a liberal state linked to a market economy, was the more plausible outcome.

Whether or not you find this convincing, to believe that you have been misunderstood for thirty years must be intensely frustrating. End or target, Fukuyama still thinks Western liberal democracy is the best form of government we have. When I met him in his air-conditioned office in Stanford University campus, he was tired after weeks spent touring his latest book, *Identity: The Demand for Dignity and the Politics of Resentment*, in which he acknowledges the new and rising possibility of liberal democracies 'decaying or going backwards'. The culprit? Identity politics.

Fukuyama claims that liberal democracies face the threat of decay because they have failed to satisfy the fundamental human craving for 'recognition of dignity'. He argues that the problem with identity politics is that it has become a 'cheap substitute' for progressives to focus on, rather than dealing with underlying economic issues. The left used to focus on solidarity-building between workers, and on fighting against exploitation against the capitalist class. Workers were not separated into isolated groups with separate grievances – they bonded over shared exploitation and alienation. But today, Fukuyama argues, rather than building communal identity around shared experience, we have begun to focus relentlessly on justice for minorities, and usually within elite institutions. Campaigning for transgender rights on university campuses, for equal pay for women in already well-paid industries, we have missed the underlying issues. He writes:

It is easier to argue over cultural issues within the confines of elite institutions than it is to appropriate money or convince sceptical legislators to change policies ... Many of the constituencies that have been the focus of recent identity claims, such as female executives in Silicon Valley or aspiring women actresses and filmmakers in Hollywood, are near the top of the income distribution. Helping

them to achieve greater equality is a good thing, but will do nothing
to address the glaring disparities between the top 1 percent and the
remaining 99.[44]

Identity politics does of course include highly paid, powerful people
campaigning for justice. The best example of this in Britain is the
campaign for fair pay at the BBC, in which female staff have rightly
called out the public-service broadcaster for failing to pay high-level
women the same as men.[45] But this is an isolated campaign. No one is
arguing that the primary purpose of politics is to achieve parity in
boardrooms and to achieve equal pay for TV presenters. This is a
mischaracterisation.

Moreover, attempts to achieve social justice are more than just
protest over cultural issues: often they result in real and lasting changes
to the law. At least in the UK, making life fairer for minorities has been
a key focus of progressives in, as well as out, of government. The New
Labour government, in which I was a young minister, had the most
multiculturalist agenda this country has ever witnessed. In Tony Blair's
first term, the Labour government introduced The Race Relations
(Amendment) Act; abolished the tough Primary Purpose rule that
blocked entry to the UK for thousands of spouses married to British
citizens; introduced faith schools for Muslims and other religions;
published the Macpherson report which directly tackled institutional
racism; and added religion to the census in recognition of the varied
religious make-up of modern Britain. In government, the Labour Party
was so successful at bringing social justice onto the agenda that to some
extent the Conservative government that followed kept to the same
path. In 2015, I was asked by Conservative Prime Minister David
Cameron to conduct a review into racial bias in the criminal-justice
system.[46] This would have been unthinkable in previous administrations. When my review was published in 2017, it found significant
evidence of racial discrimination and unconscious bias at every level. I
made thirty-five recommendations to help build trust, fairness and
responsibility. Many are being implemented.[47]

Is it fair to say that by focusing on justice for minority and oppressed
groups, we have failed to answer why inequality within countries has

grown so fast in the past three decades? This is where Fukuyama's criticism stings. While we have made progress on social justice, we have allowed inequality to rise, even when nominally left-wing governments have been in power, and in doing so have failed to provide a coherent message that unites people. During Blair and Brown's three terms in power, the gap between rich and poor widened slightly.[48] It was not as though we made no attempt to reduce inequality: tax reforms, high investment in public services, and the introduction of Sure Start and the national minimum wage were specifically designed to make our society more equal. We even had major successes. The number of children living in relative poverty in the UK at the end of Labour's time in government in 2010 was 800,000 fewer than when Blair took power in 1997.[49]

The key reason that inequality rose despite this is not what was going on at the bottom end of income distribution, but at the top.[50] The fundamental driver of inequality in the modern world is the fact that capital grows at a faster rate than wages over time.[51] It can pay more for a wealthy person to sit on their wealth than it does for a hard-working person to work ten hours per day. New Labour never fully confronted this fact. Therefore, the wealthier got multiples richer, even as the rest made small progress. A similar story occurred in the USA, where Bill Clinton accepted the fundamental logic of laissez-faire economics and facilitated the continuation of rising inequality that had begun under Ronald Reagan.[52]

We have failed to tackle inequality over the past three decades, but how much of this can really be linked to campaigning for minority rights? If identity politics has played the role of an alluring and noble distraction from a more inclusive politics, this is a problem. And if it has allowed the left to seize the moral high ground without thinking deeply about how to reorganise society to help every working person, this is also a problem. But identity politics and a redistributive economic policy are not mutually exclusive. At heart, Fukuyama's first criticism of the left is not really about identity politics. It is about a failure of the left to provide a politics separate from identity.

Politics based on group identity is not itself a bad thing. Indeed, it is vital for oppressed groups to organise and mobilise against their oppressors. So many of the great achievements of the twentieth and twenty-first centuries have been achieved through it. Yet, this does not mean that identity politics is the solution to every problem in our society, or that it does not sometimes cause unwelcome friction. I recognise that not everything is about systemic racism or sexism. Not all politics is about identity. If we are to unite as a nation, we need a means for people of different identities to arbitrate disputes, make compromises and forge a common path.

Identity politics becomes a problem when it is the *only* politics. When people see their lives only through their perspective of oppression and intersectionality, they can forget the common identities we share as human beings and as citizens of a nation state. We do not need to call for an end to identity politics, then, but for the start of a new politics of the common good. This requires the thoughtful construction of what it means to come from Tottenham, while also being a Londoner, English, British, European and, even, a citizen of the world. This would be an opportunity for us to take pride in our myriad personalities, while recognising that as citizens we have something in common, too. A chance to share a unifying story that brings people together after years of division, built on an honest reckoning of our nations' histories, warts and all.

HOW BELONGING CAN MAKE SOCIETY

Encounter Culture

Empowering our neighbourhoods

'We cannot live only for ourselves. A thousand fibers connect us with our fellow men.'

Henry Melville

Wigan, on the edge of Greater Manchester, does not get much coverage by journalists or attention from politicians. These days the town is probably most famous for its sporting prowess: the rugby-league team is one of the best in the world, and the football team competes in the second tier of the English football league. For many, though, it remains the town that symbolises post-industrial poverty in twentieth-century England. It owes this reputation to George Orwell, who in 1937 wrote *The Road to Wigan Pier* about living in squalid lodgings above a shop that sold 'great white folds of tripe'. He chose the place not because it represented average living conditions for Wiganers, but because it was particularly dirty and he thought the room in his previous hostel was too clean.

Orwell described the worst of poverty, ill-health and decay in 1930s Wigan, but he framed it as if it were normal. The lanky Old Etonian socialist claimed to 'like Wigan very much – the people, not the scenery'.[1] Yet he described little hope or humanity in the people he met. The former miners had foreheads 'veined like Roquefort cheeses'. His landlord had 'permanently dirty hands'. The place where tripe was stored was supposedly swarmed by 'blackbeetles'. One of the two permanent lodgers he lived with 'only got out of bed on the days when he went to draw his pension'. Even the title of Orwell's book, *The Road to Wigan Pier*, relies on the conceit that the jetty was ever anything more than a joke. 'Alas! Wigan Pier has been demolished,' Orwell wrote, 'and even the spot where it used to stand is no longer certain.' Presumably, the disappearance of the mythical pier was supposed to represent the image of decline in the northern towns that Orwell set out to document.

Some writers who describe poverty without having lived through it tend towards expressing too much pity, overcompensating for their own privilege. A 2019 *Sunday Times* feature did its best to highlight poverty in the Broadwater Farm Housing Estate in Tottenham.[2] It did a good job of this and managed to raise an impressive £300,000 for children from a local school.[3] It failed, however, to show the human side of deprivation. It is important to recognise that with struggle comes laughter, comedy, pathos and sarcasm.

The oversimplification of poverty happens on the left and the right. The former London mayor Ken Livingstone attempted to blame the 2011 riots on austerity when he said: 'If you're making massive cuts, there's always the potential for this sort of revolt against that.' The truth was that in 2011 the depth of austerity had not yet been felt. The mere fact that you are poor does not mean you will break and steal things. In my own working-class upbringing two streets away from the Broadwater Farm Estate, life was sometimes stressful, hard and confusing. My parents argued about money, often could not afford to send me on school trips and sometimes there was very little in the fridge. But deprivation is never as simple as some portray it. On the whole, I felt stable and happy. Most importantly, I had the steady love of a wonderful mother, who taught me and my siblings to have pride, dignity and self-worth.

Today in Wigan, you will find none of the 'plumes of smoke', 'bargemen' or 'foul water' that Orwell described. After dozens of closures in the 1920s and '30s, just twenty-five coal mines survived by the time of nationalisation in 1947.[4] By the end of the 1960s, only two remained.[5] Slag heaps from the mining days are still visible, but vegetation has returned, reclaiming land scarred by the area's industrial past. In the post-war years, many found employment in new industries: factories, weaving sheds, steelworks and on the railways. These days industrial-sized kitchens are the region's largest private employers. They include Heinz, famous across the world for its baked beans and ketchup; Waterfields, a baker of bread, pies, pasties and cakes; Bakkovar, maker of Indian, Chinese, Thai, Italian, Moroccan, Mexican and traditionally British ready meals; and AB World foods, manufacturer of Patak's, Blue Dragon, Levi Roots and other supermarket classics. Wigan's town centre is attractive. Mock Tudor façades sit alongside red-brick Edwardian buildings. Though its changes have been controversial, a £60-million redevelopment, including bars, a cinema and a restaurant, first approved by the council in 2014, is nearing completion.[6] HS2, the high-speed rail link, should shorten travel times from Wigan to London to less than one and a half hours instead of nearly two.[7]

The worst of life in Wigan is still grim. More than one quarter of children in the city live in poverty. From 2010 to 2017, council spending in Wigan fell by 43 per cent, almost double the national average. In total, its budget was cut by more than £160 million. To make things worse, the town was a pilot area for the disastrous roll-out of universal credit, which tipped struggling families into despair. Unemployment and underemployment have left many to rely on foodbanks and denied people the pride that follows a full day's work.

On the day I visited Wigan, the local MP Lisa Nandy told me she had just received a report from a mother who had been on her way to drop her kids off at school. In broad daylight, behind some shops, she found a drug addict with his pants down and needles sticking out of his groin.

I hear similarly bleak stories from the people of Tottenham. Just a month earlier a mother of six had collared me in the street to describe how her home had become surrounded by crack dens. She described dealers jumping over her fence to bury drugs in her garden, as well as being kept awake by addicts shouting, vomiting and fighting. At night, she saw prostitutes on the street outside. In the morning, she regularly found crack pipes outside her door. Because she lived in council housing, she had no way to leave without the help of her council. She was not free to move because she couldn't afford to. It is the same story whether you are poor in a former industrial town or a deprived area of a big city. Every day, my own children walk down Stroud Green Road, passing under the Finsbury Park bridge on the way to school. Several men and women live underneath it. Many of them walk around barefoot. The stale and pungent smell of Spice, the new drug of choice, is hard to ignore.

Many of the causes of social crises in both Wigan and Tottenham are, at root, economic. If there were more jobs in our neighbourhoods, far fewer individuals would become drug addicts in the first place. If there were positive places for young people to develop interests, skills and connections, they would not need to find meaning in more destructive groups. Our problem is rooted in economic injustice, for sure, but it is also a crisis of families, communities, culture, expectations and belonging. No one experiments with drugs wanting to become an addict. No one starts selling them hoping that one day they will be stabbed on the street. No one wakes up one day as a child and dreams of life without a purpose. These are the ways of life desperate people living on the fringes turn to when we offer them nothing better. When they are isolated, alone and afraid and have nowhere to belong.

Place is fundamental in creating and preserving our identities. The landscape, architecture, smells, culture, shops, food and feeling of where we live are powerful factors in determining who we are as individuals. When two strangers meet, the first question they will ask one another after 'What is your name?' is often 'Where are you from?' Each individual's answer will not only determine what the other thinks of them, it will shape their own sense of self.[8] When I first started university and answered 'Where are you from?' with 'Tottenham', I felt strong pride in the multicultural community my family had raised me in, as well as the football team. I was also aware of the judgements some would make of a young, black man from a place they had only seen in the news in relation to riots. Once we categorise ourselves as coming from a certain place, we inevitably take on elements of that place's history. Others make assumptions of us, but we also make them of ourselves.

As the places we identify with change, inevitably our conceptions of ourselves shift, too. Psychological studies show that when we become vulnerable, we are likely to shrink the size of our in-group. Human social networks in Palaeolithic groups were defined by three tiers. The first tier is the immediate household or family, the second is made up of four or so close households, and the third is the wider tribe. Individuals will prioritise helping other people in that order. If they are feeling happy and well-off, they may offer food to any of the 150 members of the wider tribe. If they are hungry and insecure, they will only share with close family and friends. If we feel confident about our own neighbourhood, we are more likely to feel secure in ourselves and generous to others. If we perceive decline around us, we will feel uneasy and defensive towards outsiders. The resurgence of tribal identities in places like Wigan, then, is at least in part a result of industrial decline, local government cuts and the degradation of neighbourhoods.

For years, populist nationalist right-wing groups have been the only political movements to recognise the importance of place on our identities. Yet rather than providing solutions to the unease people feel at those places changing, they have done their best to exploit it. In 2015, protesters in a National Front rally in the Wigan town centre waved flags that read: 'We must secure the existence of our people and a future for white children' and 'White Pride'.[9] It should be noted that these extremists do not represent anything more than a tiny fringe. Stephen Yaxley-Lennon (aka Tommy Robinson) for example, the far-right, anti-Islam activist who set up the English Defence League, received just 2.2 per cent of the vote when he ran to be MEP for the north-west region, which includes Wigan, in 2019.[10] Despite Yaxley-Lennon's failure, other less extreme anti-establishment, right-wing movements have been more successful in the town. In 2016, dissatisfaction with the status quo led Wigan to deliver the most adamant endorsement for Brexit in the whole of Manchester and Merseyside, with 64 per cent of voters opting for Leave.[11] And in the same European election that roundly rejected Yaxley-Lennon, Nigel Farage's Brexit Party received 41 per cent of the vote, pushing Labour into second place.

In the 2019 general election, Lisa Nandy was able to hold onto her seat as MP for Wigan, but her majority was slashed from 16,000 in 2017 to less than 7,000. The nearby constituency of Leigh, which had been represented by a Labour MP for almost 100 years, elected a Conservative for the first time. The seaside town of Redcar, and the former mining communities of Sedgefield, once represented by Tony Blair, Workington and Bishop Auckland were other striking examples of Labour's collapse in once-safe seats in northern England and the Midlands. For many in these constituencies, as in the rest of the country, Brexit identities displaced once strong party loyalties.[12] Following the election, some close to the Labour leadership tried to blame the defeat squarely on Labour's support for a People's Vote, a result of overwhelming pressure and years of campaigning from party members. However, suggesting that Labour's worst result since 1935 can be blamed on the party's begrudging and last-minute support for a new referendum is simply not backed up by data. Even in constituencies that voted for Leave in 2016, most potential Labour voters are pro EU.[13] Moreover, if the defeat can be explained by the party appearing too Remain, why did our vote share plummet in most Leave and Remain voting constituencies alike?[14] Jeremy Corbyn's personal decision to take a neutral stance on Brexit, the biggest national issue of the generation, convinced Leavers he was a Remainer and left Remainers believing he supported Leave. The result was that we lost support from Remainers and Leavers in almost all constituencies.

'If you want to understand Brexit, you've got to understand the buses,' Lisa told me, over barm cake, beef and chips at a Wigan social-enterprise café. She explained that the decline in local services is a huge part of why people feel the status quo is not working: 'In the last decade, we've lost about 20 per cent of the bus network, but it was already a problem. It's really common if you are trying to get somewhere to wait for over an hour for a bus. Sometimes it might not come at all, so you just have to go home. It's really common for there to be one bus that goes to a place of a day and one bus that comes back. If it's the wrong way round, you just can't do it. You can get there, but you can't get back. And it costs a fortune as well. Often it's cheaper to get a taxi. You are very cut off, basically. It's really difficult to see people and remain connected to your own community . . . People are pissed off.'

The populist mood in Wigan is palpable. It is one of several pressure points in a country where trust in politicians is at an all-time low.[15] The Brexit Party enjoyed popularity in Wigan because its message tapped into this feeling of distrust. It is understandable that voters in Wigan feel let down by the establishment. Years of globalisation, which have coincided with our EU membership, have not been good for them. Economic growth has been concentrated in city centres, not industrial towns. Much has been written about the economic and social effects of austerity on local services. The second and arguably deeper cut has been to individuals' pride in where they come from. Where once people found belonging in their communities, years of erosion in public services and neighbourhood cohesion have pushed individuals to find belonging somewhere else. In Tottenham, this might leave you vulnerable to the attractions of a gang. In Wigan, it is more likely that you will be drawn to the populist nationalist right. As Lisa told me: 'If we do not get it right, we could have fascism in five years.' As the world continues to change, the most effective way for us to fight back is to restore our citizens' pride in their neighbourhoods.

THE EROSION OF MUNICIPAL BRITAIN

It is hard to believe today, but Britain's local governments were once the envy of the world. If you walk around English cities, you can still see this history commemorated in stone. Grand town halls stand as cathedrals to the effect that placing power in local areas can have. Standing nearly seventy metres tall, Leeds town hall, completed in 1858, has a grandeur equal to many national parliaments. Birmingham's town-hall building was modelled on a classical temple when it was built in the 1830s, as its imposing columns reveal. Manchester town hall, completed in 1877, is a neo-Gothic megastructure that epitomises civic bombast. Liverpool's town hall, completed in 1754, is one of the grandest of all civic buildings.

The golden era for municipal government began in the late Victorian era. During the industrial revolution, towns quickly realised that they needed to build infrastructure to take advantage of the new industries that were emerging. Municipal governments therefore became highly innovative, using local tax-raising powers to respond rapidly to the needs and ambitions of their areas.[16] As many people moved to cities, poverty and social inequality became more visible on the streets. With national government unprepared and unwilling to step in, a revolution at the local level began. Municipalities evolved to provide what became known as 'public goods' – services that benefit everyone but that the private sector will not provide.[17]

Across the country, municipalities transformed services that were previously thought of as the job of government: supplying homes with running water, building sewers and installing streetlights. They built libraries, hospitals, houses, parks and even swimming pools.[18] Many were powerful enough to purchase electricity, gas and transport companies, thereby providing local people with vital services that were efficient and affordable.[19] The effect was a rapid improvement in the quality and length of people's lives, particularly for the urban poor. The country's death rates began to improve for the first time in decades.

Over the decades that followed, power drifted away from the municipal to the national and the private. Politicians in Westminster waged a war of attrition on local control, seeing it as getting in the way of national policy decisions.[20] The political left believed the concentration of power at the local level led to inequalities – what today we call post-code lotteries – between different municipalities. Meanwhile, the right attacked local government as an example of the superfluous influence of the state. In 1928, then Chancellor Winston Churchill captured a growing consensus when he said: 'It is a matter of vital importance to secure that any taxation of industry is taken out of the hands of local bodies.'[21]

In the decades that followed, public provisions increasingly shifted from local to central government. Following the destruction of the Second World War, Clement Attlee's 1945 Labour government rightly provided national solutions to a national crisis. Attlee did not simply move services from the local to the state level, he also created entirely new services. The National Health Service is the most treasured example of Atlee's post-war programme of nationalisation. By the 1950s, gas, local hospitals, roads and electricity were all under central governmental control. As the sixties became the seventies, sewer and water supplies joined them.[22] Their profits went to national government too.[23] Instead of being the primary provider of public goods, the role of local government morphed into a secondary service that filled gaps left by national government. Many of the fundamental services local government historically provided – water, streetlights, gas, roads and hospitals to name a few – were made the responsibility of national government. In effect then, much of local government's purpose became redistributive, rather than for the whole community.[24] While everyone relies on their council for bin collection, street cleaning, maintenance and planning, many other local government services are mostly beneficial to the worst-off. Wealthy people do not need public leisure centres because they are members of private gyms. Those with big gardens depend less on the local park. If you have the spare cash to buy books from Amazon, your local library will matter to you less. In effect, then, as power was taken away from local government, a large chunk of society started to have contact with it less and less.

When I was growing up in the seventies, local government's role in maintaining our neighbourhood still felt important. The local authority of Haringey had only been founded seven years before I was born, after absorbing the municipal boroughs of Tottenham, Wood Green and Hornsey, which had previously been part of the historic county of Middlesex. Haringey council began life with ambition, determined to make its mark on this corner of north-east London. Amidst the optimism and energy of the Swinging Sixties, it commissioned new council estates around the Tottenham Hotspur football stadium. Inspired by the modern architecture of Le Corbusier, the construction of Broadwater Farm Estate began in marshland that had previously been used for allotments. My parents relied on my elder cousin Beverly for childcare, so I spent many hours, days and nights on the top floor of the Croydon block of the development in my cousins' flat. It felt new and fresh compared with our cold, damp two-up, two-down terrace a couple of streets away.

I learned to ride a bike in Lordship Rec Park next door to the estate. The park housed a unique model traffic area: a scaled-down road network in which you could hire bikes for just twenty pence. Around the corner was the Tottenham lido. In the hot summers of the seventies, the freezing-cold pool provided hours of cheap municipal fun. I remember queuing with my mother to collect her pay cheque at the imposing Tottenham town hall. We would wait politely for hours for that brown envelope, but we felt more than rewarded afterwards as we raced round the shops for the week's supplies. The Cub Scouts were based at High Cross Reform Church and the Boy's Brigade at the Miller Memorial Church, and there was tap-dancing in Kemble Hall by the Spurs stadium. The vibrant civic life of Haringey was very real for me in the 1970s and early '80s.

When Margaret Thatcher took office in 1979, she saw municipal government as a natural enemy. Local power was a barrier to controlling inflation through monetary policy, and more broadly to free-market policies. When local authorities missed centrally imposed targets, she penalised them with reduced grants.[25] In defiance of her hostile agenda, in the early 1980s Labour-run councils deliberately overspent. Councils in Lambeth, Islington, Sheffield, Liverpool and Haringey flat-out refused to set any budget at all. My predecessor as MP for Tottenham, Bernie Grant, was one of the most ardent opponents of Conservative 'rate-capping' during his time as leader of Haringey council.[26]

In 1986, the Conservative government abolished the domestic-rates system and replaced it with the Community Charge, otherwise known as the poll tax. It was part of Margaret Thatcher's aim to dismantle what she believed was a bloated welfare state. She wanted to foster the notion of the 'active citizen', whereby individuals are independent economic citizens but at the same time politically responsible within the wider community. By ensuring that everybody paid a fee, Thatcher claimed the intention of the poll tax was to stop those who did not contribute to public services from putting 'their hands into other people's pockets, for any purpose which they think fit'.[27]

In principle, a poll tax could have given local authorities extra control over taxing and spending, restoring some level of autonomy to the local level. The tax soon became known as 'the most celebrated disaster in post-war British politics'.[28] The major problem was that it was grossly regressive. Millionaires and those living in poverty were required to pay the same amount. This left most people paying significantly more than they had under the previous system, with discounts going to the wealthiest households. Huge public anger ensued. Many people, including one third of taxpayers in Scotland in its first year, simply refused to pay. As a School of Oriental and African Studies student, the blatant unfairness of the poll tax became only the second issue I protested about, after the anti-apartheid marches I'd joined in the 1980s. Ultimately, the poll-tax disaster contributed to Thatcher's downfall, and the tax was replaced by the new Prime Minister John Major in March 1991.

When the New Labour government took office, it devolved significant power to Scotland, Wales and Northern Ireland, but not to the English regions. The government had planned to offer referendums on devolution to North East England, Yorkshire and the Humber and North West England. The only one of these referendums to go ahead, the North East, delivered a landslide rejection of the idea, by 77.9% to 22.1%.[29] National investment, not local government, was therefore seen as the way to guarantee fair opportunity across the country. To some extent, New Labour continued the Conservative policy of privatisation, by contracting out certain aspects of public services, including private finance intiatives private-finance initiatives. Local government's power was further eroded by the market.

For more than a century, then, there has been a steady drift away from local government autonomy. The current impotence of local government in Britain is unprecedented. We are now one of the most centralised democratic societies in the developed world. Decision-making overwhelmingly happens in Whitehall. In the UK, just 5.8 per cent of taxes are raised at the local level.[30] More than 70 per cent of all public spending is under the direct control of the prime minister and his or her cabinet. The comparable figure in Germany is a mere 20 per cent.[31]

England's regions suffer the most. The spending local government enjoyed as recently as a decade ago has been decimated. Since 2010, the government has almost halved its funding to English local authorities.[32] Across the country, libraries are closing, and parks are being sold off to developers. Meanwhile, youth, homelessness, social and community centres have been forced to shut their doors. Councils that once acted as guardians, protectors and developers of each neighbourhood are increasingly forced to stop all spending that is not vital. This is not only reflected by the fact that 130 public libraries closed in 2018.[33] Local museums and art festivals, which once provided a cultural fabric to remote areas without the galleries and music venues of bustling cities, are now facing the threat of extinction. There has been £400 million in cuts to culture and arts spending since 2010.[34] In 2018, Northamptonshire council effectively went bankrupt.[35]

The distribution of cuts has been vastly unequal, with the most deprived areas hit significantly harder than wealthier regions that might have been more able to absorb the loss of funding. Barnsley suffered a £688 drop per head in funding over the eight years since 2010, for example, which is far greater than the £100 per person cuts to Oxford's local government.[36] Reduced funding for youth and social services, education and housing provision, employment and opportunities for people to develop skills, play a part in explaining why knife crime in England and Wales is at its highest levels since records began.[37] The number of rough sleepers on London's streets is greater than ever before in modern times.[38] The worst-hit schools across the country are now open for only four and a half days per week.[39]

The total impact of shrinking local government on our communities is challenging to quantify. Nevertheless, it was well articulated by the UN special rapporteur Philip Alston, who was commissioned to write a report on poverty in the UK in 2018. He concluded: 'The bottom line is that much of the glue that has held British society together since the Second World War has been deliberately removed and replaced with a harsh and uncaring ethos.'[40] The report emphasised that those who had been affected by recent economic upheavals would have received 'at least minimal protection' in terms of social security in the past.

The loss of power of local government – and dramatic cuts to local services – help to explain the feeling of unease across the country. From Wigan to Peterborough to Tottenham, the wealth, strength and identity of every neighbourhood is being diluted. How can people feel as if they have a say in local democracy when councillors from all parties are bound by nine years of funding cuts? How can young people be persuaded to stay in their home towns as they watch their libraries, parks, youth centres and museums close? What does it do to your self-esteem if the public services you rely on can no longer support you? How can you have faith in supranational institutions like the EU if the local institutions around you are getting worse?

SUNSHINE HOUSE

Despite signs of an emerging tribalism in Wigan, there is still a tangible sense of community there that holds its people together. The main purpose of my visit to Lisa Nandy's constituency was not to witness poverty or social deprivation, but to understand how, despite all this, that shared sense of community had been maintained. Lisa told me that much of the answer for it lay in the area's enduring sense of local identity. People depended on each other when facing life's challenges. They formed close bonds with one other, in order to survive. Because of these close and mutual relationships, they belonged.

Lisa had arranged for us to meet at Sunshine House, a community centre that started as a residents' association in 1996 but has since grown into a home for social enterprises, care services and creative groups, as well as an entertainment venue. The area surrounding Sunshine House is filled with rows of neatly stacked, red-brick terraced houses that are typical of northern England. Many were demolished in the 1960s and '70s, but those that survive are only distinguishable from what George Orwell must have seen by the satellite dishes and hatchback cars that sit outside.

'The best thing about Wigan is the people,' Barbara Nettleton, manager of Sunshine House, told me over a cup of tea. 'We look after each other. There is still a really strong sense of where we are from and what that means.' It is this resilience and community strength that makes people in Wigan so prepared to support Brexit, Barbara believes. 'The toughness means we can get through it,' she said. 'We can do this on our own. We don't need something else. We're resilient. We can build industry. Why can we not build industry? Why do people keep saying that?'

There is no doubt that the area has shown incredible strength over the past decade. The acceleration of austerity cuts following the financial crisis forced Wigan Council into making huge savings. The council decided to do this unconventionally, with the ambition to improve services despite the massive losses in funding. It closed several existing service centres and invested the remaining money in community organisations. The idea was that the people of Wigan would have more of a say over how council funds were spent. This new arrangement became known as 'The Deal'. The plan was to get local community leaders and charities to fill in where local government no longer could. One of the most significant and dedicated contributors to this effort has been Sunshine House.

The difference Sunshine House has made is evident when you walk into the Scholes shopping precinct next door to the town centre. For years it was home to a supermarket, a fish and chip shop, a post office, a butcher's and other local shops. All of these closed a few years ago, leaving the precinct abandoned. The one remaining commercial business is Betfred, a gambling shop. Sunshine House has begun to replace the abandoned shops one by one. The most popular is the food pantry. Unlike at a foodbank, people pay a £2 yearly membership fee for access to heavily discounted food and household supplies. This changes the dynamic for users from being a receiver of charity to being a member of a social enterprise. It now has 600 members. More recently, a 'Mums Babies & Tots' shop and a clothes shop have sprung up next door.

Inside Sunshine House, I sat down with a group of pensioners. Each had been bussed from their homes across Wigan to spend the afternoon in each other's company. They played games, listened to music, drank tea, ate biscuits, chatted and laughed. One of the women, Sara, who suffers from social anxiety, told me that before coming to Sunshine House, she saw almost nobody. 'When I first came here, I was very nervous and could hardly speak,' she said. 'Now it feels like a home away from home. I feel so much happier.'

It is not only the members of Sunshine House who benefit from the interactions provided by this social base. For the volunteers, it is an opportunity to meet people and build confidence, too. One of the volunteers I met was, until last year, sleeping rough. After months of volunteering, Sunshine House offered him a paid position at the centre as a supervisor. Typically, the paid workers start off as volunteers. I asked one of them why they worked more than forty hours a week for free. The answer was simple: 'I love it here. I am a people person. This gets me out of the house.'

It is difficult to assess the impact of Sunshine House through data. What is certain is that without this community centre, the lives of many of its members would undoubtedly be less stable, more isolated and lacking in connection. Hubs that foster social cohesion are not unique to Wigan. They exist across the country. In this age of disconnection, they are the exception, rather than the rule. We need to properly fund our local government again, to give them the power to help people form communities. But funding is only part of the solution. As well as the capacity to strengthen local bonds, a newly municipal Britain needs a vision.

TOWARDS AN ENCOUNTER CULTURE

We are living in a time of unprecedented social segregation. Increasingly it feels as though we live as collections of strangers, rather than in communities and neighbourhoods. Part of this is explained by the decline in industries and the collapse of local services, but much of it is to do with the fact that we are simply mixing less. The death of community spaces and civic pride has coincided with technology that has enabled us to retreat into online groups where others think, look and live the same as we do. To fix it, we are going to have to create events, space and opportunities for people to spend time with others they would not otherwise meet.

All across Britain, there are examples of people who are weaving social bonds in tough circumstances, and in spite of the new tribalism. Local heroes who recognise it is not pursuing individualistic success through money, power or fame that leads to a happy life. Instead, they understand that good relationships, social contact and belonging are the foundation of being content. Those who run community centres like Sunshine House provide clear examples for how to build what I call an 'encounter culture', which allows previously isolated individuals to meet. But many others foster bonds between people in less obvious ways, viewing it as just a normal part of everyday life. Volunteering in a local library, offering to share the school run with local parents, coaching a local Under-11 football team, organising a pub quiz or a Parkrun are some of many ways the civic-minded among us contribute to bringing individuals closer together, after decades of hyper-individualism.

A long-standing tenet in the field of social sciences is that encounters between different groups of people help improve social cohesion. The 'contact theory' was first articulated by the eleventh-most-often-cited psychologist of the twentieth century, Gordon Allport.[41] The argument is simple: positive encounters between people from different groups can push them to understand each other better, which in turn can lead to reduced conflict in society. As a result of this insight, many policymakers mistakenly assumed that all encounters were necessarily positive. This was the argument used by the advocates of 'positive gentrification'. If people from higher and middle socio-economic groups moved to an area traditionally lived in by lower socio-economic groups, some suggested, there would be an 'urban renaissance' that would pull the whole community upwards.

In fact, even when people from different social groups live next to each other, it has, for the most part, not led to higher social mixing. Research shows that so-called gentrifiers often hold different attitudes to the established residents of the neighbourhoods and communities to which they have moved. They tend to show less engagement in their local area. Many new-build developments are gated communities that provide most services sought after by their residents within them. Even in the most urban areas, wealthy residents can avoid ever needing to step onto the pavement outside, with the help of underground car parks. Gentrification, therefore, often reinforces rather than diminishes a lack of concern for the neighbourhood at large.[42] Even liberal-minded gentrifiers who consciously seek out social mixing most often end up self-segregating whilst pushing out the locals.[43]

The failure of social-cohesion policies is down to several flawed assumptions. The most important is that simply putting different social groups closer together will lead to meaningful encounters between the new neighbours. For encounters across difference to be positive, there are a few prerequisites. Impressively, it seems that Allport summarised these conditions accurately early on. First, those engaging in an encounter need to have an equal status. Second, the engagement needs to be realistic rather than artificial. And, third, encounters need to have the support of the wider community.[44] This rule of three may appear to be just another abstract set of principles, but it turns out to be a pretty good indicator of whether an encounter is likely to be meaningful.

Foodbanks provide a good illustration of this. Over the past decade, foodbanks in Britain have provided a lifeline to struggling families and hard-up individuals left hungry by austerity. In 2018, they provided a record of 1.6 million food parcels.[45] They are also a space for encounters across class: often between middle-class volunteers and working-class users. The volunteers at foodbanks in the UK perform at least £30 million per year of unpaid work, expressing genuine compassion and kindness.[46, 47] There is little doubt that foodbanks have the support of the wider community. The encounters that occur inside them pass the second and third conditions. In this charitable exchange, users and volunteers do not have equal status.[48] Volunteers are givers of charity, while users are receivers. Of course, there are exceptions: there will be examples of meaningful bonds being made at foodbanks, and we should celebrate them. The power relation at play makes it difficult for the different social groups to mix meaningfully. Sunshine House's 'Food Pantry' concept, where users pay a nominal yearly membership fee, radically reforms the dynamic. Staff and customers have something more like equal standing.

Strong ties are not all we are looking to foster in an encounter culture. Bringing together people from diverse backgrounds, who look, sound and behave differently to one another, is also about allowing people to form a multitude of weak ties. The importance of these 'weak ties' has been highlighted by the American sociologist Mark Granovetter.[49] His argument is that the strong relationships we have with our families, friends and closest work colleagues are vital for our everyday lives. You call your mother to help babysit your young child if you have to stay late at work. Your best friend is the one you will rely on for a pint of beer after a hard week. Your desk partner will cover for you when you have to take a day off sick. But strong ties are not useful in every situation. If you are looking for a job in a new area, for example, your friends who all live nearby are not likely to know much more than you do. In contrast, an acquaintance who lives and works in another city or country is likely to be much better at helping you to identify new opportunities. This is why university is so valuable. It is not only about learning essay-writing skills, but also the contacts we make with people from all over the country. But only around half of us get the chance to go to university. So, what about everyone else?

Most people would accept that developing a healthy balance between strong and weak ties will help an individual to achieve a productive life. But some critics might disagree with the idea that it is the role of government to attempt to influence the relationships we form with other citizens. Whether we like it or not, the state is fundamental in creating the opportunities and structures within which we live our lives. Local government must be given the power and resources to restore funding to libraries, youth services, community gardens and social services, as well as be given the inspiration to create new institutions and services. Existing centres for local engagement must be restored and then developed. It is right that youth services are targeted at disadvantaged groups, but we should supplement them with initiatives that are not just a measure to soften the blows of inequality. Youth clubs unrelated to background or income – though actively recruiting from disadvantaged communities – could provide a way to bring young people from different parts of the same neighbourhoods together in one space.

Nevertheless, reforms to our democratic structure and government initiatives can only ever form part of the answer to the crisis of belonging we are experiencing at a local level. To become less tribal, the most fundamental revolution we need to aspire to is cultural. How do we encourage communities that bring people together, rather than push them into isolation and towards the toxicity of tribes? The answers will come from private individuals and groups, as well as from the state. We need to explore different spaces where such encounters can be fostered: from public spaces to educational, work and socialisation spaces. There are many ways to foster more meaningful encounters.[50] The ideas and inspiration are already out there. The biggest challenge is working out how to promote and spread them.

We should not underestimate the value of local and inclusive group activities. These can be completely ordinary. Group cycling, Parkrun events, walking clubs, board-game evenings and open-mic nights are all low-cost, low-commitment events that can bring together people from all backgrounds. They reduce social isolation and foster feelings of collective endeavour. There are also much more original ideas out there that can serve the same purpose, many of the best of which have been highlighted by the *Guardian* columnist and author George Monbiot.[51] 'Men's Sheds' bring men together to construct things in workshops (there is no reason we could not create Women's Sheds too).[52] Food Assemblies allow people to order groceries from local producers, before coming together in one space to pick them up.[53] An initiative called 'Playing Out' turns streets into temporary playgrounds. This creates a rare space for children and parents to mingle with the neighbours – a valuable activity that has grown increasingly rare.[54] A few communities have set up 'Street Olympics' and certain small residential areas in Kent have 'Village Olympics', where neighbours can compete in a range of activities from serious sports to light-hearted games. Secular services, which replicate the virtues of religious services, can bring people from all belief systems together under one roof to sing, chat and listen to thought-provoking ideas.[55] 'Songs & Smiles' brings people of all ages together through singing. The 'Chatty Café' scheme creates tables for customers to sit at if they are happy to talk to others. 'GoodGym' is a community of runners who stop off in the middle of their runs to perform physical tasks to help more vulnerable members of the community.

For many years, I have been a champion of Chance UK, a London-based organisation that creates meaningful relationships between children in tough situations and older mentors. Adult volunteers create bonds with a specific child for a year-long period, encouraging them to set goals, try new activities and get closer to family members. It is not just the mentored who benefit from the experience. One volunteer mentor at Chance UK, a young professional in a city job, recently told me: 'I feel blessed for doing this. It has opened my eyes to a world and culture I would never have known.'

Historically, from villages to urban centres, pubs have provided a meeting place where social networks are built and deepened over the social lubricant of cold lager, warm ale and refreshing gin and tonics. For generations, pubs have provided the setting for informal evening conversations, as well as formal community events. It is no coincidence that Britain's most popular soap operas have set many of their greatest plotlines in the pub. The Queen Vic in *Eastenders*, The Rovers Return in *Coronation Street* and The Woolpack in *Emmerdale* may be fictional, but they are a testament to the importance of your local drinking hole to community life.

It is a tragedy that eighteen pubs in Britain are closing every week.[56] Pubs are not only places for roast dinners and boozing. National government should act fast to protect them as rare places of community-building. As recommended by the IPPR think tank, we should apply a 50 per cent business rate relief for pubs and other 'centres of community'.[57] Pubs should be able to apply for loans and grants from the third sector to develop the community-oriented side to their businesses.[58] And the loophole that allows pubs to be demolished without planning permission should be scrapped.[59]

Centres for learning and education often provide more value than just the content of the courses that they offer. When my own mum arrived in the UK in the 1970s, she lacked skills and was uncertain how to gain them. When she found out she could go to our local college in the evening, after she finished work as a home help, her whole life path changed. She trained in typing and shorthand. Thirty years later she was able to celebrate her retirement from a management position at Haringey Council. She was never trained in management, but college classes allowed her to bridge the gap from unskilled to skilled work. Most important, they established a route for her ambition to follow. An encounter culture must be about more than social spaces: it should offer all parts of society the chance to dream big and grow. We desperately need to bring back night schools and introduce new-technology learning centres. This will help ambitious people with full-time jobs to catch up with the changing times. If we can close the gap between 'the educated' and 'the uneducated', 'skilled' and 'unskilled', 'winners' and 'losers', we could help make 'Two Englands' become one.

A UNIVERSAL CITIZENS' INCOME

Susan, who came to my constituency advice surgery one Friday in 2018, is typical of many single mothers in Tottenham. She has two children, aged ten and four. The four-year-old is disabled and relies on splints to walk. When she got in touch, Susan worked four Sundays a month for a catering contractor, which provided just enough extra cash, combined with a couple of other income sources, to put food on the table.

Out of the blue one month, her employer demanded that she give them money back for an 'overpayment' that they claimed had occurred a few months earlier. Susan had not been aware of receiving any extra pay. She had no savings and knew that sending her employers the £156 they demanded would send her into the red. Wanting to do the right thing, she offered to pay back the difference in manageable chunks, at £52 per month. She would have to live even more frugally than usual for the next few months, but, ultimately, she could survive. This was not good enough for the catering company, which responded by refusing to pay her for the entire month of March. The result was that Susan had no money left to pay for heating, electricity or food. She told me she felt ashamed having to rely on a foodbank, which she thought should not be for 'working people' like her. Over the Bank Holiday weekend, she could not even afford to buy her children the most basic Easter egg. This made her feel like a failure as a mother, she told me.

The reality, these days, is that foodbanks have become a necessity for many who are low-paid, working in the gig economy or facing any kind of unforeseen cost. Shockingly, 32 per cent of the UK's workers have less than £500 in savings.[60] This leaves them just one unfortunate event (a family bereavement, a broken dishwasher, a car crash, an unnoticed overpayment by their employer or an illness) away from having no savings at all. In this state of precariousness, individuals have no choice over the work they can accept. Our current economic system creates a poverty trap from which it is almost impossible to escape.[61] Individuals living in deprivation have no opportunities to retrain, go to university or spend hours applying for a new job. And they certainly have no time or energy to actively participate in the civic life our society desperately needs. If people lack economic security, then it is difficult for community relations to flourish.

The economy we have built is based on technology that has connected people across the world, but this same technology has also made it easier for power and wealth to accumulate in the hands of the super-rich. While the rich have got richer, the poor have stagnated, and the inequality gap has widened. Despite the massive technological advances we have made, only 40 per cent of people think they have good opportunities to progress. Economic polarisation is only going to deepen as advances in artificial intelligence and automation further concentrate power in the hands of a few. If we do not take radical steps, there will always be a class of people who are too economically precarious to participate in society. It will be impossible to totally heal the divisions that exist today if we do not address inequality.

Reducing inequality will require a wide range of local, national and global reforms, which would require at least an entire book to explore systematically. One much-hyped, redistributive reform that could be transformative, in terms of depolarising our society, is what I will call a universal citizens' income (more often called a universal basic income). This would involve every adult citizen, regardless of income, receiving a monthly cash payment from the government. Being universal, it would immediately break down the stigma of receiving payments from the state. Meanwhile, because the payment would be the same to everyone, it would progressively benefit the worst-off the most. If Susan's wage was supplemented by the government, she would have been able to repay her employer without being thrown into the indignity of debt. She would not have been forced to live on charity. She could have treated her children over the Bank Holiday weekend with a modest Easter egg.

Lifting precarious individuals out of poverty is the most fundamental purpose of a universal citizens' income. The gains will be much wider than this – they will run across all sections of society. This is the other purpose of making the income 'universal' rather than targeting only the worst-off in society, as in a welfare system. You do not have to be in poverty to benefit from the freedom a universal citizen's income would provide. Everyone who works full-time, either in the professional world or domestically, would have the opportunity to use the extra cash to pursue new education, interests or leisure activities. For the civic-minded among us, an extra afternoon off per week, funded by the citizens' income, would be the perfect chance to take part in events, activities or clubs that bring our neighbourhoods closer together.

The knee-jerk response to a universal citizens' income is that it would be vastly expensive and make people lazy, encouraging them to sit at home watching daytime TV instead of working. Some have suggested it would lead to people guzzling cans of beer, necking bottles of wine or even snorting their way to class-A drug addictions to pass the time. The problem with both assumptions is that they are based on a fundamentally flawed, and overly negative, view of human nature. Places where forms of universal income have been trialled have shown reductions, not increases, in depression and addiction. It should be unsurprising that humans want to create fulfilling lives. Addiction is most often the result of trauma, isolation and alienation, not freedom, learning and new opportunities to mix with people.

While a universal citizens' income is undeniably a radical idea, in every single part of the world where ideas like it have been tested, it has worked. Alaska has been providing a universal income to every man, woman and child living in the state since 1982. The annual dividend is funded by state-owned oil revenue. It has ranged from around $800 per year when the price of gas was low, up to a record $2,072 in 2015. In 2018, social scientists from the University of Chicago and the University of Pennsylvania, Damon Jones and Ioana Marinescu, completed a study on how the annual windfall had affected Alaskan's attitude to work. Did it make them lazier? Absolutely not. The academics found that, on balance, 'the dividend had no effect on employment'. It did manage to eliminate extreme poverty almost entirely, give people more financial freedom and unlock new opportunities for people from all backgrounds.

Not every nation has vast oil reserves to turn into a state investment fund (the UK did, but Margaret Thatcher spent it on tax cuts for the well-off). Universal-income schemes have been trialled in many other places, from Kenya to India, North Carolina, parts of Canada and Finland, with remarkable success.[62] With Britain more divided than ever, it is time for us to trial a universal citizens' income of our own.

Given there is no prospect of a new state-owned investment fund, we will have to find funding from the richest parts of society. It will be a small price to pay for a more cohesive and united society.

COMING HOME

There was something special about the British summer of 2018. For politicians, it marked a blissful break between the seemingly endless referendums and general elections that marked 2014, 2015, 2016 and 2017. But most important, blistering sun combined with a surprisingly successful England World Cup run to create a carnival atmosphere. Pints flowed to crowds bursting out of pubs. Parks were filled with raucous children running around and playing 'it' as though this would be their last summer holidays. Bosses let workers out for longer-than-usual lunches. For a month or so, a divided nation felt as if it might forget its differences and come together.

England beating Colombia on penalties to reach the quarter-finals was the high point. This was the moment we became united by the surreal feeling that football genuinely could be 'coming home' after more than half a century of 'hurt'. It does not come around often. The last time I remember feeling as optimistic about England's World Cup chances was when David Beckham slotted home a penalty against Argentina back in 2002. What I found so warming about the 2018 campaign was the sheer number of people loving a sport that for the other eleven months of the year, and the three years before that, they frankly do not give a toss about.

It is a cliché that football has a magical capability to unite people of different creeds and colours, but it is true. I was lucky enough to meet Eric Dier, a versatile defensive midfielder for Tottenham and England, and the scorer of the winning penalty in the World Cup clash with Colombia. As an insufferable Spurs fan, I've watched him play since he joined us in 2014, scoring on his debut against West Ham. Showing him around parliament, I could not help thinking back to the winning penalty and how it felt like that goal was exactly what a divided England needed.

When we chatted about it, though, Eric reminded me that football does not always bring people together in the way that his goal against

Colombia had. Sometimes it feels like anything but an antidote to tribalism. He told me a story from when Tottenham were playing the German team Borussia Dortmund in the Champions League to illustrate this. Tottenham were 1–0 up, but all he could hear was 'Stand up if you hate Arsenal' reverberating around the stadium. It was as if the defining feature of supporters' identity was how much they detested their London rivals. And despite an emphatic 3–0 victory, there was a small section of fans who were more interested in hurling abuse at the away section than celebrating the result. Eric was looking for the word to describe the atmosphere, to describe the relationship between fans of opposing teams, to describe English football. That's when he said 'tribalism'.

As somebody who is much further away from the pitch than Eric, I offered my own two cents about the fierce rivalries that have come to define English football. I told him how for some fans I believe it is about power. In other areas of their life, many have experienced loss – a loss of their stake in society, a loss of control over their own circumstances. Football offers something bigger to identify with. So, when your team scores, you get a real sense of euphoria. And if you feel like you are winning, you will sure as hell let the ones who are losing know about it. The paradox of belonging exists in football as it does in society: what brings a group together also has the potential to divide that group from the rest.

Other times, though, it's less about yearning for a sense of agency and more about taking it away from others, as a means of confirming hierarchies of status. It is common for the away fans at Liverpool and Everton to sing 'Feed the Scousers' to the tune of 'Do They Know It's Christmas'. This is an appalling example of how, sometimes, football can be used as an excuse to express the most hateful kind of bile, all in the name of 'banter'. At times like these, it is hard to try and understand what is going on inside these fans' heads.

This kind of club tribalism, however, is reflected in brain activity. Areas in the frontal and subcortical regions of the brain differ significantly between supporters of opposing teams watching the same game.[63] These areas are associated with reward, self-identity and control of bodily movement. Different sets of supporters literally develop a different understanding of the same experience.

Oddly enough, there is not as much tribalism during a World Cup as there is in the Premier League. You might think that if you throw a bunch of Swedes into a London pub showing the England game, the combination of patriotism and alcohol probably wouldn't make for the most welcoming of atmospheres. But even the most insulting chant during that game – 'You're shit but your birds are fit' – though undoubtedly sexist, was at least intended by England fans to be good-humoured. During a World Cup, there is a genuine sense of cross-national solidarity, in addition to pride in one's own team – a recipro-cal recognition that we are here to watch the game we love. The majority are joined by our mutual love of football first. We are patriots second.

I'm under no illusion that this is everybody's experience, though, and for that reason I'm still undecided whether I buy in to the roman-tic notion that the World Cup brings people together. Sometimes, it instead appears more like an outlet for primitive nationalism. Rinus Michels, the coach of Netherlands when they lost to Germany in the 1974 final, once famously said 'football is war'. This was literally the case when a qualifier for the Mexico World Cup triggered a war between El Salvador and Honduras in 1969, leading to 2,000 deaths in 100 hours.[64]

During the 2018 World Cup, I watched Portugal play Spain at the Marchmont Community Centre in Bloomsbury. As I approached, pubs were packed with Portuguese and Spanish fans, eating, drinking and laughing together as they cheered on their national teams. I was there for an event hosted by North London Cares, a social enterprise that aims to bring together young adults with their older neighbours for social events to combat isolation, foster inter-generational solidar-ity, share skills, establish connections and improve well-being.

Based in Camden and Islington, North London Cares has hosted more than 2,000 social clubs since they opened in 2011, receiving international recognition for its contribution to the community. The socials range from film screenings and pub quizzes to cooking clubs, dance lessons and, that summer, World Cup screenings. The initiative has since spread across the country. The Cares Family now includes South London Cares, East London Cares, Manchester Cares and

Liverpool Cares, and has plans to grow further. If there is one organisation that uses the principles of meaningful encounters to bring people together who would not otherwise meet, it is the Cares Family. I have known its founder Alex Smith, a former staffer for Ed Miliband, for years. We got to know each other through politics, as well as, so it happened, a mutual love of football. I was happy to give Alex a glowing reference in his successful application to become a fellow at the Obama Foundation.

Usually when I watch a match, I am either with my kids at home or at White Hart Lane, surrounded by rowdy half-drunk men. At Marchmont Community Centre, I was mixing with a different crowd. The atmosphere was warm and welcoming, rather than tense and buzzing. I sat down and quickly started chatting with one of the older members of the group. Maria, eighty-two years old, reminisced about recent times when isolation and depression had left her spending most of her time at home with not much desire for anything. She only paused a few times, one of which was to announce the prize for the sweepstake: a fridge magnet from her recent trip to Barcelona. The beauty of such charities is their relative simplicity. Their sole purpose, both simple and powerful, is to bring people together to socialise. For Maria, North London Cares had become her family. Such an organisation can represent a lifeline for older people. Nationwide, 17 per cent of pensioners see friends and family less than once a week and 11 per cent less than once a month.[65]

While older people are the most vulnerable to loneliness, those aged between twenty-one and thirty-five are the second most at risk. Indeed, suicide is the biggest killer of men under forty-five, and one in five young mothers have stated that they 'always' feel lonely.[66] Crucially, the Cares Family is as much aimed at benefiting the young adults that come to its events as it is at the older generation. Especially in a large city like London, one can quickly feel isolated from the local community. I spoke to a group member in her late twenties called Jennifer, a young professional working for Lloyds Bank. While her job provided her with great financial stability, she struggled to feel proud of its social value. Giving up some of her time to North London Cares gave her a role that was meaningful in a way that her job was not.

That evening reminded me of the importance of having physical, meaningful interactions across generations. Despite being an obsessive football fan, I found myself quickly forgetting there was a match on at all as I became engrossed in conversation with others in the room. Among them was Elizabeth-Ann, a bright eighty-seven-year-old lady who told me of the last football match she attended at a stadium: the 1966 World Cup final at Wembley. She went on to tell me her life story, from being a journalist, a teacher and a film producer to working with the Spanish embassy under Franco. We could have kept our conversation flowing for hours.

The point of the Cares Family events is not just to create 'any encounter', but 'meaningful encounters', as highlighted by Gordon Allport all those years ago. For that to happen, participants of all ages have to attend on an equal footing. This is not young people volunteering to look after old people; it is young and old people actively choosing to share time together. It embodies a resistance to the narrative that the elderly and the young must live parallel lives. Both groups have a lot to learn from each other.[67] Young people get advice about careers and financial proficiency. Pensioners gain insights into technology and the latest trends in the modern world. Before arriving, I wondered why young adults were willing to spend their Friday night with older neighbours they had never met. This was not how I spent time off in my twenties. The answer was that the young get as much from the elderly as the elderly do from the young.

What is worrying, though, is that outside of organisations such as these, the gap between young and old is widening – 64 per cent of millennials (aged eighteen to thirty-four) do not have a single friendship with an age gap of thirty years or more. This is unsurprising in a society in which meaningful inter-generational interaction is barely part of the social fabric.

The success of the Cares Family is one of social entrepreneurship and friendships being formed across generations, but charitable organisations are too often operating as a last resort for individuals who have been rejected from society by cuts in adult care and public services, along with the decimation of their social networks. This institutional void can go some way to explaining the inter-generational divide.

Caring for the well-being of the elderly should matter to all of us, not because we should sacrifice some of the rewards that we receive from an individualistic economic system that otherwise goes unchallenged, but because we should all aspire to grow old in a supportive environment.

As the French Republic recognises in its national motto, liberty and equality are fundamental, but we need to stand up for fraternity, too. In addition to those relationships the state has with the individual, we need to consider how individuals interact with each other, how we build meaningful connections among ourselves. We are social beings, who are as dependent on our social communities as much as we are on our desires and capacity for hard work.

Given the importance of relationships in our lives, they must form a fundamental part of our politics, too. In addition to winning rights and liberation for families – such as women's rights, and mandatory maternity and paternity leave – we need to provide a story about the value of strong relationships. It is time to build an ethic of care as well as liberation. This is as true in the politics of the workplace as it is in the politics of the family. Workers' rights are fundamental. Companies owe their staff fair pay, holiday leave, sick leave, flexible working hours, development opportunities and more. But fostering solidarity between workers is of vital importance, too. The bonds we form with our classmates, colleagues, bosses, bus drivers, postmen, neighbours, families, friends and strangers are as vital to the good life as the rights we accrue. How we treat each other matters. We are mutually dependent.

We are all being pushed to our tribal extremes by a combination of a political economy that prioritises efficiency over cooperation and well-being; technology and social media that amplifies disagreement and encourages polarisation as much as it connects us; and a lack of community institutions that encourage people of all ages, ethnicities and backgrounds to interact. The destruction of our local communities is at the root of the tribalism we are experiencing. If we do not give people diverse, constructive and positive places to have meaningful encounters, they will inevitably satisfy their need to belong by some other means.

RADICAL LOCALISM

It is arguably too generous to suggest that the number of popular Conservative politicians in Liverpool can be counted on one hand. Since the 1970s, the northern city has become synonymous with anti-Tory sentiment.[68] BBC Radio 5 Live's reports that the 2012 Conservative mayoral candidate for Liverpool finished behind a candidate in a polar bear costume turned out to be false, but they were not far wrong.[69] The Conservative candidate finished seventh with a mere 4.49 per cent of the vote.[70] It may seem odd, then, that the long-serving Conservative cabinet minister and former deputy prime minister, Michael Heseltine, was awarded the freedom of the city of Liverpool in the very same year.[71] As a recipient of the city's highest honour, Heseltine now sits in an exclusive club along with the Beatles and William Gladstone. The Labour winner of the 2012 mayoral election gave it to Michael in recognition of his role in the 'renaissance' and 'regeneration' of Liverpool.[72]

Lord Heseltine's special relationship with Liverpool began when he became environment minister. Succeeding Labour's Peter Shore, he continued the Environment department's 'city partnership scheme', which required it to have oversight of seven cities deemed to be suffering from 'urban stress'. Like Shore, Heseltine took personal responsibility for Liverpool and Merseyside. The city was struggling in the post-industrial economy. It suffered from poor housing and education and a 60 per cent unemployment rate among black youth.[73] In his first eighteen months, the energetic, young cabinet minister laid plans to create a development corporation, listed the Albert Dock and announced the first annual garden festival to regenerate derelict land.

The relationship between police and the black community was strained, after disproportionate targeting of minorities in stop and searches under the 'sus' laws. These laws enabled police to stop and search people whom they suspected of loitering in a public place with an intent to commit an offence.[74] Legally, this meant they could be in breach of Section 4 of the 1824 Vagrancy Act, which states that 'every suspected person . . . frequenting . . . any place of public resort; with an intent to commit an arrestable offence' can itself be an offence'.[75]

This gave the police huge discretionary power to decide what they deemed to be 'suspicious'.[76] One hot summer evening in July 1981, the arrest of twenty-year-old Leroy Cooper sparked riots that lasted for nine days.[77] Amid the chaos, 500 people were arrested, 450 police injured and seventy buildings destroyed.[78]

Following the Toxteth riots, Conservative Chancellor Geoffrey Howe privately urged Prime Minister Margaret Thatcher to consider the option of 'managed decline' for the city. Howe wrote in a private letter: 'We must not expend all our limited resources in trying to make water flow uphill.'[79] Fortunately, Howe's advice was not taken. Instead, Heseltine was allowed to go on a three-week fact-finding visit to Liverpool.[80] He spoke to black community leaders and the police, visited council estates, and returned to cabinet with a paper entitled *It Took a Riot*, detailing his proposal for locally driven regeneration.

My first meaningful encounter with Lord Heseltine came during the 2011 riots in my constituency of Tottenham. At around 5.30 p.m. on Saturday, 6 August, a group of around 120 people arrived at Tottenham police station, having marched from the Broadwater Farm Estate. What began as a peaceful protest descended into absolute, unadulterated mayhem. Stones and bottles were thrown at the police station, a police car was torched and police officers were attacked. Rioters in the streets looted and vandalised shops and buildings. Some even attempted to set shops alight. When the chaos subsided, I could hardly recognise my constituency any more. The streets were littered with burned-out cars, broken glass from smashed-up shops and ash.[81]

No two riots are the same, but social and economic deprivation, heavy-handed policing, and feelings of alienation are often underlying causes. In 2011, the catalyst was the shooting of Mark Duggan by the police. The protest that followed culminated in a riot that led to looting and destruction across my home patch. Over the following days, the riots spilled over to Hackney, Brixton, Peckham, Enfield, Battersea, Croydon and other parts of London. Then there were 'copycat' riots across England – as far away from Tottenham as Birmingham, Liverpool, Manchester and Leeds. Michael Heseltine was one of many people to make contact with me during the riots. He called to ask if I could show him around. I remember him being struck by the size of

Tottenham in comparison with Toxteth. His experience was invaluable in coordinating a response.

Now eighty-six, Heseltine spends his time between the House of Lords and the business world, where he is still actively involved in the running of the Haymarket Media Group, a publishing company he set up in the early 1960s. I met him in his office overlooking Victoria Street in central London. He shares the space with an investment firm, as his publishing business is based elsewhere.

I was running late, but when I was shown into his office by his assistant, Michael was engaged in a phone call. When he got off the phone, he told me he still worked seven days a week: 'I wouldn't have it any other way.'

We sat down around a meeting table. After exchanging gossip on Brexit, I began by asking him to recount what it was like going into Liverpool after the riots. He said a conversation with a junior minister before the visit stuck in his mind: 'We've got to talk to these people. Get into the middle of it. Sort it out.'

'Yes, Secretary of State,' the junior minister replied, 'that is very desirable, but who are you going to talk to?'

'Well, find the leaders.'

'Secretary of State, it's not quite as simple as that. There is a Mr Big. Everyone knows who he is. He has got a large white Rolls-Royce. He owns the girls, he owns the drugs and he runs that community with a rod of iron. You won't talk to anyone in that community unless he gives the nod.'

'I can't do that,' Heseltine replied. 'I can't be seen by the *Daily Telegraph* talking to someone who's a drug runner.'

Though he avoided 'Mr Big', Heseltine did manage to sit down with some local leaders. 'I will never forget the first meeting,' he told me. 'The leaders of the black community turned to my special guard and took his gun away. That was the beginning of the meeting,' he said, laughing. 'It gives you a feeling of the atmosphere.'

'The key to that, in my experience, is what you've just said – you'll never forget the first meeting,' I said. 'Because there was a second and a third and a fourth and a fifth. What these communities don't tend to see is the individual, associated with the establishment, particularly

Westminster, coming back and making relationships over a sustained period. Not just stopping by and saying: "Bye, I'll leave my officials to it." '

Indeed, no meeting was as tense as the first. Heseltine made it his role to return to Liverpool on an almost weekly basis throughout the next year. Dubbed the 'Minister for Merseyside', he helped revitalise the city by working closely with the local council and making partnerships between the public and private sector. This was most notable through his 1990s City Challenge programme. At a time when the chancellor Geoffrey Howe was arguing for a policy of 'managed decline' for Liverpool, Heseltine refused to allow one of England's greatest regional cities to disappear. For starters, he cleaned up the river and used his garden festivals initiative to reclaim polluted land. He knew this was necessary to revitalise investment, particularly in the property market.[82] Heseltine worked to improve the Radburn housing estates of Cantril Farm and Netherley and the Georgian area of Canning, as well as the high-rise housing that had replaced Everton's Georgian terraces.

There remain real pockets of poverty and isolation in and around Liverpool.[83] More than 93,000 children are growing up in poverty within the city region.[84] Areas like Riverside, Walton and Birkenhead are hardest hit. Much of the blame for this deprivation is still attributed to Margaret Thatcher's governments, of which Heseltine was a key part, for failing to support declining industries. Notwithstanding the serious difficulties that persist, Liverpool is now home to powerful business infrastructure, truly global universities, medical schools and vibrant centres of manufacturing that were hard to imagine just decades before. So, what lessons can we learn from the successes and failures of regeneration in Liverpool to apply to the communities that feel left behind today?

'It's totally clear in my mind,' Heseltine said. 'In too many places, there's no one in charge. There's much too much functional monopoly from London. The functional monopoly is reflected at the local level in functional power.'

'Too much bureaucracy?' I ask.

'It is more precise than that. It is functional power. You have a chief constable, you have a social worker, you have a highways person, you have a housing [officer]. And there is no coordination.'

The failure to have one leader who can coordinate decisions across all areas produces no single person to take responsibility. Those with 'functional' control over a specific area, be it crime, housing or infrastructure, can simply blame someone else. There is no recognisable figure who can be held adequately accountable.

'That's why I feel so strongly about directly elected mayors,' Heseltine continued. 'To get elected in a city, you have to appeal to all parts of it. It's not like becoming a councillor . . . You've got all these safe Tory seats and all these safe Labour seats. [The language is:] "These are our people, bugger the rest." But if you have one person who has got to get elected for the whole community, it is much harder.'

I partly disagreed with Michael's analysis here. Majoritarian politics still leaves room for the mistreatment of minorities. As well as leaders like mayors, we need gatekeepers to hold them to account. This is the system in the capital, where the power of the mayor is scrutinised by London Assembly members. All the same, I am pleased that in recent years there has been real progress in terms of devolution to English regions. The creation of 'metro mayors' in Greater Manchester, Cambridgeshire and Peterborough, Liverpool City Region, Tees Valley, Sheffield City Region, the West Midlands, and the West of England has taken at least some power out of London. Democratically elected mayors, several of them with established media profiles, are responsible for devising and managing strategies for their region's economy, and with some control over skills, housing and transport.[85]

Steve Rotherham, metro mayor for Liverpool, has used his powers to create an online apprenticeships portal for the region. It is a single space for people to find training opportunities and for employers to market them in an area where many have few or no qualifications. Andy Burnham has focused a significant part of his metro-mayoral agenda on addressing homelessness in the Greater Manchester region. Burnham introduced a 'Social Impact Bond' that partners the local authority with social landlords to house rough sleepers and provide them with emotional support and training. If the social landlords are successful, they get paid. The scheme was oversubscribed in its first year. Rough-sleeping figures have stabilised or gone down in eight of

Greater Manchester's ten boroughs.[86] In Wigan, the number of rough sleepers has almost halved.[87]

Metro mayors have the potential to be the start of a radical process of devolution of power across England that could help to make people feel more empowered at the local level and encourage identification with our regions. More than half of England is still without metro mayors, or any devolution at all.[88] Those metro mayors that do exist have minimal powers over spending and taxation. This should be addressed. We should invest as much power over skills, housing, policing, schools, employment and economic strategy in the hands of mayors as possible.

Metro mayors are responsible for large regions that go far beyond the city centres and into neighbouring areas. But there also needs to be stronger leadership within small towns. As Lisa Nandy wrote: 'Only real devolution will provide a remedy, not the city-centric model created by George Osborne, which concentrates investment in cities in the hope trickle-down effects will be felt by surrounding towns.'[89] We must continue to pour energy and resources into city regeneration for as long as urban poverty and deprivation remain a part of life. Nearly four decades since Michael Heseltine first brought back *It Took a Riot* to cabinet, we have to recognise that towns are in deep trouble, too.

It is hard to think of two politicians with less in common than Lisa Nandy and Michael Heseltine. One is young, left-wing, mixed race, has a northern accent, was educated at a comprehensive school and represents a deprived area in the North of England. The other is a right-wing multimillionaire, former boarding school boy, well into his eighties, who now sits in the House of Lords. Lisa's political perspective is focused on structural inequalities and the insecurities of working-class people. On the other hand, Michael's worldview is more paternalistic, viewing the maintenance of public order as the priority. Yet both recognise the same key problem in modern Britain. At a local level, people have too little control over what goes on. As local government has been eroded, people have been left without strong local voices to represent them. Most people do not know the name of their MP, let alone their local council leader. This disconnect is a key part of the breakdown of our neighbourhoods.

The first step to addressing the crisis of belonging is empowering local communities. To do this, we must redress the balance of responsibility and leadership between different levels of government. Research has demonstrated that leaders play a huge role in setting the tone and agenda for the rest of the community. When individuals see one leader behaving in a certain way towards those outside of their group – either positively or negatively – this will have a cascade effect on members of that group's future interactions with outsiders, even if they were not involved in the initial interaction.[90] After each action or pronouncement, leaders can move their followers' views further in one direction.[91] Consider a Republican voter in 2016. Initially, she might not have liked Donald Trump's more extreme policy proposals (such as the plan to build a border wall) but saw them as an acceptable campaigning tactic that would help secure what she considered to be desirable economic reforms. Since voting for Trump, she now feels a tribal allegiance to Trump as a moral and political leader. By 2019, she is defending Trump's statement that non-white congresswomen should 'go back' to where they came from.[92]

Alienated individuals in tough neighbourhoods have every right to be angry. But the lack of strong leadership on local issues has left them vulnerable to sweeping populist solutions at the national level that will not help. New local leaders have the potential to direct their community's frustration towards the root causes of decline in their areas and turn this into positive energy to rebuild and renew.

John F. Kennedy told Americans: 'Ask not what your country can do for you – ask what you can do for your country.'[93] We should apply the same mantra to our neighbourhoods. Living in a community should come with responsibilities as well as rights. We should not expect perfect roads, regular bin collection, schools that cater to exactly what we desire and beautiful public spaces if we put no effort into creating them. Shockingly, however, when asked to vote, many of us do not even bother. In 2018, just 24.4 per cent of registered voters in Hartlepool's local elections bothered to use their ballot.[94] Across England, the average was 35 per cent.[95]

Part of the reason for this is the lack of national attention given to the role that councils play in the UK. Politics is framed solely as a national phenomenon, fuelling the notion that Westminster is the only place where political change can occur. Although this is clearly not the case, the perception that it is true has the power to generate apathy in people, the majority of whom do not feel like their councillors make a difference, which in turn dissuades them from voting in local elections. This compounds the broader, national forces of apathy that starve all UK elections of healthy turnouts, namely a widespread lack of trust in politicians, which became particularly potent following the expenses scandal.[96] More broadly, there is a perceived lack of representation. Some citizens think politicians 'are all the same', and others simply do not identify strongly enough with any of the available choices.[97] A less cynical view is that apathy is a product of rationality. Your individual act of voting will, of course, almost never make a difference to the outcome. And without a proportional representation system, which I have called for, it is often ignored entirely. When reasoning like this is combined with disinterest and a lack of information, voter turnout plummets.

If people will not voluntarily take part in the democratic process, we should consider making them. In Australia, where there is compulsory voting at the federal level, turnout is around 95 per cent.[98] For most of us, it costs very little effort to turn up to a local polling station every few years. For those with disabilities or particularly gruelling work schedules, we should make remote and proxy voting as accessible as possible. Any penalty for failing to vote must not be overly harsh, and citizens should be allowed to protest by voting for no one at all. The best way to do this would be to add an option on the ballot for 'none of the above'. The reform would massively boost turnout, increase engagement, and get people discussing and thinking about what it means to be part of a local area. And the increase in legitimacy that would come with it would further strengthen our case for more devolution from central government.[99]

But we need more than compulsory voting to make people feel as if they have a stake in their neighbourhoods. Almost no one has heard of them, but local authority constitutions already exist. Currently, they contain dry details regarding a council's standing orders, codes of conduct and other miscellaneous information.[100] These bureaucratic documents do not do justice to the potential benefits of a real, local-level constitution. Building on a new codified national constitution (which I will make a case for in the next chapter), we should allow local people to decide the values and aims that they believe could bring people together in their area.

The details of these constitutions should not be dreamed up by councillors or other politicians. Instead, we should have local constitutional conventions where everyday citizens determine what is uniquely important in their area through debate and discussion over public submissions. Participants should be selected randomly by a lottery process to produce a representative demographic sample of the local area in terms of age, gender, ethnicity and social group. Once the founding convention has occurred, this could become a regular event, perhaps every five years. At each forthcoming convention, a new group of delegates could make amendments, or add new values and goals to the local constitution, based on how the town has evolved. To foster more participation at the local level on a more regular basis, we can make use of more US-style town hall meetings, in which local people can discuss and debate local issues in a publicly provided platform. Another reform that would give people more faith in local government is to reform Council tax bands to make them both progressive and fair. It is scandalous that someone living in a Nottingham bungalow worth just £150,000 should face a higher council tax bill than the wealthy owner of £17 million, seven-bedroom, grade II-listed Westminster mansion.[101]

The result of handing more power to local communities to shape their own destinies will inevitably mean that some gravitate towards certain economic and social policies, while others move towards the polar opposite. I doubt that the people of Tottenham will embrace the same agenda as those from Wigan, Peterborough or Belfast. This raises the potentially harmful prospect of segregation and further division between communities. One local authority area will not only look different, sound different and celebrate different cultural events, it will now be encouraged to have different local values and policies. Some areas will be monocultural, holding on to their traditions and way of life as long as possible, while others will be multicultural, particularly in urban centres.

Before committing to a policy that gives municipalities more freedom to diverge from the national norms, it would be worth considering whether encouraging local communities to express their social, cultural and political differences might become a threat to, rather than a means of, achieving unity. The truth, however, is that diversity between communities already exists. It is just that currently these identities are not formally recognised. By allowing local areas to define and own their local identities, we will not necessarily drive them apart from others. Different levels of identity do not need to contradict each other. By re-emphasising the ability of communities to define themselves at the local level, they could become more comfortable with inclusive conceptions of national identity. Radical localism is a key ingredient for addressing the crisis of belonging that is pushing lonely and isolated individuals into new tribes. We are not going to fix isolation, withdrawal, loneliness and disconnection between communities purely by focusing on what goes on at a local level. In order to avoid increasing division, we need a new national narrative that can bring newly empowered local communities together around a broader, civic purpose: a national story we can all be a part of and believe in.

8

Rebuilding England

How we can create pride in a civic nation state

'We are not born for ourselves alone, but our country claims for itself one part of our birth.'

Cicero

Weaving left, I raise my arms to the sky, leaving just enough room for my friend to duck underneath my red ribbon. Weaving right, I crouch underneath their strip of blue. Each time, I wince in anticipation for the inevitable crash that never comes. The blur of colour lulls me into a soothing trance, as I skip around the ten-foot wooden pole. I am dizzy, nauseous and dazed. But I am smiling. I am a black boy on my school playing field in north London dancing around the maypole. I am no longer in control of where I am going, but I find comfort in the knowledge that elsewhere, in the Cotswolds, in Manchester, in Warwickshire, in Leeds, other boys and girls who I have never even met are enjoying the same organised chaos. I grip my ribbon so tightly that my hand begins to ache, because I do not want to let go of this feeling. The pattern is disorienting, but it is shared. I am lost, but I belong.

Belong to what, though? When I relive the memory of country dancing as a child, I feel English. But am I just looking back on my childhood in an overly nostalgic way? Am I convincing myself of something that was never really there? What I do know is that I get a similar feeling when I'm eating fish and chips on the south coast, when I'm watching Spurs beat Arsenal at White Hart Lane or when I'm having a pint of beer with an old friend in a creaking country pub. In these moments, the ribbon is in my grasp – I feel English.

The first time I became conscious that my English identity was distinct from British identity was when I lived and worked in the USA. As is common for many, it was only by living in a foreign country that I became aware of how my home country had formed and shaped who I am. As soon as I opened my mouth, Americans would label me English before anything else. That my Received Pronunciation flowed out of a black man's mouth only made me seem quainter and more exotic in my Californian law firm. They would ask me about Mr Bean, the Queen and the Spice Girls as if I shared tea and cake with each on a weekly basis.

Living in California, I missed everything about home. Part of what I longed for could fit within the broader experience of Britishness, but much of it was distinctly English. I spent days pining after Walkers' Crisps, cups of tea, the English countryside, Ribena and the grey rain of a typical English autumnal afternoon. I could not help thinking of the hot summers in the 1970s, swimming and splashing in the Tottenham Lido. I fondly remembered my first pints, aged just 17, while playing darts and snooker with other sixth formers at the Farmers' Arms pub in Peterborough.

I became most aware of my Englishness while living in America, but in my earlier life in Tottenham, I felt more British than English. My parents were at ease with Britishness. Although never directly articulated, for them this was a pluralistic identity, which they had always been familiar with, having grown up in part of the British Empire. British identity is represented by institutions and traditions we share – the Monarchy and the NHS, the army and Remembrance – as well as the winning arguments that have become values in our society – from religious tolerance and free speech to universal suffrage and anti-discrimination laws. My parents proudly subscribed to each of these. They were less comfortable with Englishness, which felt like a birthright they lacked a claim to. There is a part of me that is still the child of West Indian parents obsessed with the royal family. They liked the fact that Princess Margaret had a holiday home on the Caribbean island of Mustique, returning there twice a year for three decades. My mother was particularly obsessed with Princess Diana and became addicted to collecting her memorabilia. This was the British Caribbean world I grew up in. Today, when there is a royal wedding, I am glued to the screen along with most of the nation.

Although there were rare flashes of feeling English, too, just as when I danced around the maypole, it was not until I went to boarding school in Peterborough that I truly began to absorb a sense of Englishness. The rigid hierarchy and the emphasis on tradition at school marked its character as clearly distinct from the flexible, multi-cultural primary school I had started in. Each summer afternoon I spent playing cricket and eating strawberries and cream, each time I sang hymns in the city's cathedral, and each Sunday roast I was offered at a friend's house further cemented my new-found Englishness. The fact that I was a cathedral chorister played a large role. From a young age, right up until I left school, I became entrenched within Church of England mores and sensibilities.

I credit my formative years in Peterborough with making me one of the 80 per cent of people who live in England and strongly identify as being English. When I'm in a group of English peers, I become acutely aware of the kind of things we laugh at, the kind of knowledge we are impressed by and the shared cultural experiences to which we respond. Fundamental to Englishness is a profoundly silly, and sometimes bawdy, sense of humour. From Dick Emery, Benny Hill and Alan Partridge all the way to James Corden and David Mitchell, English comedians rarely fail to leave me in stitches. Watching Spurs, first with my father and now with my two sons, is a quasi-holy experience. So is the tingling feeling I get every four years when England play in the World Cup. Through making friends at university, I got to see so many parts of the country I would never have visited otherwise. Many were not Londoners. Grant from the Wirral, Simon from Berkshire, Phil from Kent, Steve from Norfolk and Andy from Jarrow showed me new corners of England that I came to love and I will never forget.

Nevertheless, whether I am allowed to identify as English sometimes feels like an open question. For some, it is an identity to which I am simply not entitled. 'Why don't you get in your canoe, and paddle back to N***** land' is just one piece of hate mail addressed to me in recent years, but it is sadly typical of what I receive in my email inbox, on Twitter and via the Royal Mail routinely as a black MP. These messages are designed to make me question my English identity. They tell me that I am not allowed to feel connected to the traditions and customs of this country because my skin is black, not white. They make me feel as if the ribbon is out of reach. Or rather, someone is trying to snatch it away from me.

Even with those who hold no ill will towards me, I often feel as if I have to earn, or at least prove, my Englishness. When I first entered public life, the eternal refrain of 'Where are you from?' chipped away at me. Often asked with the best of intentions, this question denies me the Englishness that others who look different are ascribed by default. It is a refusal, consciously or otherwise, to afford me the same identity that they afford themselves. It doesn't matter if I'm faced with a polite grin or a menacing stare, when my Englishness is so questioned, I cannot help but see a little Englander looking back.

When I first arrived in Westminster, I felt I had almost as much in common with the new MPs from Kent and Essex (who arrived unexpectedly in the 1997 landslide) as I did with my London colleagues. Their middle England worldview reminded me of life in the Fens. Working as an MP, you feel strongly rooted to the patch of land you represent. By this point it would have been impossible to deny my Englishness. Yet even as a young MP, I could never have expected to feel as English as I did when kneeling in front of the Queen, trying to keep my balance, after staying up all night to watch my friend become the first black president of the United States of America. Becoming a privy councillor in 2008, I demonstrated not only that I could feel English, but that I had been accepted as being English. I had become not only a part of this society, but an immensely privileged part of it. I belonged in England. I was found.

ENGLISH OR BRITISH?

In the United Kingdom, our sense of national identity is naturally complex. Each of us lives within one of four nations that exists within one broader state. The promotion of Englishness, Scottishness, Welshness or Northern Irishness inevitably affects our sense of Britishness, and vice versa. Promoting one may risk eroding another. Ignoring one may allow another to flourish. It is a difficult balancing act.

The introduction of devolution, under the first New Labour government, was a pivotal moment in the ongoing shaping of the United Kingdom's overlapping identities. The Scottish, Welsh and Northern Irish identities grew stronger as a result of being given their own political institutions. The creation of the Scottish Parliament in Holyrood, the Northern Irish Assembly at Stormont and the Welsh Assembly in Cardiff created formal civic centres for each identity. England was left out. England's separation from the new project of devolution, while every other constituent nation's identity was encouraged, has been an important factor in causing a kind of national identity crisis. About one third of people in England say they are 'English or more English than British'. Another third consider themselves to be 'equally English and British', while 22 per cent of people identify as being 'British or more British than English'.[1] English men and women are not decided on whether to call themselves English, British or both.

There is clear and revealing regional variation. In places like Lincolnshire and the Midlands, more than nine in ten people feel strongly English. In London, Oxford and Cambridge, this ranges from just 32 to 45 per cent. Only half of people in Liverpool and Manchester feel pride in being English, compared with around two thirds of people in coastal and former industrial towns. Those who feel most strongly English are those who fit the 'left behind' label. Britishness has started to represent a more inclusive, cosmopolitan national identity – represented most clearly by Danny Boyle's 2012 Olympic opening ceremony. This complexity is nothing new. Tom Nairn, a Scottish political theorist and academic, wrote that the UK has:

A variety of titles having different functions and nuances – the UK (or 'Yookay' as Raymond Williams relabelled it), Great Britain (imperial robes), Britain (boring lounge-suit), England (poetic but troublesome), the British Isles (too geographical). 'The country' (all-purposes within the Family), or 'This small Country of Ours' (defensive Shakespearian).[2]

As the meaning of each title bends and takes on new meaning, it affects how UK citizens identify and see themselves. The job of a state controlling a union as complex as our own is not to prioritise one of these identities over another. It is to make sure we are comfortable with our layered identities, balancing what it means to be English and British, for example, at the same time.

In recent years, UK governments have worked hard to promote Britishness, as well as Welshness, Scottishness, and Northern Irishness, but Englishness has been somewhat forgotten. This imbalance is one of the major causes of the instability in the union today. The 2016 Brexit vote, for example, was largely a decision by people in England, many parts of which voted overwhelmingly to leave the EU in protest at the way the country has in their eyes changed.

Following the Tory landslide in England and the SNP's landslide in Scotland at the 2019 general election, the break-up of the UK has never felt more probable. In the wake of the results, SNP leader Nicola Sturgeon, who had just won 48 out of 59 seats in Scotland, said, 'it's very clear that Scotland wants a different future to the one chosen by much of the rest of the UK' and outlined plans for a second independence referendum. The confrontation between Scottish nationalism and a rising ethnic English nationalism, without enough common ground to be united by the broader British identity, is just one existential tension that has been exposed. Boris Johnson's election victory also guaranteed the implementation of his withdrawal agreement and the creation of a border between Northern Ireland and the rest of the UK. This separation increases the chances that Northern Ireland will unite with the Republic of Ireland one day in the not-so-distant future.

If we are to address dissatisfaction, political tribalism and imbalance in the UK, we need to rebuild, or at least reimagine, England. My goal in this chapter is to work out what reforms at the English level, and at the UK level, can help us to do this. It is impossible to fix Englishness in isolation from Britishness, as the two are so intimately interlinked. Therefore, some of my ideas will target England directly, such as a new English citizens' assembly. Others, like my call for a new, codified constitution, are explicitly at the UK level, though they will fundamentally depend on a new role for England, recognising the complexity of a multinational UK.

CIVIC NATIONALISM VS ETHNIC NATIONALISM

The tension between my feeling English and others' attempts to deny my Englishness comes from a conflict between two competing understandings of what it means to have a nationality.

Ethnic nationalism is the idea that the nation is defined as the natural home of a people whose ancestors all come from one place and from one specific ethnic group. It is racially chauvinist, and it legitimises the prioritisation of individuals with certain 'native' characteristics over those perceived as being different. Ethnic nationalists emphasise the 'common roots' or 'blood' its people share. They talk about the emotional attachment to a place they were born into, rather than the rational attachment to a society they choose. Ethnic nationalism is the root of the new populist nationalist right – it explains much of the politics of Donald Trump, Boris Johnson and Nigel Farage. Its logical consequences include increased hate crimes, Theresa May's 'Go Home' deportation vans and the racist abuse that black public figures like me receive daily.

Civic nationalism, on the other hand, suggests that a common national identity can be built around shared values and national institutions. It says citizens can find pride in what the people of one nation have built together, but also what they want to build in the future, in the vision of their shared ideals. Civic national identity relies on the construction of public spaces in which people engage with other people who look, sound, think and live differently from themselves. Close variations of civic nationalism include multicultural nationalism and progressive patriotism.[3] For any or all to work, there needs to be literal and metaphorical common ground for people from different backgrounds, generations, religions and regions to come together and share different points of view.

While ethnic nationalism comes from a nativist desire to return to some mythologised time, civic nationalism comes from a reformist desire to build and improve society around shared values and the realities of modern life. The USA is a prime example of a civic nation. There is no such thing as an 'ethnic American'. The country is instead built around shared values of freedom, democracy, cooperation and entrepreneurial initiative. While the rise of Donald Trump has raised questions around whether ethnic nationalism is now taking hold, in the recent past America provided an example of how people of varying ethnicities can unite around what they have in common, rather than their genetic roots.

Meanwhile, leaders from across the political spectrum have, in recent years, resisted a civic Englishness, presumably worried that it would cause offence to the smaller nations of Scotland, Northern Ireland and Wales. Politicians in Westminster have done their best to ignore the burgeoning English identity, focusing on what it means to be British. Following Tony Blair's Cool Britannia, Prime Minister Gordon Brown explicitly tried to promote a British identity over an English one, in part to address questions about his suitability, as a Scot, to lead a country with a population dominated by the English.

In the 2016 referendum, Britain Stronger in Europe campaigned in Scotland as Scotland Stronger in Europe, in Wales as Wales Stronger in Europe, but in England as simply Britain Stronger in Europe.[4] Similarly, political parties in Westminster act as though devolution of key policy areas never happened. As John Denham observed, in Labour's 2018 policy consultation on issues that largely affected England, only one of eight of the policy papers even used the word 'England'. English men and women with patriotic pride in their country would be forgiven for thinking there is a political conspiracy to avoid speaking about 'England' until everyone forgets about it entirely.

This is not helped by the fact that any use of 'England' that is not strictly necessary is airbrushed out by the media. During the 2018 World Cup, manager Gareth Southgate proudly proclaimed: 'We're a team with our diversity and our youth that represents modern England.'

The *Guardian* headline following the interview was 'England team represents modern Britain'. As Denham also pointed out, this is not just 'lazy reporting'.[5] It is an example of the press eradicating the last remnants of acceptable English identity and replacing it with something more palatable: Britishness.

With few or no legitimate outlets for civic Englishness, a sharp rise in English ethnic nationalism, tied to an ugly, anti-migrant, right-wing ideology, has been able to fill some of the gap. It would be easy to mistake the collapse of both the English Defence League and the British National Party as a collapse of the far right more broadly. Relying on broad and directionless anti-Islam rhetoric, disputes over both groups' concrete beliefs and policies made their eventual fracture inevitable.[6] Unfortunately, however, the demise of these groups does not mean the death of the English far right. Rather, the members holding these views simply hitch a ride with the next racist vehicle until it breaks down, at which point they stick out their thumb waiting for another driver.

In 2018, thirteen supporters of the British white supremacist National Action group were convicted under terrorism legislation.[7] The former head of the Metropolitan Police's counter-terrorism unit, Mark Rowley, warned: 'For the first time since the Second World War, we have a domestic terrorist group. It's right wing, it's neo-Nazi, it's proudly white supremacist, portraying a violent and wicked ideology.'[8] In June 2018, Britain saw its largest far-right demonstration since the 1970s, with 10,000 marching down Whitehall to protest the imprisonment of Tommy Robinson. UKIP, which at least used to attempt to distant itself from the overtly racist views held by many of its members, is 'now explicitly a far-right party', according to the anti-fascist organisation, Hope Not Hate.[9]

It is important not to exaggerate the closeness of the link between English nationalism and the far right. Half of English people identify their Englishness as being seven out of seven in strength.[10] Only a tiny minority of them are far-right supporters. Regardless, it is a national tragedy that we have allowed the far right to exploit the vacuum at all, and to appropriate our English flags, symbols and national anthem around an ethnic idea of what it means to be English. It is bitterly ironic, given that our nation's greatest moment in the twentieth century was defeating fascism, that we now have home-grown fascists running around claiming our country's symbols as their own. If we do not counter this toxic ethnic nationalism clearly and effectively now, it could destroy much of the tolerance and peace we have spent years building as a society. We need to construct an attractive civic nationalism to go in its place.

THE NATION STATE

While it is impossible for most of us to imagine how life was structured before nation states were first established, they are novel in the scale of human history. They developed through centuries of evolving laws and systems, as well as economic and political principles. Revolutions, wars and power grabs undermined and reformed individual states, until relatively stable nations first began to emerge in Europe. Nations replaced previous trading entities such as city states, kingdoms and other economic clusters that operated in the thirteenth, fourteenth and fifteenth centuries.[11] As global trading routes grew in the sixteenth century, from the Mediterranean and ultimately across the Atlantic, the nation state matured, culminating in the Treaty of Westphalia in 1648, which ended the Thirty Years' War. This agreement outlined several key principles in the transference of sovereignty to the nation, many of which have survived to this day.[12] Westphalia enshrined the idea that one nation should not interfere in the domestic affairs of another and that only states – not churches or other entities – could exercise political power, as well as introducing the notion of diplomatic immunity.

The French revolution in 1789 marked the creation of the first major modern state. The nation became a vehicle for defending the sovereignty of every citizen, or 'the people', against the monarchy. Emmanuel Joseph Sieyès, one of the leading political theorists of the French Revolution, wrote: 'The Nation exists before all things and is the origin of all. Its will is always legal, it is the law unto itself.'[13] In its infancy, then, the nation state was not built on ideas of ethnic purity, or even shared language and culture.[14] In fact, France in the late eighteenth century was made up of various groups, some of whom spoke different languages: Breton, Norman, Alsatian and Corsican, for example. From its birth, the nation state was about bridging divides between different tribes. The nation was a political project that sought to unite a diverse population around a common culture and aspirations for a shared future. It was a great equalising force, which maintained that whether you were an aristocrat or a farmer, you were a citizen.

In Britain, however, change was less far-reaching. Our own 1688 revolution did not take sovereignty away from the royal family and hand it to the public. Instead it remained a top-down constitutional arrangement, with sovereignty moving from the crown to a government accountable to parliament under the crown. As before, power rested with the elites in charge, rather than citizens themselves. The dominance of the royals in the UK has admittedly receded in practical terms, but through names, titles and language, the British public are repeatedly reminded of secondary status. We are subjects first and citizens second. We are part of a 'kingdom', not a 'republic'. Our national anthem is 'God Save the Queen', not 'God Save the People'. If you want to go for a picnic in London, you will most likely choose from one of eight 'royal' parks. Venture out of the capital and you can visit Royal Tunbridge Wells, Royal Leamington Spa or Royal Wootton Bassett. We send our letters in the Royal Mail. Homeowners have nothing but an interest in the monarch's land. When I became an MP, my first duty was to swear my allegiance to the crown, not to the public.

It was not until nearly a whole century after the birth of the first modern nation state in France that nationalism began to take on a less liberal, more ethnocentric streak. Right-wing intellectuals began to think about the nation state in terms of racial or cultural purity in reaction to, and in defence against, a fast-moving and fragmenting world. The backlash to the first wave of globalisation arguably fertilised the roots of ethnic nationalism, which wreaked havoc in the twentieth century and shares many parallels with populist resurgences today. Ethnic definitions of the nation began to dominate in late nineteenth-century Europe, as new countries, including Italy and Germany, started to form out of regional states under one common national identity.

Ethnic nationalism, not defined by membership of a specific political project, but by ethnicity and roots, is based on an assumption that minority cultures are inherently in conflict with the national culture.

For this reason, migrants and foreigners are treated as a threat to be resisted, rather than potential fellow citizens to be welcomed. The father of English ethnic nationalism in the modern era is the late Conservative politician Enoch Powell. His 'Rivers of Blood' speech in 1968 articulated the racially constructed concept of the nation. He warned that by embracing mass migration, the country had gone 'literally mad' and that 'in fifteen or twenty years' time the black man will have the whip hand over the white man'.[15]

This speech was not the first occasion ideas of ethnic nationalism had been considered by leading figures in the Conservative Party. In fact, ahead of the 1955 general election Winston Churchill privately told his cabinet that 'Keep England White' was a good slogan.[16] Powell's public articulation of these supremacist ideas had the power to legitimise ethno-nationalism in this country for decades to come. Just one year before she became prime minister, in 1978, Margaret Thatcher said 'the British people who have given so much to the world' were understandably afraid of being 'swamped by alien cultures'. Echoes of this worldview were obvious throughout the rise of UKIP, which at various times called for the end of laws that prohibit discrimination on the grounds of race or colour[17] and described the 'Islamification' of Britain as a 'serious existential crisis', while its most recent leader, Richard Braine, has argued that Muslims arriving in the country should be subject to a special 'security-based screening policy'. The 'Powellite' cry to send ethnic minorities 'back to where they came from' remains an all-too-common refrain in modern Britain.[18]

England has a long history of migration that is inconsistent with an ethnic understanding of our nationality. After the Romans left Britain, around AD 400, our island was characterised by a clash between different cultures and tribes: from the French to the Germanic, Celtic and Norman. This melting pot forged the new society that would become modern Britain and England today. It explains the English language – itself a mixture of Germanic languages, Latin, the language of the Viking invaders, Old Norse and Anglo-Norman French.

Our country has been a refuge for endangered peoples throughout history. During the years of Louis XIV's reign, around 50,000 French Huguenots crossed the Channel to make their homes in Britain, becoming England's 'first refugees'.[19] Persecution of Protestants throughout the eighteenth century swelled this number further. The impact of the Huguenots on English culture was vast. Many were skilled craftsmen, watchmakers, weavers and silversmiths, as well as professional doctors, soldiers, teachers and clergy. In the late 1800s, Britain welcomed 120,000 Jews fleeing Tsarist Russia. Before the outbreak of the Second World War, the UK had accepted 70,000 refugees from Hitler's Germany. After that war, more than 250,000 from across Europe settled in England. In the late sixties and early seventies, 70,000 Kenyan and Ugandan Asians found sanctuary on British shores. Eleven thousand Vietnamese boat people followed a few years later. Meanwhile, roughly 10,000 Cypriots fled to the UK in the mid-seventies.[20]

Critics of the argument that Britain has a history of immigration suggest that previous migrations were fraught with tension. Indeed, the *Anglo-Saxon Chronicle*, which describes the various groups that made up the people of 'Engla Lond' around the turn of the first millennium, are filled with blood and violence, as native groups tried to resist invasion from the Danes and the Normans.

It is true that the scale of immigration in modern Britain has risen over past decades, with a peak in net migration of 336,000 in the year ending June 2016.[21] The point, however, is not to argue that levels of immigration are the same as in previous centuries. Instead, it is first to observe that immigration has been a part of every stage of our history, and second to argue that we are now in a historically unprecedented position to accept higher numbers of immigration than before.

The world is far wealthier, connected and more reliant on free movement of labour than in previous centuries. The UK's ageing population and gaps in public services make it dependent on high levels of migration. This is a truth that previous British governments have acknowledged. After World War Two, tens of thousands were invited from the Commonwealth to help build the institutions, like the NHS, of which we are most proud. In 2004, the UK was one of only three countries that refused to put restrictions on migration from the eight countries joining the EU. And before the introduction of the Aliens Act in 1905, there was not even a system of immigration controls for those arriving in Britain. We do need immigration controls in the modern world. However, renewing a spirit of openness will not undermine our nation, it will strengthen it. The most compelling form of patriotism is not closed; it reaches out and welcomes willing volunteers from outside its borders to join in on the national project.

BUILDING A CIVIC NATION

A civic nation can only develop when there are enough shared values and preferences among its citizens.[22] This kind of coherence between a nation's people can evolve organically. Nation building – the art of constructing a national identity using the power of the state – can also have a role to play. In the modern era, nation building has most often been used as a means of preventing civil war and conflict and for new nations forming in complex historical contexts.

All the same, the logic of nation building can also be applied to developed modern democracies.[23] Shared ideals and a common narrative within a nation are always broadly beneficial to a nation's citizens, regardless of whether there is a threat of violence. Better transport links will prevent certain citizens or regions from becoming disenfranchised and isolated. The teaching of a shared language will make it easier for all citizens of one nation to get along. A diverse curriculum based on shared principles in schools will promote more tolerance and better understanding across society. The state, civil society groups, businesses and ordinary communities all have roles to play in encouraging a new sense of collective responsibility for making a good society. From the top down and the bottom up, there is work to do.

As the late Stuart Hall explained, nations are largely 'symbolic communities'. National symbols and institutions provide a way of constructing shared meaning. This in turn can influence how individuals in a society act.[24] At their most powerful, civic institutions and symbols can foster a sense of 'national destiny'.[25] An institution or symbol can be used to prioritise one set of values over another, or to exclude other key values within a nation. The Union Jack, which merges the Cross of Saint Andrew with the Cross of Saint Patrick, around the Cross of Saint George, shows how powerful symbols can be: by merging the patron saints into one flag, the message of unity is clear. The same symbolism was repackaged and updated for the vision of Team GB, which reflected the better sense of ourselves in the summer Olympics of 2012.

In order to build a civic nation, a coherent national culture must be established. The French state accepted this truth before many others, using the preservation and promotion of historic monuments as part of a deliberate strategy to create 'myths and symbol about "the French nation"'.[26] Cultural heritage policies are a direct way for the state to define, emphasise and mobilise cultural history to make its citizens more united. The Canadian Liberal governments between 1993 and 2006 similarly used national symbols, including street names, banknotes, rituals, flags and state ceremonies, 'to inform and shape the content of a collective national identity'.[27] They also published a citizenship guide entitled *A Look at Canada,* which promoted the narrative that Canada is a multicultural nation of immigrants, with two official languages, and a country of regions.[28] These initiatives appeared to have been successful: Canadian national identity became intertwined with a strong feeling of internationalism.[29]

Canada is also an example of how nation building is an inescapably political endeavour. In 2009, the Conservative government replaced this citizenship guide with a new one, entitled *Discover Canada.* This included a markedly increased emphasis on the military and warfare – the term 'war' is mentioned forty-six times.[30] It was mentioned just twice in the previous guide. It also gave much greater attention to Canada's relationship to the British monarchy, discussed the responsibilities of citizenship, and emphasised the importance of law and order.[31]

Post-Soviet states have relied heavily on projects and processes of nationalisation to differentiate themselves from each other as they abandoned homogenisation and entered the globalised, liberal, democratic world order. Estonia is a prime example of how a national civic identity can be rebuilt and 'rebranded' in the modern era. The country only declared independence from the Soviet Union in 1991, but now has a very plausible claim to being the most digitally advanced state in the modern world.[32]

As early as 2005, the country became the first to facilitate online voting in national elections, using blockchain technology to do this even before it was used as a decentralised ledger for Bitcoin. In 2014, Estonia introduced e-residency, which through an identity card, a cryptographic key and a PIN code allows citizens to access national documents – ranging from educational documents to health records, tax details and property details – digitally. It even welcomes non-Estonian nationals to become e-residents, allowing them to register EU-based companies entirely online.[33]

Estonia has therefore built a new civic pride around being at the forefront of technological change. Speaking to other European leaders at an EU Digital Summit in Tallin, Estonia's capital, in 2018, the President, Kersti Kaljulaid, said '"I am President to a digital society." Continuing, she put forward a vision of a footloose, cosmopolitan and global national identity, "Our citizens will be global soon . . . We have to fly like bees from flower to flower to gather those taxes from citizens working in the morning in France, in the evening in the U.K., living half a year in Estonia and then going to Australia."

Though few nations have rebranded as distinctively as Estonia in recent years, nation branding has become a booming business world-wide. With almost 200 countries in the world today competing for the same investment, tourism and trade, many have been turning to consultancies that work with governments and politicians to brand cities, regions and nations.

The concept of a nation's 'brand' as opposed to its 'identity' is used as a metaphor to apply the logic of corporate brands to the form and content of a nation. A nation's 'brand' therefore is its 'image, reputation, style, identity, public opinion, influence, trust, mediatization, exhibition, visualization, self-representation, symbolic value, coordinated messaging, diplomacy, publicity, international cooperation, promotion, and even – with strong implications – culture'.[34]

The Institute for Identity (Instid) is one such consultancy taking advantage of the new demand for nation branding. One of the firm's most successful projects is its rebranding of Tatarstan, a republic of the Russian Federation with a population of just under 4 million. Commissioned by the government to produce a new way to market the region, Instid went further than a typical PR agency, by looking deep into the place's history. Settling on the time of the Bulgar kings, who ruled from the seventh to the thirteenth centuries, they produced an account of Tatarstan that they argued persisted to this day.

Undoubtedly, the purpose of nation branding is clearest in newer countries, like those formerly part of the Soviet Union and African nations post-independence. Nevertheless, the purpose of defining national identity is not only to shape how a place is perceived externally by holidaymakers and investors. It is also about finding common ground within the nation to encourage internal cohesion around an honest story about a place's history – a common journey that its people will pursue in the future.

'In England, there's an absolutely palpable need for someone to come and say: "This is what we are," ' Natasha Grand, one of Instid's founders, told me in a Portcullis House meeting room, overlooking the Palace of Westminster. She continued: 'We need to know who we are in this twenty-first-century information age, where there are young people travelling all around the world and people coming here in [their] thousands.'

Applying the techniques of a corporate entity to a nation has understandably faced criticism as a strategy and should be treated cautiously by those looking for deep reform.[35] With hindsight, New Labour's 'Cool Britannia' branding by supportive think tanks, which wrote about 'Rebranding Britain', was superficial and failed to bind the country's citizens in a deep and lasting way.[36] It also suffered from the ephemerality of fashion that makes branding very difficult to sustain. You can never guarantee that what captures an audience one week will draw a different crowd the next.

Instead of branding, then, we should think about refreshing our concept of England through nation building. To do this we need to look deeper than appearance and style. Crucially, it should not come top-down from a consultancy or PR agency; it has to result from a bottom-up national conversation. What are English values? Why are these values English? Why are they a desirable part of the good society? And how do we promote them?

Rebuilding the English identity, in a civic fashion, will affect, and require reform of, the whole of the UK. Some of the values I discuss in relation to Englishness will, unsurprisingly, also ring true for other parts of the UK. Similarly, some of the reforms will require new UK-level institutions and ideas. Together, we must work out the core of what makes England, Wales, Scotland and Northern Ireland individual nations, as well as one United Kingdom.

THE ENGLISH

Defining Englishness is notoriously difficult. Many have tried and failed, and most definitions that have been put forward are contradictory in one way or another. Many of the earliest attempts to define Englishness relied on ethnic nationalism: viewing the English as a group of people with the same ancestors and skin colour living on the same island. Yet as early as 1701, Daniel Defoe ridiculed the idea of English racial purity – and as a result ethnic nationalism – in his satirical poem 'A True Born Englishman'. In it, Defoe defined the English as a nation of immigrants, describing 'a mongrel half-bred race . . . Infus'd betwixt a Saxon and a Dane'.

Two and a half centuries later, George Orwell tried a different tack in his essay 'England Your England'. Orwell himself admitted: 'National characteristics are not easy to pin down, and when pinned down they often turn out to be trivialities or seem to have no connexion with one another.' Indeed, his own attempts to define the English as 'not gifted artistically' and 'not intellectual' do not hold true today. Orwell's descriptions of life in England now feel dated rather than universal. His account of '(t)he clatter of clogs in the Lancashire mill towns, the to-and-fro of the lorries on the Great North Road, the queues outside the Labour Exchanges, the rattle of pin-tables in the Soho pubs, the old maids biking to Holy Communion through the mists of the autumn mornings' would sound foreign to any teenager growing up in England today.

As Michael Kenny has noted, the practice of making lists – 'often without comment or justification' – to capture some shared essence of the national experience is in itself revealing about English culture.[37] Peter Ackroyd, Stanley Baldwin, Christopher Hitchens and Jeremy Paxman are among other public figures who have attempted to define what it is to be English through the power of a list.[38] The problem with these lists of symbols and objects is that no purely descriptive attempt to detail what it means to be English will satisfy everyone or chime with our vastly different individual experiences. Society is malleable, especially as one of the four nations of the UK, where flexibility is reflected in an unwritten constitution that allows for legislative and social elasticity. Neither will they provide a coherent guide around which the state can focus its work and reforms for a better society.

Others have attempted to solve the Englishness problem by suggesting values instead of objects and characteristics. Often the problem is that they are simply desirable rather than particularly English. When Ed Miliband listed 'a willingness to do things for others, without recognition or reward' in a speech about 'the essence of English identity' it felt more like an expression of what it means to be a good person. It is pointless to cite certain values that we like and then frame them as if they are somehow archetypically English if they have no connection to our history or way of life.

In 2014, the Department for Education announced that schools in England would be required to promote 'fundamental' values to their pupils. This attempt to define and develop the national character was based around fundamental British, rather than English, values. It chose 'democracy, the rule of law, individual liberty, and mutual respect and tolerance for those of different faiths and beliefs'. While it is difficult to take issue with any of these, it is clear they are deliberately broad and vague. Indeed, they could apply to any liberal democracy. They are no more British than they are French, German, Canadian, Norwegian or American. While this was a smart way to avoid controversy, it meant that the values felt cold and without character.

The language chosen by the British government was itself lifted from the 2011 Prevent strategy for combating extremism. Some critics have suggested that requiring schools to teach fundamental values prescribed by the government, without any consultation from the public, 'is likely to generate suspicion toward the "other" '.[39] Deciding on the values that will come to define England, and the whole of the UK, as it moves forward, should not be the job of any one politician or government. Crucially, in my view, it must result from a detailed and deliberative bottom-up process, involving representative groups across age, social class, gender, sexuality and ethnicity. In fact, this should be the first task of a new English citizens' assembly.

A descriptive list of national symbols and stereotypes will quickly expire in relevance and offer little guidance to citizens considering how they ought to live their lives. Meanwhile, a set of values that strays too far into vague, moral prescription will often not ring true or will fail to pick out anything unique about a national culture. A more useful articulation of Englishness should be both aspirational and grounded in reality. It should recognise that there are qualities that are particularly abundant and valuable within England, even if they are not universal. It should be about trying to find the best of England, not the worst. These values should come under regular scrutiny and be ready to adapt to changing times.

It is a daunting task. No definition of Englishness will satisfy everyone. None will hold perfectly true in 100 years' time. Despite the difficulty of defining Englishness, we should not be afraid of suggesting ideas to begin a national conversation. Three values I believe have a strong case for being considered fundamental to Englishness are Creativity, Openness and Fair Play. They are intended to be provocative rather than prescriptive, and suggestive rather than exhaustive. Any final shortlist of English values should be discussed, debated, edited and finally rubber-stamped by the English public.

CREATIVITY

What do the chocolate bar, the jet engine, the cat's eye, soda water, stainless steel, the World Wide Web and the light bulb all have in common? All are English inventions. Modern ingenuity owes much to Britain in general and England in particular. The emergence of reason, individualism, scientific rigour and exploration from the late seventeenth to the early nineteenth century transformed European society. Rejecting custom and tradition in favour of a more creative outlook, the Enlightenment has its roots in the English Civil Wars.[40] Following years of bloody conflict, philosophers like John Locke studied ancient Roman and Greek civilisations to consider how a good society might be better organised. Locke argued persuasively that human consciousness provided a path to understanding the world better, rejecting 'the notion that human knowledge was somehow pre-programmed and mystical'.[41]

But it is not only in science and technology that England has been a world-leading creator. Our language is the second-most widely spoken across the world, with 983 million speakers, and is the global lingua franca. From the Beatles to One Direction, English musicians have always had the power and social capital to dominate the world's charts. Our literature, plays, films, and television – from the high art of Shakespeare to the crass amusement of *Top Gear* – have continuously punched above their weight, entertaining and enlightening people across the globe. We are the only country, other than the USA, to have three universities in the world's top ten.[42] Our comedians have continued to export laughter, with remakes of sitcoms like *The Office* the greatest flattery, and prime-time US talk-show hosts John Oliver and James Corden both born in England.

Our cultural and creative capital is vast. As a former cathedral chorister, married to an artist and having enjoyed my two years as culture and arts minister more than any other brief, there is no doubt I am biased. But in direct opposition to Orwell's damning verdict of the English as 'not artistic', I believe any understanding of what it means to be English must include our incredible power of creation.

A progressive English identity should be steeped in a proud recognition of the nation's role at the root of the best parts of Enlightenment thinking. The Enlightenment represented a new dawn for values such as liberty, personal freedom, logic and reason. While at the time these values were only applied to a small elite and property-owning class, justifying imperialism and colonialism, since then they have proliferated across society. At our best, we are innovators, and our focus on liberty and personal freedom has advanced many spheres of human achievement. From art to science, from literature to technology, and from television to philosophy, we are world leaders. I believe any reimagined English identity should be founded in a commitment to creativity.

OPENNESS

The openness of England has always been a paradox. While we know it as British, the roots of Empire from this island are very much English. The colonial expansion which eventually became known as the British Empire emerged during the sixteenth and the beginning of the seventeenth century with the English settlement of parts of the Caribbean and North America.[43] This was a time at which 'British' was close to meaningless to most inhabitants of the British Isles.[44] As well as oppression and domination, the Empire that came out of England was also about discovery and exploration. It meant trading teas, spices, fruits and fabrics with new corners of the globe, and, although the exchange was weighted far too much in one direction, it meant exchanging cultures, language and customs with new people.

As Krishnan Kumar found in *The Making of English National Identity*, the fantasy of an ethnically pure England is a recent construction. England has never been homogeneous in culture or had a strong tradition of nationalist celebration. This leaves the possibility for the creation of 'an open, expansive and diverse society' welcoming 'new peoples, cultures and ideas'. England, Kumar noted optimistically, 'typically looked outward from itself to the world'.[45] Peter Ackroyd, a prominent observer of English culture, similarly wrote: 'Englishness is the principle of diversity itself. In English literature, music and painting, heterogeneity becomes the form and type of art. This condition reflects a mixed language comprised of different races.'[46] And Billy Bragg agrees that England is defined by 'what we've achieved with our diversity' and how 'on the whole we rub along better than most, the way we react to people from a different background is more open'.[47]

On the one hand Kumar, Ackroyd and Bragg are right. But the uncomfortable truth is that not all of England is tolerant and inclusive. Public sentiment to immigration remains negative across Britain, but particularly in former industrial areas of England. Overall, 63 per cent of people think immigration into the country over the past ten years has been too high.[48] Government policies and slogans have tapped into anti-migrant rhetoric, cynically exploiting it as a vote winner. This has not only come from the right. Even the Labour Party has not been able to resist the lure of anti-migrant rhetoric. Ed Miliband will never live down the 'controls on immigration' mug produced in the 2015 general election. Five hundred years of colonial expansion cemented in the minds of some Englishmen a superiority to foreigners that is neither open nor tolerant.

This should not blind us to the fact that our country is far more tolerant than so much of the rest of the world. I believe we can work to create a society that moves beyond structural and systematic prejudice. My fundamental optimism about this does not come from statistics, but from meeting people from across England. During the 2019 general election, I had the pleasure of speaking to Englanders from Bolton, Bury, Birmingham, Cambridge, Watford, Wakefield, Halifax, Dewsbury, Croydon, Solihull and West Bromwich and across London. As I find every election, the English are far more open-minded than some statistics indicate. While certain politicians court and entrench divisions, most are just interested in improving their own lives. A clear majority of the public is motivated to vote based on hope for a better society far more than on distrust of others.

The Labour activists in my constituency of Tottenham epitomise this. Each election, they spend hours and days travelling across Britain to marginal constituencies – from Croydon to Derby, Hastings, Milton Keynes and Norwich – to campaign for a Labour government. The people in the Tottenham constituency Labour Party come from all races, ages, social backgrounds, but they are united around a common purpose. They do not do this unpaid campaigning for personal advantage. They do it because they want a more inclusive and just country. These activists represent the open-minded, civic spirit we can build on.

Another paradox of England's openness is the royal family. Archaic, class-based and in many ways not fit for the modern world, parts of it are more reflective of twenty-first-century modern England and Britain than many of our other institutions. The royal family has a female boss, whose son and successor is on his second marriage, and whose grandson has married a mixed-race American woman and is determined to break the stigma of mental health.

Parts of England are open and parts are closed, but the most successful parts of the country are often those which are the most open. The urban theorist Richard Florida provides a hypothesis for why this might be. Florida showed that the high presence of Bohemians – who tend to be creative, as well as promoting creativity, openness and diversity – in a place attract other talented people. In turn, this attracts more innovative and hi-tech jobs.[49] Indeed, this is one of the reasons why London – diverse, open-minded and with some of the highest levels of migration in Europe – is by far the most productive place in the UK and the second-most powerful city in the world – behind only New York.[50] Openness is a value that is worth pursuing and one that the state ought to promote.

If England is to flourish in the twenty-first century, we need to embrace the open side of our nature, not retreat into the closed-mindedness that has at times held us back. It is disingenuous to describe England as open and its people as open-minded without caveat, but there is enough precedent to make it our target. If a refreshed English nationalism is to be civic and not ethnic, to be forward-looking and not sentimental, it has to be open.

FAIR PLAY

The English are mocked for queuing, for our sense of justice on matters as trivial as reserving a sun-lounger at a hotel swimming pool and our visceral anger at an 'unsportsmanlike' dive during a football match. It is a cliché that the English are obsessed with fairness, but behind it lies a truth.

One of the country's most loved and respected institutions is the National Health Service – a universal healthcare system established by Clement Attlee's government in the wake of the Second World War. Even when Britain was exhausted and impoverished by the bloodiest conflict the world has ever witnessed, there was a drive to make sure that no one would die because they could not afford to pay a bill. Behind only New Zealand and the Australian state of Queensland, the UK was one of the first places to establish a universal healthcare system. In so doing, we helped to set a trend that would later spread across Scandinavia, Japan, Canada and elsewhere. Our enthusiasm for the NHS has not waned over time – in fact, spending has increased remarkably since Sylvia Diggory became the NHS's first patient on 5 July 1948. Yearly spending per head has grown from the equivalent of £260 in 1950 to £2,273 today.[51] The NHS has come to represent something deeper than just healthcare in this country. It speaks to the fundamental idea of who we want to be. Everyone who is able to work pays in, so that help is there for everyone when they need it, whether they can work or not.

To an extent, the English sense of fair play extends beyond our borders. We are the world's fourth-largest contributor of foreign aid, routinely fulfilling the UN mandated figure of 0.7 per cent of GDP. English Common Law is the most widespread legal system, covering 30 per cent of the world's population and used in 27 per cent of the world's 320 legal jurisdictions.[52]

Fairness is one of the reasons our country remains a popular destination for migrants. Indeed, according to Transparency International's 'Corruption Perceptions Index', the UK is the eleventh-least corrupt nation in the world.[53]

'Becoming British is a very important event in my life, because I feel that this country treats people like human beings,' Orlena Lavrenchuk, who migrated from Ukraine, told the BBC on becoming a British citizen.[54] Rather than needing to start with money and power to be successful, Lavrenchuk perceived Britain, and England where she lived, as a society where if you are 'honest and have enough skills' you will be able to do well. 'If I do things correctly,' she added, 'I can get success. In our country it is different.'

England has not always been fair. The truth remains that if you are born poor in the UK, you are likely to die poor. And though we do our best to erase these incidents from our history, we are a nation that played a major role in some of the greatest indignities the world has witnessed. Estimates for the number of those killed in the partition of India range from 200,000 to 2 million, while between 10 and 20 million people were displaced. Though this brutal episode had complex causes, the British Empire's strategy of divide and rule must take the lion's share of the blame.[55] Similarly, our role in the concentration camps in the Boer War, and our exploitation and transport of Africans to the Caribbean for slavery, cannot be whitewashed from our history.

At home in England, racial prejudice is still rife. There is a greater disproportion in the number of black people in UK prisons than in the USA.[56] As of 2019, 51 per cent of inmates in Young Offender Institutions are from ethnic minorities, nearly four times their representation in the general population. Ethnic minorities are three times as likely to have been thrown out or denied entrance to a restaurant, bar or club in the last five years.[57] They are more than twice as likely to encounter abuse or rudeness from a stranger.[58] And they are more than twice as likely to have been treated as a potential shoplifter.[59] These are unfair differences we cannot ignore.

Despite the contradictions that exist in our history and in our present, there remains something characteristically English about fair play. In rebuilding England, we need to put fairness front and centre. We should own up to our past mistakes. We should continue the fight to end racial, sexual and other inequalities at home. And we urgently need to rebalance wealth across the country, not let inequality fester and grow.

GIVING ENGLAND A VOICE

England is one of the most centralised countries in Europe and the entire Organisation for Economic Co-operation and Development.[60] While Scotland, Wales and Northern Ireland secured some level of devolution from the first New Labour government, England has been left without its own national political institution. Recent devolution to regional metro areas has been welcome, but they have been given limited new powers. Moreover, regional devolution does not solve the problem of there being no central crucible for English political debate.

The 'take back control' narrative in the 2016 Brexit referendum was so persuasive in England because English people are further from real power than their counterparts in the rest of the UK. The fact that England dominates the union through sheer number of MPs matters little to a powerless man in Wigan who has lost his job and has seen his local industries destroyed by changes he never voted for, with no choice or effective lever to pull.

In 2016, English Votes for English Laws reforms were introduced which gave further powers to MPs who represent English constituencies. The reforms meant that now when a bill – or part of a bill – is deemed to affect only England, a new stage is added to the law-making process at which only MPs for English constituencies can vote. This adds an important veto power for English MPs, but it still fails to give England a voice.

Many on the right of British politics, and an increasing number on the left, have started to argue that the solution to England's lack of voice is to create an English Parliament. This would give English citizens the same level of representation as Scottish, Welsh and Northern Irish citizens. It would also create a distinct English voice and help foster a stronger sense of English civic identity. To further break down the London-centric establishment in Britain, a new English Parliament could be based in the North, bringing jobs, status and power to a whole new region of the UK.

While the idea of an English Parliament is appealing in principle, it becomes deeply problematic once you start asking detailed questions. Should we hold separate elections for members of such a new parliament, or should Westminster send delegates to the new institution? If the former, would the English Parliament now compete with the British Parliament for power, given the huge imbalances in population between England, Scotland, Wales and Northern Ireland? If the latter, how would MPs have time to sit in two chambers at once? Would there be a first minister of England to mirror the first minister of Scotland? How would the dual mandate of the English first minister and the British prime minister be reconciled? Would the creation of an English Parliament lead to formal federalism and require stronger intergovernmental arrangements? How many members of the new parliament should there be? What form of electoral system would be used to elect the English Parliament? Should it rely on first past the post or bring in a proportional system? Would this reform raise questions about the worth of the House of Lords?

None of the many supporters of an English Parliament have proposed serious answers to these questions and set out in detail how it might work.[61] Indeed, having a separate English Parliament that represents 85 per cent of the UK population might just be too destabilising and cause the final split in an already fracturing United Kingdom.

Citizens' assemblies, which are becoming increasingly popular tools to supplement representative democracy across the modern world, are one potential alternative. They have been variously useful in Australia, the USA and on a small scale in the UK. Random samples of citizens gather in one place over a limited period of time to discuss a specific policy issue. Reflective of the nation or area's population in terms of demographics and relevant attitudes, these assemblies have two main advantages. First, they offer lawmakers a rare opportunity to gain in-depth understanding of public opinion on complex issues, and second, through reasoned, calm debate, they increase the possibility of achieving political consensus.[62]

The most publicised citizens' assembly in recent times was commissioned by the Irish government to untangle the complex and tense debate surrounding the right of women to have abortions. For years, politicians in Ireland had been reluctant to discuss or reform abortion laws, seeing it as a divisive and politically risky issue. In the groundbreaking citizens' assembly, ninety-nine ordinary citizens were coordinated by a chairperson appointed by the government. Over the course of five weekend sessions between November 2016 and April 2017, they discussed, debated and reviewed 300 submissions (of 12,000 received) from various interest groups and other citizens, as well as hearing from twenty-five experts with views from across the political spectrum.[63]

So far, citizens' assemblies have generally been used to find solutions to specific, tense policy debates. There is no reason why we cannot create a permanent citizens' assembly to reside in England. A new institution, including a symbolic building, a secretariat of civil servants and a media centre, could sit in Manchester or Newcastle or Sheffield, providing a voice for England, working on various policy issues, one at a time.

Just as in jury duty, adult citizens could be called up at random to form a representative sample of England. During their stint in the citizens' assembly, they would listen to policy experts, hold question-and-answer sessions and have round-table debates on one controversial policy issue for two to four weeks at a time. Lodged in hotel rooms and introducing new people from across the country, this common space for citizen debate would hopefully lead to reasoned verdicts on controversial issues.

While a permanent English citizens' assembly would not have the power to make law, and therefore might be criticised by the strongest English Parliament activists, it would provide written reports with policy recommendations for MPs in Westminster. The influence of this form of advice and agenda-setting must not be underestimated. The

Irish citizens' assembly delivered surprisingly radical recommendations on liberalising abortion, including calling for a referendum on whether or not to remove the Eighth Amendment of the Irish constitution, which effectively banned abortion. Just two years later, the country held a referendum. In the vote, 66.4% of the public voted 'Yes' for the Amendment to be repealed.[64]

The cost of a permanent English citizens' assembly would certainly be significant, but it would be smaller than creating a whole new English Parliament, with all the additional staffing and infrastructure that would entail. The value it would bring to the nation would be immeasurable, balancing rather than destabilising the complex union we find ourselves in following devolution.

REPENTANCE AND RE-EDUCATION

I remember sitting in history lessons at school in Peterborough in the 1980s. We learned about Henry VIII, the defeat of the Spanish Armada and of course Britain's victories in the First and Second World Wars. Great stories of British successes inculcated the founding myth of our nation. We are a small island that at various points in history has wielded outsized and global influence. We conquered half of the globe and spread our language with us. We helped to defeat Germany and its allies in a world war, not once but twice in one century. Our kings were so powerful that one was even able to break away from the Roman Catholic Church in its heyday.

History was not a compulsory subject in British schools until the dawn of the twentieth century. When the subject finally did become a staple in our education system, it was a based on a 'convergence of ideas of military conquests, patriotic support for imperial dominance and racial superiority'.[65] The American Civil War and slavery were largely airbrushed, with pupils taught to believe that Britain's expansionism served the colonised as much as it did the British.

After the Second World War, there was a reorganisation of the education system. At the time policymakers used their energy and powers to reshape local authority and school structures, rather than worrying 'about changing views and attitudes concerning the British Empire and its aftermath'.[66] Nevertheless, education about Empire was sorely needed. In 1948, one survey found that while 62 per cent of the British were confident that those living in the colonies were largely 'coloured', only 49 per cent could name a single British colony.[67]

In the second half of the twentieth century, education about British history hardly improved. In 1964, the Commonwealth Immigrants Advisory Council dismissively declared that 'a national system cannot be expected to perpetuate the values of immigrant groups'.[68] The standard textbook in this era, *New World Geographies*, claimed that 'mankind is usually divided into three races: (1) The Caucasian or White Race, (2) The Mongoloid or Yellow Race, (3) The Negro Race'.[69] This perpetuated the Social Darwinist classifications that for decades had provided the false intellectual justification for white supremacy. This textbook was still used widely in the 1970s when Theresa May and Boris Johnson were themselves at school.[70]

When I was at school, the question of why I – or other people who look like me – were in Britain was a subject that was never talked about. How could I be English when I was so clearly separate from those great kings and queens, and when all the world-war soldiers who appeared in textbooks were white? The subject of colonialism and Britain's history of exploitation and enslavement was rarely dealt with explicitly and is still not to this day. The only time people who looked like me were studied in school was in geography lessons. I remember feeling a mixture of shame and embarrassment whenever we were shown photographs of the African 'savages' living in mud huts and wearing ceremonial dress. The textbooks used simplistic stereotypes to portray Africans as peculiar, exotic and often downright inferior. As the only black person in the classroom, I felt I somehow had to explain what was going on in those pictures, as though they showed something deeply uncivilised about me and my family. It was a heavy burden to bear, and it became heavier and heavier with every set of eyes that caught mine as the teacher read the text aloud.

Throughout this period, the abuses of the British Empire were covered up, distorted or spun so as to paint British imperialism as beneficial to the people colonised. During the brutal partition of India, for example, contemporary British press reports blamed 'gangs of Muslims assaulting Hindus' as the fault of the Indian people, hardly mentioning the role or responsibility of the British.[71] Archival material that would have provided damning evidence of British misdeeds on foreign soil was frequently burned and even dropped into the sea to destroy evidence.[72] This practice most likely continued later in the twentieth century, with documents from the Falklands War in the 1980s and from the Irish troubles from the 1970s also 'lost'.[73] Collaboration between the British government, education system and media meant that the British public was never properly educated on the source of its wealth – and remains unclear to this day.

It was not only the British Empire's abuses on foreign soil that have been covered up by a jingoistic and distorted telling of our national history. Internal colonisation by the English created the United Kingdom as we know it today. England bound itself to Scotland in an Act of Union in 1707, nearly two centuries after its annexation of the whole of Wales in the Wales Acts of 1535 and 1542. It was not until 1922 that the United Kingdom of Great Britain and Northern Ireland came into existence. These histories of the foundation of our nation are filled with tales of conquests and conflicts over culture, religion and language that are hardly covered in English schools – outside of the occasional end-of-term playing of Mel Gibson's *Braveheart*.

Given the standard of history education in Britain throughout the twentieth century, it is no surprise that a poll in 2016, the same year as the Brexit referendum, found that more than 44 per cent of the respondents were proud of Britain's record of colonialism, with just 21 per cent who regretted it.[74] Indeed, history education in British schools still lacks an accurate confrontation with our past. An honest telling of English and British history requires re-education. For as long as we tell British history through the lens of 'white past opposed to a multicultural present', we perpetuate the feelings of loss among large segments of the population. If we are to create a progressive, civic Englishness founded on the vision of a good society, we need to address, not ignore, our complicated multi-ethnic past, which is deeply tied to our multi-ethnic present.[75]

Promoting civic nationalism cannot be an excuse to whitewash the UK's history of discrimination and oppression. In fact, civic nationalism should help us learn from our history. We need to confront our nation's mistakes as well as our successes, in the syllabi of our schools and universities, but also in new national institutions that stand alone.

TRUTH AND RECONCILIATION

Britain is in no way unique in needing to deal with a violent and divisive past to create a common civic identity. We can learn by understanding how other modern democracies have confronted wrongdoings of the past.

In 2015, Canada finally confronted its dark history of abuse against thousands of native aboriginal children in the forced schooling system. The six-year inquiry heard from more than 150,000 former pupils of the 'residential schools' – many of whom were raped, beaten or otherwise abused at the hands of the residential school authorities. Thousands of children died in the schools, which were open from 1876 to 1996, with the true number unknown after the Canadian government stopped recording the shocking statistics in 1920. Justice Murray Sinclair, who was appointed head of the country's first Truth and Reconciliation Commission, boldly declared: 'Canada clearly participated in a period of cultural genocide.'[76]

'It feels like our story is validated at last and is out there for the world to see,' fifty-eight-year-old Cindy Tom-Lindley, executive director of the Indian Residential School Survivor Society in British Columbia, told the *Guardian* after these findings were announced: 'We were too scared as children to speak out. So to give our testimonies to the commission was liberating and emotional.'[77]

Following his election in the same year, Liberal Prime Minister Justin Trudeau created a National Council for Reconciliation to help enact the Commission's ninety-four recommendations and pledged $8.4 billion over five years towards policies that help the aboriginal communities, as well as $10 million in funding for the University of Manitoba's National Centre for Truth and Reconciliation – set up to document Canada's cultural genocide.

Canada's example shows that alongside national pride it is fitting and appropriate to build a recognition of national shame. It is now time for Britain and England to follow Canada's example by creating its own institutions that recognise the British Empire's peculiar dependence on slavery and oppression. And within the UK, England must be honest about its aggressive actions against the other nations in our union, as well as Britain's role in the oppression and domination of Ireland. If we are to restore the United Kingdom as a healthy union of equals, Britain and England must be honest about their own history and their broader role in the world.

I am not arguing that modern Britons or the English should take responsibility for the gross sins of those who lived on these islands before us, but simply that we confront our nation's past mistakes as well as its successes. National pride will mean so much more if it is accompanied by appropriate recognition of national shame. It offers the opportunity for Britain to stand in the world as a confident nation, at ease with its past and open about its future.

Once we develop the maturity and humility to reconstruct an accurate collective narrative, there will be little choice but to accept that we have a responsibility to tell our nation's story honestly. We can begin by accepting that colonial history is British history. We can teach the history of the first UK slave ships sent to exploit and enslave African men and women for profit. We can teach the history of colonisation, of how Britain took control of much of the world through force. We can teach the history of how we reconciled this past with a future based on universal values and respect for all people. How we built modern Britain out of the past.

We already have a brilliant International Slavery Museum in Liverpool, but why not augment it with a permanent National Museum of Migration?[78] This would bring Britain in line with France's National Museum of the History of Immigration, and Ellis Island in the USA.

COMPULSORY NATIONAL CIVIC SERVICE

In the trenches, the battlefields and the air-raid shelters of the twentieth century's two world wars, many of Britain's deepest divides were broken down. Through the adversity of war, people were brought together through a shared purpose. Soldiers from the all over England, Scotland, Northern Ireland, Wales and across the Commonwealth, and from all social classes – from alumni of Britain's top private schools to those from mining towns without any formal qualifications – shared rations, spirit and goals. While men were abroad fighting to protect the freedom of the nation, women stepped in at home, completing the vital work that was left behind. As women proved they could work in the fields and in the factories at least as well as men, there was no justification for them to be denied the right to vote or to work when peacetime returned. Similarly, there was no excuse to treat those from poorer backgrounds, or those whose skin was black or brown, as worth any less.

The indignity of poverty, the senseless violence and the broken families caused by the world wars are the great tragedy of the twentieth century, but this doesn't mean we cannot learn anything good from this common national experience. Mobilising Britain's Dunkirk spirit is a concept that has been constantly touted by British Eurosceptics, advocating a hard 'No Deal' Brexit, who have suggested that a period of pain may help bring the country together again. They miss the point. It was not the squalid conditions, or the lack of food and vital resources, that united Britain during its two world wars. We were brought together by obligations, such as rationing and conscription, that showed everyone they had a stake in society – responsibilities as well as rights.

We can start by reintroducing a form of compulsory national service. Conscription into the British army was phased out gradually in the United Kingdom from 1957. But compulsory community service is a public good that can be shared equally across classes, races, genders and regions. If done correctly, it would allow us to break down the divides that are becoming entrenched in modern society. Women and men, black or white, poor or rich, from Tottenham or Torquay, would mix as equals.

I first proposed the idea of national civic service in 2006.[79] In 2009, as Labour's higher-education minister, I broke ranks to support the think tank Demos's report *Service Nation*, which put forward detailed proposals for the idea. Very quickly I was slapped down by Prime Minister Gordon Brown, whose liberal urges were deeply offended by the idea that any national service for young people should be compulsory.

Brown's successor as prime minister, David Cameron, introduced the National Citizen Service (NCS) for fifteen- to seventeen-year-olds in England and Northern Ireland in 2011. I have been supportive of the scheme, which offers teenagers from diverse backgrounds the opportunity to contribute to society with a social-action campaign, learn hard skills that set up ambitious youngsters for their future careers, and soft skills through living and working with strangers.

In its current form, the NCS is voluntary. Over 500,000 young people have taken part, but many more have not.[80] Without compulsion, there is no obligation. And without obligation, there is no duty. The whole notion of civic service is founded on the perception that a nation is made up of 'independent but interdependent citizens' who have a duty to one another.[81] This is an idea that is centuries old and can even be traced back to Cicero, who said: 'We are not born for ourselves alone, but our country claims for itself one part of our birth, and our friends another.'

This insight suggests that we are more than just cosmopolitan citizens of the world. Instead we owe special care to those with whom we share a nation. A compulsory civic national service is a way of encouraging and institutionalising the maxim that those who are fit and able must give something back to their country, as well as looking after themselves.

While the work citizens do will benefit society, the major benefit of a national citizens' service is for those participating, not those receiving the benefits of their labour. Taking part in national civic service for one year would allow individuals to create strong and weak ties with new acquaintances, as well as allowing them to develop skills and knowledge outside their normal network. This could have vast and surprising benefits and should not be limited to middle-class people who spend three or four years at university.

The national civic service could become a powerful tool for creating social mobility. For those from poorer backgrounds, it could present the first opportunity to leave their deprived environment and mix with people of different backgrounds, perspectives, races and religions. Many of the skills that graduates gain at university are not analytic, but social. By encouraging a national service for everyone, we could make the playing field more level between graduates and non-graduates, breaking down the ugly divide behind the highly educated and the left behind.

After the Second World War, Britain introduced a form of peace-time conscription for all able-bodied men between the ages of eighteen and thirty.[82] This was primarily to allow for the occupation of post-war Germany and Japan. When the Suez Crisis of 1956 forced Britain to reassess its use of the armed services, the necessity of national service was called into question. It eventually ended in 1963.

The biggest criticisms of military national service are moral and practical. Morally, it is extremely controversial to force individuals to put their lives at risk for the sake of national security. Practically, soldiers cost the tax-payer thousands of pounds per month. My proposal neutralises these concerns. First of all, I am suggesting a national *civic* service – individuals would not be forced to join the army, but rather a much broader range of institutions in the public sector. For the same reason, costs would be much lower overall, seeing as many of the young people taking part would be contributing to the very public services that require public expenditure.

We cannot hide from the fact that polling suggests some form of compulsory national civic service is popular only among those who are too old to face conscription. There's no doubt it could initially be unpopular with many of the teenagers asked to take part. Why would they want to spend a year learning how to complete military exercises, working in a care home or maintaining public spaces when they could start university or be getting their first job to earn real money?

While a national civic service should be compulsory, it does not need to be prescriptive. In the spirit of English creativity, young people should be encouraged to choose and design their own experi-ences as far as possible. Service classes throughout school years could be used for students to learn about different opportunities. As Demos suggested in their *Service Nation* report, young people should be able to choose when to complete their national service: any time between sixteen and twenty-four. Depending on their age and experience, there could be different options, from traditional army conscription to vocational training that might lead to qualifications, structured volunteering for students across the summer months of university holidays and schemes like TeachFirst for graduates. Students should be able to choose what type of national service they perform, each service option should be as inclusive as possible and every form of service should involve the mixing of people across region, race, social class and education level. And of, course, there should be exceptions to the compulsory aspect of the new citizens' service. Those who have medical or other compelling reasons to avoid it would be able to do so without sanction.

While national service was phased out in this country generations ago, other European nations maintained the practice for considerably longer. Italy, the Netherlands, Belgium and France maintained a form of national service until the 1990s, while Sweden only abolished compulsory national service in 2010 and Germany in 2011. In recent years, many countries have begun to reintroduce the draft. Lithuania in 2015 and Sweden in 2017 both reinstated conscription due to fears of Russian aggression and expansionism. French President Emmanuel Macron has recently reinstated compulsory national service for all sixteen-year-olds, encouraging them to work 'in an area linked to defence and security', but with the option to work in heritage, the environment or social care.

One often-cited criticism of the idea of national service is that it would be too expensive. Indeed, money was one of the main reasons the British government abandoned obligatory national service. President Macron too has hit the wall of financial constraints, forcing the compulsory element of his plan to last for a month only, with an additional three to twelve months being optional. Macron's plan is estimated to cost $1.8 billion per year. Given that France's population is similar to the UK's, it's reasonable to suggest that the cost in Britain would be at least as much.

This would be a serious investment but worthwhile. The return on a national citizen's service would no doubt be slow, and hard to perceive at first, but the links it would foster between kids from Glasgow and Greenwich, from Tunbridge Wells and Wakefield, would continue to pay dividends for decades to come. We would not be able to value such a programme in the short term. The skills learned on a compulsory national service programme would be hugely beneficial to the economy. In both Israel and Finland, which have for different reasons made national military service compulsory for decades, those who have performed conscription are highly valued. While only 60 per cent of the country's adult population are former conscripts, they make up 90 per cent of workers in Israel's flourishing technology sector.[83] A year's compulsory service would be an invaluable tool for young people to create networks and connections, as well as to learn social and practical skills, that would inevitably benefit them later in their careers.

WRITING IT ALL DOWN

Who are the English, the Scottish, the Welsh and the Northern Irish? What does it mean to be a citizen, or a subject, of the United Kingdom? What separates us from one another? What holds us together? When should decisions be made that apply to every country in our union? When should they be made regionally or locally? What type of society are we working towards? And what are our most fundamental values?

These are all questions to which we currently have no straightforward response, but which need to be answered if we are to build a new civic identity, or set of identities, according to each country within our union. Ours is one of just five nation states without a codified constitution. Along with Canada, Israel, New Zealand and Saudi Arabia, the United Kingdom does not have a single set of documents that define the most fundamental rules, values and aspirations that bind us. We do have an *unwritten* constitution, based on a body of laws, precedent and principles that have evolved over hundreds of years, but it is ephemeral and bendable at the will of the politicians of the day.

The main argument for our constitution, which exists but at the same time does not, is this flexibility. The UK in the twenty-first century is not bound by a historical document created by leaders, like America's founding fathers, whose lives are in many ways unrecognisable from our own. Walter Bagehot's *The English Constitution*, published in 1867, set out just such a justification for our idiosyncratic legal basis made up of blended common law and custom. British political debate is not set by fixed parameters that mandate the right to bear arms or whether or not a woman has the right to remove an unwanted foetus from her body.

Unlike the USA, which is in Abraham Lincoln's words 'a government of the people, by the people, for the people', the United

Kingdom's sovereignty lies in Parliament under the ultimate authority of the monarch. The executive of government is accountable to both chambers of Parliament – the Commons and the Lords – under the crown. The 2016 referendum on the UK's membership of the EU acted like an explosive device underneath the established constitutional structures within which we make decisions. Legally, the referendum was always advisory to parliament, where sovereignty lies. Yet David Cameron sold the referendum to the public as though its result were a binding commitment. This was hugely irresponsible, given the Leave option was left vague, and built on a series of lies and contradictory promises.

When, on 23 June 2016, a slim majority voted in favour of Brexit, these contradictions were bound to be exposed. Initially, Theresa May tried to carry out Brexit with as little scrutiny from Parliament as possible. Those who stood up against this executive power grab, including the High Court judges who ruled that the UK government would need the consent of Parliament to give notice of Brexit, were labelled 'Enemies of the People'. MPs like me who argued against leaving the EU despite the referendum result were accused of 'treachery' as well as much worse. Fulfilling our role, as defined by Edmund Burke, to act as 'trusted representatives' of our constituents rather than 'unthinking delegates' conflicted with what Brexiters perceived as the new sovereign popular will.

These constitutional tensions deepened even further when Theresa May's withdrawal deal was rejected three times by Parliament and she was replaced by Boris Johnson as leader of the Conservative Party and Prime Minister. In his first few weeks as Prime Minister, Boris Johnson expelled 21 Conservative MPs from the parliamentary party, described safety concerns of MPs as 'humbug', and was found to have unlawfully suspended parliament to avoid scrutiny, by the Supreme Court, the highest court in the land.

In societies with a written constitution, the government is subject to it, but in those with an unwritten constitution it is the constitution that is subject to the government. A codified constitution acts as a safeguard against the whims and partisan strategies of a government of the day. The rigidity of a codified constitution that is onerous to amend is a virtue, not a vice. Changing the most fundamental principles of society should be difficult, requiring careful thought and established consensus. Requiring a super-majority of more than one half for amendments is the means to avoid the tyranny of a simple majority.

A new written UK constitution is necessary if we are to climb out of the quagmire and renew the United Kingdom around a civic sense of who we are, before ethnic nationalism and supremacy get there first. A new constitution must do three things. First, it needs to establish the rights and responsibilities of UK citizens. Building on, rather than abandoning, the European Convention on Human Rights, a fresh and modern Bill of Rights should establish democratic and minority rights, as well as personal liberties.

Some might suggest that this is already covered by Magna Carta and our 1689 Bill of Rights, but these great and historic documents do not perform the functions we need today. Magna Carta establishes principles of the relationship between twenty-five barons, while the 1689 bill focuses on the liberties of parliamentarians, not the everyday man or woman on the street. The European Convention, signed in 1950, does better, but only establishes the bare minimum – such as free speech, fair trial and human dignity – while obviously and understandably failing to articulate all the values of a modern UK. An additional British Bill of Rights would give proper clout to certain liberties, protecting them against the often partisan and shifting will of Parliament.

Second, a written constitution must establish where power lies. It would divvy up decision-making between our four nations and the UK – and define how we share power with Europe, regardless of whether we leave or remain. Doing so would offer the opportunity to create and codify a clear framework for all the city and county regions, devolving more power to local decision-makers and decentralising the behemoth of the British state. In addition, this process would clarify any ambiguities between the separation of powers, defining what power lies with the executive, the legislature and the judiciary.

Third, a new UK constitution must establish the fundamental tenets of our shared values. These must be aspirational, rather than descriptive. All existing constitutions do this. The USA aspires to 'life, liberty and the pursuit of happiness', the French motto '*Liberté, Egalité, Fraternité*' was written into the 1958 constitution and the South African constitution specifically includes non-racialism in its founding values. I have put forward some of the values that I perceive as uniquely English, but the establishment of values in a UK constitution must result from a much more thorough and collaborative operation than this.

Writing a UK constitution fit for a multi-ethnic, politically diverse kingdom of four countries will be no easy task. The process of its construction offers an opportunity for national healing and a level of mutual understanding that we have never had before. This undertaking should involve not only lawyers and politicians, but teachers, artists, manual workers and the unemployed. We need to make sure that the principles agreed, and the rights secured belong to all citizens equally, rather than to the same old elite.

To do this we need to set up a convention, not unlike the citizens' assembly described above but at the UK level, to draw up the refreshed and updated principles of our kingdom. As Alan Renwick, a professor of politics and proponent of this idea, suggests in his blueprint for a UK Constitutional Convention, the randomly drawn but representative sample of the UK should go through three stages.[84] First, they should receive tuition from experts of various nationalities with opposing perspectives. Second, the delegates should travel the country, meeting other citizens and discussing what they have learned. It is only in the third stage that, with the assistance of a secretariat qualified to draft legal texts, the first draft of a new British constitution would emerge.

FINDING CONSENSUS

An ethnic Englishness, tied to toxic assumptions of group supremacy, has put down deep roots in recent years. Allowing this to take hold would result in a vision of England too ugly to imagine. The development of a civic and progressive Englishness is a vital task for anyone looking to ensure a healthy and balanced United Kingdom. We must use this moment of crisis as an opportunity to refresh our identity and come together. A recognition of those values we share is the starting point from which we can rebuild. It is only by doing this that we can create an inclusive English identity, where our great range of identity groups can belong in a common space.

To be clear about how we can come back together, we must have a transparent analysis of how our politics has become so divided. To do this, it is necessary to untangle two different forms of polarisation. On the one hand there is polarisation based around our emotions, and on the other there is polarisation on specific policy issues. Emotional polarisation concerns the extent to which we consider ourselves members of exclusive groups, from which we denigrate, distrust or dislike those outside. This is close to the phenomenon of tribalism I diagnose at the beginning of the book. On this measure, the UK appears very polarised, along the lines of our attitudes to the European Union: 44 per cent of Britons say their Brexit identity is very strong, compared to just 9 per cent who strongly identify with a political party.[85] Less than half of Remainers say they are happy for their children to marry a Leaver, and vice versa.[86] This is deeply concerning. Our democracy depends on all sides respecting the legitimacy of the others, even when they disagree.

Fortunately, there are reasons to be optimistic that we are not as polarised as we might expect, at least in terms of policies. According to new research by Demos, the British public agrees on specific issues more often, rather than less.[87] For example, 79 per cent of the public now agree that 'we need to combat climate change by any means necessary'. Meanwhile, 72 per cent believe 'people should not be allowed to post hateful, offensive or inciting language on social media'. And, 76 per cent think the National Health Service should be 'given whatever public funding it needs'.

We can find consensus, then, even if some of us do not like each other very much. The more we focus on fixing these issues, the more agreement we can reach. Once we remember how to identify as citizens with differing views inside one society, rather than as part of opposing tribes that happen to live on the same island, we can restore legitimacy to our democracy.

There are other reasons for hope. While Britons are losing faith in the political class, their trust in each other is at a record high.[88] And two thirds of the public believe that people across the world have more in common with us than what separates us.[89] Rebuilding England will require us to recognise the worst aspects of our nature, but the process will fail if it does not also set its target on the best. To heal, we need to move outside of our tribal groups, but we also need to decide, together as a nation, what it is we want to build.

9

Beyond Tribes

*Why and how we must move beyond tribes
and replace them with communities*

'Because this is the other thing about immigrants ('fugees, émigrés,
travellers): they cannot escape their history any more than you yourself can lose your shadow.'

Zadie Smith[1]

This book ends where it started, with my DNA results. Not at my
kitchen table this time, but in a grand, white stucco-fronted building
overlooking St James's Park: the home of the Royal Society, the oldest
national scientific organisation in the world. I was there to meet four
world-leading scientists: Dr Ewan Birney, a member of the society and
the director of the European Bioinformatics Institute; Dr Aylwyn
Scally, an expert in human evolutionary genetics at the University of
Cambridge; Dr Adam Rutherford, a science writer and broadcaster for
BBC Radio 4; and Dr Stuart Ritchie, a postdoctoral research fellow at
the Centre for Cognitive Ageing and Cognitive Epidemiology. If
anyone could explain the links between DNA, group membership,
psychology and the scientific basis for tribes, it was them.

I had not yet told them about the DNA test that inspired my

journey to my ancestral home. Instead, after we had settled around an oval table in a conference room, I began by asking them about how modern genetic science is changing our world.

'Something none of us predicted is the rise of genetic ancestry testing, which has become a multi-billion-dollar industry,' Adam said. 'Our best estimate is that 26 million kits have been sold, the majority by two different companies. Most geneticists agree that the science involved is somewhere between sketchy and bogus.'

'I don't think so,' Ewan murmured.

'I think you're more hostile to this programme than most,' Aylwyn added. 'It varies a lot by company.'

'The big companies like the ones that are selling most of the kits – like 23andMe – are not pseudo-scientific,' Stuart said. 'I would argue they do a good job on their website of explaining exactly what they mean.'

It seemed Adam had got at least one thing wrong: 'most geneticists' did not agree. Not one to back down easily, he replied: 'My point is what they are selling . . .'

'They are sort of selling a myth,' Ewan conceded.

'Yes, that's right,' Aylwyn said.

'If they accurately described what product you're buying, no one would buy it,' Adam continued. 'The marketing says: "Find your roots. Find out where you come from." It says you can be 40 per cent German, right? It's literally impossible to be 40 per cent German, because being German involves having a German passport. So, all of those things about where your ancestral roots come from are pseudo-scientific mythmaking, coupled with a misunderstanding about how ancestry and genetics actually works.'

'So, what do these tests show?' I asked.

'They say that 40 per cent of your genome looks like a lot of people who currently live in Germany,' Aylwyn explained. The results do not reveal any connection to your ancestors or 'roots', as 'Roots4Real', the company I used, implies in its name. They simply show where other people with similar DNA to your own currently live. Worse, your genome is compared only to that of people who have previously chosen to take the company's test, not an objective sample of the population of each region.

'There are even companies which will say: "We can trace a tribe, or even a village, where your ancestors came from," ' Adam said. 'I think it is profoundly unethical to tell people you can establish an individual's geographical and ancestral origins, from somewhere like West Africa through to transatlantic slavery. It is very, very broadly true, but fundamentally the science is profoundly stupid.'

At this point, I had to come clean. I told them everything. About the ancestry test I took during the anniversary of the Abolition of the Slave Trade Act 1807. The results which singled out specific tribes and towns in Niger, Sierra Leone and South Africa, and even said I was five per cent Scottish. I showed them a picture of me in the long white turban and robes in which Alhousseini had wrapped me in Niger.

We all burst out laughing. I had done the seemingly impossible: I'd made the geneticists agree. They said it was ludicrous for a DNA-testing company to suggest their results could identify a specific village my ancestors lived in. The idea that some came from the Highlands was even less likely. The test I had taken identified two parallel lines of ancestry. But the method used less than 2 per cent of my total genetic make-up. I had been sold a fantasy.

My imagined heritage was snatched away just as quickly as it had been given. I thought about all the family members I had shared it with and how excited we had been. It had been a mistake to be seduced by dreams of my ethnic roots.

This is not to say our ethnic identities are a fiction. Race exists – not because different human skin colours have any innate significance, but because of the material differences between the ways people with different skin colours are treated. It is real because of humanity's long history of classification and oppression according to pigmentation. It is just that, on a biological level, skin colour is no more linked to other characteristics than is our height or the colour of our hair. The recent surge of interest in genetic ancestry runs counter to this. Adam worries it 'has effectively fuelled a sense of biological essentialism in the demos, in the people, that we thought had gone away'.

THEM AND US

It is not only biological essentialism we have to worry about. Across society, many people are starting to use one element of their identity to define themselves as members of a 'tribe' that is essentially distinct from the rest. In a time of rapid change, they are finding comfort in exclusive groups that claim superiority over outsiders. Some groups are based on race, and this explains the resurgence of white supremacism on our streets and on the internet. It has, as Donald Trump's call for four non-white congresswomen to 'go home' showed, even infected the US presidency. Others have found tribal belonging in extreme distortions of their religion. Think of Anwar and his journey to join ISIS, and thousands of others like him. Still more are seduced by the fast money and quick status that comes with life in a gang.

Most of us have not been pushed to the extremism of a religious terror group, an urban gang or outmoded forms of racism. But this does not mean we are immune to the new tribalism. Fractured into the increasingly distant tribes of right and left, liberal and conservative, Leave and Remain, mainstream political discourse in the UK has become toxic. Inclusivity, bipartisanship and common purpose have become increasingly rare. We assume the worst of our opponents, while turning a blind eye to the wrongdoing of those we perceive to be on our side. The idea that our rivals are not only wrong, but evil, has blocked cooperation and made compromise impossible.

A new tribalism based around our cultural, political and ethnic identities has arisen. This has happened because our societies have become more individualistic, isolated and atomised. We are in the middle of a loneliness crisis that is affecting young and old people alike. This can in part be explained by a culture that has lost the clear demarcations of traditional classes, is losing faith in the religions that once held us together, and in which both local and national civic institutions have been eroded.

Another key driver of the new tribalism has been rapid growth in technology and a revolution in how we communicate. The internet, smartphones and social media have for ever changed how we live, and it will take decades for us to grasp the full extent of the effects. It is already clear that they have provided a platform for people to connect with groups of like-minded individuals with whom they share no geographical space. Online, polarisation is thriving. Atomised individuals are becoming radicalised, while hostile powers are creating bot factories to further sow division.[2]

The communications revolution has had the effect of pouring gallons of petrol onto an already burning forest fire. Social media has replaced traditional media, offering each of us a distorted filter through which our own biases determine how we see the rest of the world. Algorithms ensure that our feeds are filled with the information that is most likely to elicit an emotional response, often negative and adversarial. Fake news and lying politicians have eroded trust in the institutions and public servants whose job it is to look for a solution.

Counterintuitively, this has created a crisis of loneliness. Meaningful interactions have been replaced by the synthetic rush of notifications and 'likes'. Depression, anxiety and despair are numbed through the wide prescription of antidepressants. For far too many young people, isolation and disconnection ends in suicide. Without the strong communities our ancestors evolved to depend on, many of us feel alone. We seek belonging wherever we can find it. We have replaced communities with the toxicity of tribes.

ECONOMIC ROOTS

Explaining how we have arrived at this place is not easy. Yet because of the changes we are witnessing, there is a growing recognition among some people that capitalism must be checked by a politics that focuses on belonging as well as on growth, that technology must be harnessed sustainably, and that we need to put more emphasis on building meaningful relationships in the physical spaces of our communities and neighbourhoods.

Indeed, many of the roots of the new tribalism are economic. Following the Second World War, Keynesian high investment facilitated decades of remarkable growth which tangibly improved people's lives. An economy based on manufacturing grew, salaries rose, new household appliances reduced chores, transport infrastructure linked up distant places, and the creation of the welfare state and public-health provision raised standards of living. But nothing can go up and up for ever. When our industrial economies began to falter and stagnate, inflation started to get out of control.

A new economic worldview, neoliberalism, soon replaced Keynesianism. In Reagan and Thatcher's experiment, free markets and finance were treated as the solution and government regulation as an obstacle. Labour unions tried to resist the brutality of the reforms, but they were defeated. Traditional industries collapsed under the weight of competition. For a while at least, neoliberal economics seemed to have benefits of its own. After recession in the early eighties, growth returned. In Britain, relaxed regulations meant council tenants were provided the means to buy their own homes. Their values rocketed. Homeowners felt more well off.

The Third Way governments that followed tried to marry certain economically liberal policies with social justice. The aim was to check the cruelty of the market, while keeping its benefits. Again, this seemed to work for a while. Growth continued and centre-left governments made it their mission to pour massive investment into schools, hospitals and other vital services. In Britain, millions of children and pensioners were lifted out of poverty, waiting times in NHS hospitals were cut by two thirds and state schools were immeasurably improved.[3] Yet with hindsight, the conditions of crisis were looming.

We have not yet got over the shock of the financial crisis that culminated in the crash of 2008. There is no obvious way out of the stagnation that has marked the more than decade since. The economic pain that followed has been endured not by the bankers who created it, but by the communities that were already being eroded throughout the decades before. There are many places like Wigan and Peterborough, not only in the UK, but across the Western world – places that once benefited from good wages and reliable incomes in the economies of old. We must be honest with them. There is no way for us to bring these jobs back. The vast majority have been lost to technological progress, not foreign labour.[4] But we have to recognise that people's cultural anxieties about the loss of their way of life are real and justified. The economy that once gave them security and pride no longer exists. This unease has been made worse by an understandable feeling that a distant governing elite, whether in Brussels, Westminster or Washington, has been ignoring them.

THE NEW POPULIST NATIONALIST RIGHT

One of the reasons the new tribalism has been so destructive is that no political movement on the mainstream left or right has created a new politics capable of going beyond the neoliberal consensus of recent decades. We have not provided political answers to the question of how disenfranchised individuals can find belonging in a fast-changing, modern world.

The only significant attempts at answers have come from a new breed of populist nationalist right party that has roots in the old far right. Nigel Farage in the UK, Matteo Salvini in Italy, Marine Le Pen in France, Geert Wilders and Thierry Baudet in the Netherlands, Jimmie Åkesson in Sweden, Viktor Orbán in Hungary, Jair Bolsonaro in Brazil and Donald Trump in the USA are just a few who have attempted to fill this void. Each has found support by leading movements that provide straightforward answers to communities that feel cultural loss. Rather than engaging in real and complex policy solutions, the populist nationalist right argues that our nations and identities can be fixed simply by rejecting foreigners and outside influences. Populist leaders, either in completely new parties or from the fringes of existing ones, have achieved success by creating a false and baseless nostalgia for a time of ethnic and religious uniformity. They use this replacement narrative to stoke anger at the side effects of technological advancement and globalisation.

Broadly, national populists blame demographic change for rising house prices, overrun hospitals and overstretched schools. Specifically, they target the Muslim family that just moved in up the road, the Eastern European men on their local construction site, as well as civil servants with foreign accents living in Brussels or working at the UN. High immigration figures correlate closely with the rise of national populist parties in Europe.[5] During the 2019 European Parliament elections, Austria's then deputy chancellor, Heinz-Christian Strache, said that his populist nationalist Freedom Party was resisting the 'replacement' of Europe's 'native' population.[6] When challenged by the interviewer, Strache added: 'We don't want to become a minority in our own country. That's legitimate and fair and deeply democratic.'[7] In this exchange, Strache relied on pre-existing definitions of 'we' and 'our'. This created a self-legitimising statement: those entering the country are automatically excluded from the collective unit that is being changed. Strache's language implied that his primary determinant of 'we' was ancestry – an insistence that migrants and their descendants cannot become part of 'our' country purely because of arbitrary differences in their DNA.

The term 'great replacement' originates in a 2012 book *Le Grand Remplacement* by Renaud Camus, a French author and supporter of Marine Le Pen's populist nationalist right National Rally. The conspiracy theory contends that rising immigration combined with low birth rates among white women means that white people are under threat of existential decline and even extinction. This demographic analysis is deeply flawed: white people are not going to become extinct. This is not to deny the realities of how demographics are in constant flux. In the USA, racial and ethnic minority populations are growing faster than the white population.[8] It is projected that by 2044 no single ethnic group will be a majority.

Demographic change, then, will continue, giving rise to populist replacement narratives in both the USA and Europe. The narrative of replacement, even if not the specific language, has been used by national populist parties across Europe. When Nigel Farage stood in front of a poster covered in brown faces of non-European refugees with the caption 'breaking point' during the 2016 EU referendum, he was conveying the same xenophobic message. This narrative has even been accepted by large swathes of what was traditionally thought of as 'mainstream' opinion. In 2019, a poll found that 60 per cent of Conservative Party members believe that Islam is a threat to Western society.[9]

The USA differs from Europe in that it is truly a nation of immigrants. Nevertheless, in recent years a similar narrative has been able to take hold. Donald Trump has received strong support from a growing movement of white nationalists, who marched on the streets of Charlottesville in 2017 chanting 'Jews will not replace us'. As Trump goes into campaign mode to try and win a second term as president in

2020, he has begun to use European ideas of ethnic purity: as well as telling the 'squad' of non-white Democratic Congresswomen to 'go back' to 'the totally broken and crime-infested places from which they came', Trump also used racist tropes against black Representative Elijah Cummings by calling his district a 'rat and rodent infested mess'.

The new populist nationalist right's campaign against migration is designed to appeal to our lowest tribal instincts. It switches on the wiring in our brains that makes us enjoy feeling part of an in-group that carries positive characteristics, in contrast to the out-group with negative traits. Trump played on this when he smeared Mexicans as 'rapists' and 'criminals', as did Poland's Jarosław Kaczyński when he announced that immigrants may bring 'parasites' and 'diseases'.

The national populists' second answer to the erosion of our communities and identities in an era of globalisation is to blame international institutions. In Europe, the EU has been the main target. It is easy to vilify anonymous bureaucrats, by painting them as agents determined to erode communities and undermine the traditional nation state. Until a few years ago, many described the EU as a shining example of how to unite different nations around a shared purpose. In recent years, it has been deeply wounded by the Greek crisis and Brexit. Meanwhile, President Trump has made significant cuts to the UN's funding,[10] pulled out of important international agreements, branded NATO 'obsolete' and threatened to tear up the North American Free Trade Agreement.[11]

The sad irony of this second target is that to properly address many of the greatest challenges we face, international cooperation and the supranational institutions like the EU that facilitate it have never been more important. Many of the biggest problems we face are coordination problems. Think of each nation as a player in a game that must choose a plan of action based on the information they have available. Each player can either cooperate or act selfishly. If every player cooperates, this would be the best outcome for every player. If some players act selfishly, it becomes in the best interest of other players to act selfishly, too. If players cannot know how the other players will act in advance, they have to make a judgement over whether to act selfishly or cooperate.

Consider how this applies to the climate crisis. A global reduction in carbon emissions is in every country's economic interests. There is also economic incentive for an individual nation to rely on other countries making the sacrifice in carbon output. If an individual country can continue exploiting carbon as an energy source without limit, while other nations respond effectively to the climate emergency by making sacrifices, the selfish individual country will benefit. Without the guarantee that other nations will also act to reduce their carbon emissions, nations are incentivised to underinvest in green alternatives. It is for this reason that environmental legislation is more powerful if it applies at the federal level to all fifty states in America, rather than just a few liberal enclaves by the coast. Such rules are even more powerful if they apply to every nation across the world. Global rules, tied to adequate punishment for those who fail to keep to them, eliminate the incentive for individual nations to act selfishly.

The mass movement of people is another coordination problem. The world would be a considerably fairer place if every country took their share of refugees fleeing war, persecution, violence or environmental destruction. Many nations have a political incentive – due to anti-migrant sentiment – to act selfishly and close their borders. Tax avoidance presents a similar dilemma. Except for tax havens, every national government would benefit from businesses and wealthy individuals paying their fair share of taxes. However, as soon as one nation facilitates tax avoidance, it becomes beneficial for others to do the same. National governments cannot stop tax avoidance on their own. Environmental solutions to the climate crisis will only be fast enough if we work together. Sharing the burden of housing refugees across those nations with the capacity to support, train and integrate them will reduce strain on existing communities. Regulating footloose tech companies and legislating to reduce harm on social media will only be effective at the supranational level. The solutions to coordination problems rely on moving beyond our tribal and national interests.

THE CLIMATE CRISIS

The 280-mile concrete wall that runs along Guyana's coastline stands as a man-made protection against the Atlantic Ocean. It was constructed by Dutch settlers in the nineteenth century. Since then the wall has become far more than an obstacle to nature. The sea wall is where Georgetown's children first encounter the open water as they face up against the tide on slippery jetties. It is where they later catch crabs and small fish. On sunny days, the sand beside the wall off Camp Street transforms into a cricket pitch. Teenage boys bowl fast and the batsmen try to keep their sixes out of the water. Both of my parents talked warmly of late-night strolls on the sea wall. This is the location where generations of young couples have shared their first kiss.

Usually, when I return to Guyana's capital, I force myself to wake up uncharacteristically early, around five, at least once. I go for a jog along the sea wall as the sun rises. In the early morning light, the boundary between the sea and the city becomes blurred and, in the moment, you feel almost as though you are running on water. The cool morning air feels light against the concrete floor.

On one of my recent visits a few years ago, however, there was no way I was running on the wall. I visited not long after the high tide had breached it, causing chaos and terror in Georgetown. Traffic was moved into one lane as waves splashed over the barrier and swamped coastal roads.[12] Nervous townspeople worried that it would seep further into their city. Before long, the entire roadway flooded. A family friend who had been driving towards the affected road at the time told me: 'It was really terrifying. It felt like this time the sea was going to swamp us. The floods are happening more and more now.'

Guyana is one of the most vulnerable countries on earth to the effects of climate change. Sea levels are rising much faster than the global average.[13] An estimated 80 per cent of the population already live and work in the low-lying coastal plains. Many residential areas already lie below sea level.[14] The remaining areas suffer from highly unseasonal weather patterns of long *el niño* droughts and intense '*la niña*' rainy seasons. The Rupununi region, which takes up more than a quarter of Guyana's land, suffers from long droughts that increase the occurrence of savannah fires, cause floods and damage subsistence crops. Coastal plains are made habitable by a complex network of drainage and irrigation canals linked to conservancies behind agricultural lands. The East Demerara Water Conservancy, which sustains the largest portion of the country's population, can hold 250 million cubic metres of water.[15] When waves overcome the sea walls, or there are heavy rains, flooding happens. If this means the canal takes in more water than it was designed to hold, the dam which holds it together can collapse and cause even more extreme flooding. In the colonial period, agricultural lands were drained using natural gravitational flow controlled by sluices that were opened at low tide and closed at high tide. This system is no longer viable, as the rate of drainage is too slow. Pumps now have to be used.

It has never been possible to avoid water in Georgetown. In fact, the name 'Guiana' is rumoured to be derived from an Amerindian word meaning 'land of many waters'. Yet there is little doubt that in recent years its people's battle with the sea has intensified.[16] No flood in recent years has come close to the scale of the crisis in 2005. Houses were submerged, businesses ruined, possessions destroyed and dead cows sent floating down the river. The rainfall average in Guyana at the time was seven inches per month, but by the middle of January twenty-seven inches of rain had already fallen.[17] Extreme rainfall broke the region's flood defences. An estimated 200,000 people were affected and 35,000 became homeless.[18] Medical equipment and drug supplies were soaked, forcing health centres to close. Many people were forced to survive without adequate food supplies and drinking water.[19] It cost an estimated $465 million in damage – equal to roughly 59 per cent of the country's GDP at the time.[20] Thirty-four people died.[21]

Guyana has contributed relatively little to the creation of the climate crisis, yet it is one of the countries facing the most serious threat. According to the latest figures, the annual carbon dioxide emissions per head in the country are around 2.6 metric tons. This compares with 16.5 metric tons per head in the USA. There are more extreme examples of this injustice. Haiti, for example, is another of the most vulnerable nations to climate change, yet it emits just 0.2 metric tonnes of carbon dioxide per person. This is a pattern repeated across the globe. The poorest countries, with the least consumption, will generally suffer the most in the years to come. With the notable exception of Australia, it is usually the countries with the lowest GDPs whose temperatures will rise the most. But it is not the global south that will bear the only impact of the climate breakdown, even if our most selfish inclinations might wish this to be so. In fact, the USA, along with India and Saudi Arabia, will be one of the countries hit hardest by the climate crisis.[22]

Humanity is pumping out carbon at a rate that is one hundred times faster than before the industrial revolution.[23] As a result, there is one third more carbon in the world's atmosphere than at any time in the past 800,000 years.[24] More than half of the carbon released into the atmosphere by burning fossil fuels arrived in the last three decades – that is, since Margaret Thatcher stepped down as prime minister during my own university days.[25] In this time, we have sown such havoc across our planet that we are now destined to heat the world up by *at least* two degrees Celsius by 2100. Scientists from the UN Meteorological Agency say it will be more like three to five degrees.

Global temperature rises of between two and five degrees may sound modest in the abstract, and even appealing to a Brit tired of mild summers. But the reality is catastrophic.

As David Wallace-Wells has written, even in the best-case scenario of a two-degree rise in global temperature, some major cities will become uninhabitable. Heatwaves will kill thousands of people each year and hundreds of millions more of us will endure water scarcity. If global temperature rises four degrees by 2100, the effects will be even more catastrophic. Saharan deserts will spread through southern and central Europe, whole equatorial regions will become unliveable, and much of the human population will be forced to live in northern parts of the globe, including Scandinavia, Alaska, Siberia and Canada.[26]

Given the scale of the climate crisis, there is no way we can fix it as individual nations. So far, the most significant international effort to tackle it has been the Paris Climate Agreement, COP21. It did not, however, go nearly far enough. Most overdeveloped nations are not on target to reduce emissions to the extent they promised in 2015,[27] while others – including Turkey and Russia – have set unambitious targets.[28] The global response to the climate crisis has strengthened in rhetoric, but this has been accompanied by failure to act. Ten years ago, for example, the G20 committed to phasing out fossil-fuel subsidies.[29] In reality, subsidies tripled for coal-fired power plants in just three years, to $47 billion.[30]

Much of the Paris agreement's failure is down to doubt over whether it is legally binding. The reality is that some parts are mandatory, while others are not. Some requirements use the modal verb 'should', others 'may', as well as the one that obliges signatories to act: 'shall'. There are 117 uses of 'shall' in the text of the climate accord. Most 'shalls' are vague enough to avoid tying countries to anything specific. For example: 'Parties shall take into consideration in the implementation of this Agreement the concerns of Parties with economies most affected by the impacts of response measures, particularly developing country Parties'.[31] It is not clear what actions 'take into consideration' actually requires.

Given climate breakdown does not discriminate against borders, we need to engage at a supranational level if we are going to save our planet. This is one of the many reasons why I campaigned for the UK to keep its seat at the top table of Europe. The EU has recently committed to cut greenhouse gas emissions by at least 40 per cent by 2030 and boost the share of renewable energy to at least 32 per cent. Eighteen of the EU's members are now ready to support the European Commission's proposed carbon neutrality objective for 2050. The EU Commission, backed by eight member states, is pressing for a quarter of the EU budget to be spent on measures to combat climate breakdown.

Many populist nationalists – including Donald Trump, the Sweden Democrats and the True Finns – are working to prevent action to lessen the climate crisis. For them, it has become a new front in the culture wars. Rather than recognising the climate issue as a global one, these politicians attempt to frame any reform as a gift from the developed to the developing world. This plays on the very worst of our tribal instincts, and must be overcome if we are to respond to this global emergency.

The truth is that nothing erases the false dividing lines of tribes more indiscriminately than the climate emergency, which makes no distinction based on race, political affiliation, religion, identity or worldview. To face the broad threat of the climate emergency, we must be motivated to work together, as part of the human race. If we cannot move beyond our tribalism on this of all issues, we risk our world's future environmental collapse.

MASS MOVEMENT OF PEOPLE

'If I return home, they will kill me without a doubt,' said Ahmed, a twenty-seven-year-old Iranian with thick black hair and a limp. We were standing outside his tent in a small, improvised campsite on some scrubland near the sand dunes in Calais. I had been led there by guides from a British charity. We arrived hot from a ten-minute walk down a track in the heat of the midday summer sun. I could smell sweat and cigarettes around me. Beside us, water for tea was coming to the boil over a campfire.

Ahmed spoke the best English of the group of Kurdish men who huddled around me. 'My application for asylum was rejected in Denmark,' he explained. 'I can't go forward to the UK . . . I can't go anywhere. I'm stuck.'

At its peak in 2015 and 2016, it is estimated that around 10,000 refugees lived together in the infamous Calais 'jungle' camp. In autumn of 2016, after much anger from Calais residents and local politicians, the camp was officially destroyed and fenced off. When I visited in the summer of 2019, however, I met dozens of refugees sleeping rough on the dry ground between bushes and trees in the Sangatte area, not far from the Channel Tunnel. There are now an estimated 1,300 refugees spread across northern France hoping to reach the UK.[32]

Most nights, Ahmed and dozens of others in his campsite attempt to climb on to the back of a lorry that will board a P&O ferry or cross the Channel via the tunnel. Others take an even greater risk, buying rubber dinghies and attempting to sail across. In 2018, at least 539 migrants made the perilous trip on small boats.[33] Most attempts ended in failure.

Ahmed told me his problems began three years ago, when he was at university in Tehran. Raised as a Muslim, during his early adult-hood he began to question his faith and became interested in Christianity. One day at an academic conference his university was hosting, he entered into an argument with another audience member, stating his view that it is wrong to execute people who renounce Islam. He had discussed his views before, but only in private. When he took the step to speak out publicly, he was reported to the authorities by other attendees.

In 2017, Iran executed at least 507 people, which accounted for 6 out every 10 confirmed executions in the Middle East that year. The Iran Human Rights Documentation Center, a non-profit organisation that gets funding from the US and Canadian governments, says the number may be even higher because the state often conducts executions in secret.[34] A majority of those killed were guilty of violent crimes, but others were killed for drug offences, adultery, homosexuality, apostasy and imprecise crimes like 'sowing corruption on Earth'.

Ahmed was right to be worried. Not only did he denounce the execution of apostates, he had lost his faith in Islam and converted to Christianity. The persecution of Christians in Iran is orchestrated from the highest levels of the government. In October 2014, President Hassan Rouhani's senior adviser on Ethnic and Religious Minority Affairs publicly reaffirmed that 'converting to different sects is illegal in our country'. The phone calls, emails and Skype conversations of known Christian converts in Iran are monitored by the Ministry of Intelligence and Security (MOIS). Christians are routinely arrested and detained for interrogation.[35] During long spells in detention centres, they are abused physically and mentally, and receive threats of execution. Punishments for converts often include dozens of lashes, but in the most extreme cases they have included capital punishment.

The primary intention of the MOIS treatment of Christians in Iran is to force the religious minority into fleeing the country as refugees. Indeed, Ahmed told me he felt he had little other choice. He gathered all the money he could find, said an emotional goodbye to his loved ones, and travelled to Iraq and then Turkey, before crossing the border into Europe.

> I first tried to claim asylum in Denmark. The process was very slow. While I was seeking asylum, I broke my leg playing football. The doctor refused to give me an operation before I had secured the right status . . . I tried to pay the doctor, I even offered them my phone in return. He did not allow it.
>
> I waited for months to get an answer, but when it finally came back, I got a 'no' . . . My leg is still in so much pain.

Refugees in Calais stick closest to those from the same country or ethnic group. Divisions are not as precise as in the old 'jungle' camp, where Eritreans, Sudanese, Syrians and Afghanis each lived in separate zones. Ahmed was living with other Kurds, mainly from Iran and Iraq. A few hundred metres away, there was another camp. About two dozen black Africans were smoking and chatting around an extinguished fire under a blue tarpaulin sheet held up by sticks. Their seats were made of an old pine chest of drawers, some crates and various blocks of concrete and plastic crates. Although it was midday, many others were asleep in their tents, resting in preparation for planned attempts, later that evening, to reach England.

Yusef, a volunteer from the charity which had organised my trip, introduced me, in French, to the group. I was invited to settle in under the tarpaulin. 'It's a fucking life, my brother. We are living like animals in the bush. This fucking life,' said a young Gambian man wearing sunglasses, orange Nike shorts and a green camouflage jacket. 'No one expected these conditions. I have been here almost five months now . . . When I call my friends in Africa, they will not believe the state I am living in and they will not expect any of us [are] living like this.'

I asked the young men where they were from.

'Gambia,' said one. 'Ivory Coast,' said another. Then, 'Senegal,' 'Mali,' 'Burkina Faso,' 'Niger,' 'Guinea.' Another man cut in: 'We are West Africans.'

Each of them had a unique story to tell about how they had arrived in France, but their experiences in Calais painted a similar picture of suffering. These days refugees living in Calais are woken up two or three times a week by police, who tear down their tents, confiscate their possessions and force them to move on. On average, French police conduct camp evictions against refugees in the port area more than once a day. There had been 803 forced evictions in the previous year.[36]

Reports of intimidation, verbal abuse and physical violence, as well as intrusive surveillance against both refugees and the aid workers trying to help them, are common.[37] Much of this heavy-handed police work is funded by the British government, which gave France £44.5 million in 2018 for 'additional security measures to prevent the reconstruction of refugee camps in Calais'.[38] Between 2015 and 2018, under the French–British Touquet Agreement, the British government paid £150 million. Felipe González, the UN special rapporteur on migrants, has described the situation as being the result of 'regressive migration policies'. He described conditions in northern France as 'inhumane and substandard'.[39]

There is a common misconception in parts of the British press and among the public that every refugee entering Europe wants to come to the UK. This is simply not true. At the peak of the refugee crisis, in 2015, 1.1 million asylum seekers registered in Germany.[40] In the same year, the UK received just 32,733 refugees.[41] Britain is a considerably less popular destination among asylum seekers than the British public thinks.[42] Millions of refugees do not attempt to enter Europe at all: 80 per cent of the world's 26 million refugees live in countries neighbouring their own country of origin.[43] Since 2011, Lebanon has become home to 1.5 million Syrians and Palestinian refugees from Syria, meaning that refugees now constitute 30 per cent of Lebanon's population.[44]

The minority of refugees who do travel to northern France to reach the UK usually have a specific reason for doing so. They almost always either speak the language or have friends or family here already. A couple of the men I met in the campsites dotted around Sangatte said they hoped to become professional footballers or boxers. The overwhelming majority said they wanted to study before finding a job.

'What is the message you want me to transmit to the British public?' I asked the group.

There was a moment of silence. Then the young Gambian piped up: 'We are not bad people. We are not criminals. We want to integrate.'

Around forty minutes' drive from Calais is the city of Dunkirk. Before I visited, I associated Dunkirk with the immense bravery of the ordinary British people and soldiers who evacuated Allied troops from the beaches during the Second World War. Today it is home to around 88,000 people, including several hundred refugees. The commune of Grande-Synthe, near Dunkirk, hosts 500 refugees inside the public gymnasium and outside in tents that line the car park. This gym has become the prime destination for predominantly Kurdish refugees, fleeing Iraq, Iran and Turkey.

The refugees in Grande-Synthe have limited access to showers and toilets, but these were designed for thirty or forty gym users, not 500 residents. The tents are cramped and hot, but certainly beat the conditions of the desolate scrubland around Calais, where refugees are afraid each night that the police will wake them and confiscate their tents.

At a stand in the centre of the Grande-Synthe camp, loud music was blaring from a large black speaker. Kurds were selling kebabs, chicken and bread, alongside ice-cold Coke, reminding me of Green Lanes in the constituency I represent in London. Tottenham is home to the largest Kurdish community in the country. I have spent countless afternoons in Kurdish homes and community centres.

As soon as word travelled that I was a British member of parliament, men, women and children surrounded me. Many were sick. Some had unhealthy skin conditions. I found it hard to hold back tears as two mothers with severely autistic sons asked for help. One of the mothers introduced me to her young son. His eyes were closed and his arms flailing. 'Before, I was able to see a doctor with him at least once every month,' the mother told me, 'but here we have nothing. Everything [is] worse.'

'I have never been so emotional as I feel at this time,' the family's father said. 'I will swim across the water if it means we can get to England.'

When I imagine the borders of the United Kingdom, I picture images of the white cliffs of Dover, the peaceful Outer Hebrides, the Welsh coast and the border on the island of Ireland. The UK government has outsourced our main border to France. It is this externalisation that has allowed Britain to feel detached from the trauma and human suffering on its edge. These days, British media coverage of Calais is scarce. Public attitudes remain fixed. Compared with a mere 18 per cent who say we are doing too little, 30 per cent of the British public believe the British government offers refugees too much help.[45] Only a quarter of the public believes we should let more people 'fleeing persecution or war' come to the UK.[46] Britain's aversion to refugees is not unique. In Germany, two out of three people have negative attitudes towards asylum seekers.[47] Globally, the proportion of people who believe borders should be kept open to refugees has fallen from 51 per cent in 2017 to 46 per cent in 2019.

The drivers of the refugee crisis are only going to intensify over the next century. The UN estimates that there will be 200 million climate refugees by 2050. Those made stateless by environmental changes are not currently covered by the UN Refugee Convention, which was designed for those fleeing war, violence and persecution. If we are to honour the spirit of the definition, this must be broadened to include climate refugees.

As of 2019, no institution can enforce the Refugee Convention at the global level.[48] Burden-sharing between countries will only be fixed with the sharpening of the United Nations High Commissioner for Refugees' teeth or enforcement by other institutions at the supranational level. The EU has made the most effort to do this, but its member countries are further bound by the 2013 Dublin Regulation, which requires a refugee arriving in the EU to request asylum in the first country in which they arrive. The result is that the burden weighs disproportionately on countries on Europe's long sea borders, such as

Italy and Greece. This is simply not fair. A common European asylum policy should allow EU member states and close partners to share responsibilities and resources for asylum applications. It is unacceptable that a country of the UK's size and wealth housed just 121,837 refugees and had 40,365 pending asylum cases between the beginning of the Syrian refugee crisis and the end of 2017, given the scale of the global demand. This is just one quarter of 1 per cent of the UK's population.[49] The contribution of each nation state – measured by the numbers of refugees housed, the financial support and manpower provided, overseas aid contributions and diplomatic efforts – should be proportionate.[50] A more systematic approach should be developed for wealthier nations to pay into a fund for countries, like Lebanon and Kenya, who host huge numbers of refugees, disproportionate to their own resources and population.

It is important to separate refugees – those fleeing violence, persecution or war – from other migrants who wish to move to a new country for economic or social reasons. However, the debate around all forms of human movement has become vexed because it plays into tribal divisions – this is, at least in part, because of the perceived uneven way these issues hit certain groups within host countries. While the net effect of migration on a host nation is positive, anti-migrant politicians emphasise the risk of foreign labour putting pressure on low-skilled workers' salaries and public services. All the evidence suggests that if this effect on low-skilled workers' wages exists, it is tiny – and it could easily be made up for through a small redistribution of the overall net gains to a host society.[51] This analysis also ignores the extent to which our public services depend on high levels of migration. Take the National Health Service, for example: 13.1 per cent of its staff are not British citizens. Just imagine how much worse the crisis in our hospitals would be without them.

The scapegoating of migrants for national policy failures must end. It is my view that we should celebrate migration, rather than get defensive about it. And we should address the root causes of anti-migrant feeling through sound investment in our public services, rather than succumb to indulging an anti-migrant narrative that lacks an evidential base. Some of my peers in the Labour Party think differently. Stephen

Kinnock MP and former MP Emma Reynolds have argued that, by failing to argue for reduced migration, Labour has 'left a vacuum for the right to fill'.[52] Stephen and Emma have called for a two-tier visa system after Brexit, in which low-skilled and semi-skilled workers have their access restricted to the UK labour market, determined by sector-based quotas. The problem with caps on immigration is that they are necessarily rigid and inflexible. Arbitrarily limiting the number of migrants arriving in the UK will leave gaps in the workforce, potentially forcing businesses to close and reducing funding for our public services for no clear benefit.

One way we might be able to de-toxify the immigration debate, without mimicking the policy prescriptions of the populist nationalist right, is to move it to the local and regional level. In the UK, one of the most centralised countries in the developed world, we assume that policies on issues like immigration must always be set at the national level. However, this is not the case elsewhere. Denmark has given its ninety-eight municipalities discretion over managing integration policies, allowing them to establish local integration councils that consult on and debate integration issues. Similarly, in Finland, municipalities have responsibility over planning, developing and monitoring integration at the local level. Belgium goes further, by devolving responsibility over economic migration largely to its regions.[53] There are two other major countries with significant regional variation in migration policy: Australia and Canada. Both nations have federalised structures that allow decisions on migration policy at the local level.

There are two ways in which devolving migration policy to the sub-national level could work. First, there could be 'modest variation' between regions which would have mostly similar eligibility criteria but with one region having lower salary requirements, for example. The alternative is a 'large variation' system which would allow entirely different visa types and requirements between different areas.[54] At present, the UK's political structures are too centralised for either version. Devolving migration policy to the sub-national level would require a radical decentralisation of the UK, with newly empowered metro mayors and regional assemblies.

If a significant devolution of power out of Westminster does occur, allowing regions more influence over migration policy may allow local people to feel more ownership and control over the rate of change in their community. It would also enable policymakers to consider local factors rather than relying on a one-size-fits-all approach. The substantial regional variation in attitudes towards immigration would be more accurately reflected, and local authorities could make appropriate spending commitments in related areas like integration and housing.

To be clear, I would prefer the whole of the UK to embrace a position that is welcoming to migrants from across the rest of the world. However, given the toxicity of the migration debate at the national level, it is worth at least considering how devolving some migration policy decisions to the regional level might work. This change would not necessarily lead to stricter or more flexible immigration rules, but simply change the level at which decisions are made. It seems likely that initially in cosmopolitan centres, like London, Manchester, Liverpool and parts of Scotland, migration rules would be relaxed; while in other regions migration controls may be tightened. If this devolution was enacted, I hope that areas which initially opted for tighter migration controls would change their minds, once they see the economic, social and cultural benefits to those areas which chose more flexible migration rules from the start.

INEQUALITY

As of 2019, the world's richest twenty-six people have as much wealth as the 3.8 billion people who make up the poorest 50 per cent of the world's population.[55, 56] The economic gap has widened both within and between countries. In large part, this is because the rate of return on capital has been considerably higher than the rate of economic growth.[57] The effects of inequality are made worse by the fact that this is a time of unprecedented ease of travel and instant communication between people from different continents. The global poor can see on their smartphones how the rich live.

What's worse is that the super-rich can avoid and evade tax with ease. According to wealth detective Gabriel Zucman, $7.6 trillion is held in tax havens, most of which is undeclared.[58] Legal loopholes in our global taxation system mean that even some of the richest are asking to pay more. The billionaire Warren Buffett admitted to CNBC that he pays a lower effective tax rate than anyone in his office. This includes those on modest salaries, like his secretary. 'I'll probably be the lowest-paying taxpayer in the office,' Buffett said.[59] Primarily, he does this by 'donating' huge sums of money to certain organisations so that he can take advantage of the maximum 30 per cent charitable deduction for appreciated property.[60] National governments are bad at preventing tax avoidance on their own. A global company can simply move its HQ to the neighbouring country. A wealthy individual can buy citizenship or residency somewhere with more relaxed rules.

One way to stop global inequality from deepening is to introduce a global wealth tax. Estimates vary on how much this would raise, and they depend on the threshold and rate. Even a small wealth tax of 1 per cent on the world's billionaires would raise an estimated $100 billion annually.[61] Another report has shown that a tax of half a per cent on the richest would be enough to provide health treatment that could save 3.3 million people from early death. Alternatively, it could be used to pay for the education of all 262 million children currently denied access to school.[62] In addition to a new global wealth tax, we need a new infrastructure of global rules and institutions to prevent both tax avoidance and tax evasion. If we do so, the gains of technological innovation and economic growth can be far more evenly spread.

Once revenues have been raised through closing legal loopholes, raising taxes for the super-rich and strictly enforcing anti-tax-evasion rules, we will have access to vast resources that can be spent on further reducing global inequality. Britain can be proud that it is one of the few big economies that meet the UN's global aid target of 0.7 per cent of GDP.[63] This means that for every £100 made in the UK, seventy pence goes towards foreign aid and development. A wealth tax offers the opportunity either to redistribute more wealth to the rest of the world or to provide a new way of funding our existing commitment. Creating a global wealth tax would, of course, be difficult. It would require supranational cooperation on a larger scale than we have previously witnessed, at a time when it has become unfashionable. Nevertheless, we must take hope from the fact that great acts of international cooperation have been achieved before.

Following the Second World War, Europe was exhausted and broke, and millions of its working-age men had been killed. The continent's victorious and defeated alike faced bleak economic prospects. In response, US Secretary of State George C. Marshall designed the Marshall Plan, which provided $15 billion to help finance the redevelopment of broken industries, infrastructure and flattened cities in Europe. The UK was its greatest beneficiary, receiving around 25 per cent of the total funds. In the decades that followed this four-year plan for strategic development, economists and historians have debated the impact of the funds. While it is difficult to know the precise impact of the funding, by the end of the plan in 1952, economic growth was higher in the beneficiary countries than it was before the war.

European countries should cooperate more on foreign aid and introduce linked-up strategic plans in the spirit of the Marshall Plan for underdeveloped regions of the world. Rather than providing aid just for crises, modern Marshall Plans should focus on setting up infrastructure, industry and innovation in those countries. The intention should be to eradicate the need for international aid. Let me be clear: I believe that aid is a moral duty of rich countries in an unequal world. But governments wishing to reduce migration can also be motivated to provide aid for selfish reasons. Though the extent of this effect is debated, by providing financial assistance to poorer nations that want to develop further, we reduce the incentive for people to migrate.[64] Modern, globally coordinated Marshall Plans will be far more effective at addressing inequality than the actions of any individual nation state. They could also find support on both the left and the right.

If we can smooth over the harshest edges of inequality nationally and globally, tribalism will inevitably decline. Those with the least will feel less vulnerable and more secure. And hopefully there will be a growing recognition, across our societies, that we are strongest when we face the world's challenges together.

A NEW POLITICS OF BELONGING

It is not only that tribalism makes it very difficult to deal with problems relating to migration, the climate crisis and inequality. It is also the case that each of these issues plays into tribal divisions because of the uneven way they hit different groups. Tackling climate change is perceived by many in the developed world as requiring transfers to the underdeveloped world. Nationalist populists, from Trump to the True Finns and the Sweden Democrats, are framing attacks on climate reform as though it is in opposition to working-class interests. This is even more clear when it comes to migration, which, while beneficial to host countries as a whole, makes the worst-off in these countries feel as though migrants undercut their own wages and put pressure on public services, even when this is not the case.

I do not claim to have all the answers. There is no simple solution to move beyond tribalism, defeat the new wave of populist nationalism and tackle the global challenges humanity faces. I believe the place to start is by filling the vacuum of leadership on belonging, identity and community.

One answer to the crisis of belonging is to construct a global identity to sit on top of our local and national identities. An argument for it goes something like this. Identities are built as layers on top of one another; they do not always compete for the same space. Just as my pride in Tottenham does not make me any less of an English patriot, neither should my fundamental belief in the equality of all people. Believing that countries which have sufficient resources and institutions should provide sanctuary for the stateless is not an attempt to undermine a nation's existing citizens. Instead, generosity and openness to the world can be a source of pride. So, what is stopping us from building a global identity that spans humanity?

The problem with putting forward a global identity as the solution to our crisis of belonging is that while it may be desirable, it is unrealistic. Fostering solidarity between Barking and Blackpool is difficult enough, let alone between Berlin and Barbados. As much as some of us may will it, globalism is unlikely ever to be as powerful as the pushes and pulls of our local communities and neighbourhoods. The democratic nation state is still the primary unit for forging common purpose and solidarity. Therefore, the main political means for overcoming the antagonisms and conflicts caused by the new tribalism can be found locally and nationally.

The UK has always been a place of contradiction, political paradox and layers of identity. Nearly 20 per cent of our population is not 'White British'.[65] Just 14 per cent identify as members of the Church of England.[66] More than 3 million non-UK EU citizens live in the UK.[67] There are more than 300 languages spoken in London schools alone.[68] In the political and media class, we too often forget it, but we are a union of four nations. At times of strength, our Scottish, Northern Irish, Welsh and English identities have been able hang together within a broader Britishness.

We can take courage from moments in our history. In the past, we have overcome far more bitter, bloody and divisive conflicts than the culture war we are fighting over Brexit today. Just a few hundred years ago, Britain was split between Catholics and Protestants. In 1780, Lord George Gordon led a protest of 60,000 to the Palace of Westminster to present a petition urging the repeal of the Catholic Relief Act of 1778, which Protestants claimed threatened the Church of England and encouraged 'popery'.[69] The anti-Catholic riots that followed became the deadliest in British history, with around 1,000 people killed.[70] In 1605, Guy Fawkes had attempted to blow up Parliament and the Protestant King James I in a brutal expression of loyalty to the Catholic faith. Moving beyond these tribal divisions took centuries of effort. In most of modern Britain, Catholics and Protestants live next to each other in relative harmony, alongside Jews, Sikhs, Muslims, Buddhists and Hindus. I am a member of the Church of England, but by tradition the high church I follow is Anglo Catholic. In 2017, at a service attended by Protestants and Catholics in Westminster Abbey to mark five centuries since the reformation, the Archbishop of Canterbury Justin Welby, said, 'We have learned to love one another again.'[71]

Sport is another of the ways in which the flexibility of these identities has been shown to be Britain's strength. The purist left and the communitarian right alike have criticised metropolitans for harking back to the 2012 Olympics as the epitome of an open, inclusive Britishness. Still, in many ways it was: the opening ceremony celebrated Britain's history, from the village green and maypole dancers, to the smoky chimneys of the industrial revolution, the arrival of the *Empire Windrush*, the creation of the NHS, and a modern-day love story which highlighted the power of social media, with a nod to Tim Berners-Lee, the British inventor of the World Wide Web.

Since 2012, we've seen enough flashes of this civic spirit to be sure it still exists. In many of the summers since, English crowds have found pride in a dour Scot whose skill and determination took him to the top of tennis and gave Britain its first men's singles Wimbledon winner in eight decades. When England's World Cup-winning cricket captain, Dublin-born Eoin Morgan, was asked whether he thought the 'luck of an Irishman got England over the line', Morgan replied: 'We had Allah with us as well. I spoke to Adil [Rashid, the team's Muslim leg spinner]. He said Allah was definitely with us. I said we had the rub of the green.' Alongside the tribal identities that have begun to dominate our four nations, an inclusive, civic spirit has run in parallel, offering a potential song of redemption.

There are two options for Britain. Many nations across the world face the same stark choice. The first is to dive more deeply into a nation-hood that defines itself by ethnicity, the illusion of genetic purity and ancestral supremacy. If we choose this tribal path, we commit ourselves to decades of cultural, political and moral strife. The abstract ideal of ethnic nationalism will inevitably clash with the reality of a multi-national, multi-racial, socially and religiously diverse union. In this future vision of Britain, those with characteristics that mark them out as different will be tolerated at best. At worst they will be denigrated.

The second choice is to reimagine a civic patriotism that brings together our union's diverse tribes into one super-community. An inclusive identity that brings the four nations, social classes, ethnicities, and cities and towns together. Revitalised localities coupled with a new culture of encounter beyond them. A municipal Britain working together, with the recognition of our diversity, to prepare for the new challenges and vast opportunities of the next century.

Our history reminds us that we have always done best when standing up straight, with our shoulders back and reaching outwards to the world. The Empire was built with supremacy, domination and subjugation. But, paradoxically, this has left us as a multicultural Britain with footprints, ties and relationships across the planet. If we honestly tell the stories of our past mistakes, confront and reconcile with them, we can look forward with wisdom and humility. A new inclusive national identity will restore the spirit of optimism and generosity we have lost. A future beyond tribalism, with shared spaces and institutions where we all belong.

MORE IN COMMON

Besides, we may have more in common than it seems. In the political realm, we have been pushed into tribes based around identities such as Leave and Remain, and Republican and Democrat, as well as ethnically and religiously rooted identity groups. While this has been happening, there is evidence that on specific issues we are starting to find large areas of agreement. A national study in the USA revealed that Democrats and Republicans wildly overestimate the extremity of their opponents' political opinions. Democrats guessed that only half of Republicans would consider racism still to be a problem in America today, but the true figure is eight out of ten. Republicans guessed half of all Democrats would agree with the statement 'most police are bad people', but in reality only 15 per cent believe this.

In modern Britain, there is increasing consensus on social issues. There is now a clear and growing majority in favour of same-sex relationships, opposition to racial prejudice and support for gender equality.[72] The percentage of the population that agrees with the statements 'a man's job [is] to earn money' and 'a woman's job [is] to look after the home and family' has decreased from more than 40 per cent in 1980 to less than 8 per cent today.[73] There is even growing consensus over public policy priorities. Leave and Remain supporters alike prioritise more investment in health and social care and providing more support for families living in poverty.[74]

Perhaps more surprising is that, despite our new political divides, we are becoming more trusting of people in general. Between 1998 and 2014, the percentage of the public that said they believe 'people can be trusted' remained steady at around 45 per cent. In 2017, it jumped to 54 per cent. While our political tribes have pushed us to become more polarised around certain identities, this is encouraging evidence that it has not been accompanied by a wholesale breakdown in trust outside of politics.

We can use these areas of agreement to help us visualise what our nation could look like in a new age of connection. One built on radical localism threaded together by a shared national story and values. Municipal governments pursuing different approaches to shared challenges and goals. Businesses working to maximise welfare as well as profits. Communities held together by a state that sees its role as fostering connection as much as efficiency.

Centralised Britain must loosen its grip on the purse strings that are strangling our towns and regions. People should be represented by local leaders who look, sound and live like them. Giving each region a metro mayor with increased powers and the ability to tax and spend is a good start. Allowing regions to vary their immigration policies will make them feel in control. In our neighbourhoods, we can commit to mixing with other generations beyond simply our family members. Older people should be encouraged to teach children and young adults their area's social history in our schools. Neighbours can be inspired to help each other because they are part of the same community, not benefactors to a 'service' or a charity. We can make a concerted effort to speak civilly to those with different viewpoints, even when we disagree.

To foster a radically localised encounter culture, in which people have meaningful interactions, we have to go beyond the political. We should encourage initiatives where people who share postcodes and neighbourhoods spend time with each other and build solidarity in real time and space. New community initiatives – from food assemblies to secular services and street Olympics – can complement a restoration of the local libraries, youth services and community gardens that have been starved of resources for too long. In our neighbourhoods, we can begin looking up from our smartphones and towards each other. Let us remember how to have conversations on trains, buses and cafés, instead of spending all our time on Twitter. Why not abandon the pain of the treadmill for the community struggle of the Parkrun? Instead of retreating into the comfort of a Netflix subscription, why not put the same money each month into a community outdoor film screening?

Imagine these newly empowered local communities as the bricks held together by the mortar of a new civic Britain, itself made up of four proud nations but united around a common purpose. A newly confident England, with a permanent citizens' assembly, at last with its own voice, will provide balance with the devolved nations of Scotland, Wales and Northern Ireland. Together we can agree on aspirational values, like creativity, openness and fairness, to put at the root of our decision-making. We can replace a complicated and uncodified British constitution with a new document setting out our inalienable rights, freedoms and guiding principles. New generations of young people will be bound together by a year of compulsory national civic service, in cohorts mixed up according to gender, geography, educational background, ethnicity and social class. This can all be founded on an honest telling of our national history that reflects and learns from our historic failures as much as our successes.

A world beyond tribes will not work if it is a world without belonging. It is only through finding meaning in strong local and national identities that we will have the collective confidence to challenge the problems that go far beyond them. Our era of loneliness can be replaced by an epoch of meaningful connection. Hope can overtake fear. Competitiveness replaced by cooperation. Compassion before argument. Communities instead of tribes.

Postscript

On a mild April night in 2005, seventeen-year-old Charles Osei-Bonsu was hanging out with a group of teenagers on the street beside the Broadwater Farm Community Centre in Tottenham. Contrary to stereotypes, the group were not causing trouble. In fact, they were some of the hundreds of guests attending the Ghanaian Community Education Awards that evening. Earlier, I had presented Charles with a prize for his outstanding exam results. As so often happens at these community events, by the end of the night, the young people had separated from their parents and the rest of the party to spend time with their peers. All was calm, until just after midnight, when a silver Fiat Punto approached at high speed. Inside the car, as I later learned, were members of the 'MOB' gang from nearby Wood Green. Mistaking the crowd of teenagers for the rival 'Farm Boys' gang, they opened fire.

When we heard the gunshots from inside the community centre, a group of community elders and I immediately sprinted outside. Shocked, pumped up and filled with adrenalin, we experienced the kind of tunnel vision that only comes during a moment of crisis. We found Charles sprawled on the pavement. He was squirming in agony, with blood pouring out of his body. Several of us frantically dialled

'999'. A man ripped off his shirt, converting it into a bandage to stop more blood from draining out onto the tarmac. A woman wiped the sweat off his forehead with a handkerchief. Two others held his hands and told him it would all be OK. We kneeled around Charles waiting for the ambulance to arrive. At first, he was screaming and moaning loudly, but after a few minutes his voice became weaker as he lost consciousness.

After what felt like an hour, but was probably no more than twenty minutes, we heard the ambulance sirens approaching. Absurdly, the police blocked the road, preventing the ambulance from reaching the crime scene. I could not believe it. With my white shirt and suit soaked in blood, I began running up the road. A passing car picked me up and took me the final few hundred metres to the police and paramedics. I begged them to come and help my severely wounded constituent. I was told that the police were afraid the shooter was still active and did not want to put their lives at risk.

Fortunately, Charles survived the drive-by shooting. If it had been left to the emergency services that night, he may well have bled to death. Charles was saved by the bravery, love and care of normal citizens. People who did not think twice about running towards the gunshots to help rather than keeping a safe distance away. This is the kind of inner-city story you rarely hear about. Too often we focus on the derangement of a killer as evidence of the fundamental evil of human nature. In doing this, we forget the much larger section of the population that is horrified by violence, filled with empathy for its victims and desperate to help whenever they can.

In this book I have focused on the antagonistic side of human nature, but this is not the full story. Of all mammals, human beings are uniquely social.[1] Studies in evolutionary biology, psychology and neuroscience suggest we are an extreme outlier in the animal kingdom when it comes to cooperation.[2, 3, 4] Working together in much larger groups than any other animals tolerate is, in part, what makes us human. This gets to the crux of an old debate. Thomas Hobbes saw humans as a naturally chaotic and violent species made civil by society. Jean-Jacques Rousseau disagreed, arguing instead that people are instinctively peaceful but corrupted by malign influences in society.

Are we naturally violent or peaceful? Are we inherently tribal or cooperative? The truth is a paradox: we are both.

Darwinian biologists initially viewed cooperation as difficult to understand in terms of evolution.[5] It was believed that natural selection benefits those who behave selfishly. Survival of the fittest means looking after yourself. Cooperation, which involves the sacrifice of one individual to increase the fitness of the other, goes against this logic. This ignores the fact that cooperation does not always involve a sacrifice. In fact, a group of individuals working together can produce a better outcome for every individual than if they had each worked by themselves.[6]

Imagine you are out in the forest, on your own, hunting for rabbits. Suddenly you see a stag in the distance. The stag is a much better catch than a rabbit – it could feed you for weeks rather than a day or two – but you cannot kill the stag on your own. At the same time, another hunter is also looking for rabbits when they spot the same stag. You decide to team up to catch it. The result of your cooperation is that you both end up with far more and better food from the stag than if you had hunted for a rabbit on your own. The 'stag hunt parable' applies far beyond stag hunting and across human society.[7] Rather than working in opposition to natural selection, cooperation lies at the centre of both our everyday interactions and the greatest human endeavours. The Eiffel Tower was not built by one man. Some of the best music is made by bands and orchestras. Happiness is most often found in social relations, not individual success.

If we are to overcome tribalism with a new project of cooperation, it cannot be overly partisan. There are reasons to support a new politics of belonging from both the left and the right. Small 'c' conservatives who value tradition, family values and place should be invigorated by the opportunity to restore pride in our localities. Left-wingers who value solidarity, the social fabric and equality should spot it as a chance to create opportunity and hope for the many. I hope people from all sides of the political spectrum can understand and even agree with the principles of this book. Moving beyond polarisation does not mean compromising our values. Instead it means focusing a little more on the ideals we already share, rather than those that separate us. There is inherent joy and happiness to be found in working together, even when there are important subjects on which we disagree.

The only people a new civic politics of belonging will work against are the charlatans who cynically use fear to divide us. The ethnic nationalists who cling to unscientific theories of racial superiority to ease their own insecurities. The populists who offer the false solution of animosity to solve the real problems of our time. The extremists who groom the young, vulnerable and alienated, offering them hate as a replacement for meaning.

At the same time, we can demonstrate understanding of people's anxieties without agreeing with them. We should treat those who have been duped by the lies of these toxic tribes with understanding, respect and compassion. There are legitimate reasons for their anger and unease at a fast-changing world which has not been good to them. They have been pulled towards the comfort of tribal identities because we have failed to construct healthy, inclusive and civic spaces where belonging and community can thrive.

Our job now is to win them over by creating hope. We can do this by telling the positive story of humanity. A tale of extraordinary creatures who have a unique capacity for compassion and cooperation. A species that has evolved and succeeded, throughout human history, by working together in ever larger groups. From our humble beginnings in Palaeolithic tribes of one hundred or so, we formed villages, towns and independent city states. Eventually, we created the modern-day Westphalian nation, and, in recent decades, we have worked to bind these nations closer through supranational institutions and international communities. Reaching out across tribal lines is not something to be dismissed as unnatural. It is as fundamental to our human nature as our desire to feel we are part of a group in the first place.

Together we can build a society that provides opportunity for all classes, ethnicities, genders, sexualities and identity groups. Together, we can feel part of a coherent whole, instead of being just another atomised part. Together, we can replace tribes with inclusive and dynamic communities of which we can be proud. Together, we can find spaces and places to belong.

Acknowledgements

Amidst these extraordinary political times, this book simply could not have been completed without the considerable work, tenacity and impeccable dedication of Will Heilpern.

David Matthews, thank you for being a true friend and helping me to find my voice throughout this project.

The book needed a lot of heavy lifting to get it off the ground. Thank you so much to Gillian Stern, Morgan Mackinnon and James Kirchick.

Dear sweet friends who never tired of me asking for literary and editorial favours: Lara Pawson, Miranda Pyne, Kate Critchley, Ian Critchley, Simon Gow, Sabrina Broadbent and Ewan Birney.

Thank you to a dedicated team of current and former staff who support me superbly in Westminster. Jack McKenna, Oliver Durose, Josh Kaile, Gavin Cowings and Austin Cook.

I was hugely assisted by researchers, Isabel Ryan, Chris Edis, Jonty Leibowitz and Clément Julien in the early stages of the project.

Jonathan Rutherford, Dylan Kerrigan and Alex Smith, who have read early drafts and sections of the manuscripts throughout. Thank you for all your comments and suggestions.

Thank you also to Brendan Cox, Joe Jervis, John Denham, David Olusoga, Guy Standing, Afua Hirsch, David Cummings, Ben Rhodes, David Miliband, Anthony Painter, Tom Kibasi, Mark Leonard, Kwame Anthony Appiah, Mike Phillips, James Kirchick, Sunder Katwala, Julian Richards, Paul Gilroy, David Singh, David Mosse, Robert Weisberg, Hugh Gusterson, Amitai Etzioni, Gina Rippon, Henry Louis Gates Jr., Abby Wolf, Krishna Lewis, Mohammadou Saye, Alan Stone and Pat Carrington, Tanya Meadows and Sarah Clarkson at City College Peterborough.

For sacrificing your valuable time to feature in this book, thank you to Ian and Judy Gow; James Hopgood and Tricia Hopgood; Sarah Mathewson, Alhousseini Iktam, Ali Bouzou, the board and staff of Timidria, as well as Moustapha Kadi, Agouzoum and Koulouwiya and other slavery survivors; Paul Fitzjohn, David Stock, Andrew McGilivray, Diane Munday, Mark Thurston and the rest of the staff at Forterra brickyard; Amani Simpson; Adain McQuade; Ben Nimmo; Bernie Sanders; Francis Fukuyama; Lisa Nandy; Barbara Nettleton and the volunteers at Sunshine House; Eric Dier; Michael Heseltine; Natasha Grand; Clare Moseley and volunteers at Care4Calais; Dr Ewan Birney, Dr Aylwyn Scally, Dr Adam Rutherford and Dr Stuart Ritchie; Eileen Adams; Damian Wawrzyniak; Geethika Jayatilaka; the people of Hopetown village, Guyana and so many more.

Thank you to my publisher Andreas Campomar for putting your faith in me and for your insights on the text throughout, as well as Andrew Gordon my literary agent for making *Tribes* happen. Finally, thanks must go to my editors Paul Murphy and Una McGovern.

METHOD

As a politician, it is unsurprising that the ideas covered in this book are broad, but not covered in great depth. Many of the concepts have been borrowed from academics, as well as other thinkers and experts. If you are interested in a specific topic or theory which I discuss, I recommend using the sources provided as a starting point. For the more personal sections of the text, I relied on memory, records and conversations with friends and family members. For the more scientific and historical sections of this book, I benefited from the help of several academics, listed above, who read and checked the relevant parts of the manuscript.

My biases, as an elected and active Member of Parliament for the Labour Party, are obvious. However, in the spirit of overcoming tribalism, I did my best to put partisan politics aside, in favour of objective reporting of facts combined with honestly held opinion. Many will disagree with my analysis, as well as my policy ideas. I welcome constructive criticism and debate.

Many of the names of those who are not public figures have been changed to protect their anonymity. Interviews have been edited for the purposes of clarity and concision.

Notes

1. A NEW TRIBALISM

1 Baz Lecocq, *Disputed Desert. Decolonisation, Competing Nationalisms and Tuareg Rebellions in Northern Mali*, Brill Publications, Leiden, 2010, p. 3.

2 Susan Rasmussen, 'Re-formations of the sacred, the secular, and modernity: nuances of religious experience among the Tuareg', *Ethnology*, Vol. 46, Iss. 3, (Summer 2007): 185–203.

3 Karl-G. Prasse, *The Tuaregs: The Blue People*, Museum Tusculanum Press, University of Copenhagen, 1995.

4 Robert Siegel and Bruce Waterhouse, *Nomadic 'Blue Men' of Sahara Receive New Attention With Mali Fighting*, National Public Radio, 23 January 2013.

5 R. Boyd and P. J. Richerson, 'Culture and the evolution of human cooperation'. *Philos Trans R Soc Lond B Biol Sci.* 2009;364(1533):3281–3288.

6 Ibid.

7 Amy Chua, *Political Tribes: Group Instinct and The Fate of Nations*, Bloomsbury Publishing, London, February 2018.

8 Aidan W. Southall, 'The Illusion of Tribe', *Journal of Asian and African Studies*, Vol. 5, No. 2, 1–2, 1970.

9 Michel Maffesoli, *The Time of the Tribes: The Decline of Individualism in Mass Society*, SAGE Publications, London, 1996.

10 Kevin Hetherington, *Expressions of Identity: Space, Performance, Politics*, SAGE Publications, London, 1998, p. 49.

11 Wojciech Dohnal, 'Tribalism of Our Times', CzasKultury/English 4-5/2007.

12 H. Tajfel, M.G. Billig, R.P. Bundy and C. Flament, 'Social categorization and intergroup behaviour'. *Eur. J. Soc. Psychol.*, 1: 149–178. 1971.

13 R. F. Baumeister and M. R. Leary, 'The need to belong: Desire for interpersonal attachments as a fundamental human motivation.' *Psychological Bulletin*, 117, 497–529. 1995.

14 Meagan M. Patterson and Rebecca S. Bigler, 'Preschool children's attention to environmental messages about groups: social categorization and the origins of intergroup bias', *Child Dev.*, Vol. 77, No. 4, 2006, pp. 847–60.

15 P. Valdesolo and D. DeSteno, 'Moral Hypocrisy: Social Groups and the Flexibility of Virtue', *Psychological Science*, 18(8), 689-690.

16 Ibid.

17 John F. Kennedy, 'Address at Rice University on the Nation's Space Effort', Rice University, Houston, 12 September 1962.

18 Calculations based on: one year as 1,000 years; one month as eighty-three years; one week as twenty years; one day as 2.857 years.

19 'Key elements of the EU-Japan Economic Partnership Agreement – Memo' https://trade.ec.europa.eu/doclib/press/index.cfm?id=1955

20 Johan Norberg, *Progress: Ten Reasons to Look Forward to the Future,* Oneworld Publications, London, 2017.

21 Ibid.

22 Ibid.

23 Office for National Statistics, *How Has Life Expectancy Changed Over Time?*, 9 September 2015.

24 Johan Norberg, *Progress: Ten Reasons to Look Forward to the Future,* Oneworld Publications, London, 2017.

25 Thomas Piketty, *Capital in the Twenty-First Century*, The Belknap Press of Harvard University Press, Massachusetts, 2014, p. 1.

26 Ministry of Housing, Communities & Local Government, *Rough Sleeping Statistics Autumn 2017, England (Revised),* 16 February 2018, p. 1.

27 National Vital Statistics System, *Mortality,* National Center for Health Statistics/ Centre for Disease Control and Prevention, Atlanta, 2018.

28 OECD Data, Youth unemployment rate.

29 Theresa May, 'The New Centre Ground', The Birmingham International Convention Centre, Birmingham, 5 October 2016.

30 BBC World Service/GlobeScan, 'Global citizenship a growing sentiment among citizens of emerging economies shows global poll for BBC World Service', 27 April 2016.

31 Lawrence H Summers, 'U.S. Economic Prospects: Secular Stagnation, Hysteresis, and the Zero Lower Bound', *Business Economics*, April 2014, Volume 49, Issue 2, pp. 65–73.

32 Cal Newport, *Digital Minimalism: Choosing a Focused Life in a Noisy World*, Portfolio, New York, 2019.

33 ReportLinker, 'Smartphone Statistics: For Most Users, It's a "Round-the-Clock" Connection', 12–13 January 2017.

34 Audit Bureau of Circulations, *National newspaper circulations for January 2019,* 2019.

35 Ivan Dylko et al., 'The dark side of technology: An experimental investigation of the influence of customizability technology on online political selective exposure', *Computers in Human Behavior*, Vol. 73, Nos. 181–190, 2017, pp. 181–190.

36 Geraldine Bedell, 'Teenage Mental-Health Crisis: Rates of Depression Have Soared In Past 25 Years', *Independent*, 27 February 2016.

37 Katharine Sadler et al., *Mental Health of Children and Young People in England, 2017*, NHS Digital/Government Statistical Service, November 2018.

38 Office for National Statistics, *Loneliness – What characteristics and circumstances are associated with feeling lonely?*, April 2018.

39 Stephanie Russell-Kraft, 'The Rise of Male Supremacist Groups', *The New Republic*, 4 April 2018.

40 Kevin Schofield, 'Lammy's whammy', *Sun,* March 2014.

41 Tony Blair, Labour Party meeting, 7 May 1997, cited in Andy McSmith, *Faces of Labour: The Inside Story,* Verso, London, 1997, p. 11.

42 Martin Luther King Jr., 'Address Delivered at the National Biennial Convention of the American Jewish Congress', Miami Beach, Florida, 14 May 1958.

43 'Tottenham Labour Party Members Only' Facebook group, March 2018.

44 'Clacton versus Cambridge', *The Economist,* 6 September 2014.

45 Sean M. Theriault, *Party Polarization in Congress*, Cambridge University Press, New York, 2008.

46 Ibid.

47 David E. Hoffman, *The Dead Hand: The Untold Story of the Cold War Arms Race and Its Dangerous Legacy*, Anchor Books, New York, 2009.

48 Cynthia R. Farina, 'Congressional Polarization: "Terminal Constitutional Dysfunction"', *Columbia Law Review,* Vol. 115, No. 7, 2015, p. 1694.

49 Terry Gross, 'How Newt Gingrich Broke Politics', *National Public Radio,* Philadelphia, 1 November 2018.

50 Newt Gingrich, 'Address to the College Republicans', Atlanta Airport Holiday Inn, 24 June 1978.

51 Newt Gingrich cited in David Osborne, 'Newt Gingrich: Shining Knight of the Post-Reagan Right', *Mother Jones Magazine,* November 1984, p. 15.

52 Samuel Earle, 'The terrifying rehabilitation of Nazi scholar Carl Schmitt', *New Statesman,* 10 April 2019.

53 Carl Schmitt, *The Concept of the Political: Expanded edition*, University of Chicago Press; Enlarged edition, 2007.

54 Raphael Gross, *Carl Schmitt and the Jews: The "Jewish Question," the Holocaust, and German Legal Theory*, University of Wisconsin Press, 2007.

55 Toby Helm, Michael Savage and Stefan Boscia, 'Whistleblowers to sue Labour as antisemitism row deepens', *Observer*, 13 July 2019.

56 Mark Townsend, 'Britain First says 5,000 of its members have joined Tories', *Observer*, 28 December 2019.

57 Michiko Kakutani, *The Death of Truth,* Tim Duggan Books, London, 2018.

58 Morning Consult/POLITICO, *National Tracking Poll,* 20–24 July 2017, p. 7.

59 The Policy Institute at King's College London/Ipsos MORI, *Brexit Misperceptions*, October 2018.

60 Glenn Kessler and Meg Kelly, 'President Trump made 2140 false or misleading claims during his first year', *Washington Post*, 20 January 2018.

61 Heather Stewart, Jennifer Rankin and Lisa O'Carroll, 'Johnson accused of misleading public over Brexit deal after NI remarks', *Guardian*, 8 November 2019.

62 Peter Bull and Will Strawson, 'Can't Answer? Won't Answer? An Analysis of Equivocal Responses by Theresa May in Prime Minister's Questions', *Parliamentary Affairs*, 2019, pp. 1–21.

63 Ibid.

64 'The politics of apathy,' *The Economist*, 29 June 2000.

65 David Lammy, 'House of Commons Debate on Public Expenditure', *Hansard*, 20 July 2000.

66 Francis Fukuyama, *The End of History and the Last Man*, Free Press, New York, 1992.

2. JERUSALEM

1 David Pilditch, 'Britain's migrant squatter shambles', *Daily Express*, 11 August 2010.

2 'Peterborough: A city crumbling under pressure from immigrants', *Daily Mail*, 20 September 2007.

3 Plan International UK, 'Walking Alone After Dark', 11 October 2016.

4 Persil, 'Dirt Is Good: The Campaign for Play'/One Poll, 2016.

5 Matthew Reville, 'Forza Peterborough! Peterborough's strong links with the Italian community', *Peterborough Today*, 27 September 2012.

6 'The history of Peterborough's development', *Peterborough Today*, 12 May 2008.

7 Office for National Statistics, *Migration levels: What do you know about your area?*, 24 August 2017.

8 Stewart Jackson MP, 'House of Commons Debate: Community Cohesion', *Hansard*, 14 July 2006.

9 Will Jennings et al., 'The Decline in Diffuse Support for National Politics: The Long View on Political Discontent in Britain', *Public Opinion Quarterly*, Vol. 81, Issue 3, Fall 2017, pp. 748–58.

10 Matthew Goodwin, 'The end of trust in our political class', *New Statesman*, 1 May 2019.

11 Paul Lewis et al., 'Revealed: One in four Europeans vote populist', *Guardian*, 20 November 2018.

12 Carl Baker, 'NHS Staff from Overseas: Statistics', Commons Library Briefing Paper, 8 July 2019.

13 Office for National Statistics, *Migrant Labour Force within the Construction Industry: June 2018*, 19 June 2018.

14 Polly Simpson, *Public Spending on Adult Social Care in England*, Institute for Fiscal Studies, 3 May 2017.

15 Anthony Barnett, *The Lure of Greatness: England's Brexit and America's Trump*, Unbound, London, 2017.

16 Office for National Statistics, Index of Production.

17 Richard Florida, *The New Urban Crisis*, Basic Books, New York, 2016.

18 Michael Bruter and Sarah Harrison, 'Understanding the emotional act of voting', *Nature Human Behaviour*, Vol. 1, 2017, pp. 1–3.

19 Office for National Statistics, *The probability of automation in England: 2011 and 2017*, 25 March 2019.

20 Valentina Romei, 'UK unemployment rate drops to lowest level since 1974', *Financial Times*, 14 May 2019.

21 Gavin Jackson, 'How much underemployment is left in the labour market?', *Financial Times*, 19 August 2018.

22 'Luke Raikes, Arianna Giovannini and Bianca Getzel, State of the North 2019, Institute for Public Policy Research, November 2019.

23 Olivia Bailey and Lewis Baston, *For the Many?*, Fabian Policy Report, 2018, p. 4.

24 Tim Lambert, 'A Brief History of Peterborough', *Local Histories*.

25 Josh Holder, 'High street crisis deepens: 1 in 12 shops closed in five years', *Guardian*, 30 January 2019.

26 Ibid.

27 'London Brick Company in Stewartby', Bedford Borough Council.

28 The Monopolies and Mergers Commission, *Building Bricks: A Report on the Supply of Building Bricks*, Her Majesty's Stationery Office, London, 1976.

29 Tim Page, 'The decline of UK manufacturing is devastating – it's time to change course', *TUC*, 17 April 2018.

30 GMB Union, 'Almost 600,000 manufacturing jobs lost in decade', 3 June 2018.

31 Ofcom, *Children and Parents: Media Use and Attitudes Report 2018*, 29 January 2019, p. 7.

32 Office for National Statistics, *Official Labour Market Statistics*, 2018.

33 Jon Burnett, *The New Geographies of Racism: Peterborough*, Institute of Race Relations, London, 2012, p. 11.

34 Ibid.

3. BABYLON

1 Andrea Levy, *Small Island*, Headline Review, London, 2004.

2 Home Affairs Select Committee, 'Update on the work of the Home Office in relation to Windrush', 12 November 2018.

3 Geoff Alston, 'A Forgotten Diaspora: The Children of Enslaves and "Free Coloured" Women and Highland Scots in Guyana', *Northern Scotland*, Edinburgh University Press, Vol. 6, No. 1, 2015, pp. 49–69.

4 Jane Joseph, 'Pompey Joseph and the emancipation of slaves in Hopetown, West Coast Berbice, British Guiana', Sapodilla Press, 2015.

5 Ibid.

6 Dorothy P. Josiah, 'After Emancipation: Aspects of Village Life in Guyana, 1869–1911', *Journal of Negro History*, Vol. 82, No. 1, 1997, pp. 105–21.

7 Ibid.

8 Jane Joseph, 'Pompey Joseph and the emancipation of slaves in Hopetown, West Coast Berbice, British Guiana', Sapodilla Press, 2015.

9 Alvin O. Thompson, *Unprofitable Servants: Crown Slaves in Berbice, Guyana, 1803–1831*, University of the West Indies Press, Jamaica, 2002.

10 Shammane Joseph, 'The Liberated Africans of Berbice, 1841–1865', *History This Week*, August 2010.

11 Ibid.

12 Dorothy P. Josiah, 'After Emancipation: Aspects of Village Life in Guyana, 1869–1911, *Journal of Negro History*, Vol. 82, No. 1, 1997, pp. 105–21.

13 Joy Moncrieffe, *Ethnic Diversity and State Response in the Caribbean*, United Nations Development Programme, 2004, p. 4.

14 Basdeo Mangru, 'Indian Labour in British Guiana', *History Today*, Vol. 36, No. 4, 1986.

15 Lomarsh Roopnarine, 'The Repatriation, Readjustment, and Second-Term Migration of Ex-Indentured Indian Labourers from British Guiana and Trinidad to India, 1838–1955', *New West Indian Guide*, Vol. 81, Nos. 1–2, 2009, p. 71.

16 Lomarsh Roopnarine, 'East Indian Indentured Emigration to the Caribbean: Beyond the Push and Pull Model', *Caribbean Studies*, Vol. 31, No. 2, 2003, p. 102.

17 Raymond T. Smith, ' "Living in the Gun Mouth": Race, Class, and Political Violence in Guyana', *New West Indian Guide*, Vol. 69, No. 3/4, 1995, p. 234.

18 Stephen G. Rabe, *U.S. Intervention in British Guiana: A Cold War Story*, cited in https://foreignpolicy.com/2015/07/31/guyana-cia-meddling-race-riots-phantom-death-squad-ppp/

19 Jagan served as president from 1980 to 1985 following a change in the constitution.

20 Johannes Gerrit de Kruijf, *Guyana Junction: Globalisation, Localisation, and the Production of East Indianness*, Rozenberg Publishers, Amsterdam, 2006, p. 82.

21 Raymond T. Smith, ' "Living in the Gun Mouth": Race, Class, and Political Violence in Guyana', *New West Indian Guide*, Vol. 69, No. 3/4, 1995, p. 224.

22 People's Progressive Party, 'Our Cause Is Just', *Thunder*, Vol. 34, No. 1, 1999, p. 33.

23 Lomarsh Roopnarine, 'The Repatriation, Readjustment, and Second-Term Migration of Ex-Indentured Indian Labourers from British Guiana and Trinidad to India, 1838–1955', *New West Indian Guide*, Vol. 81, Nos. 1–2, 2009, p. 71.

24 Kirk Smock and Claire Antell, *Guyana*, The Globe Pequot Press Inc., Connecticut, 2018, p. 18.

25 Ibid.

26 Ibid.

27 David Cameron cited in *The Economist*, 16 June 2007, p. 58.

28 Trevor Phillips, interviewed by Andrew Marr, *The Andrew Marr Show*, London, 6 February 2011.

29 Trevor Phillips, *Race and Faith: The Deafening Silence*, Civitas, London, 2016, p. 14.

30 Trevor Phillips, speaking at a Policy Exchange think-tank meeting, London, 26 January 2016.

31 Ministry of Housing, Communities & Local Government, *Integrated Communities Strategy Green Paper*, 9 February 2019, p. 7.

32 Alastair Ager and Alison Strang, *Indicators of Integration: Final Report*, Home Office Development and Practice Report, 2004, p. 3.

33 Office for National Statistics, *English Language Skills*, 7 February 2018.

34 Office for National Statistics, *Ethnicity and the Labour Market*, November 2014.

35 70 per cent of Indians in the UK are in employment. The average across the population is 71 per cent.

36 Office for National Statistics, *Ethnicity and the Labour Market*, November 2014.

37 NHS Digital, 'Patient experience of primary care: GP services', March 2019; A higher percentage of Caribbeans also reported a positive experience of GP out-of-hours services – Office for National statistics, 'Patient satisfaction with GP out-of-hours services', 10 October 2017; 93.7 per cent of Black Caribbeans reported successfully booking an NHS dental appointment, just below the average of 94.6 per cent, cited in NHS Digital, 'Access to NHS dental services', March 2019.

38 Stephen Jivraj, 'The Dynamics of Diversity: evidence from the 2011 Census', *Joseph Rowntree Foundation and University of Manchester Centre on Dynamics of Ethnicity*, 2012.

39 Office for National Statistics, *Age Groups*, 22 August 2018.

40 Ibid.

41 Geoff Parker and Miri Song, *Rethinking 'Mixed Race'*, Pluto Press, London, 2001, p. 2.

42 Ibid.

43 Office for National Statistics, *2011 Census Analysis*, 3 July 2014.

44 *Evening Standard* (London), 25 May 2005, p.12.

45 Edouard Machery and Luc Faucher. 'Social Construction and the Concept of Race.' *Philosophy of Science*, vol. 72, no. 5, 2005, pp. 1208–19.

46 Afua Hirsch, *Brit(Ish): On Race, Identity and Belonging*, Jonathan Cape, London, 2018.

47 Ibid.

48 Winthrop D. Jordan, 'Historical Origins of the One-Drop Racial Rule in the United States', *Journal of Critical Mixed Race Studies*, Vol. 1, No. 1, pp. 98–132.

49 Office for National Statistics, *2011 Census Analysis*, 3 July 2014.

50 David Owen, *Ethnic Minorities in Great Britain: Patterns of Population Change, 1981–91*, Centre for Research in Ethnic Relations, Warwick, December 1995.

51 'The next generation', *The Economist*, 28 January 2016.

52 Office for National Statistics, *Population of England and Wales*, 1 August 2018.

53 According to the 2011 census, 989,628 individuals in England and Wales specified their ethnicity as 'Black African', 594,825 as 'Black Caribbean', and 280,437 as 'Other Black'.

54 Department for Education, *Pupil Exclusions*, 28 September 2018.

55 Feyisa Demie and Christabel McLean, 'The Achievement of Black Caribbean Pupils', Schools Research and Statistics Unit, Brixton, 2017, p. 2.

56 Ibid.

57 Department for Education, *Destinations of Students After Key Stage 5 (Usually Aged 18 years)*, 9 May 2019.

58 Office for National Statistics, *Confidence in the Local Police*, 7 December 2018.

59 David Lammy, *The Lammy Review*, 8 September 2017, p. 6.

60 Ibid., p.3.

61 Office for National Statistics, *Household Income*, 4 July 2019.

62 Office for National Statistics, *Homicide in England and Wales: Year Ending March 2018*, 7 February 2019.

63 Joan Moore, cited in *Dying to Belong,* The Centre for Social Justice, London, 2009, p. 81.

4. OUT OF AFRICA

1 United Nations Development Programme – Human Development Index, 2019.

2 Dr Saul David, 'Slavery and the "Scramble for Africa", BBC History.

3 Stig Forster, Wolfgang J. Mommsen, Ronald Robinson, *Bismarck, Europe and Africa: The Berlin Africa Conference, 1884–85, and the Onset of Partition*, Oxford University Press, 1989.

4 Lord Salisbury quoted in Muna Ndulo, 'The Democratization Process and Structural Adjustment in Africa', *Indiana Journal of Global Legal Studies*, Volume 10, Issue 1, Article 12, Winter 2003.

5 Chris Blattman and Edward Miguel, 'Civil War', *Journal of Economic Literature*, Vol. 48, No. 1, 2010, pp. 3–57.

6 'Niger condemned for slavery', *Anti-slavery*, 27 October 2008.

7 Afua Hirsch, 'Mali's conflict and a "war over skin colour"', *Guardian*, 6 July 2012.

8 Yvan Guichaoua, 'Circumstantial Alliances and Loose Loyalties in Rebellion Making: The Case of Tuareg Insurgency in Northern Niger (2007–2009)', In: Yvan Guichaoua (eds) *Understanding Collective Political Violence: Conflict, Inequality and Ethnicity*, Palgrave Macmillan, London, 2012.

9 'Mali, Niger, Tuareg rebels pledge peace: Libya', Reuters News Agency, 7 October 2009.

10 Anti-Slavery International, 'Niger condemned for slavery', 27 October 2008.

11 Women's UN Report Network, 'Wahaya – Fifth Wives: Young Girls Sold Into Slavery', 31 January 2013.

12 Mary E. Modupe Kolawole, 'An African View of Transatlantic Slavery and the Role of Oral Testimony in Creating a New Legacy', in Anthony Tibbles (ed.), *Transatlantic Slavery: Against Human Dignity*, Liverpool University Press, Liverpool, 1994, p. 101.

13 Daniel B. Domingues da Silva, *The Atlantic Slave Trade from West Central Africa, 1780–1867*, Cambridge University Press, Cambridge, 2017, p. 125.

14 James L. A. Webb Jr, 'Ecology & Culture in West Africa', in Emmanuel Kwaku Akyeampong (ed.), *Themes in West Africa's History*, Ohio University Press, Athens, 2006, p. 49.

15 Greg Timmons, 'How Slavery Became the Economic Engine of the South', *History,* 6 March 2018.

16 Alvin O. Thompson, 'Race and Colour Prejudices and the Origins of the Trans-Atlantic Slave Trade', *Caribbean Studies,* Vol. 16, No. 3–4, pp. 29–59.

17 Munyae M. Mulinge, 'Botswana, Africa's Haven of Ethnic Peace and Harmony: Status and Future Prospects', *African Journal of Sociology*, Vol. 4, No. 1, 2008.

18 Southern African Regional Poverty Network, presentation speech on Draft National Development Plan 9 by Hon. B. Gaolathe, Minister of Finance and Development Planning, delivered to the National Assembly, 21 November 2002.

19 Bastian Berbner, 'Beer Summit – Act One: One More For My Baby and One More For the Road', *This American Life*, NPR.

20 M Nei, 'Genetic support for the out-of-Africa theory of human evolution', Proceedings of the National Academy of Sciences of the United States of America. 1995; 92(15):6720–6722.

21 Charles Darwin, On the Origin of Species, 1859.

22 Y. Cheng, '"Is Peking Man Still Our Ancestor?" – Genetics, Anthropology, and the Politics of Racial Nationalism in China', *The Journal of Asian Studies*, 76(3), 575–602, 2017.

23 Nicholas Wright Gillham, *A Life of Sir Francis Galton: From African Exploration to the Birth of Eugenics*, Clarendon Press, Oxford, 2001.

24 R. B. Freeman, 'Darwin's negro bird-stuffer', *Notes and Records of the Royal Society of London*, Vol. 33. No.1 (Aug 1978), pp. 83–86.

25 Adam Rutherford, 'Why racism is not backed by science', *Observer*, 1 March 2015.

26 Simon Heffer, *The Age of Decadence*. Windmill Books, London, 2018.

27 Dominic Cummings, 'Some Thoughts on Education and Political Priorities', published in full on the *Guardian*, 11 October 2013.

28 Adam Rutherford, *How to Argue With a Racist: History, Science, Race and Reality*, Orion, London, February 2020.

29 Steve Jones, 'There's much more to IQ than biology and DNA', *Telegraph*, 14 October 2013.

30 Kevin Mitchell, 'Why genetic IQ differences between "races" are unlikely', *Guardian*, 2 May 2018.

5. ALONE

1 Dr Offord, 'UK Nationals returning from Syria', *Hansard*, Vol. 654, 18 February 2019.

2 Jytte Klausen et al., 'Radicalization Trajectories: An Evidence-Based Computational Approach to Dynamic Risk Assessment of "Homegrown" Jihadists', *Studies in Conflict & Terrorism*, 2018, pp. 1–28.

3 Cressida Dick, answering questions from the Joint Committee on Human Rights, 8 May 2019.

4 Ibid.

5 Celia de Anca, *Beyond Tribalism: Managing Identities in a Diverse World*, Palgrave Macmillan, London, 2012, p. xxii.

6 The Co-operative and the British Red Cross, *Trapped in a Bubble: An Investigation into Triggers for Loneliness in the UK*, Kantar Public, December 2016, p. 18.

7 TNS survey for Age UK, April 2014.

8 Ibid.

9 Cigna, *Cigna U.S Loneliness Index: Survey of 20,000 Americans Examining Behaviours Driving Loneliness in the United States,* May 2018, p. 3.

10 'Japan home to 541,000 young recluses, survey finds', *Japan Times,* 7 September 2016.

11 J.K. Rilling et al., 'Social cognitive neural networks during in-group and out-group interactions', *Neuroimage,* Vol. 41, No. 4, 2008, pp. 1447–61.

12 Julianne Holt-Lunstad et al., 'Social Relationships and Mortality Risk: A Meta-analytic Review', *PLoS Med,* Vol. 7, No. 7, 2010, pp. 1–20.

13 Jacqueline Olds and Richard S. Schwartz, *The Lonely American: Drifting Apart in the Twenty-first Century,* Beacon Press, Boston, 2009, p. 8.

14 NHS Digital, *Prescription Cost Analysis: England 2018,* 28 March 2019.

15 NHS Business Services Authority, *Antidepressant Prescribing,* 2018.

16 Centers for Disease Control and Prevention's National Center for Health Statistics, *NCHS Data Brief,* 15 August 2017.

17 L. Scholl, 'Drug and Opioid-Involved Overdose Deaths – United States, 2013–2017', *Morb Mortal Weekly Rep.,* 21 December 2018.

18 Jacqueline Olds and Richard S. Schwartz, *The Lonely American: Drifting Apart in the Twenty-first Century,* Beacon Press, Boston, 2009, p. 8.

19 Nielsen Book Research, 2019.

20 Kara Cutruzzula, 'The Last 100 Years of Self-Help', *TIME,* 9 August 2016.

21 Jacqueline Olds and Richard S. Schwartz, *The Lonely American: Drifting Apart in the Twenty-first Century,* Beacon Press, Boston, 2009.

22 Ibid.

23 Jeffrey M. Jones, 'U.S. Church Membership Down Sharply in Past Two Decades', Gallup, 18 April 2019.

24 Neha Sahgal, '10 key findings about religion in Western Europe', Pew Research Center, 29 May 2018.

25 Robert D. Putnam, *Bowling Alone: The Collapse and Revival of American Community,* Simon & Schuster Paperbacks, London, 2000.

26 http://cityobservatory.org/wp-content/files/CityObservatory_Less_In_Common.pdf

27 House of Commons Library Briefing Paper 06152, *Business statistics,* 12 December 2018.

28 David Lammy, *Out of the Ashes: Britain After the Riots,* Guardian Books, London, 2012.

29 David Baddiel, Twitter, 10 December 2018. https://twitter.com/baddiel/status/1072168951847755776

30 John Maynard Keynes, *The General Theory of Employment, Interest and Money (1936),* Macat, London, 2017.

31 Margaret Thatcher, interviewed by *Women's Own* magazine, 31 October 1987.

32 'The Impact of the September 2008 Economic Collapse', Pew Research Center, 28 April 2010.

33 Chartered Institute of Personnel and Development, January 2010

34 'Chart Book: The Legacy of the Great Recession', Center on Budget and Policy Priorities, 6 June 2019.

35 'The Impact of the September 2008 Economic Collapse', Pew Research Center, 28 April 2010.

36 'GDP up by 0.6% in the euro area and by 0.5% in the EU28', Eurostat, 29 April 2016.

37 Northern Mine Research Society, government data.

38 Charles Taylor, 'A Different Kind of Courage', *New York Review of Books,* April 2007.

39 Ibid.

40 Guy Standing, *The Precariat: The New Dangerous Class*, Bloomsbury Academic, London, 2011.

41 Andre Gorz, *Farewell to the Working Class: An Essay on Post-Industrial Socialism*, Pluto Press, London, 1982.

42 Mike Kelly, 'North East named zero-hours contract capital of the UK as calls are made to end "blackspot"', *Chronicle Live*, 16 August 2017.

43 The TUC, 'UK's gig economy workforce has doubled since 2016, TUC and FEPS-backed research shows', 28 June 2019.

44 House of Commons Science and Technology Committee, *Robotics and Artificial Intelligence*, October 2016, p. 11.

45 Ibid.

46 PWC, *UK Economic Outlook,* March 2017, p. 30.

47 Jean M. Twenge and Joshua D. Foster, 'Birth Cohort Increases in Narcissistic Personality Traits Among American College Students, 1982–2009', *Social Psychological and Personality Science*, Vol. 1, No. 1, 2010, pp. 99–106.

48 F. S. Stinson et al., 'Prevalence, correlates, disability, and comorbidity of DSM-IV narcissistic personality disorder: results from the wave 2 national epidemiologic survey on alcohol and related conditions', *Journal of Clinical Psychiatry*, Vol. 69, No. 7, 2008, pp. 1033–45.

49 Ibid.

50 Susie Khamis, Lawrence Ang and Raymond Welling, 'Self-branding, "micro-celebrity" and the rise of Social Media Influencers', *Celebrity Studies*, Vol. 8, No. 2, 2017, pp. 191–208.

51 Horatia Harrod, 'The rise and rise of the ultra-influencer', *Financial Times,* 16 November 2018.

52 Google I/O – Keynote, 2014.

53 Mikey Smith and Dan Bloom, 'Jacob Rees Mogg is now part of the Cabinet – let's remind ourselves of his views', *Mirror*, 25 July 2019.

54 Matthew Holehouse and Tim Wigmore, 'Jacob Rees-Mogg's shock at dinner with group that want to repatriate black Britons', *Telegraph*, 8 August 2013.

55 Peter Walker, 'Rees-Mogg defends promotion of German far-right AfD video', *Guardian*, 1 April 2019.

56 'Grenfell Tower: Jacob Rees-Mogg criticised for "insulting" comments', BBC News, 5 November 2019.

57 Carole Cadwalladr, Steve Bannon: '"We went back and forth" on the themes of Johnson's big speech', *Observer*, 23 June 2019

58 'EU Referendum: Boris Johnson stands by Hitler EU comparison', BBC News, 16 May 2016.

59 Paul Mason, 'David Lammy is right to encourage the left to unite against the far right', *New Statesman*, 15 April 2019; Suzanne Moore, 'David Lammy was right to name and shame the ERG', *Guardian*, 15 April 2019; Sunny Hundal, 'David Lammy is spot on – the British right is tumbling into extremism and we should call it out before it's too late', *Independent*, 15 April 2019.

60 Albert Evans, 'Michael Heseltine backs David Lammy's Brexit Nazi comparison, saying similarities to 1930s are "chilling"', *I*, 15 April 2019.

61 Mark Townsend, 'Britain First says 5,000 of its members have joined Tories', *Observer*, 29 December 2019.

62 David Lammy, Jon Trickett and Mary Creagh, 'Labour: After the debacle, what comes next?', *Observer*, 21 December 2019.

63 Masha Gessen, 'How Trump Governs by Tweet: Start with Outrage, Then Escalate', *New Yorker*, 11 October 2017.

64 Fran O'Malley, 'A Taxonomy of Tweets', *The Democracy Project*, University of Delaware, pp. 1–6.

65 Robert S. Mueller, Special Counsel's Office Department of Justice, *The Mueller Report: Report on the Investigation Into Russian Interference in the 2016 Presidential Election*, Melville House Publishing, 30 April 2019.

66 Jack Nicas, 'How YouTube Drives people to the Internet's Darkest Corners', *Wall Street Journal*, 7 February 2018.

67 Paul Lewis and Erin McCormick, 'How an ex-YouTube insider investigated its secret algorithm', *Guardian*, 2 February 2018.

68 Zeynep Tufekci, 'YouTube, the Great Radicalizer', *New York Times*, 10 March 2018

69 Cass R. Sunstein, 'The Law of Group Polarization', *Law & Economics Working Papers*, No. 91, 1999.

70 Ibid.

71 Lucy Wood, 'Jacob Rees-Mogg supporters would make the National Front blush', *Morning Star*, 4 March 2019.

72 Ibid.

73 Ibid.

74 Matt Honeycombe-Foster, 'Tories suspend 14 members after Islamophobic comments found on pro-Jacob Rees Mogg Facebook Page', *Politics Home*, 6 March 2019.

75 Rebecca Lewis, *Alternative Influence: Broadcasting the Reactionary Right on YouTube*, Data & Society Research Institute, 2019.

76 Ibid.

77 Ezra Klein, 'The rise of YouTube's reactionary right', *Vox*, 24 September 2018.

78 Zephoria Digital Marketing, 'The Top 20 Valuable Facebook Statistics', 24 July 2019.

79 Statistica, *Number of Monthly Active Twitter Users in the United States from 1st Quarter 2010 to 1st Quarter 2019 (in Millions)*, 2019.

80 Damien Cave, 'Australia Passes Law to Punish Social Media Companies for Violent Posts', *New York Times*, 3 April 2019.

81 Philip Oltermann, 'Tough new German law puts tech firms and free speech in spotlight', *Guardian*, 5 January 2018.

6. IDENTITY CRISIS

1 Jack Simpson, 'Grenfell-style cladding removed from only three private residential blocks' *Inside Housing*, November 2018.

2 Equality and Human Rights Commission, *Summary of Submissions Following Phase 1 of the Grenfell Tower Inquiry*, March 2019, pp. 7–8.

3 David Lammy, interviewed by Sophy Ridge, Sky News, London, 2 July 2017.

4 Ben Cobley, *The Tribe*, Imprint Academic, Exeter, 2018.

5 Ibid.

6 Mark Rice-Oxley, 'Grenfell: The 72 victims, their lives, loves and losses', *Guardian*, 14 May 2018.

7 Lord Chief Justice of England and Wales and Senior President of Tribunals, *Judicial Diversity Statistics 2018*, 12 July 2018, p. 1.

8 Robin Diangelo, 'White Fragility', *International Journal of Critical Pedagogy*, Vol. 3, No. 3, 2011, pp. 54–70; Robin Diangelo, *White Fragility*, Allen Lane, London, 2018.

9 Martin Luther King Jr., 'I Have a Dream', March on Washington for Jobs and Freedom, 28 August 1963.

10 George M. Fredrickson, *Racism: A Short History*, Princeton University Press; New Ed edition. 22 July 2003.

11 'Racist behaviour is declining in America', *Economist*, 1 September 2017.

12 Data released under the Freedom of Information Act, December 2010.

13 Christopher Hitchens, *Blood, Class, and Empire: The Enduring Anglo–American Relationship*, Nation Books, New York, 2004, pp. 63–4.

14 David Lammy, 'Africa deserves better from Comic Relief', *Guardian*, 24 March 2017.

15 Kitty Wenham-Ross, 'Comic Relief's Vision of Africa Isn't Funny', *Foreign Policy*, 15 March 2019.

16 Norwegian Students and Academics International Assistance Fund, interviewed by the *Guardian*, 4 December 2017.

17 Richard Borowski, 'The Hidden Cost of a Red Nose', *Primary Geography*, Vol. 75, 2011, pp. 1–20.

18 Robin Diangelo, *White Fragility*, Allen Lane, London, 2018, pp. 9–13.

19 Erik Erikson, *Childhood and Society*, 2nd ed., W. W. Norton, New York, 1963, p. 279.

20 Abraham Maslow, 'A Theory of Human Motivation', *Psychological Review*, 1943.

21 Kwame Anthony Appiah, *The Lies that Bind: Rethinking Identity*, Liveright Publishing, New York, 2018.

22 Erik Erikson, *Identity: youth and crisis*, W. W. Norton & Co, New York, 1968.

23 Robert Haws (ed)., *The Age of Segregation: Race Relations in the South, 1890–1945*, University Press of Mississippi, Mississippi, 1978.

24 Moin Syed, 'Revisiting Erik Erikson's Legacy on Culture, Race, and Ethnicity',

An International Journal of Theory and Research, Vol. 18, No. 4, 2018, pp. 274–83.

25 Ibid, p. 295.

26 Keeanga-Yamahtta Taylor, *How We Get Free: Black Feminism and the Combahee River Collective*, Haymarket Press, Chicago, 2017.

27 The Combahee River Collective, 'The Combahee River Collective Statement', in Barbara Smith (ed.), *Home Girls: A Black Feminist Anthology*, Kitchen Table: Women of Colour Press, New York, 1983.

28 Bernie Sanders, Berklee Performance Center, Boston, 20 November 2016.

29 Mark Lilla, 'The End of Identity Liberalism', *New York Times*, 18 November 2016.

30 Mark Lilla, *The Once and Future Liberal: After Identity Politics*, Hurst & Co., London, 2017.

31 Mychal Denzel Smith, 'What Liberals Get Wrong About Identity Politics', *New Republic*, 11 September 2017.

32 Salma El-Wardany, 'What Women Mean When We Say "Men Are Trash"', Huffington Post, 3 May 2018.

33 Bahar Mustafa Facebook post, 15 April 2015, cited in an interview with Taylor McGraa, VICE, 3 November 2015.

34 Alana Conner, cited in German Lopez, 'Research says there are ways to reduce racial bias. Calling people racist isn't one of them', *Vox*, 30 July 2018.

35 Ibid.

36 Ibid.

37 Sheri Berman, 'Why identity politics benefits the right more than the left', *Guardian*, 14 July 2018.

38 Jeremy W. Peters, 'As Critics Assail Trump, His Supporters Dig in Deeper', *New York Times*, 23 June 2018.

39 Hope Not Hate, 'State of Hate', January–February 2018, p. 3.

40 Hope Not Hate, 'Societal Attitudes to Islam and Muslims', August 2017.

41 Hope Not Hate, 'State of Hate', January–February 2018.

42 Francis Fukuyama, 'The End of History?', *The National Interest*, Summer 1989.

43 Francis Fukuyama, *The End of History and the Last Man*, Free Press, New York, 1992.

44 Francis Fukuyama, *Identity: The Demand for Dignity and the Politics of Resentment*, Farrar, Straus and Giroux, New York, 2018, p. 115.

45 'Timeline: How the BBC gender pay story has unfolded', BBC News, 29 June 2018.

46 David Lammy, *The Lammy Review*, 8 September 2017.

47 Justice Committee, 'Progress in the implementation of the Lammy Review's recommendations', House of Commons, 26 March 2019.

48 Mike Brewer, David Phillips, Luke Sibieta, 'Living Standards, Inequality and Poverty: Labour's Record', Institute for Fiscal Studies, April 2010.

49 'Poverty: up or down?', *Full Fact*, 30 November 2016.

50 Ibid.

51 Thomas Piketty, *Capital in the Twenty-First Century*, The Belknap Press of Harvard University Press, Massachusetts, 2014, p. 1.

52 David Jacobs and Lindsey Myers, 'Union Strength, Neoliberalism, and Inequality: Contingent Political Analyses of U.S. Income Differences since 1950', *American Sociological Review*, 79(4), 752–74, 2014.

7. ENCOUNTER CULTURE

1 George Orwell, *The Road to Wigan Pier,* Harcourt, Brace and Company, New York, 1958, p. 74.

2 'The children dreading their summer holidays shut away inside the Broadwater Farm estate', *Sunday Times*, 30 June 2019.

3 Eleanor Mills, 'A thank you to *Sunday Times* readers from Broadwater Farm', *Sunday Times,* 21 July 2019.

4 Northern Mine Research Society, 'Wigan Coalfield', *NMRS Records.*

5 Ibid.

6 Charlie Schouten, 'Wigan to sign off town centre transformation', *North West Place,* 21 January 2019.

7 HS2, 'Wigan', 2019.

8 Shukran Qazimi, 'Sense of place and place identity', *European Journal of Social Sciences Education and Research*, May–August 2014, Vol. I, Issue I.

9 'Counter protests fail to stop far-right march', *Wigan Today,* 19 September 2015.

10 *Far-right Extremism: Who Are the EDL?*, Channel 4 Productions, 28 May 2013.

11 European Parliament Liaison Office in the United Kingdom, *North West Region – 8 MEPs,* 2019.

12 Brexit and public opinion 2019, *The UK in a Changing Europe*, 22 January 2019.

13 Ed Fieldhouse, Labour's electoral dilemma, *British Election Study*, 17 October 2019

14 'Election results 2019: Analysis in maps and charts', BBC News, 13 December 2019.

15 Combined data from Department of Employment Statistics Division, 'Trade union members in the UK (in millions) 1892–1974', and Certification Office, '1974–2015'.

16 Tony Travers and Lorena Esposito, *The Decline and Fall of Local Democracy: A History of Local Government Finance,* Policy Exchange, London, 2003, p. 10.

17 D. A. Dawson, 'Economic change and the changing role of local government', in M. Loughlin et al. (eds.), *Half a Century of Municipal Decline*, Allen & Unwin, 1985, pp. 26–49.

18 Tom Crewe, 'The Strange Death of Municipal England', *London Review of Books,* Vol. 38, No. 24, December 2016, pp. 6–10.

19 Ibid.

20 Tony Travers and Lorena Esposito, *The Decline and Fall of Local Democracy: A History of Local Government Finance,* Policy Exchange, London, 2003, p. 11.

21 Allan McConnell, *The Politics and Policy of Local Taxation in Britain*, Tudor Business Publishing Limited, Newcastle upon Tyne, 1999, p. 14.

22 A.D. Dawson, 'Economic change and the changing role of local government', in M. Loughlin et al. (eds.), *Half a Century of Municipal Decline*, Allen & Unwin, 1985, p. 31.

23 Tom Crewe, 'The Strange Death of Municipal England', *London Review of Books*, Vol. 38, No. 24, December 2016, pp. 6–10.

24 Richard Jackman, 'Local Government Finance', in M. Loughlin et al. (eds.), *Half a Century of Municipal Decline*, Allen & Unwin,1985, p. 153.

25 Tony Travers and Lorena Esposito, *The Decline and Fall of Local Democracy: A History of Local Government Finance*, Policy Exchange, London, 2003, p. 50.

26 'Bernie Grant: A controversial figure', BBC News, 8 April 2000.

27 Richard Murgatroyd, 'The Popular Politics of the Poll Tax: An Active Citizenship of the Left?', PhD thesis, Brunel University, 2000, p. 14.

28 David Butler et al., *Failure in British Government: The Politics of the Poll Tax*, Oxford University Press, Oxford, 1994.

29 Hélène Mulholland, 'North-east voters reject regional assembly', *Guardian*, 5 November 2004.

30 Grace Blakeley, 'Why we must empower local government', *New Statesman*, 8 May 2019.

31 Jon Trickett, 'This is one of the most centralised countries in the world. It is also one of the most unequal', *LabourList*, 11 December 2016.

32 Comptroller and Auditor General of the National Audit Office/Ministry of Housing, Communities & Local Government, *Financial Sustainability of Local Authorities 2018*, 5 March 2018, p. 4.

33 Chartered Institute of Public Finance and Accountancy, *Annual Library Survey*, 7 December 2018.

34 County Councils Network Analysis based on comparing Office for National Statistics data on 'budgeted' *Local Authority Revenue Expenditure and Financing: 2017–18* (June 2017) with actual *Provisional Outturn* (23 August) data for the same year.

35 Northamptonshire County Council, 'Immediate spending controls put in place at Northamptonshire County Council', 2 February 2018.

36 Centre for Cities, press release, 28 January 2019.

37 Office for National Statistics, *Crime in England and Wales: Year Ending March 2018*, 19 July 2018.

38 CHAIN, *Annual Report, Greater London, April 2018–March 2019*, 2019.

39 Freddie Whittaker and Jess Staufenberg, 'More schools could be forced to cut teaching hours, union warns', *Schools Week*, 8 March 2019.

40 United Nations General Assembly, *Visit to the United Kingdom of Great Britain and Northern Ireland, Report of the Special Rapporteur on Extreme Poverty and Human Rights*, 23 April 2019.

41 Steven Haggbloom et al., 'The 100 most eminent psychologists of the 20th century', *Review of General Psychology*, Vol. 6, No. 2, 2002, pp. 139–52.

42 Mark Davidson, 'Love thy neighbour? Social mixing in London's gentrification frontiers', *Environment and Planning*, Vol. 42, No. 3, 2010, pp. 524–44.

43 Loretta Lees, 'Gentrification and Social Mixing, towards and inclusive urban renaissance', *Journal of Urban Studies*, Vol. 45, No. 12, 2008, pp. 2449–70.

44 Gill Valentine and Joanna Sadgrove, 'Biographical Narratives of Encounter: The Significance of Mobility and Emplacement in Shaping Attitudes towards Difference', *Urban Studies*, 25 September 2013, pp. 1979–94.

45 Trussell Trust, press release, 25 April 2019.

46 Trussell Trust/Independent Food Aid Network, joint study, 17 October 2017.

47 Andrew Williams et al., 'Contested space: The contradictory political dynamics of food banking in the UK', *Environment and Planning*, Vol. 48, No. 11, 2016, pp. 2291–316.

48 Kayleigh Garthwaite, '"I feel I'm Giving Something Back to Society": Constructing the "Active Citizen" and Responsibilising Foodbank Use', *Journal of Social Policy & Society*, Vol. 16, No. 2, 2017, pp. 283–92.

49 Mark S. Granovetter, 'The Strength of Weak Ties', *American Journal of Sociology*, Vol. 78, No. 6, 1973, pp. 1360–80.

50 Aneta Piekut and Gill Valentine, 'Spaces of encounter and attitudes towards difference: a comparative study of two European cities', *Social Science Research*, Vol. 62, 2017, pp. 175–88.

51 George Monbiot, *Out of the Wreckage. A New Politics for an Age of Crisis*, Verso, London, 2017, pp. 78–9.

52 The Men's Sheds Association, www.menssheds.org.uk

53 The Food Assembly, www.thefoodassembly.com

54 Playing Out, www.playingout.net

55 Sunday Assembly, www.sundayassembly.com

56 The Campaign for Real Ale, *Total Pub Closures January–June 2018*, August 2018.

57 Rick Muir, *Pubs and Place. The Social Value of Community Pubs*, Institute for Public Policy Research, London, January 2012, p. 3.

58 Ibid.

59 Ibid.

60 'Revealed: The Seven New Classes of Worker in the Modern British Economy', The Royal Society of Arts, 25 January 2018.

61 Anthony Painter, 'The Case for Basic Income Is Growing. Scotland Can Take It Forward', The Royal Society of Arts, 8 May 2019.

62 Karl Widerquist, 'Current UBI Experiments: An update for July 2018', Basic Income Earth Network, 1 July 2018.

63 'It's a beautiful game, but how you see it is all in the mind . . .', York University, October 2018.

64 Steve Bunce, 'How a World Cup qualifier and the suicide of a young girl launched the bloody 100 Hour Football War,' *Independent*, 20 June 2018.

65 C. R. Victor, J. Bond, S. Scambler and A. Bowling, 'Loneliness, social isolation and living alone in later life', Economic and Social Research Council, 2003.

66 South London Cares, *Annual Report 2016/17*, London, p. 12.

67 Andrew Scott and Lynda Gratton, 'What younger workers can learn from older workers, and vice versa', *Harvard Business Review*, 18 November 2016.

68 David Jeffrey, 'The strange death of Tory Liverpool: Conservative electoral decline in Liverpool, 1945–1966', *British Politics*, Vol. 12, No. 3, pp. 386–407.

69 Felicity Morse, 'Penguin Candidate Beats Liberal Democrats in Edinburgh', Huffington Post, 4 May 2012.

70 Liverpool Council, *Election Results for Whole District: Mayoral Election*, 5 May 2016.

71 'Lord Heseltine gets the Freedom of Liverpool at town hall ceremony', *Liverpool Echo*, 14 March 2012.

72 Martin Wainwright, 'Michael Heseltine is given the Freedom of Liverpool', *Guardian*, 13 March 2012.

73 Simon Parker et al., 'Disorderly cities and the policy-making field: the 1981 English riots and the management of urban decline', *British Politics*, pp. 1–18.

74 Alexander Cockburn, *Corruptions of Empire: Life Studies & the Reagan Era*, Verso, London, 1988, p. 65.

75 Ibid.

76 Ibid.

77 John Belcham, *Before the Windrush: Race Relations in Twentieth-century Liverpool*, Liverpool University Press, Liverpool, p. 251.

78 Ibid., p. 252.

79 Geoffrey Howe, quoted in Margaret Thatcher cabinet documents, *National Archives: 1981 Files*, 2011.

80 Geoffrey Howe, quoted in Margaret Thatcher cabinet documents, *National Archives: 1981 Files*, 2011.

81 David Lammy, *Out of the Ashes: Britain After the Riots*, Guardian Books, London, 2012.

82 Andrew Dewdney et al., *Post Critical Museology: Theory and Practice in the Art Museum*, Routledge, London, 2013, p. 24.

83 Poverty in Liverpool, House of Commons Library, Number CDP-2018-0226, 23 October 2018.

84 Ibid.

85 The exact powers metro mayors have depends on the terms agreed in the devolution deal with government.

86 Ministry of Housing, Communities & Local Government, *Rough Sleeping in England: Autumn 2018*, 21 January 2019.

87 Ibid.

88 Christopher Caden, *Metro Mayors Are a Good Start*, Institute for Government, 2 May 2018.

89 Lisa Nandy, 'The key to reuniting our two Englands? Towns with power', *LabourList*, 15 October 2018.

90 James H. Fowler and Nicholas A. Christakis, 'Cooperative behaviour cascades in human social networks', *PNAS*, Vol. 107, No. 12, 2010, pp. 5334–8.

91 Simon Kuper, 'Trump, Johnson and the new radical tribes of politics', *Financial Times* magazine, 25 July 2019.

92 *USA Today*/Ipsos Poll, July 2019.

93 John F. Kennedy, 'Inaugural Address', Washington D.C., 20 January 1961.

94 Hartlepool Borough Council, 'Results of the Hartlepool Local Government Elections', 3 May 2018.

95 Electoral Commission, *Local Elections in England, May 2018*, August 2018, p. 3.

96 Committee on Standards in Public Life, *Public Perceptions of Standards in Public Life in the UK and Europe*, March 2014, p. 9.

97 Poll by Survation, *Apathy in the UK? A Look at the Attitudes of Non-voters*, 28 February 2014.

98 Gary Johns, 'Does Compulsory Voting Distort Electoral Outcomes?', *Agenda: A Journal of Policy Analysis and Reform*, Vol. 5, No. 3, 1998, pp. 367–72.

99 Lisa Hill, 'On the Justifiability of Compulsory Voting: Reply to Lever, *British Journal of Political Science*, Vol. 40, No. 4, 2010, pp. 917–23.

100 Local Government Act 2000, Section 37.

101 Patrick Collinson, 'Council tax should be fair and progressive. Ours is neither', *Guardian*, March 2018

8. REBUILDING ENGLAND

1 YouGov/BBC Survey Results, 'Young people are less proud of being English than their elders', 2018.

2 Tom Nairn, *The enchanted Glass*, Vintage, New York, 1994, p. 93.

3 Tariq Modood, 'Multicultural Nationalism', *Open Democracy*, 13 August 2018; Marc Saxer, 'Progressive Patriotism', International Politics and Society, 2 April 2019.

4 Professor John Denham, 'A nation divided? The identities, politics and governance of England', Speaker's House, House of Commons, London, 27 June 2018.

5 Ibid.

6 Mark Wilding, 'The Rise and Demise of the EDL', *VICE*, 12 March 2018.

7 Nick Lowles (ed.), 'The People vs the "Elite"? State of Hate 2019', Hope Not Hate, p. 36.

8 Mark Rowley, 'UK underestimating risk of far-right extremism', ABC News, 19 August 2018.

9 David Lawrence, interviewed by Peter Walker and Josh Halliday, *Guardian*, 3 March 2019.

10 John Denham, 'The left must stop stereotyping the English as racist', *The Staggers*, 2017.

11 Matthew Horsman and Andrew Marshall, *After the Nation State: Citizens, Tribalism and the New World Disorder*, HarperCollins, London, 1994, p.4.

12 Derek Croxton, 'The Peace of Westphalia of 1648 and the Origins of Sovereignty', *The International History Review*, Vol. 21, No. 3, 1999, p. 569.

13 Emmanuel Sieyès, *Political Writings*, Hackett Publishing, Indianapolis, 2003, p.134.

14 Matthew Horsman and Andrew Marshall, *After the Nation State: Citizens, Tribalism and the New World Disorder*, HarperCollins, London, 1994, p. 6.

15 Enoch Powell, 'Rivers of Blood', Conservative Association meeting, Birmingham, 20 April 1968.

16 Vernor Bogdaner, 'Winston Churchill, 1951–1955', *From New Jerusalem to New Labour*, pp. 23–41, 2010.

17 Nigel Farage, interviewed by Trevor Phillips, LBC, 12 March 2015.

18 Caryl Phillips, *A New World Order*, Vintage, New York, 2002, p. 248.

19 Randolph Vigne, 'Testaments of Faith: Wills of Huguenot Refugees in England as a Window on Their Past', in David J. B. Trim (ed.), *The Huguenots: History and Memory in Transnational Context: Essays in Honour of Walter C. Utt*, Koninklijke Brill NV, Leiden, 2011, p. 263.

20 Kika Orphanide, 'The Cypriot Community in Britain', *Race & Social Work*, London, Routledge, 1986, pp. 80–7.

21 The Migration Observatory, University of Oxford.

22 Alberto Alesina and Bryony Reich, 'Nation-building', National Bureau of Economic Research Working Paper, 2015.

23 Ibid.

24 Stuart Hall, 'The Local and the Global: Globalisation and Ethnicity', in Anthony D. King (ed.), *Culture, Globalisation and the World-System: Contemporary Conditions for the Representation of Identity*, University of Minnesota Press, Minnesota, 1996, p. 200.

25 Gabriella Elgenius, *Symbols of Nations and Nationalism: Celebrating Nationhood*, Palgrave Macmillan, Basingstoke, 2011.

26 Mark Thatcher, 'State production of cultural nationalism: political leaders and preservation policies for historic buildings in France and Italy', *Nations and Nationalism*, Vol. 24, No. 1, 2018, p. 65.

27 Tim Nieguth and Tracey Raney, 'Nation-building and Canada's national symbolic order, 1993–2015', *Nations and Nationalism*, Vol. 23, No. 1, 2017, p. 88.

28 Loleen Berdahl et al. (eds.), *Canada: The State of the Federation, 2012 – Regions, Resources and Resiliency*, Queen's University Press, 2012.

29 Don Munton and Tom Keating, 'Internationalism and the Canadian public,' *Canadian Journal of Political Science* 34, No. 3 (2001): 517–49.

30 Government of Canada, *Discover Canada*, 2012.

31 Ibid, pp. 38–41.

32 Richie Etwaru, *Blockchain: Trust Companies*, Dog Ear Publishing, Indianapolis, 2017, p. 171.

33 Ibid.

34 Melissa Aronczyk, 'Nation Branding: A Twenty-First Century Tradition', in Carolin Viktorin et al. (eds.), *Nation Branding in Modern History*, Berghahn Books, Oxford, 2018. p. 236.

35 Neil Brenner et al., 'Neoliberal urbanism: Models, moments, mutations', *SAIS Review*, Vol. 29, No. 1, 2009, pp. 49–66.

36 Mark Leonard, *BritainTM: Renewing Our Identity*, Demos, London, 1997.

37 Michael Kenny, *Politics of English Nationhood*, Oxford University Press, Oxford, 2014, p. 9.

38 Ibid.

39 https://theconversation.com/the-problem-with-teaching-british-values-in-school-83688

40 Matthew White, 'The Enlightenment', The British Library, 21 June 2018.

41 Ibid.

42 Times Higher Education, 'World University Ranking 2018', 2018.

43 Nicholas Canny, *The Origins of Empire: The Oxford History of the British Empire Volume I*, Oxford University Press, Oxford, 1998.

44 Ibid, p.1.

45 Krishan Kumar, *The Making of English National Identity*, Cambridge University Press, Cambridge, 2003, p. 272.

46 Peter Ackroyd, *Albion: The Origins of the English Imagination*, Chatto & Windus, London, 2002, p. 237, p. 448.

47 Patrick Rhamey, '2018 State of World Liberty Index', 2018.

48 Alana Lentin, 'Why racism is so hard to define and even harder to understand, *The Conversation*, November 2018.

49 Richard Florida, 'Bohemia and economic geography', *Journal of Economic Geography 2* (2002) pp. 55-71.

50 Richard Florida, *Who's Your City?*, Basic Books, New York, March 2008.

51 Rachael Harker, *NHS Funding and Expenditure*, House of Commons Library Briefing Paper, 3 April 2012.

52 Professor Philip Wood, *Maps of World Financial Law*, Sweet & Maxwell, London, 2008.

53 Transparency International, Corruption Perceptions Index 2018.

54 Orlena Lavrenchuk, interviewed by John Humphreys, BBC *Today*, 14 October 2010.

55 Alex von Tunzelmann, *Indian Summer: The Secret History of the End of an Empire*, Pocket Books, London, 2008.

56 David Lammy, *The Lammy Review*, 8 September 2017, p. 3.

57 ICM Unlimited/*Guardian*, 'Bias in Britain BAME Polling', 3 December 2018.

58 Ibid.

59 Ibid.

60 'UK "almost most centralised developed country," says Treasury chief', Institute for Government, 27 January 2015.

61 Meg Russell and Jack Sheldon, 'Options for an English Parliament', *The Constitution Unit*, University College London, March 2018.

62 What is a citizens' assembly?', Commons Select Committee, UK Parliament website.

63 Michela Palese, 'The Irish abortion referendum: How a Citizens' Assembly helped to break years of political deadlock', Electoral Reform Society, 29 May 2018.

64 'Eighth Amendment repealed as Irish President signs bill into law,' BBC News, 18 September 2018.

65 Torsten Bell, 'How to solve the UK's wealth inequality problem', *New Statesman*, 8 February 2018.

66 Ibid., p. 81.

67 David Kynaston, *Austerity Britain 1945–1951*, Bloomsbury, London, 2007, p. 272.

68 Commonwealth Immigrants Advisory Committee, Third Report, HMSO, London, 1964.
69 J. H. Stembridge, *New World Geographies: Europe*, Oxford University Press, Oxford, 1951, p. 1.
70 Sally Tomlinson, *Education and Race*, Policy Press, Bristol, 2019, p. 80.
71 Jason Rodrigues, 'From the archive: how the *Guardian* reported the partition of India 70 years ago', *Guardian*, 14 August 2017.
72 Ian Cobain, *The History Thieves: Secrets, Lies and the Shaping of a Modern Nation*, Portobello, London, 2016.
73 Ian Cobain, 'Files on Britain's most controversial episodes vanish from archives', *Guardian*, 26 December 2017.
74 YouGov Survey Results, 'The British Empire is "something to be proud of"', 26 July 2014.
75 Jack Black, 'Celebrating British multiculturalism, lamenting England/Britain's past', *Nations and Nationalism*, Vol. 22, No. 4, 2016, pp. 786–802.
76 John Barber, 'Canada's indigenous schools policy was "cultural genocide", says report', *Guardian*, 2 June 2015.
77 Mali Ilse Paquin, 'Canada confronts its dark history of abuse in residential schools', *Guardian*, 6 June 2015.
78 There is a non-permanent Migration Musuem in Lewisham Shopping Centre, which stages exhibitions, events and workshops.
79 David Lammy, 'Close Encounters', *Prospect*, 23 April 2006.
80 National Citizens Service website. Accessed via: https://www.ncsyes.co.uk/what-is-ncs
81 Sonia Sodha and Dan Leighton, *Service Nation*, Demos, London, 2009.
82 'What was National Service?', National Army Museum website. Accessed via: https://www.nam.ac.uk/explore/what-was-national-service
83 Elizabeth Braw, 'The benefits of conscription are economic as well as military', *Financial Times*, 10 September 2017.
84 Alan Renwick and Robert Hazell, 'Blueprint for a UK Constitutional Convention', The Constitution Unit, University College London, June 2017.
85 Bobby Duffy et al., 'Divided Britain? Polarisation and fragmentation trends in the UK', The Policy Institute at King's College London, 2019.
86 Ibid.
87 Demos research, publication upcoming.
88 2018 British Attitudes Survey.
89 2018 BBC Global Survey.

9. BEYOND TRIBES

1 Zadie Smith, *White Teeth*, Hamish Hamilton, London, 2000.
2 Marco T. Bastos and Dan Mercea, 'The Brexit Botnet and User-Generated Hyperpartisan News', *Social Science Computer Review*, Vol. 37, No. 1, October 2017, pp. 38–54.

3 Robert Joyce and Luke Sibieta, 'An assessment of Labour's record on income inequality and poverty', *Oxford Review of Economic Policy*, Vol. 29, Issue 1, Spring 2013, pp. 178–202; Polly Toynbee, 'NHS: The Blair Years', *British Medical Journal*, 334, 2019, pp. 1030–1.

4 Ibids.

5 Lewis Davis and Sumit S. Deole, 'Immigration and the Rise of Far-Right Parties in Europe', *ifo DICE Report*, Vol. 15, 2017, pp. 10–15.

6 Heinz-Christian Strache, statement given to *Krone* newspaper, Austria, 28 April 2019.

7 Ibid.

8 Sandra L. Colby and Jennifer M. Ortman, 'Projections of the Size and Composition of the U.S. Population: 2014 to 2060', United States Census, March 2015, pp. 25–1143.

9 YouGov on behalf of Hope not Hate, 'The Conservative Crisis Over Islamophobia', 24 June 2019.

10 'President Confirms He Threatened to Withdraw from NATO Over Funding', C-SPAN, 21 August 2018.

11 Hassan Damluji, *The Responsible Globalist: What Citizens of the World Can Learn from Nationalism*, Allen Lane, London, September 2019.

12 'High Tide Swamps Lower East Coast Road in Guyana', *Stabroek News*, 14 January 2013.

13 'Climate Hot Map – Global Warming Effects Around the World – Guyana', Union of Concerned Scientists. Accessed via: https://www.climatehotmap.org/global-warming-locations/guyana.html

14 Ibid.

15 Neil Marks, 'Climate change and floods, the uninvited guests of Guyana', UNDP, 4 December 2015.

16 Melinda Janki, 'Water is Everywhere in Georgetown, Guyana – Our Disrespect for It Will Kill Us', *The Nature of Cities*, 27 May 2018.

17 'Floods in Guyana January 2005 – Situation Report, 25 Jan 2005', Pan American Health Organization, 25 January 2005.

18 'Children in danger as rainstorms flood Guyana', Unicef, 26 January 2005.

19 'Floods in Guyana January 2005 – Situation Report, 25 Jan 2005', Pan American Health Organization, 25 January 2005.

20 Neil Marks, 'Climate change and floods, the uninvited guests of Guyana', UNDP, 4 December 2015.

21 'Floods in Guyana January 2005 – Situation Report, 25 Jan 2005', Pan American Health Organization, 25 January 2005.

22 Katharine Ricke et al., 'Country-level social cost of carbon', *Nature Climate Change*, Vol. 8, 2018, pp. 895–900.

23 David Wallace-Wells, *The Uninhabitable Earth: A Story of the Future*, Allen Lane, London, 2019, p.4.

24 Ibid.

25 'WMO climate statement: past 4 years warmest on record', World Meteorological Organization, 29 November 2018.

26 Gaia Vince, 'The heat is on over the climate crisis. Only radical measures will work', *Observer*, 19 May 2019.

27 'Emissions Gap Report 2018', UN Environment, 27 November 2018.

28 Ibid.

29 Jeff Mason and Darren Enis, 'G20 agrees on phase-out of fossil fuel subsidies', Reuters, 26 September 2009.

30 Ipek Gencsu et al., 'G20 coal subsidies: tracking government support to a fading industry', Open Data Institute, June 2019.

31 'Paris Agreement', United Nations, 2015, p. 5.

32 Mark Townsend, 'Record refugee evictions at camps in France to halt Channel crossings', *Guardian*, 22 June 2019.

33 Robin Sykes, House of Lords Library briefing – English Channel Migrant Boat Crossings, 7 March 2019.

34 'The Iranian Judiciary: A Complex and Dysfunctional System,' Iran Human Rights Documentation Center, 2018.

35 https://appgfreedomofreligionorbelief.org/media/APPGs-report-on-Persecution-of-Christians-in-Iran.pdf

36 Mark Townsend, 'Record refugee evictions at camps in France to halt Channel crossings', *Guardian*, 22 June 2019.

37 Tom Steadman, 'Report reveals excessive police violence and intimidation of aid workers in Northern France', Help Refugees, 8 August 2018.

38 Alan Travis and Heather Stewart, 'UK to pay extra £44.5m for Calais security in Anglo-French deal', *Guardian*, 18 January 2018.

39 'UN urges French government to provide for basic needs of migrants and asylum seekers in Northern France', European Council on Refugees and Exiles, 6 April 2018.

40 Cynthia Kroet, 'Germany: 1.1 million refugee arrivals in 2015', *Politico*, 1 June 2016.

41 Georgina Sturge, *Asylum Statistics – Number SN01403*, House of Commons Library Briefing Paper 6 March 2019.

42 Victoria Waldersee, 'The UK is less popular among asylum seekers than we think', YouGov, 2 June 2018.

43 'Figures at a Glance', The UN Refugee Agency. Accessed via: https://www.unhcr.org/uk/figures-at-a-glance.html

44 https://ec.europa.eu/echo/where/middle-east/lebanon_en

45 Another 35 per cent say they don't know and 17 per cent say refugees are getting the appropriate amount of support; Francesca Sheeka, 'World Refugee Day 2018: How does the British public feel about refugees?' YouGov, 20 June 2018.

46 Francesca Sheeka, 'World Refugee Day 2018: How does the British public feel about refugees?' YouGov, 20 June 2018.

47 'German attitudes towards asylum seekers increasingly hostile: report', *The Local*, 25 April 2019.

48 Hassan Damluji, *The Responsible Globalist: What Citizens of the World Can Learn from Nationalism*, Allen Lane, London, September 2019, p. 97.

49 'Facts About Refugees', Refugee Action. Accessed via: https://www.refugee-action.org.uk/about/facts-about-refugees/

50 Susi Dennison, 'A new deal on EU burden-sharing', European Council on Foreign Relations, 3 March 2016.

51 Migration Advisory Committee, *EEA migration in the UK: Final report*, September 2018.

52 Stephen Kinnock and Emma Reynolds, 'People are worried about immigration – Labour must devise a fair system and reunite the country', *The Observer*, 8 Jan 2017.

53 Ninke Mussche, Vincent Corluy and Ive Marx, 'Determining labour shortages and the need for labour migration from third countries in Belgium', European Migration Network, 2015.

54 Office for National Statistics, *Migration Statistics Quarterly Report: February 2019*, 28 February 2019.

55 Max Lawson et al., *Public Good or Private Wealth?*, Oxfam GB, Oxford, 2019.

56 Ibid.

57 Thomas Piketty, *Capital in the Twenty-First Century*, The Belknap Press of Harvard University Press, Massachusetts, 2014.

58 Ibid.

59 Chris Isidore, 'Buffett says he's still paying lower tax rate than his secretary', 4 March 2013.

60 Robert Green, 'How Buffett Saves Billions on His Tax Return', *Forbes*, 17 August 2011.

61 Professor Jeffrey Sachs et al., 'Closing the SDG Budget Gap', Move Humanity, December 2018.

62 Patricia Espinoza Revollo et al., 'Public Good or Private Wealth? Methodology Note', Oxfam, 2019.

63 Dominic Kennedy, 'Only Britain meets UN overseas aid target among big economies', *The Times*, 10 April 2018.

64 Michael A. Clemens and Hannah M. Postel, 'Deterring Emigration with Foreign Aid: An Overview of Evidence from Low-Income Countries', Center for Global Development, 2018.

65 Office for National Statistics, *Population of England and Wales*, August 2018.

66 Ibid.

67 Office for National Statistics, *Population of the UK by country of birth and nationality*, May 2019.

68 National Association for Language Development in the Curriculum.

69 'The Gordon Riots', The National Archives.

70 Antonia Fraser, 'London's anti-Catholic riots were the bloodiest in British history', *Catholic Herald*, 17 May 2018.

71 'Archbishop of Canterbury Justin Welby's pain at broken communion', *Anglican News*, 30 October 2017.

72 D. Phillips et al., *British Social Attitudes 35*, The National Centre for Social Research, 2018.

73 Ibid.

74 'Challenges facing Britain: research into the public's priorities and attitudes on key issues', BritainThinks, 2019. Accessed via: https://britainthinks.com/news/challenges-facing-britain-a-report-for-engage-britain

10. POSTSCRIPT

1 George Monbiot, *Out of the Wreckage. A New Politics for an Age of Crisis*, Verso, London, 2017.

2 Keith Jensen et al., 'The Emergence of Human Prosociality; Aligning with Others through Feelings, Conserns and Norms', *Frontiers in Psychology*, 5, July 2014.

3 Henrike Moll and Michael Tomasello. 'Cooperation and human cognition: the Vygotskian intelligence hypothesis', *Philosophical Transactions of the Royal Society of London*, Series B, biological sciences, Vol. 362, 1480, 2007: pp. 639–48. doi:10.1098/rstb.2006.2000

4 G. Tabibnia and M. D. Lieberman, 'Fairness and Cooperation Are Rewarding: Evidence from Social Cognitive Neuroscience', *Annals of the New York Academy of Sciences*, Vol. 1118, Issue 1, pp. 90–101.

5 Stuart A. West et al., 'Evolutionary Explanations for Cooperation', *Current Biology*, Vol. 17, Issue 16, 2007.

6 Michael Tomasello et al., 'Two Key Steps in the Evolution of Human Cooperation – The Interdependence Hypothesis', *Current Anthropology*, Vol. 53, No. 6, December 2012.

7 Brian Skyrms, *The Stag Hunt and the Evolution of Social Structure*, Cambridge University Press, Cambridge, 2004.

Index

Abrahamsen, Karla 168–9
Ackroyd, Peter 248
AfD 143, 144
Africa 102–9, 162–4, 256
African Americans 87, 171
Ahmed (Iranian refugee) 285–7
Åkesson, Jimmie 277
Alaska 209
Alhousseini (Timidria NGO) 98–9,
    113, 115
Ali, Muhammad 112
Alio (Timidria NGO) 100
Allport, Gordon 202–3, 214
Alston, Philip 198
Angelou, Maya 112
Anti-Slavery International 100, 101,
    115
Anwar (ISIS) 120–2, 127, 128, 131,
    151, 274
Arendt, Hannah 145
Attlee, Clement 194
Australia 153, 223, 282, 292

Baddiel, David 134
Bagehot, Walter 265
Bannon, Steve 144, 155
Bantu tribe 2–3
Barnett, Anthony 45
Barnsley 198
Baudet, Thierry 277
BBC 181
Beckham, David 210
Belgium 263, 292
Benesch, Susan 153
Beverly (cousin) 195
Birmingham 193
Birney, Ewan 271–3
Blair, James 75
Blair, Tony 1, 19, 135–6, 181, 234
Bohemians 250
Boko Haram 96
Bolsonaro, Jair 277
Botswana 105–8
Boyle, Danny 231
Bragg, Billy 248
Braine, Richard 238

Brammer, Bram 42

British African community 86

British Caribbean 27, 70, 81–3, 85–8, 94, 171

British Empire 248, 256, 257, 299

British National Party 235

Broadwater Farm Estate 14, 155, 188, 195, 303

Brooke, Rupert 156

Brown, Gordon 234, 261

Bruno, Frank 81

Buffett, Warren 294

Burke, Edmund 265

Burnham, Andy 157, 220

Burnham, Forbes 77, 78

Calais 'jungle' camp 285–6, 287–9, 290

California 130–1, 228

Cameron, David 80, 181, 261, 265

Camus, Renaud 278

Canada 241, 258–9, 292

Cares Family 212–13, 214

Caribbean 66, 68–9, 75–6

Carnegie, Dal 130

Carol (Botswanan teacher) 107–8

Central Africa 102–3

Chamberlain, Neville 156

Chance UK 205

Charlottesville 278

Chaslot, Guillaume 147

China 109

Christchurch, New Zealand 153

Christie, Linford 81

Churchill, Winston 143, 194, 238

Cicero 227, 261

Clinton, Bill 21

Clinton, Hillary 176

Clive (friend) 39, 40–6, 48–9, 50–1

Cobley, Ben 158–9

Colombia 92–3, 210–11

Combahee River Collective 173–4, 175, 176

Comic Relief 162–6

Conner, Alana 178–9

Conservative Party 142, 149

Cool Britannia 234, 243

Corbyn, Jeremy 20, 26, 142, 145, 192

Cosmopolitans 70

Cox, Brendan 123

Cox, Jo 20–1, 123, 149

Cummings, Dominic 110–11

Curtis, Richard 165–6

Darwin, Charles 108–9, 110

David (father) 67–8, 69, 74, 168

Defoe, Daniel 244

Dembélé, Siriki 51

Democratic Republic of Congo 104

Demos 261, 263, 268

Denham, John 234

Denmark 292

Desmond (brother) 69

DiAngelo, Robin 159

Dick, Cressida 123

Dier, Eric 210–11

Dooley, Stacey 162, 164

Dublin Regulation 2013 290–1

Duggan, Mark 217

Dunkirk 260, 289

East Demerara Water Conservancy 281–2

Eastern European workers 59, 61

Edmonstone, John 110

El-Wardany, Salma 177

Eliot, T. S. 95

Elizabeth-Ann (North London Cares) 214

England

    cultural and creative capital 247

    devolution referendums 197

    giving a voice to 252–5

    internal colonisation 257

    local government spending 197–8

    nation branding 243–4

    openness 248–50

    racial prejudice 252

    refugees 238–9

    teaching British values 245–6

English Defence League 191, 235

Ennis, Jessica 81
Erikson, Erik 167, 168–71
Estonia 241–2
European Research Group (ERG) 142, 144
European Union (EU) 20–1, 154, 279, 284–5, 290

Facebook 139, 141, 148–9, 152, 153
Fafa, Niger 95–6
Falklands War 67, 257
Farage, Nigel 25, 44, 142, 145, 233, 277, 278
Fawkes, Guy 297
Finland 264, 292
Florida, Richard 250
Food Assemblies 205
France 215, 236–7, 259, 263, 288
Freud, Anna 169
Fukuyama, Francis 28, 179–81, 182

Gaborone, Botswana 107
Galton, Francis 110–11
Garnett, Alf 35
Gentleman, Amelia 71
Geoff (Dorothy Nelson's son) 64–5, 87
Georgetown, Guyana 281–2
Germany 153, 288, 290
Ghanaian Community Education Awards 303
Gingrich, Newt 21–2
Goldsmiths, University of London 178
González, Felipe 288
Goodwin, Matthew 43–4
Gordon, Lord George 297
Gove, Michael 25, 110
Grand, Natasha 243
Grande-Synthe, Dunkirk 289–90
Granovetter, Mark 203
Grant, Bernie 79, 196
Greece 13
Grenfell Tower 143, 155–60, 166
Guyana 26, 69, 75–8, 280–2
Guyanese immigrants 66–7

Hall, David 123–7, 128, 131, 149, 151
Hall, Stuart 79–81, 240
Han ethnic group 109
Hannan, Daniel 103
Haringey Council 195–6, 206
Harlem 83
Harrison, Stephen 55
Hartlepool 222
Heseltine, Michael 145, 216, 217–20, 221
Hirsch, Afua 84
Hobbes, Thomas 304
Holmes, Kelly 81
Homburger, Theodor 169
Hopetown, Guyana 74–5
Howe, Geoffrey 217
Huguenots 238–9

Iger, Bob 153
India 77–8, 251, 257, 283
Instagram 139, 140
Iran 286–7
ISIS 121–2
Islamic extremists 96–7, 128
Israel 264
Italy 263

Jack (parliamentary researcher) 71
Jackson, Michael 33
Jackson, Stewart 42
'The Jacob Rees-Mogg Supporters Group' 149–50
Jagan, Cheddi 77
James, C. L. R. 81
Jamieson (school friend) 35, 38–9, 40, 52, 54–5
Japan 129
Jennifer (North London Cares) 213
Johnny (brick stacker) 58–9
Johnson, Boris 23–4, 25, 144, 145, 233, 265–6
Johnson, Linton Kwesi 81
Johnsons of Hopetown 75
Jones, Aled 33–4

Jones, Damon 209
Jones, Steve 111

Kaczyński, Jarosław 279
Kadi, Moustapha 101–2
Kakutani, Michiko 24
Kaljulaid, Kersti 242
Kardashian, Kim 140
Kathy (friend) 39, 40–6, 48
Kennedy, John F. 11–12, 222
Kenny, Michael 245
Khama, Seretse 106
Khan, Adil 126, 127
Khan, Sadiq 149
King, Martin Luther, Jr 1, 19, 112, 160, 171
The King's Cathedral School (Peterborough) 34–8
Kinnock, Stephen 292
Kipling, Rudyard 162
Koulouwiya (former slave) 101
Kumar, Krishnan 248
Kurdish refugees 289–90

Labour Party 23, 142, 145, 148, 181, 192, 249
Lakoff, George 146
Lamb-Shapiro, Jessica 129
Lavrenchuk, Orlena 251
Le Pen, Marine 277
Lebanon 288
Leeds town hall 193
Leigh 192
Leyton 64
LGBT+ 161, 171
Liberia 163
Lilla, Mark 175–6
Lincoln, Abraham 265
Liverpool 193, 216, 217, 219, 220
Livingstone, Ken 188
Locke, John 247
London 250
London Brick 52, 54, 55, 58–9
Lone Man (Teton Sioux) 119
Long, Jackie 157

Longthorpe, Peterborough 42
Lorde, Audre 173

Macron, Emmanuel 263
Maffesoli, Michel 7–8
Major, John 197
Mali 104
Manchester 193, 220–1
Mandela, Nelson 143
Manhattan 83
Marchmont Community Centre 213
Maria (Marchmont Community Centre) 213
Marinescu, Ioana 209
Marley, Bob 112
Marr, Andrew 143, 144
Marshall, George C. 295
Maslow, Abraham 168
Maureen (white East Ender) 70
May, Theresa 14, 25–6, 233, 265
McCray, Chirlane 173
Melville, Herman 187
Merseyside 216
Michels, Rinus 212
Miliband, Ed 18–19, 245, 249
Mitchell, Kevin 112
Molyneux, Stefan 150–1
Monbiot, George 205
Moore-Bick, Martin 157
Moore, Joan 92
Morgan, Eoin 298
Morgan, Nicky 126
Morris, Desmond 4–6
mother 2, 65–70, 73, 74, 138, 168, 206
Mustafa, Bahar 178
Muswell Hill, London 14

Nairn, Tom 231–2
Nandy, Lisa 189, 192, 199, 221
National Action group 235
National Citizen Service (NCS) 261
National Front 73, 191
National Health Service 44, 194–5, 250–1, 291
NBC 146

Nelson, Dorothy Monica 64
Netherlands 263
Nettleton, Barbara 199
New Labour 136, 181, 182, 197, 231, 243
New York 83
Niamey, Niger 95, 96, 114
Nicola (wife) 83–4, 156
Niger 98–102, 104, 108, 112, 115
Nimmo, Ben 142
North London Cares 212, 213
Northeastern University 9–10
Northern Ireland 231, 232, 257
Nunn, Sam 21

Obama, Barack 22, 85
Olds, Jacqueline 129, 131–2
Orapa diamond mine (Botswana) 105–6
Orbán, Viktor 277
Orwell, George 187–8, 199, 244, 247
Osei-Bonsu, Charles 303–4
Oxford 198

Parks, Rosa 112
Peterborough 39–42, 59–60, 169
    Brexit 44
    census 2011 50
    development 1970's 49
    drug dealers 90–1
    immigration 62
    inflexibility 94
    population 48
    unemployment 45–6, 47, 60
    'white flight' 48
Peterborough Cathedral 34
Peterborough United ('the Posh') 50–1
Phillips, Jess 149
Phillips, Trevor 80–1
Piketty, Thomas 13
Portugal 108, 212
Powell, Enoch 73, 126, 238
Putnam, Robert 132–3

Queensgate Shopping Centre, Peterborough 49

Rashid, Adil 298
Reagan, Ronald 8, 172, 276
Redcar 192
Rees-Mogg, Jacob 142–3, 145, 149
Renwick, Alan 267
Republic of Ireland 232, 254
Reynolds, Emma 292
Rhodes, Cecil 33
Ridge, Sophie 158
Ritchie, Stuart 271–3
Rob (London Brick supervisor) 52–3, 54, 55
Robinson, Tommy 191, 235
Rotherham, Steve 157, 220
Rouhani, Hassan 286
Rousseau, Jean-Jacques 304
Rowley, Mark 235
Rubin, Dave 150–1
Rudd, Amber 71
Rugby School 156
Rushdie, Salmond 156
Russia 284
Rutherford, Adam 271–3

Salisbury, Robert Cecil, 3rd Marquis 98
Salomonsen, Waldemar Isidor 168
Salvini, Matteo 277
Sanders, Bernie 175
Sangatte, Calais 285–6
Sara (Sunshine House) 200
Saudi Arabia 283
Saye, Khadija 156–8
Scally, Aylwyn 271–3
Schmitt, Carl 22–3
Scholes shopping precinct, Wigan 200
Schwartz, Richard S. 129
Scotland 197, 231, 232, 234, 257
Sheeran, Ed 163
Shore, Peter 216
Sieyès, Emmanuel Joseph 236
Silicon Valley 130, 152
Simpson, Amani 89–93

Sinclair, Murray 258
Smith, Alex 213
Smith, Barbara 173
Smith, Eleanor 124
Smith, Owen 142
Smith, Zadie 81
SNP 232
Soubry, Anna 149
South Africa 106, 267
Southgate, Gareth 234–5
Spain 13, 212
Standing, Guy 138
Sterling, Raheem 81
Steve (London Brick) 55–7
Strache, Heinz-Christian 277–8
Streep, Meryl 146–7
Sturgeon, Nicola 232
Sunshine House, Wigan 199–201, 203
Sunstein, Cass 148, 150
Susan (single mother) 207, 208
Susannah (grandmother) 74
Sweden 263
Syrian refugees 291

Tariq (taxi driver, Tottenham) 119–22
Tatarstan 242–3
Temne tribe, Sierra Leone 2–3
Thatcher, Margaret 8, 135–6, 172, 196,
    217, 238, 276
Thompsons (Hopetown) 75
Timidria NGO 97–9, 101
Tom-Lindley, Cindy 258
Tottenham 27, 38, 41, 62, 169,
    189–90, 193, 249
Tottenham riots (2011) 133–4, 217–19
Toxteth riots 217
Traditional Britain Group 143
Transparency International 105, 251
Trudeau, Justin 258
Trump, Donald
    aggressive defensiveness 179
    election slogans 17
    ethnic nationalism 233, 234
    European ideas of ethnic purity
        278–9

false and misleading claims 25
populist nationalist 277
tribal allegiance to 222
tweets 141, 146–7
white supremacism 274
Tuareg people 2–3, 26–7, 96, 99,
    112–16
Tubman, Harriet 173
Tufekci, Zeynep 148
Turkey 284
Twitter 16, 141–2, 146–7, 152

UKIP 238
Underwood, Blair 130
United Kingdom
    borders 290
    centralisation 300
    confronting the past 259
    constitution 264–7
    contradictions, paradoxes and
        identity 297
    creation 257
    Empire and imperialism 72
    global aid 294
    inequality 136
    migration policies 291–3
    mixed race population 85
    national identity 231
    nationhood/civic patriotism 298–9
    religious faith 132
    social mobility 131
United States of America (USA)
    civic nation 234
    climate crisis 283
    constitution 265, 267
    Ellis Island 259
    inequality 136, 182
    loneliness 128–9
    nation of immigrants 278
    opioid crisis 13
    partisan politics 21–2
    religious faith 132
    Republicans and Democrats 299
    West Indian emigrants 68–9
University College London 110

University of Cambridge 47, 172
University of Manitoba 259
University of Oxford 47, 160, 172

Walcott, Derek 63
Wales 231, 234, 257
Wallace-Wells, David 283
Walsall Magistrates Court 123
Warner, Liz 163
Wawrzyniak, Damian 41
Weila, Ilguilas 99
Welby, Justin 297
Welshness 231, 232
West Africa 102–3
West Indian communities 86

Widdecombe, Anne 103
Wigan 187–93, 199–201
Wilberforce, William 2
Wilders, Geert 277
Windrush generation 65, 70–4, 79, 168
Wood, Tiger 85

Yaxley-Lennon, Stephen 191, 235
YouTube 141, 147–8, 150, 152–3
Yusef (volunteer) 287

Zephaniah, Benjamin 81
Zimbabwe 106
Zuckerberg, Mark 148–9, 153
Zucman, Gabriel 293